Hira-gana	Kata-kana	Rōma-ji	Hira-gana	Kata-kana	Rōma-ji	Hira-gana	Kata-kana	Rōma-ji	Hira-gana	Kata-kana	Rōma-ji	Hira-gana	Kata-kana	Rōma-ji	Hira-gana	Kata-kana
は	ハ				ma	ま	マ	ra	ら	ラ	wa	わ	ワ	n	ん	ン
ひ	ヒ				mi	み	ミ	ri	り	リ						
ふ	フ				mu	む	ム	ru	る	ル						
へ	ヘ				me	め	メ	re	れ	レ						
ほ	ホ				mo	も	モ	ro	ろ	ロ	o	を	ヲ			
ひゃ	ヒャ				mya	みゃ	ミャ	rya	りゃ	リャ						
ひゅ	ヒュ				myu	みゅ	ミュ	ryu	りゅ	リュ						
ひょ	ヒョ				myo	みょ	ミョ	ryo	りょ	リョ						

ば	バ	pa	ぱ	パ												
び	ビ	pi	ぴ	ピ												
ぶ	ブ	pu	ぷ	プ												
べ	ベ	pe	ぺ	ペ												
ぼ	ボ	po	ぽ	ポ												
びゃ	ビャ	pya	ぴゃ	ピャ												
びゅ	ビュ	pyu	ぴゅ	ピュ												
びょ	ビョ	pyo	ぴょ	ピョ												

(a) The euphonic change in the initial consonant of the second element in a compound word, as when はな and ち join to make はなぢ (nosebleed) or ゆう and つき join to make ゆうづき (evening moon).

(b) Repetition of the same sound, as in ちぢみ (crêpe) or つづく (to continue).

4. The "h" in the ha and hya groups is thought to have been a "p" in proto-Japanese. Because of this, the Japanese "h" frequently changes to a "b" or a "p," this last being given the special name of semi-sonant. Examples are in counting cylindrical things, which begins (1) ip-pon, (2) ni-hon, and (3) san-bon, or in combining stone (ishi) with bridge (hashi) to make a stone bridge (ishi-bashi).
5. For reference, please see the relevant sections of the Introduction.

森塚先生

寺村秀夫

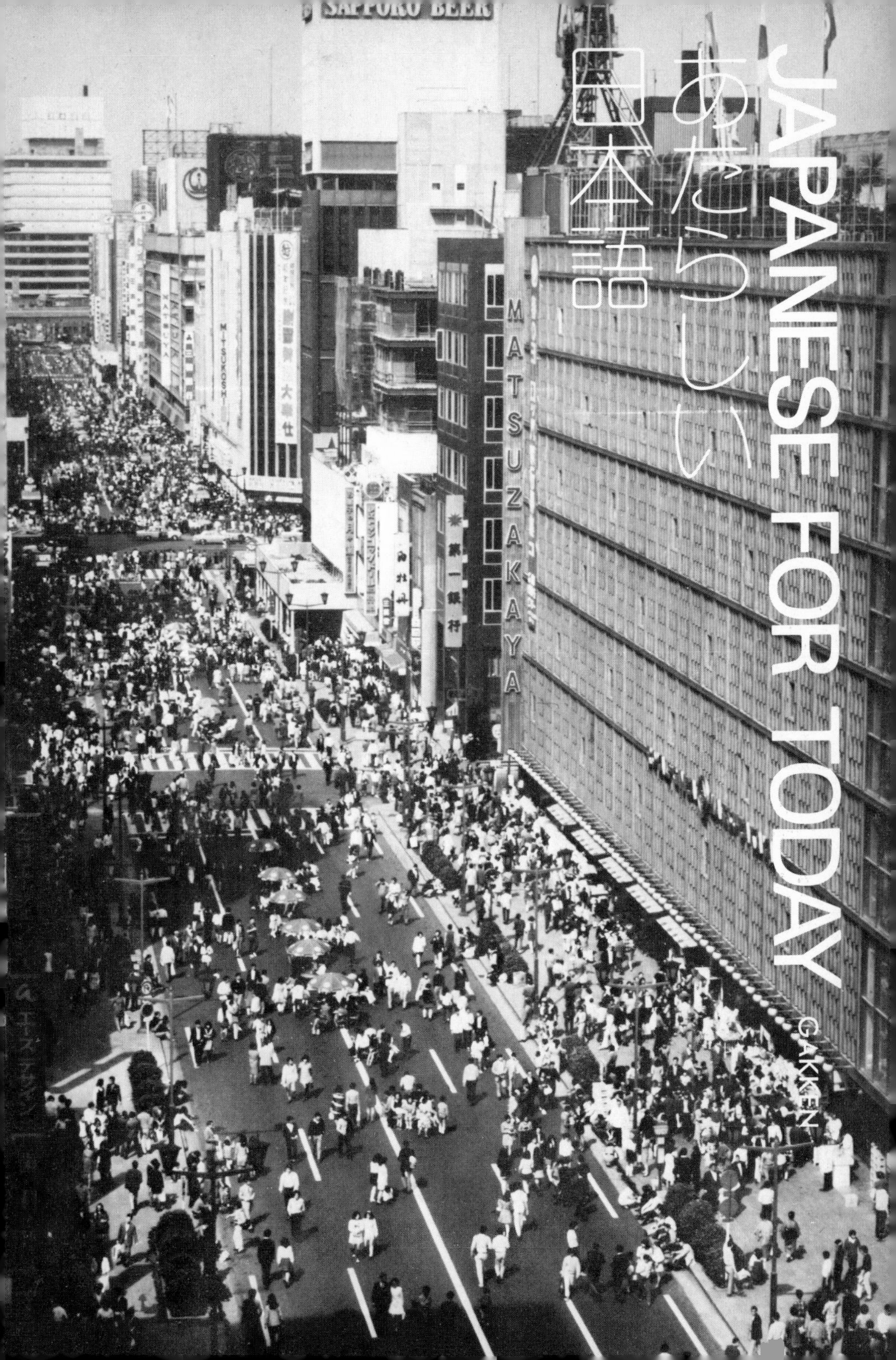
JAPANESE FOR TODAY
あたらしい日本語
GAKKEN
SAPPORO BEER
MATSUZAKAYA
MITSUKOSHI

JAPANESE FOR TODAY

4-40-5, Kami-ikedai, Ohta-ku, Tokyo 145, Japan
Library of Congress Catalog Card Number: 73-88140
Printed in Japan

EDITORIAL STAFF

Editors

Department for Foreign Students, Osaka University of Foreign Studies

Chairman	Yoshida Yasuo	Reading
Associate Professor	Teramura Hideo	Grammar
Associate Professor	Saji Keizo	Grammar
Associate Professor	Tamamura Fumio	Presentation
Associate Professor	Kuratani Naoomi	Conversation
Lecturer	Nishide Ikuyo	Exercise
Lecturer	Yamaguchi Koji	Presentation
Assistant Instructor	Okura Miwako	Exercise
Assistant Instructor	Okada Hideki	Conversation
Assistant Instructor	Haruna Makiko	Reading

Editorial Adviser
Frederick M. Uleman

Layout and Design
Imai Minoru

Gakken Co., Ltd.: Tanaka Yoshio(chief), Hayashi Hiroyuki, Yamashita Yoichi
Okubo Masayoshi, Saito Takashi

PREFACE

With the international situation as complex and Japan's role as important as they are today, there are many people wanting to learn Japanese. The Osaka University of Foreign Studies has been teaching Japanese to foreign students for over twenty years, producing in the process a flexible set of ten texts plus annual research papers. Unfortunately, however, these could not be provided to people wishing to study the language outside of the University. Thus it was with pleasure that we accepted Gakken's suggestion that this latest revision be made more widely available. Nonetheless, this also entailed condensing the existing fifty-lesson course by breaking from its exclusively classroom orientation to a dual structure suited to either the classroom or self-study.

The end result differs from other texts in utilizing living Japanese in common situations to get an understanding of contemporary Japan which transcends mere language education. Although it is impossible to "master" Japanese in only thirty lessons, a mastery of this text will allow intelligent participation in most situations and will lay the foundations for further learning. The vocabulary and characters introduced have been selected from a statistical survey of texts used in Japanese high schools, and the sentence patterns on the basis of extensive research and experience.

Each lesson having presentations, grammar explanations, practice exercises, conversations, and readings, these may be skimmed, stressed, or reordered to suit the individual's needs. In addition, there is a set of accompanying tapes which should prove extremely helpful for anyone wishing to develop his ear for and fluency in Japanese pronunciation and intonation. Yet another feature of this text is the use of romanization and Japanese script as appropriate to each section, such that conversations are in romanization alone, more advanced readings in Japanese alone, and presentations in both.

Finally, a major attempt has been made to avoid the common failing of "textbook Japanese" which is useless in daily life. Although this has at times meant using hard-to-explain and hard-to-translate expressions, the emphasis was still on having natural Japanese, and it is hoped that this will be accepted, and learned, as such.

While the time required to complete this text will obviously vary depending upon the person and study method, a total of about 200 hours should be adequate to acquire an everyday-life conversational proficiency and the ability to read real Japanese, albeit with a dictionary.

Yoshida Yasuo

吉田弥寿夫

Organization of the Lessons

Each of the thirty lessons consists of the following sections (twelve pages).

(1) **Presentation** (1st & 2nd pages): The presentation of new sentence patterns in general spoken Japanese. This is mostly in the normal polite style, except in the monolog parts where the plain style is used. The instructor is strongly urged to present the patterns orally, using whatever visual aids are available, and *not* to begin a lesson by just having the student read the presentation.

The romanized version of the Presentation is given on the 3rd page and the English translation on the 4th page.

(2) **Grammatical explanations** for self-study or review (5th & 6th pages).

(3) **Exercises** (7th & 8th pages): These exercises should also be conducted orally. Model answers to the Exercise questions are given on the 4th page.

(4) **Conversation** (9th & 10th pages): This section introduces a variety of colloquial expressions, conversational phrases, and familiar and polite styles used between people in various relationships and situations. The English translation (on the inner sides of the pages) is not a word-by-word or sentence-by-sentence translation, but is intended to give the meaning of the total conversation.

(5) **Reading** (11th page): This introduces Japanese as it is written. Beginning with Lesson 8, the normal written style is used, although phrases are separated with spaces until Lesson 20 to make it easier for the beginner to read. Here too, the English translation is to give the sense of the passage (12th page).

All new words are footnoted as they appear in each section. Verbs and Adjectives are given in their dictionary forms.

Abbreviations and Notations:

N	Noun	Adv	Adverb
Nv	Nouns which can be used as Verb bases e.g. benkyō (Nv) →'study' —(benkyō-suru) (V) 'to study'	P	Particle
		Conj	Conjunction
		PreN	Prenoun
		Pref.	Prefix
Na	'na Adjective'	Suf.	Suffix
A	'i Adjective' (All A's are indicated by '‥i' in the footnotes.)	Count.	Counter (See § 14)
		onomat	Onomatopoetic words
		Cph	Conversational phrase
V	Verb	(m)	male
Vi	Intransitive Verb	(f)	female
Vt	Transitive Verb (which takes a Direct Object)	NB	(*nota bene*) Note well.
	(A Verb is specified as Vi or Vt only when it has a formally related counterpart: e.g. hajimaru (Vi) 'begin'; hajimeru (Vt) 'begin')	Ex. or e.g.	example
		cf.	related expressions
		=	synonyms, or variants of the same word
		←	derived from
‥u	1st Group Verb (See § 42)	/	or
‥ru	2nd Group Verb (See § 42)		

CONTENTS

INTRODUCTION

I. Pronunciation

1. Syllables

Japanese syllables are "open syllables" and almost always end in a vowel. Thus "hana" is syllabicated as ha-na, and "paipu" as pa-i-pu. At the same time, the language is also isochronous so that all syllables are the same sound duration.

In all, there are seven kinds of syllables divisible into two groups.

Group		Kind	Example
i. General	i-i	Consonant+vowel (most common)	"ka"
	i-ii	Consonant+semi-vowel+vowel	"kya"
	i-iii	Semi-vowel+vowel	"yu" or "wa"
	i-iv	Vowel	"a"
ii. Special (Syllabics)	ii-i	Special nasal syllabic	"N" of "saN"
	ii-ii	Unpronounced consonant	"Q" of "iQpon"
	ii-iii	Special syllabic for the second syllable of an extended vowel	"V" of "okaVsan"

Special mention should be made, however, that i-ii takes only "y" as its semi-vowel and only "a," "o," or "u" as its vowel, while in i-i "t" and "d" appear only before "e," "a," or "o." The syllabics of Group ii can never be pronounced alone, occuring only within or at the end of multisyllabic words and never at the beginning of a word.

2. Sounds

Contemporary Japanese phonemes include 14 consonants, 2 semi-vowels, and 5 vowels.

i) Consonants: k, g; p, b; t, d; c, z; s; r; h; m, n, ŋ
ii) Semi-vowels: y, w
iii) Vowels: a, e, i, o, u

These are pronounced as shown below.

(A) Letters (representing consonants)

b [b]
ch [tʃ] as in the English "choice"
d [d]
f a bi-labial voiceless fricative, not the English labio-dental fricative, used only in "fu"
g [g] when it begins a word and [ŋ] when it is not the initial letter
h [h], but this always becomes "f" before the vowel "u"
j as in the English "join"
k [k]

m [m] and always followed by a vowel

n the common nasal [n] and [m] before [p], [b], or [m] and the syllabic "N" as in "Ki-n-e-n"

p [p]

r a sound peculiar to Japanese pronounced with the tip of the tongue moving midway in the mouth but not rolled. If the tongue is given slightly more tension, this sound easily becomes "d." It is like neither "r" nor "l" in English but is sort of between the two, like the Spanish "r" in "pero."

s [s] although this is written "sh" before the vowel "i"

sh like the English "sh" unstressed

t [t]

ts like the English voiceless affricate [ts] as in "cats" and always followed by the vowel "u"

z the voiced affricate [dz] as in the English "words" and not the "z" of the English "zoo"

NB: Unvoiced consonants usually change to voiced when they come at the beginning of the second element of compound words. In such cases, "h" often changes to "p" or "b." Ex. "yama"+"sakura"→"yama-zakura"; "ishi"+"hashi"→"ishi-bashi"

(B) Letters (representing semi-vowels)

w [w] and always followed by the vowel "a"

y as in the English "yard"

(C) Letters (representing vowels)

a as in the English "father"

e as in the French "être"

i as in the English "see"

o as in the English "comb"

u as in the English "doodling" but of shorter duration

3. Syllabics

"N," "Q," and "V" are called "syllabics" because they constitute syllables even though they are not vowels.

i) "N" is a special nasal sound written as "n" as in "pa-n" and "sa-n-po."

ii) "Q" is the special one-syllable pause represented in Japanese *kana* by the small っ or ッ. In romanization, this is usually shown by doubling the consonant which follows it, as in "Nippon" and "kitte."

iii) "V" is the second syllable of a prolonged or extended vowel. In Japanese, vowels can be either long or short, although this is not in the same sense as English "long" and "short" vowels. Rather, Japanese long vowels are double-length, two-syllable vowels, such as in To-o-kyo-o or hi-i-ta. These long vowels are indicated either by putting a line over the vowel (Tōkyō) or by writing the vowel twice (hiita).

4. Devocalization of Vowels

After a voiceless sound or between two voiceless sounds, the inaccentuated and narrow vowels "i" and "u" become voiceless, being pronounced very weakly as in "kusá," "hitó" and "áki."

5. Accent

The Japanese language has pitch accent, or musical accent, which is quite different from the stress accent in English, German, and other European languages, as well as some Asian languages. While stress accent pronounces the syllable louder, Japanese pitch accent pronounces the accentuated syllable of an independent word (not the particles or auxiliary verbs) at a higher pitch than the other syllables. In addition, the accentuated syllable should be pronounced at the same pitch throughout.

As a rule, n-syllable words can be accented in n+1 ways. For example, Japanese words of four syllables can be classified into five types according to accent pattern.

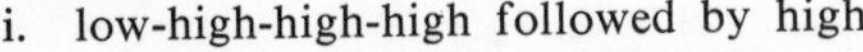

i. low-high-high-high followed by high

ii. low-high-high-high followed by low

iii. low-high-high-low followed by low

iv. low-high-low-low followed by low

v. high-low-low-low followed by low

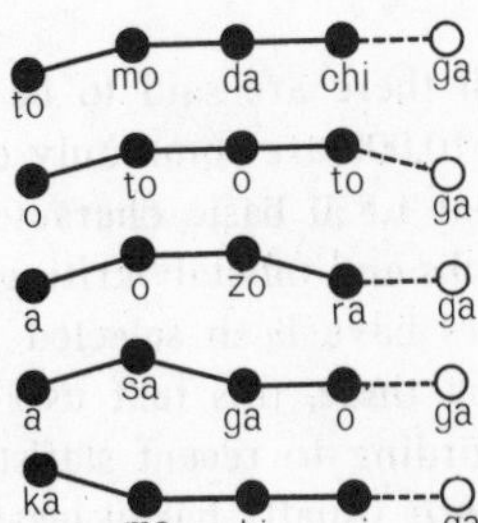

Each word has only one accent summit, although the location of this peak depends upon the word.

Japanese accent today functions more to show the unity of words than to distinguish the meanings of words which sound the same (homonyms).

II. Writing

1. General

i) Orthography in the European sense of the term is virtually non-existent in Japan, and there is very little effort made to adhere to any set standard. Thus "norikumi-in" (crew member) may be written のりくみいん, 乗り組み員, 乗組員, のりくみ員, or 乗組み員 and all are accepted as correct, each with its own rationale. Nevertheless, there is a clearly discernible trend toward orthography and the schools teach 乗組員 as "standard." Regardless, there is still little popular concern with orthography and it would be incorrect to brand different writings of the same word as deviant or erroneous.

ii) This neglect of orthography comes from the fact that Japanese everyday writing uses a combination of *kanji* and *kana* (*hiragana* and *katakana*) with even some foreign writing occasionally mixed in.

Because the early Japanese encountered great difficulties in trying to express perfectly their polysyllabic Japanese language with Chinese-origin *kanji*, at once ideographic and phonetic, they devised *kanji* cursive forms (*hiragana*) and abbreviations (*katakana*) as phonetic symbols suited to the open-syllable Japanese. In so doing, *kanji* was retained primarily for the semantemes (such as the word roots and stems) while the *kana* phonetics were used mainly for such morphemes as endings, derivated parts, fixations, and particles.

For example, 起きる and 起こす have the same 起 *kanji* stems but differ in their *kana* endings, the former being "okiru" meaning to get up (Vi) and the latter "okosu" meaning to wake (Vt). By the same token, the *kanji* 上 meaning "up" is used in 上がる (ascend), 上げる (raise), and 上る (climb).

iii) There is no established custom of separating words and/or phrases in writing.

iv) There is no system of capital letters and small letters.

v) Although the European style of writing horizontally from left to right, top to bottom, has recently come into partial use, the traditional form is still to write vertically from top to bottom, right to left.

2. *Kanji*

i) Although there are said to be some 48,000 *kanji* characters in existence, only about 5,000 to 10,000 are commonly used. After World War II, the Japanese Government designated 1,850 basic characters as "*Toyo kanji*" and these are the only ones used in textbooks and official writings. Of these 1,850 *Toyo kanji*, 996 particularly basic characters have been selected for inclusion in the elementary school curriculum. Including these, this text uses the approximately 1,000 most commonly used characters according to recent statistical surveys.

ii) Each *kanji* usually has at least two readings. One is the "*on*" reading adapted from the ancient Chinese pronunciation and the other is the "*kun*" reading of the character's meaning in Japanese. It also frequently happens that a *kanji* has two or more "*on*" readings and/or "*kun*" readings, and thus the many different readings that may be given for a single character are all correct.

iii) As already noted, *kanji* are used for the roots of nouns, verbs, and adjectives. Naturally enough, words borrowed from the Chinese and given their "*on*" readings are, in principle, written in *kanji*.

3. *Hiragana*

Hiragana is used for Japanese words to which *kanji* cannot be easily fitted, words of sound symbolism, endings of words which conjugate, such as verbs and adjectives, particles, auxiliary verbs, and the like. In addition, pronouns, adverbs, conjunctions, and names of plants and animals are better written in *hiragana* (such as ぴくぴく, わたしたち, and きつね).

4. *Katakana*

Foreign words, other than *kanji*, and onomatopoeia are written in *katakana* (such as ビール and ワンワン).

5. Roman Script

Although Western letters are not generally used, they have come into use recently for certain words such as units of measure and abbreviations. Examples are kg, Tel, PR, CM, SOS, Yシャツ, and PCB.

6. Notations

i. Sonant (ga, za, da, ba)

This is shown by ゛ to the upper right of the *kana* phonetic.

ii. Semi-sonant (pa)

This is shown by ゜ to the upper right of the *kana* phonetic.

iii. Reduplication

a. The mark ゝ indicates repetition of one syllabary.

b. The mark 々 indicates repetition of the *kanji* character.

III. Romanization

1. The romanization system adopted for transliteration in this text is the *Hyojun-shiki* (standard system), which is an adaptation of the Hepburn system.

2. The system used here has the following features.

i. Prolonged vowels are indicated by an ¯ over the vowel. However, the long "e" in all Chinese-origin words has been written "ei" and the long "i" of Japanese words as "ii."

ii. The syllabic "Q" has been shown by doubling the consonantal letter of words, such as in kitte (stamp) and kippu (ticket). However, the doubling of "ch," "sh," and "ts" have been written as "tch," "ssh," and "tts" respectively.

iii. The syllabic "N" has been consistently shown by "n" regardless of its actual sound value in the word.

iv. The hyphen has been adopted mainly to show the word structure of compound words.

IV. Outline of the Sentence Structure

1. Although the sentence structure of Japanese is strikingly different from that of English, most of the "Content words" that make up a sentence can be categorized in roughly the same way as in English: Nouns (hon 'book'), Adjectives (atsui 'hot'), Verbs (yomu 'read'), Adverbs (yukkuri 'slowly'), Conjunctions, etc.

The "Function words," however, require special attention and more careful study: (1) Particles (ga, o, ni, kara), most of which are postposed to Nouns and indicate their grammatical relationships within the sentence; (2) Auxiliaries, which are postposed to Verbs or Adjectives to show negative, passive, causative, progressive, and so on.

2. The core of the sentence is the Predicate, which is always placed at the end of the sentence. Predicates are of three types: Verbal, Adjectival, and Nominal. The Nominal Predicate consists of a Noun and the Copula desu or its variants.

Preceding the Predicate are 'Noun+Particle' phrases which indicate Topic, Subject, Object, Location, Time, etc. These non-Predicate phrases may appear in any order and may be omitted whenever they are not necessary to understanding. When a word or a clause is modified by another word or clause, the modifier always precedes what it modifies.

3. The Predicate is inflected (conjugated) for Tense and Mood (Declarative, Imperative, Conditional, Volitional, etc.), all in at least the two styles of "Plain" and "Polite."

第 1 課

これは さくらです

TAPE
No. 1
Side 1

❶ これ[1]は[2] 花(はな)[3]です[4]。 さくら[5]です。

それ[6]は もも[7]です。

あれ[8]は ばら[9]です。

❷ これは なん[10]ですか[11]。

——それは 花(はな)です。

それは 日本(にっぽん)[12]の[13] 花(はな)です。

さくらの 花(はな)です。

それも[14] さくらの 花(はな)ですか。

——はい[15]、 そう[16]です。

あれも さくらですか。

——いいえ[17]、 あれは さくらではありません[18]。

あれは ばらです。

あれは さくらですか、 ももですか。

——あれは さくらです。

語句

1 kore this See §2
2 wa (a topic marker) See §1
3 hana blossom, flower
4 desu be See §1
5 sakura cherry
6 sore that, it See §2
7 momo peach
8 are that See §2
9 bara rose
10 nan =nani what See §3
11 ka (a question marker) See §1
12 Nippon Japan (Japanese say both "Nippon" and "Nihon." They are pronunciation variants of the same word.)
13 no of See §4
14 mo also, too See §1
15 Hai Yes
16 sō so See §1
17 Iie No
18 dewa arimasen be not See §1
19 watashi I 20 *Buraun* 'Brown'
21 gakusei student
22 anata you (sing.)
23 kaisha-in company employee
kaisha company -in member
24 namae name
25 Imai (a family name)
26 Nippon-jin Japanese (person)

❸ わたし[19]は　ブラウン[20]です。　学生(がくせい)[21]です。

あなた[22]も　学生(がくせい)ですか。

——いいえ、　そうではありません。　わたしは　会社員(かいしゃいん)[23]です。

名(な)まえ[24]は　今井(いまい)[25]です。　日本人(にっぽんじん)[26]です。

彼女(かのじょ)[27]は　だれ[28]ですか。

彼女(かのじょ)は　アンナ[29]です。　わたしの　妹(いもうと)[30]です。

——かれ[31]は　だれですか。

かれは　トム[32]です。　わたしの　いとこ[33]です。

——あなたがた[34]は　カナダ[35]の　人(ひと)[36]ですか。

はい、　わたしたち[37]は　カナダ人(じん)[38]です。

* * *

❹ ここ[39]は　どこ[40]ですか。

——ここは　銀行(ぎんこう)[41]です。

郵便局(ゆうびんきょく)[42]は　どこですか。

——郵便局(ゆうびんきょく)は　あそこ[43]です。

切手(きって)[44]の　売(う)り場(ば)[45]は　ここですか。

——いいえ、　ここではありません。　そこ[46]です。

-jin　people of (nationality)
27 kanojo　she
28 dare　who　See §3
29 *Anna*　'Anna'
30 imōto　younger sister
31 kare　he　32 *Tomu*　'Tom'
33 itoko　cousin
34 anata-gata　you (pl.)
　-gata　(Plural Suf. for Human N; Polite)
35 *Kanada*　'Canada'
36 hito　man, person
37 watashi-tachi　we
　-tachi　(Plural Suf. for Animate N)
38 *Kanada*-jin　Canadian (person)
39 koko　here　See §2
40 doko　where　See §2, §3
41 ginkō　bank
42 yūbin-kyoku　post office
　yūbin　mail
　-kyoku　bureau
43 asoko　over there　See §2
44 kitte　postage stamp
45 uri-ba　place for selling
　uri ←ur·u (sell)　-ba　place
46 soko　there　See §2

Dai 1-ka

Kore wa sakura desu.

1 Kore wa hana desu. Sakura desu. Sore wa momo desu. Are wa bara desu.

2 Kore wa nan desu ka?

——Sore wa hana desu. Sore wa Nippon no hana desu. Sakura no hana desu.

Sore mo sakura no hana desu ka?

——Hai, sō desu.

Are mo sakura desu ka?

——Iie, are wa sakura dewa arimasen. Are wa bara desu.

Are wa sakura desu ka, momo desu ka?

——Are wa sakura desu.

3 Watashi wa *Buraun* desu. Gakusei desu. Anata mo gakusei desu ka?

——Iie, sō dewa arimasen. Watashi wa kaisha-in desu. Namae wa Imai desu. Nippon-jin desu. Kanojo wa dare desu ka?

Kanojo wa *Anna* desu. Watashi no imōto desu.

——Kare wa dare desu ka?

Kare wa *Tomu* desu. Watashi no itoko desu.

——Anata-gata wa *Kanada* no hito desu ka?

Hai, watashi-tachi wa *Kanada*-jin desu.

* * *

4 Koko wa doko desu ka?

——Koko wa ginkō desu.

Yūbin-kyoku wa doko desu ka?

——Yūbin-kyoku wa asoko desu.

Kitte no uri-ba wa koko desu ka?

——Iie, koko dewa arimasen. Soko desu.

Lesson 1

This is a cherry blossom.

1 This is a flower. This is a cherry blossom. That is a peach blossom. That is a rose.

2 What is this?

——It is a flower. It is a Japanese flower. It is a cherry blossom.

Is that a cherry blossom too?

——Yes, it is.

Is that a cherry blossom too?

——No, it is not a cherry blossom. It is a rose.

Is that a cherry blossom or a peach blossom?

——It is a cherry blossom.

3 My name is Brown. I am a student. Are you a student too?

——No, I am not. I am a company employee. My name is Imai.

I am a Japanese. Who is she?

She is Anna. She is my younger sister.

——Who is he?

He is Tom. He is my cousin.

——Are you Canadians?

Yes, we are Canadians.

* * *

4 What is this place?

——It is a bank.

Where is the post office?

——It is over there.

Is this the counter for postage stamps?

——No, it is not. It is over there.

ANSWERS 〈pp. 16, 17〉

I. (C) 1. Kore wa *Tomu* no *kamera* desu. 2. Kore wa anata no *tabako* desu. 3. Kore wa kanojo no kasa desu. 4. Kore wa watashi no megane desu. 5. Kore wa imōto no tokei desu. 6. Kore wa kare no denki-*sutando* desu.

IV. 1. nan 2. doko 3. nan 4. anata; dare

V. 1. (Watashi no namae wa) ___ desu. 2. (Watashi no kuni wa) ___ desu. 3. (Watashi no kuni no shuto wa) ___ desu.

●文法

§1 Identifying a Thing or Person

N_1 wa N_2 desu. 'N_1 is N_2.'

e.g. Watashi wa gakusei desu. 'I am a student.'

Negation: N_1 wa N_2 **dewa arimasen.** 'N_1 is not N_2.'

Wa is a Particle ('P') indicating that the Noun ('N') to which it is attached is the Topic of the sentence. A Topic can be anything that the speaker wants to talk about. Remember that it is not quite the same as the 'subject' in English grammar. The essential function of wa is to attract the listener's attention to the word or phrase to which it is attached.

Desu is a Copula (like 'to be' in English) used most commonly in medially polite spoken Japanese, and is inflected for negative (dewa arimasen), Past tense, etc. 'N desu' constitutes the Nominal Predicate.

Wa is replaced by **mo** when the same predicate also applies to another N.

e.g. Watashi wa gakusei desu. 'I am a student.'

Tomu mo gakusei desu. 'Tom is a student too.'

Question: N_1 wa N_2 desu **ka?** 'Is N_1 N_2?'

Ka is a Sentence-final Particle ('Ps') expressing question or doubt. In an answer to a question, the predicate alone is sufficient; the Topic may be omitted whenever it is understood.

e.g. *Tomu* wa gakusei desu ka? 'Is Tom a student?'

—Hai, gakusei desu. 'Yes, (he) is a student.'

The answer sentence can be further simplified by using **sō**, which stands for the 'N_1 wa N_2' part of the question sentence.

e.g. Anata wa gakusei desu ka? 'Are you a student?'

—Hai, sō desu. 'Yes, I am.'

—Iie, sō dewa arimasen. 'No, I am not.'

§ 2 Demonstratives

Japanese has a set of Demonstratives used for the speaker to point at or refer to a thing, place, being, or state of affairs. This lesson introduces three subsets (in boldface below).

	Nominal			Prenominal	Adjectival	Adverbial	
	thing	place	direction			(1)	(2)
I	**kore**	**koko**	**kochira**	kono	konna	konna-ni	kō
II	**sore**	**soko**	**sochira**	sono	sonna	sonna-ni	sō
III	**are**	**asoko**	**achira**	ano	anna	anna-ni	ā
?	**dore**	**doko**	**dochira**	dono	donna	donna-ni	dō

I (**ko**- series)...for whatever is near the 1st person (speaker)

II (**so**- series)...for whatever is near the 2nd person (listener)

III (**a**- series)...for whatever is near neither the speaker nor the listener, but is seen or known by both

? (**do**- series)...for a thing or state which the speaker is unable to point at, locate, or describe. This series usually appears in questions.

§ 3 Interrogative Nouns

Kore wa [hon] desu. 'This is a book.'

Sore wa **nan*** desu ka? '**What** is that?'

Kare wa [Yamada] desu. 'He is Yamada.'

Kare wa **dare/donata**** desu ka? '**Who** is he?'

Koko wa [Ginza] desu. 'This is Ginza.'

Koko wa **doko** desu ka? '**Where** is this?' or '**Where** am I?'

*nan generally before t-, d-, n-; nani elsewhere.

**more polite

§ 4 Connecting Two Nouns: N_1 **no** N_2 (roughly) 'N_2 of N_1'

e.g. Watashi no hon 'my book' (literally, 'book of I')

Nippon-go no hon 'a book of/in/on Japanese'

N_2 is sometimes omitted when it is understood.

e.g. Kore wa watashi no desu. 'This is mine.'

●練習

ANSWERS→p. 13

I. Use the chart to practice the patterns as shown in the examples.

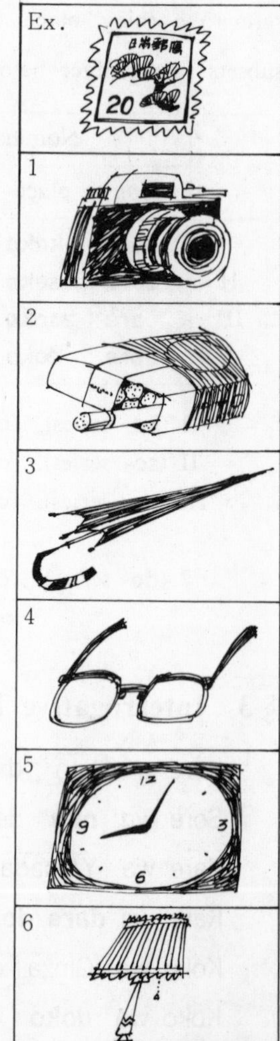

(A) Ex. (kitte) →Kore wa kitte desu.

1. (*kamera*[1]) 2. (*tabako*[2]) 3. (kasa[3])

4. (megane[4]) 5. (tokei[5]) 6. (denki-*sutando*[6])

(B) Ex. (pointing to Ex.) Kore wa nan desu ka?

—Kitte desu.

(C) (Ex.+kare) →Kore wa kare no kitte desu.

1. (1+*Tomu*) 2. (2+anata) 3. (3+kanojo)

4. (4+watashi) 5. (5+imōto) 6. (6+kare)

II. Make dialogs as shown in the example.

Ex. Q: (hon[7]) Kore wa hon desu ka?

A: (Hai) Hai, sō desu.

(Iie) (shinbun[8]) Iie, sō dewa arimasen.

Shinbun desu.

1. Q: (shinbun) A: (Hai)

2. Q: (*nōto*[9]) A: (Iie) (hon)

3. Q: (kitte) A: (Hai)

4. Q: (tokei) A: (Iie) (*kamera*)

5. Q: (sakura no hana) A: (Iie) (bara)

6. Q: (anata no kasa) A: (Iie) (kare no)

語句

1 ***kamera*** 'camera'
2 ***tabako*** 'tobacco,' cigarette
3 kasa umbrella
4 megane glasses
5 tokei clock, watch
6 denki-*sutando* desk lamp, reading lamp
 denki electricity *sutando* 'stand'
7 hon book 8 shinbun newspaper
9 ***nōto*** 'notebook'
10 byōin hospital
11 tosho-kan library
 tosho books, library
 -kan building, house
12 Tōkyō-eki Tokyo Station
 Tōkyō (the capital of Japan)
 eki station

III. Use the pictures to practice questions and answers as shown in the example.

Ex. (ginkō) →Q: Koko wa doko desu ka?

A: Koko wa ginkō desu.

1. (yūbin-kyoku) 2. (byōin[10]) 3. (tosho-kan[11])

4. (Tōkyō-eki[12]) 5. (daigaku[13])

IV. Fill in the blanks.

Ex. "Kore wa (dare) no hon desu ka?"

"Sore wa watashi no hon desu."

1. "Sore wa ( ) no hon desu ka?"
"Kore wa Nippon-go[14] no hon desu."

2. "Kore wa ( ) no shashin[15] desu ka?"
"Sore wa Kyōto[16] no shashin desu."

3. "Are wa ( ) no kaisha desu ka?"
"Are wa jidōsha[17] no kaisha desu."

4. "Kore wa ( ) no *bōru-pen*[18] desu ka?" "Iie, sore wa watashi no *bōru-pen* dewa arimasen."
"Soredewa,[19] ( ) no *bōru-pen* desu ka?"
"Sore wa *Tomu*-san[20] no desu."

V. Answer the following questions.

1. Anata no namae wa nan desu ka?
2. Anata no kuni[21] wa doko desu ka?
3. Anata no kuni no shuto[22] wa doko desu ka?

---

13 daigaku university, college
14 Nippon-go =Nihon-go Japanese (language)
-go language; word
15 shashin photograph
16 Kyōto (an old capital of Japan)
17 jidōsha automobile, car
18 *bōru-pen* 'ball-point pen'
19 soredewa well, then
20 -san (Suf. for Human N or Name) Mr., Mrs., Miss, Ms.
21 kuni country, nation; one's home land
22 shuto capital city

●会話

KONNICHI WA!

Konnichi wa.[1]

Ohayō gozaimasu.[2]

Ohayō.

Konban wa.[3]

Sayōnara.[4]

Oyasumi-nasai.[5]

Oyasumi.

Yamada[6]: Hajimemashite.[7]

Watashi wa Yamada desu.

Dōzo[8] yoroshiku.[9]

Buraun: Hajimemashite.

Watashi wa *Buraun* desu.

Dōzo yoroshiku.

Y: Kore wa watashi no meishi[10] desu.

B: Dōmo[11] arigatō[12] gozaimasu.

Y: Shitsurei desu ga,[13]

o-kuni[14] wa doko desu ka?

B: *Igirisu*[15] desu.

Hello.
Good morning. (Polite)
Morning. (Familiar)
Good evening.

Good-bye.
Good night. (Polite)
Good night. (Familiar)

Y: How do you do? (←This is the first time for me to meet you.) I am Yamada. I am pleased to meet you. (←I hope we shall become friends.)

B: How do you do? I am Brown. Pleased to meet you.

Y: This is my card.

B: Thank you very much.

Y: Excuse me, but where are you from? (←where is your country?)

B: England.

語句

1 Konnichi wa (Cph: daytime greeting)
2 Ohayō (gozaimasu) (Cph: morning greeting)
gozaimasu exist, there is, we have (Superpolite form of desu; aru, arimasu)
3 Konban wa (Cph: evening greeting)
4 Sayōnara＝Sayonara (Cph: used in parting)
5 Oyasumi(-nasai) (Cph: greeting before going to bed)
-nasai (Polite imperative form of suru)
6 Yamada (a family name)
7 Hajimemashite (Cph: when introduced)
8 dōzo please
9 (Dōzo) yoroshiku (Cph: all-purpose request for favorable consideration)
10 meishi name card

Y: (From) London?
B: Yes, London.
Y: What is your occupation?
B: I am an architect.
Y: Is that so?
My younger brother is also an architect.

....

Y: Hi, Mr. Tanaka.
This is Mr. Brown from England.
He is an architect.
T: How do you do?
I'm Tanaka.
B: I'm Brown. Glad to meet you.

Y: *Rondon*[16] desu ka?

B: Ē,[17] *Rondon* desu.

Y: O-shigoto[18] wa nan desu ka?

B: Kenchiku-ka[19] desu.

Y: Sō desu ka.[20]

Watashi no otōto[21] mo kenchiku-ka desu.

....

Y: Yā,[22] Tanaka[23]-san, kochira[24] wa *Igirisu* no *Buraun*-san desu.

Kenchiku-ka desu.

T: Hajimemashite. Tanaka desu.

B: *Buraun* desu. Yoroshiku.

11 dōmo very
12 arigatō (Cph: for expressing thanks)
13 Shitsurei desu ga (Cph) Excuse me, but...
 shitsurei (Na/Nv) being impolite/rude
 ga but
14 o-kuni nation, country
 o- (Pref. for politeness)
15 *Igirisu* 'England'
16 *Rondon* 'London'
17 Ē Yes (Informal)
18 shigoto work, job
19 kenchiku-ka architect
 kenchiku architecture
 -ka specialist
20 Sō desu ka (Cph) Is that so?
21 otōto younger brother
22 Yā Hey, Hi
23 Tanaka (a family name)
24 kochira this person/side/place See §2

▼ Mt. Fuji

ひらがな《HIRAGANA》—1

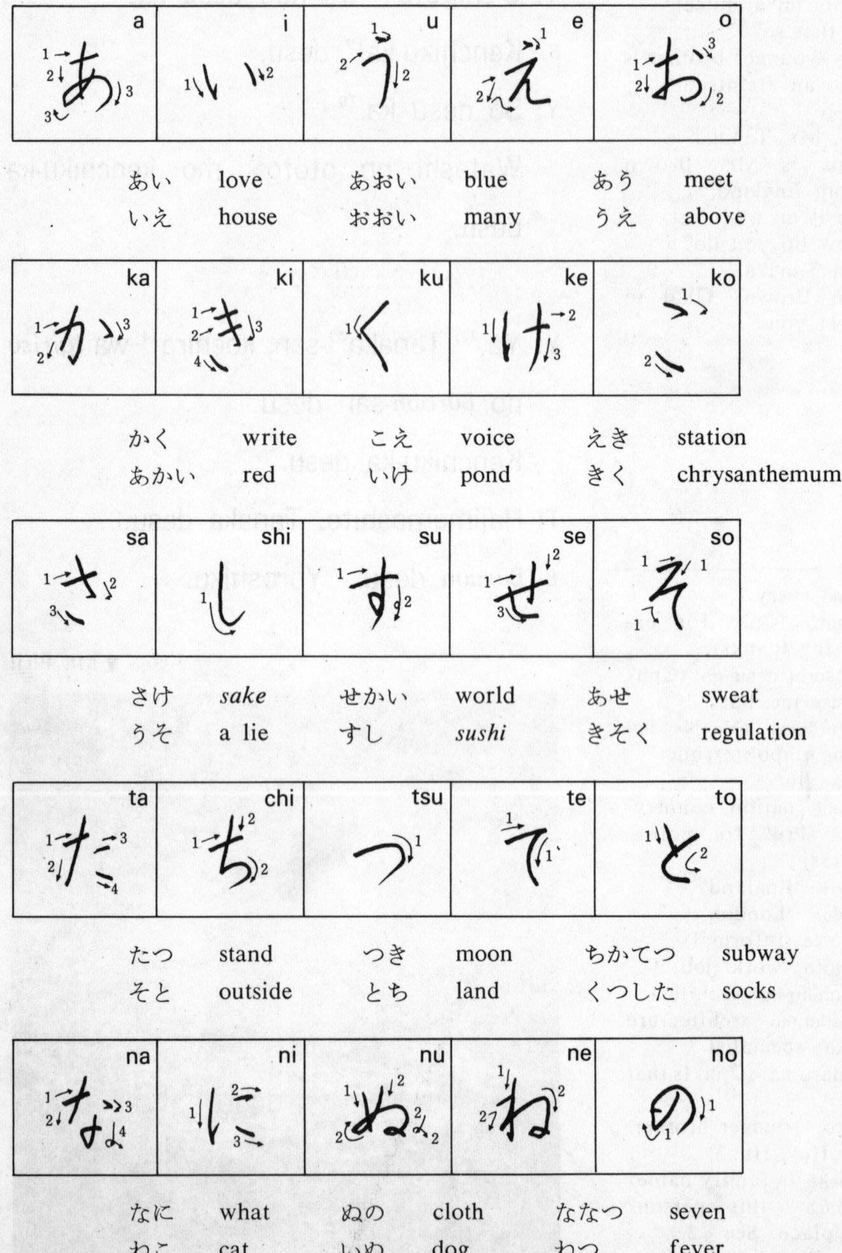

あい	love	あおい	blue	あう	meet
いえ	house	おおい	many	うえ	above

かく	write	こえ	voice	えき	station
あかい	red	いけ	pond	きく	chrysanthemum

さけ	*sake*	せかい	world	あせ	sweat
うそ	a lie	すし	*sushi*	きそく	regulation

たつ	stand	つき	moon	ちかてつ	subway
そと	outside	とち	land	くつした	socks

なに	what	ぬの	cloth	ななつ	seven
ねこ	cat	いぬ	dog	ねつ	fever

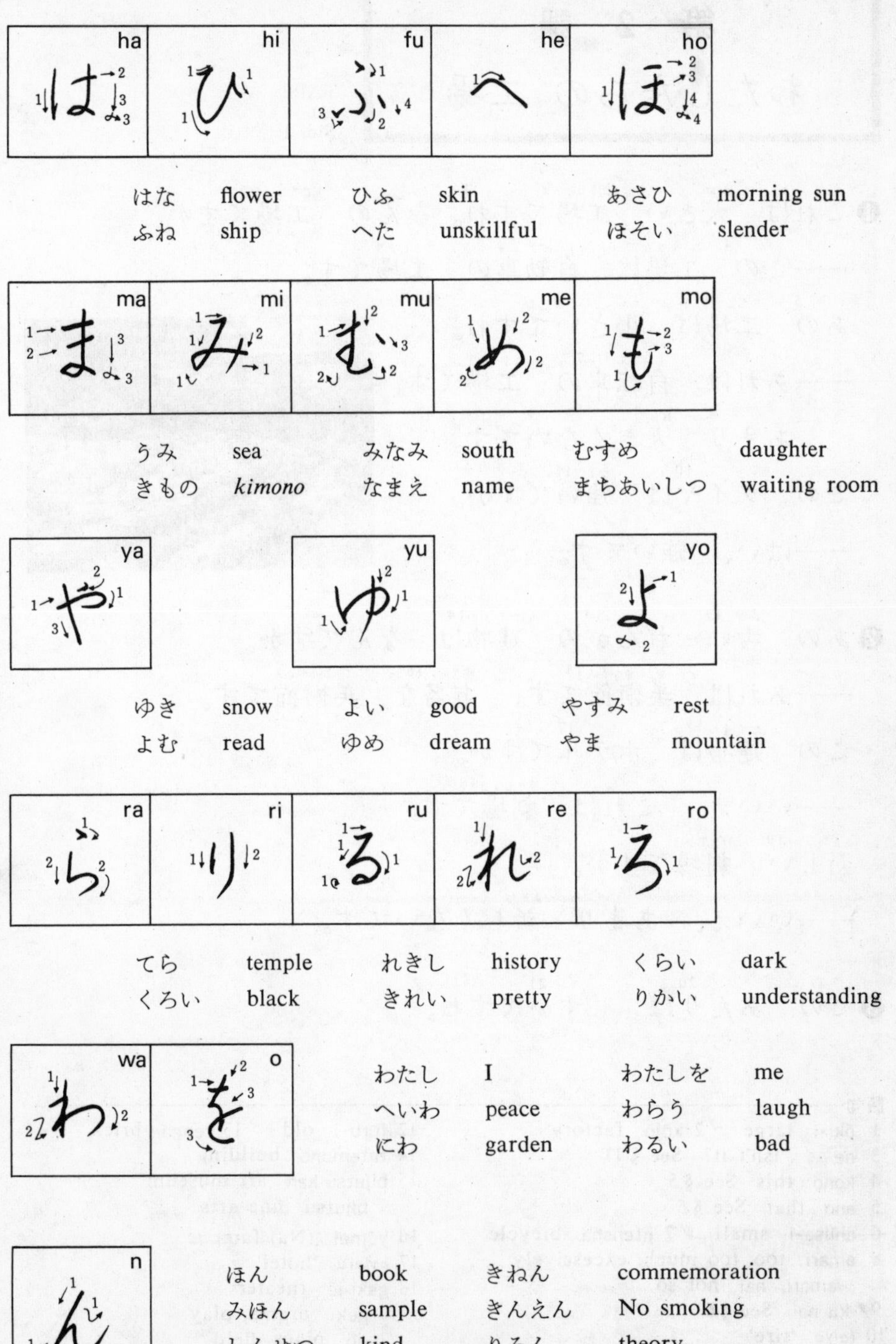

はな	flower	ひふ	skin	あさひ	morning sun
ふね	ship	へた	unskillful	ほそい	slender

うみ	sea	みなみ	south	むすめ	daughter
きもの	*kimono*	なまえ	name	まちあいしつ	waiting room

ゆき	snow	よい	good	やすみ	rest
よむ	read	ゆめ	dream	やま	mountain

てら	temple	れきし	history	くらい	dark
くろい	black	きれい	pretty	りかい	understanding

わたし	I	わたしを	me
へいわ	peace	わらう	laugh
にわ	garden	わるい	bad

ほん	book	きねん	commemoration
みほん	sample	きんえん	No smoking
しんせつ	kind	りろん	theory

第 2 課

わたしたちの 工場

TAPE
No. 1
Side 1

❶これは　大(おお)きい[1]　工場(こうじょう)[2]ですね[3]。なんの　工場(こうじょう)ですか。

——この[4]　工場(こうじょう)は　自動車(じどうしゃ)の　工場(こうじょう)です。

あの[5]　工場(こうじょう)は　小(ちい)さい[6]ですね。

——あれは　自転車(じてんしゃ)[7]の　工場(こうじょう)です。

あまり[8]　大(おお)きくない[9]です。

この　タイヤ[10]は　強(つよ)い[11]ですか。

——はい、強(つよ)いです。

❷あの　古(ふる)い[12]　れんが[13]の　建物(たてもの)[14]は　なんですか。

——あれは　美術館(びじゅつかん)[15]です。有名(ゆうめい)[16]な　美術館(びじゅつかん)です。

この　建物(たてもの)は　ホテル[17]ですか。

——いいえ、これは　劇場(げきじょう)[18]です。

新(あたら)しい[19]　劇場(げきじょう)ですか。

——いいえ、あまり　新(あたら)しくないです。

❸この　あたり[20]は　しずか[21]ですね。

語句

1 ōki·i　large　2 kōjō　factory
3 ne　..., isn't it?　See § 11
4 kono　this　See § 5
5 ano　that　See § 5
6 chiisa·i　small　7 jitensha　bicycle
8 amari　too, too much, excessively
　amari...nai　not so...
9 -ku nai　See § 6
10 *taiya*　'tire'
11 tsuyo·i　strong, powerful
12 furu·i　old　13 renga　brick
14 tatemono　building
15 bijutsu-kan　art museum
　bijutsu　fine arts
16 yūmei　(Na) famous
17 *hoteru*　'hotel'
18 geki-jō　theater
　geki　drama, play
　-jō　place, field
19 atarashi·i　new, fresh

——はい、いつも[22] しずかです。あなたの 家(いえ)[23]の あたりは どう[24]ですか。

あまり しずかではありません。

——あなたの 町(まち)[25]は どんな[26] 町(まち)ですか。

酒(さけ)[27]で[28] 有名(ゆうめい)な 町(まち)です。海(うみ)[29]に[30]も 山(やま)[31]にも 近(ちか)[32]いです。空気(くうき)[33]も 水(みず)[34]も たいへん[35] きれい[36]です。

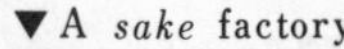

▼A *sake* factory

---

20 atari (N) neighborhood
kono atari this neighborhood
21 shizuka (Na) silent, quiet
22 itsumo always 23 ie house
24 dō how See § 9
25 machi town
26 donna what sort of See § 8
27 sake alcoholic drink, Japanese wine
28 de with, for
…de yūmei famous for…
29 umi sea, ocean
30 ni to
31 yama mountain
32 chika·i near
…ni chikai near…
33 kūki air
34 mizu water
35 taihen very See § 10
36 kirei (Na) clean; pretty

Dai 2-ka
Watashi-tachi no Kōjō

1 Kore wa ōkii kōjō desu ne. Nan no kōjō desu ka?

——Kono kōjō wa jidōsha no kōjō desu.

Ano kōjō wa chiisai desu ne.

——Are wa jitensha no kōjō desu. Amari ōkiku nai desu.

Kono *taiya* wa tsuyoi desu ka?

——Hai, tsuyoi desu.

2 Ano furui renga no tatemono wa nan desu ka?

——Are wa bijutsu-kan desu. Yūmei-na bijutsu-kan desu.

Kono tatemono wa *hoteru* desu ka?

——Iie, kore wa gekijō desu.

Atarashii gekijō desu ka?

——Iie, amari atarashiku nai desu.

3 Kono atari wa shizuka desu ne.

——Hai, itsumo shizuka desu. Anata no ie no atari wa dō desu ka?

Amari shizuka dewa arimasen.

——Anata no machi wa donna machi desu ka?

Sake de yūmei-na machi desu. Umi nimo yama nimo chikai desu.

Kūki mo mizu mo taihen kirei desu.

▼ The National Museum of Western Art

▼ Osaka's Shin-Kabuki-za

Lesson 2

Our Factory

1 This is a big factory, isn't it? What do they make here?

——This factory is an automobile factory.

That factory is small, isn't it?

——That is a bicycle factory. That is not so big.

Is this tire strong?

——Yes, it is strong.

2 What is that old brick building?

——That is a museum. It is a famous museum.

Is this building a hotel?

——No, it is not. This is a theater.

Is it a new theater?

——No, it is not so new.

3 It is quiet in this neighborhood, isn't it?

——Yes, it is always quiet. What is your neighborhood like?

It is not so quiet.

——What kind of a town is your town?

It's a town famous for *sake*. It is close to both the sea and the mountains.

Both the air and the water are very clean there.

ANSWERS 〈pp. 28, 29〉

I. (A) 6. Q: Kono machi wa umi ni chikai desu ka? A: Iie, chikaku nai desu. Tōi desu. (C) 1. Q: Ano ōkii tatemono wa nan desu ka? A: Ano ōkii tatemono wa daigaku no tosho-kan desu. 2. Q: Ano wakai onna no hito wa dare desu ka? A: Ano wakai onna no hito wa watashi no sensei desu.

II. (A) 1. Kore wa nagai shōsetsu desu. 2. Kore wa takai kitte desu. 3. Kore wa watashi no atarashii jidōsha desu. 4. Kore wa benri-na *taipu-raitā* desu. 5. Koko wa shizuka-na machi desu.

(B) 1. Kono benri-na *kamera* wa watashi no desu. Kono karui *kamera* wa dare no desu ka? 2. Kono chiisai ie wa watashi no desu. Kono furui ie wa dare no desu ka? 3. Kono shiroi kasa wa watashi no desu. Kono akai kasa wa dare no desu ka?

III. 1. Kore wa yūmei-na shōsetsu desu. Kono shōsetsu wa taihen omoshiroi desu. (Kore wa) amari muzukashiku nai desu. 2. "Ano ōkii tatemono wa nan desu ka?" "Atarashii tosho-kan desu." 3. "Kono shiroi hana no namae wa nan desu ka?" "Bara desu." 4. "Ano kirei-na onna no hito wa dare desu ka?" "Ano kirei-na onna no hito wa watashi-tachi no Nippon-go no sensei desu."

●文法

§5 Prenominal Demonstratives: **kono, sono, ano, dono**

e.g. Kono hana wa bara desu. 'This flower (here) is a rose.'

Ano hito wa *Amerika*-jin desu. 'That person (=He) is an American.'

Yamada-san wa dono hito desu ka? 'Which person is Mr. Yamada?'

§6 Describing Things—Adjectival Predicates

N wa {A / Na} desu.

e.g. Kono kōjō wa ōkii desu. 'This factory is big.'

Kono machi wa shizuka desu.

'This town is quiet.'

Question: N wa A/Na desu ka?

Negation: N wa {**A-ku nai desu.** / **Na dewa arimasen.**}

e.g. ...ōkiku nai desu. '...is not big.'

...shizuka dewa arimasen. '...is not quiet.'

Adjectives are of two kinds: 'i Adjectives' ('A') and 'na Adjectives' ('Na'). All **A** are indigenous Japanese adjectives, and they all end with '-i' in the present affirmative form (Dictionary form), e.g. ōkii 'big,' nagai 'long.' **Na** are mostly Chinese-origin words, some coming from other foreign languages, e.g. shizuka 'quiet,' kirei 'pretty,' sakan 'active, flourishing, popular,' etc. A and Na are conjugated in different ways.

§7 Using A or Na as Noun Modifiers

A / **Na(-na)** } +**N**

e.g. ōkii kōjō 'a big factory'

shizuka-na machi 'a quiet town'

When foreign words are to be used as adjectives in Japanese, they conform to the Na pattern and not to the A pattern.

e.g. Sore wa *nansensu* desu. 'That's nonsense.'

nánsensu-na hanashi 'a nonsensical story, a bit of nonsense' *modan*-na tatemono 'a modern building'

NB: ōkii and chiisai, although they are 'i Adjectives,' sometimes take the '-na form' when used as Prenominal modifiers.

e.g. ōki-na kōjō (=ōkii kōjō) 'a big factory'

chiisa-na kōjō (=chiisai kōjō) 'a small factory'

§ 8 Adjectival Demonstratives (See Table in § 2)

The Demonstratives **konna, sonna, anna** are used before N, like Adjectives, expressing 'such...,' or '...like this/that.' **Donna** means 'what kind of...'

e.g. Sono machi wa donna machi desu ka? 'What is that town like?'

—Chiisai shizuka-na machi desu. 'It's a small, quiet town.'

§ 9 Adverbial Demonstratives (See Table in § 2)

When the particle **ni** is attached to konna, sonna, etc., they function as Adverbs and are used to modify other Adjectives, expressing degree.

e.g. Itsumo konna-ni samui desu ka? 'Is it always this cold?'

Ima sonna-ni isogashiku nai desu. 'I am not so busy (as you may suppose) now.' or 'I am not all that busy now.'

Another set of Demonstratives **kō, sō, ā, dō,** are also used as Adverbs, but they are mainly used to modify Verbs, expressing manner.

e.g. Kyōto e wa dō ikimasu ka? 'How do I go to Kyoto?'

Kore wa dō desu ka? 'How is this?' or 'How do you like this?'

§ 10 Adverbs of Degree

e.g. taihen (ōkii) 'very (big)' totemo (kirei) 'very (pretty)'

taitei (ōkii) 'mostly (big)' amari (ōkiku nai) '(not) very (big)'

§ 11 Sentence-final Particles ('Ps'): ne and yo

In addition to ka (§ 1), the Ps which are most commonly used in spoken Japanese are ne and yo. The particle ne indicates that the speaker is expecting the listener's agreement, and yo that he is calling for the listener's particular attention to his statement. Others will be introduced later.

●練習

ANSWERS→p. 25

I. Make dialogs as shown in the examples.

(A) Ex. Q: (kono kaisha) (atarashii) Kono kaisha wa atarashii desu ka?

A: (iie) (furui) Iie, atarashiku nai desu. Furui desu.

1. Q: (sono[1] hon) (omoshiroi[2]) A: (iie) (tsumaranai[3])
2. Q: (sono jidōsha) (takai[4]) A: (iie) (yasui[5])
3. Q: (sono yama) (takai) A: (iie) (hikui[6])
4. Q: (Nippon-go) (muzukashii[7]) A: (iie) (yasashii[8])
5. Q: (kono *taipu-raitā*[9]) (karui[10]) A: (iie) (omoi[11])
6. Q: (kono machi) (umi ni chikai) A: (iie) (tōi[12])

(B) Ex. Q: (Tōkyō) (kirei) Tōkyō wa kirei desu ka?

A: (taihen) Hai, taihen kirei desu.

(amari) Iie, amari kirei dewa arimasen.

1. Q: (Tōkyō) (shizuka) A: (amari)
2. Q: (kono bijutsu-kan) (yūmei) A: (taihen)
3. Q: (kono kikai[13]) (benri[14]) A: (amari)
4. Q: (ano byōin no hito-tachi[15]) (shinsetsu[16]) A: (taihen)
5. Q: (kanojo) (shinsetsu) A: (amari)
6. Q: (sono shōsetsu[17]) (yūmei) A: (amari)
7. Q: (anata no machi no kūki) (kirei) A: (amari)

(C) Ex. Q: (furui) (tatemono) Ano furui tatemono wa nan desu ka?

A: (bijutsu-kan) Ano furui tatemono wa bijutsu-kan desu.

1. Q: (ōkii) (tatemono) A: (daigaku no tosho-kan)
2. Q: (wakai[18]) (onna no hito[19]) A: (watashi no sensei[20])

語句

1 sono that See §5
2 omoshiro·i amusing, interesting
3 tsumarana·i not interesting
4 taka·i expensive; high
5 yasu·i cheap 6 hiku·i low
7 muzukashi·i difficult
8 yasashi·i easy; gentle, tender
9 *taipu-raitā* 'typewriter'
10 karu·i light, not heavy
11 omo·i heavy 12 tō·i far
13 kikai machine
14 benri (Na) convenient; useful

II. Transform the following sentences as shown in the examples.

(A) Ex. Kono hon wa omoshiroi desu. →Kore wa omoshiroi hon desu.

1. Kono shōsetsu wa nagai[21] desu.
2. Kono kitte wa takai desu.
3. Kono watashi no jidōsha wa atarashii desu.
4. Kono *taipu-raitā* wa benri desu.
5. Kono machi wa shizuka desu.

(B) Ex. Kono jidōsha wa ōkii desu. →Kono ōkii jidōsha wa watashi no desu.

(atarashi) →Kono atarashii jidōsha wa dare no desu ka?

1. Kono *kamera* wa benri desu.
   (karui)
2. Kono ie wa chiisai desu.
   (furui)
3. Kono kasa wa shiroi[22] desu.
   (akai[23])

III. Put the following into Japanese.

1. This is a famous novel. This novel is very interesting. It is not very difficult.
2. "What is that big building?" "It is a new library."
3. "What is the name of this white flower?" "It is a rose."
4. "Who is that beautiful lady?" "That beautiful lady is our teacher of Japanese."

---

15 hito-tachi people
16 shinsetsu (Na) kind(ness)
17 shōsetsu novel
18 waka·i young
19 onna no hito woman, lady
onna woman, female (person)
20 sensei teacher
21 naga·i long
22 shiro·i white
23 aka·i red

●会話

KOKO WA DOKO?

Sumimasen[1] ga....

Koko wa Yotsuya[2] desu ka?

—Iie, chigaimasu.[3]

Yotsuya wa tsugi[4] desu.

Koko wa doko desu ka?

—Shinjuku[5] desu.

Ā,[6] sō desu ka. Dōmo arigatō.

—Dō itashimashite.[7]

Chotto[8] sumimasen ga....

Are wa *hoteru* desu ka?

—Iie, sō dewa arimasen.

Ano *biru*[9] wa daigaku desu.

Hoteru wa sono mukō[10] no takai *biru* desu.

Excuse me, but....
Is this (place) Yotsuya?
—No, it's not.
Yotsuya is the next station.
Where is this (place)?
—(This is) Shinjuku.
Oh, is that so? Thank you.
—Not at all.

Excuse me a minute.
Is that a hotel?
—No, it isn't.
That building is a university.
The hotel is the tall building beyond that.

語句

1 Sumimasen (Cph: apology)
2 Yotsuya (a place name)
3 Chigaimasu You're wrong. It is not.
  chiga·u be different
  -masu See §16
4 tsugi (N) next
5 Shinjuku (a place name)
6 Ā Oh
7 Dō itashimashite You're welcome. Not at all.
8 chotto a little; a while
9 *biru* 'building'
10 mukō (N) over/beyond there

2

Is it close?
—Well, let me see....
It's not all that far.
It's about 5 minutes on foot.
Thanks.
Excuse me....
Where is Mr. Ota's house?
—Let's see... Mr. Ota?
That's Mr. Ota the doctor, isn't it?
No, the painter.
—Mr. Ota the painter?
Then... Taro Ota, is it?
Yes, that's it.
Is it around here?
—Yes, it's that house with the red roof.
Is that so? Thank you.
—You're welcome.

Chikai desu ka?
—Sō desu nē[11]....
Sonna-ni[12] tōku nai desu yo.[13]
Aruite[14] go-fun[15] gurai[16] desu.
Arigatō.

Sumimasen....
Ōta[17]-san no o-taku[18] wa doko desu ka?
—Ē...to,[19] Ōta-san desu ka?
O-isha[20]-san no Ōta-san desu ne?
Iie, gaka[21] desu.
—Gaka no Ōta-san?
Ā..., Ōta Tarō[22]-san desu ne?
Hai, hai, sō desu.
Kono atari desu ka?
—Ē, ano akai yane[23] no uchi[24] desu.
Sō desu ka. Dōmo arigatō.
—Iie, dō itashimashite.

11 nē=ne See § 11
12 sonna-ni...nai not so
13 yo See § 11
14 aruite on foot
aruk•u walk
15 -fun =-pun minute
16 ...gurai about/approximately...
17 Ōta (a family name)
18 (o-)taku residence
19 Ē...to Well, let me see
20 isha medical doctor
21 gaka painter
22 Tarō (a given name (m))
23 yane roof
24 uchi=ie house, home

ひらがな《HIRAGANA》—2

ga	gi	gu	ge	go
が	ぎ	ぐ	げ	ご
za	ji	zu	ze	zo
ざ	じ	ず	ぜ	ぞ
da	ji	zu	de	do
だ	ぢ	づ	で	ど
ba	bi	bu	be	bo
ば	び	ぶ	べ	ぼ
pa	pi	pu	pe	po
ぱ	ぴ	ぷ	ぺ	ぽ

かぜ　wind

でんわ　telephone

こども　child

かぞく　family

たばこ　cigarette

さんぽ　a walk

がくせい　student

えんぴつ　pencil

しんぶん　newspaper

がいこくじん　foreigner

kya	kyu	kyo	nya	nyu	nyo
きゃ	きゅ	きょ	にゃ	にゅ	にょ
gya	gyu	gyo	hya	hyu	hyo
ぎゃ	ぎゅ	ぎょ	ひゃ	ひゅ	ひょ
sha	shu	sho	bya	byu	byo
しゃ	しゅ	しょ	びゃ	びゅ	びょ
ja	ju	jo	pya	pyu	pyo
じゃ	じゅ	じょ	ぴゃ	ぴゅ	ぴょ
cha	chu	cho	mya	myu	myo
ちゃ	ちゅ	ちょ	みゃ	みゅ	みょ
ja	ju	jo	rya	ryu	ryo
ぢゃ	ぢゅ	ぢょ	りゃ	りゅ	りょ

ひゃく　hundred

きゃく　guest

ぎじゅつ　technique

きょねん　last year

でんしゃ
electric train

りょかん　inn

さんびゃく　300

しゃかい　society

おちゃ　tea

ちゅうい　caution

Some Orthographical Rules

1. The difference between じ and ぢ (ji) and between ず and づ (zu) is not a matter of pronunciation but one of usage. じ and ず are generally used.

2. Double consonants are expressed by the small っ.

みっつ (mit-tsu) 'three' cf. みつ (mitsu) 'honey'

そっと (sotto) 'secretly' cf. そと (soto) 'outside'

もっと (motto) 'more' cf. もと (moto) 'origin'

3. (C※+) ō is usually written as (C+) o and う (u). ※consonant

ふうとう (fūtō) 'envelope'

ありがとう (arigatō) 'thank you'

べんきょう (benkyō) 'study'

Exceptions: Some are written as (C+) o and お (o).

おおきい (ōkii) 'big' おおい (ōi) 'many, much'

とお (tō) 'ten' とおる (tōru) 'pass'

とおい (tōi) 'far' こおり (kōri) 'ice'

4. The Particle wa (See § 1) is written は.

これは ほんです。'This is a book.'

はは は とうきょうに います。'My mother is in Tokyo.'

わたしは がくせいではありません。'I am not a student.'

5. The Particle e (See § 19) is written へ.

あなたは どこへ いきますか。'Where are you going?'

わたしは くにへ かえります。'I will go back to my country.'

ここへ きてください。'Please come here.'

6. The Particle o (See § 17, § 26, § 28) is written を.

わたしは にっぽんごを べんきょう します。'I study Japanese.'

あなたは ごはんを たべましたか。'Did you eat?'

とりは そらを とびます。'Birds fly in the sky.'

第 3 課

へやの 中

TAPE
No. 1
Side 2

❶ここは　営業課(えいぎょうか)[1]の　へや[2]です。
この　へやに[3]は　ドア[4]が[5]　二つ(ふた)[6]　あります[7]。
へやの　中(なか)[8]には　つくえ[9]が　たくさん[10]　あります。
人(ひと)も　たくさん　います[11]。

❷——つくえは　いくつ[12]　ありますか。
一つ(ひと)[13]、　二つ(ふた)、　三つ(みっ)[14]、　四つ(よっ)[15]、　五つ(いつ)[16]……全部(ぜんぶ)[17]で　十五(じゅうご)[18]　あります。　いす[19]も　十五(じゅうご)　あります。
——人(ひと)は　何人(なんにん)[20]　いますか。
今(いま)[21]、　一人(ひとり)[22]、　二人(ふたり)[23]、　三人(さんにん)[24]、　四人(よにん)[25]、　五人(ごにん)[26]……八人(はちにん)[27]　います。

❸——課長(かちょう)[28]さんの　つくえは　どこですか。
へやの　奥(おく)[29]です。　わたしの　つくえは　これです。
つくえの　上(うえ)[30]には、　本(ほん)[31]や　ボールペンや　電話(でんわ)[32]が　あります。
本(ほん)は　五(ご)さつ[33]、　ボールペンは　三本(さんぼん)[34]　あります。

語句

1 eigyō-ka　sales section
　eigyō　business, trade, sales
　-ka　section (smaller than -bu)
2 heya　room
3 ni　in, at　See § 12
4 *doa*　'door'　　5 ga　See § 12
6 futa-tsu　two　See § 14
7 ar·u　exist　See § 12
8 naka　(N) inside　　9 tsukue　desk
10 takusan　(N/Adv) many, much
11 i·ru　exist; stay　See § 12
12 iku-tsu　how many; how old (age)
　See § 14
13 hito-tsu　one　See § 14
14 mit-tsu　three　See § 14
15 yot-tsu　four　See § 14
16 itsu-tsu　five　See § 14
17 zenbu　(N/Adv) all, whole
　zenbu de　in all
18 jū-go　fifteen　jū　ten　go　five
19 isu　chair
20 nan-nin　how many people
　nan-　(+Count.) how many; what
　-nin　(Count. for persons)　See § 14
21 ima　now　　22 hito-ri　one person
23 futa-ri　two persons
24 san-nin　three persons
25 yo-nin　four persons

へやの　すみ[35]に　大(おお)きい　本(ほん)だな[36]が　あります。　その　横(よこ)[37]に　カレンダー[38]が　あります。

まど[39]の　そば[40]に　ロッカー[41]も　あります。

——計算機(けいさんき)[42]は　何台(なんだい)[43]　ありますか。

全部(ぜんぶ)で　三台(さんだい)　あります。　わたしの　うしろ[44]と[45]　へやの　まん中(なか)[46]と　あの　黒板(こくばん)[47]の　前(まえ)[48]に　一台(いちだい)ずつ[49]　あります。

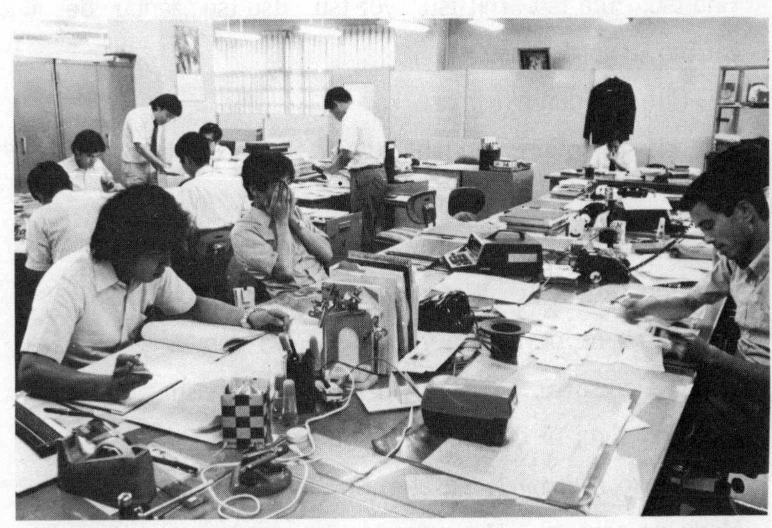

---

26 go-nin five persons
27 hachi-nin eight persons
28 ka-chō section chief -chō chief
29 oku the end of a room, inner part
30 ue top; surface; upper part See § 13
31 ya and See § 15
32 denwa telephone
33 -satsu (Count. for books) See § 14
34 -bon =-hon, -pon (Count. for cylindrical things) See § 14
35 sumi corner (seen from inside)
 cf. kado (corner from outside)
36 hon-dana bookshelf
 -dana =tana shelf
37 yoko (N) beside, by
38 *karendā* 'calendar' 39 mado window
40 soba (N) beside, close by
41 *rokkā* 'locker'
42 keisan-ki calculator, computer
 keisan calculation -ki machine
43 -dai (Count. for machines) See § 14
44 ushiro (N) back, rear
45 to and See § 15
46 man-naka center, middle
 man- =ma- at the height/center of
47 kokuban blackboard
48 mae (N) before, front
49 ...zutsu ...each

Dai 3-ka
Heya no Naka

1 Koko wa eigyō-ka no heya desu.
Kono heya niwa *doa* ga futa-tsu arimasu.
Heya no naka niwa tsukue ga takusan arimasu.
Hito mo takusan imasu.

2 ——Tsukue wa iku-tsu arimasu ka?
Hito-tsu, futa-tsu, mit-tsu, yot-tsu, itsu-tsu...zenbu de jū-go arimasu.
Isu mo jū-go arimasu.
——Hito wa nan-nin imasu ka?
Ima, hito-ri, futa-ri, san-nin, yo-nin, go-nin...hachi-nin imasu.

3 ——Ka-chō-san no tsukue wa doko desu ka?
Heya no oku desu. Watashi no tsukue wa kore desu.
Tsukue no ue niwa, hon ya *bōru-pen* ya denwa ga arimasu.
Hon wa go-satsu, *bōru-pen* wa san-bon arimasu.
Heya no sumi ni ōkii hon-dana ga arimasu.
Sono yoko ni *karendā* ga arimasu.
Mado no soba ni *rokkā* mo arimasu.
——Keisan-ki wa nan-dai arimasu ka?
Zenbu de san-dai arimasu. Watashi no ushiro to heya no man-naka to ano kokuban no mae ni ichi-dai zutsu arimasu.

Lesson 3

Inside the Room

1 This is the sales section's room.
There are two doors to this room.
There are many desks in the room.
There are also many people.

2 ——How many desks are there?
One, two, three, four, five.... There are fifteen in all.
There are also fifteen chairs.
——How many people are there?
One, two, three, four, five.... There are eight persons here now.

3 ——Where is the Section Chief's desk?
It is in the back of the room. This is my desk.
There are books, ball-point pens, and a telephone on the desk.
There are five books and three ball-point pens.
There is a big bookshelf in the corner of the room.
There is a calendar next to the bookshelf.
There are also some lockers near the window.
——How many computers are there?
There are three in all. There is one behind me, one in the middle of the room, and one in front of that blackboard.

ANSWERS 〈pp. 40, 41〉

I. (B) 1. (Tokei no migi ni) denwa ga arimasu. 2. (*Tēburu* no ue ni) ringo to *tabako* ga arimasu. 3. (Hana wa) *terebi* no ue ni arimasu. 4. (Hon wa) *terebi* no shita ni arimasu.
II. (B) 1. (Ki no shita ni) onna no ko ga imasu. 2. (Anata no yoko ni) *Tomu* to *Jon* ga imasu. 3 (Tarō wa) jidōsha no naka ni imasu. 4. (Neko wa) isu no ue ni imasu. 5. (Tori wa) ki no ue ni imasu.
IV. 1. Q: Bijutsu-kan wa doko ni arimasu ka? A: (Bijutsu-kan wa) kōen no man-naka ni arimasu. 2. Q: Tosho-kan wa doko ni arimasu ka? A: (Tosho-kan wa) daigaku no soba ni arimasu. 3. Q: Anata no kazoku wa doko ni imasu ka? A: Watashi no kazoku wa *Kanada* ni imasu. 4. Q: Byōin wa doko ni arimasu ka? A: (Byōin wa) yūbin-kyoku no mae ni arimasu. 5. Q: Ka-chō-san wa doko ni imasu ka? A: (Ka-chō-san wa) mado no soba ni imasu.

●文法

§ 12 Existence, Location, and Quantity

(Location) {N (inanimate) / N (animate)} **ga** (Quantity) {**arimasu.** / **imasu.**}

e.g. Koko ni denwa ga arimasu. 'Here is a telephone.'

Asoko ni gakusei ga imasu. 'There is a student over there.'

The Particle **ni** is attached to N denoting place and expresses the location of something that exists. Arimasu (Dictionary form aru) is used for inanimate objects or abstract N such as books, telephones, problems, causes, etc., while imasu (Dictionary form iru) is used for living beings such as people, dogs, fish, birds, etc.

When the location or quantity of a particular thing or person is the focus of the sentence, the following pattern is used.

N **wa** (Location) (Quantity) **arimasu/imasu.**

e.g. Anata no tsukue wa doko ni arimasu ka? 'Where is your desk?'

—(Watashi no tsukue wa) koko ni arimasu. 'My desk is here.'

§ 13 Relative Position

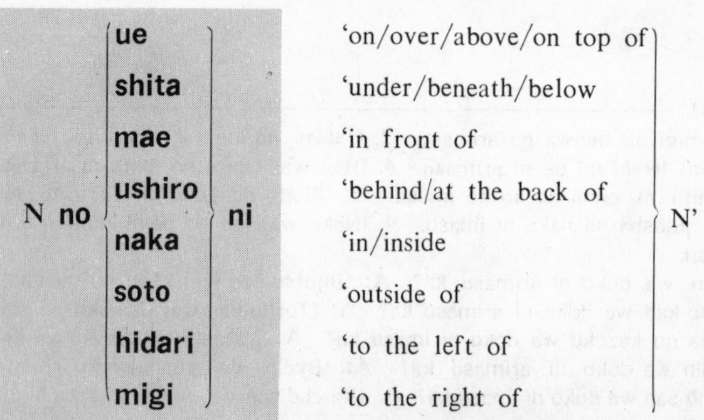

N no	**ue**	ni	'on/over/above/on top of N'
	shita		'under/beneath/below N'
	mae		'in front of N'
	ushiro		'behind/at the back of N'
	naka		'in/inside N'
	soto		'outside of N'
	hidari		'to the left of N'
	migi		'to the right of N'

§ 14 How to Count Things or Persons (See Appendix)

Japanese has two different sets of Numerals: one native Japanese ('J' in the table below) and the other of Chinese origin ('C' below).

	1	2	3	4	5	6	7	8	9	10
'J'	hito-	futa-	mi-	yo(n)-	itsu-	mu-	nana-	ya-	kokono-	tō
'C'	ichi	ni	san	shi	go	roku	shichi	hachi	ku/kyū	jū

When actually counting things, it is necessary to combine 'C' Numerals (with a few exceptions) and what are called Counters (or Counter-suffixes) depending upon the kind of thing to be counted. The Counters that are most commonly used are the following:

-mai for thin, flat objects like paper, plates, shirts, etc.

-hon for long, slender objects like trees, pencils, chalk, etc.

(h is replaced by p after 1, 6 and 10, and by b after 3. See Appendix.)

-satsu for books

-dai for automobiles, bicycles, typewriters, tape recorders, etc.

-hiki for small animals

-wa for birds (-pa after 6 and 10, and -ba after 3)

-nin for people

Exceptions: 'one person'=hito-ri; 'two —'=futa-ri; 'four —'=yo-nin

When expressing numbers in the abstract, as in mathematics, the 'C' Numerals alone are used. For things which are not clearly categorized or which are shapeless, the suffix -tsu is attached to the 'J' Numerals, e.g. stones, cups, boxes, stars, ideas, problems, etc.

§ 15 Noun-conjoining Particles: to and ya

N_1 to N_2 to N_3 'N_1, N_2, and N_3' (implying that these three things are all that there are——'exhaustive')

N_1 ya N_2 ya N_3 'N_1, N_2, and N_3' (among others——'non-exhaustive')

練習 ANSWERS→p. 37

I. Practice with the picture.

(A) Locate the things in the picture (①) as shown in the examples.

1. Tsukue no mae ni isu ga arimasu. 2. Tsukue no ue ni denwa ya tokei ya enpitsu[1] ga arimasu. 3. Denwa no hidari[2] ni tokei ga arimasu. 4. Ringo[3] no migi[4] ni *tabako* ga arimasu. 5. Mado no soba ni *terebi*[5] to *tēburu*[6] ga arimasu. 6. *Terebi* no shita[7] ni *kamera* ga arimasu.

(B) Answer the following questions.

1. Tokei no migi ni nani[8] ga arimasu ka?
2. *Tēburu* no ue ni nani ga arimasu ka?
3. Hana wa doko ni arimasu ka?
4. Hon wa doko ni arimasu ka?

II. Practice with the picture (②).

(A) Locate the people or animals in the picture.

1. Dōro[9] no soba ni kodomo[10] ga imasu. 2. Ki[11] no shita ni onna no ko[12] ga imasu. 3. Jidōsha no naka ni Tarō ga imasu. 4. Jidōsha no ushiro ni inu[13] ga imasu. 5. Ōkii ki to chiisai ki no aida[14] ni otoko[15] no ko ga imasu. 6. *Tomu* to *Jon*[16] no aida ni watashi ga imasu. 7. Watashi no tonari[17] ni *Tomu* ga imasu.

語句

1 enpitsu pencil
2 hidari (N) left
3 ringo apple
4 migi (N) right
5 *terebi* 'television'
6 *tēburu* 'table'
7 shita (N) under, beneath
8 nani what
9 dōro road
10 kodomo child(ren)
11 ki tree, wood
12 ko =kodomo child(ren)
onna no ko girl
13 inu dog
14 aida (N) between

(B) Answer the following questions.

1. Ki no shita ni dare ga imasu ka?
2. Watashi no yoko ni dare to dare ga imasu ka?
3. Tarō wa doko ni imasu ka?
4. Neko[18] wa doko ni imasu ka?
5. Tori[19] wa doko ni imasu ka?

3

III. Practice with the pictures (①, ②).

(A) Practice the following sentences.

1. Denwa ga ichi-dai arimasu. 2. Kami[20] ga ni-mai[21] arimasu.
3. Ki wa zenbu de nan-bon arimasu ka? —Rop-pon arimasu.
4. Inu wa nan-biki[22] imasu ka? —Ni-hiki imasu.

(B) Make questions such as the following and answer them.

Q: Ringo wa iku-tsu arimasu ka? —A: Itsu-tsu arimasu.

IV. Make dialogs as shown in the example.

Ex. Q: (anata no kaisha) Anata no kaisha wa doko ni arimasu ka?
A: (in Tokyo) Watashi no kaisha wa Tōkyō ni arimasu.

1. Q: (bijutsu-kan) A: (in the middle of the park[23])
2. Q: (tosho-kan) A: (beside the university)
3. Q: (anata no kazoku[24]) A: (in Canada)
4. Q: (byōin) A: (in front of the post office)
5. Q: (ka-chō-san) A: (by the window)

---

15 otoko man, male (person)
otoko no ko boy
16 *Jon* 'John'
17 tonari (N) (sitting/standing/living/placing) next (to...)
18 neko cat 19 tori bird
20 kami paper
21 -mai sheet (Count. for thin, flat objects) See § 14
22 -biki =-hiki, -piki (Count. for small animals)
23 kōen park 24 kazoku family

●会話

ANATA NO SHUMI WA?

Anata no shumi[1] wa nan desu ka?

—*Gorufu*[2] desu.

Nippon niwa *gorufu*-jō[3] ga arimasu ka?

—Ē, takusan arimasu yo.

Hap-pyaku[4] gurai arimasu.

Hohō,[5] ōi[6] desu ne.

Anata wa doko no *menbā*[7] desu ka?

—Hakone[8] *Kantori Kurabu*[9] desu.

Nan-*yādo*[10] gurai arimasu ka?

—Nana-sen-go-hyaku[11] desu.

Ōkii desu ne.

Kyadi[12] wa nan-nin gurai imasu ka?

—Hyaku-go-jū-nin[13] gurai desu.

Mina[14] ii[15] *kyadi* desu.

Mina otoko no *kyadi* desu ka?

—Iie, Nippon dewa[16] *kyadi* wa taitei[17] onna desu.

Tokorode,[18] anata no shumi mo *gorufu* desu ka?

Iie, watashi no shumi wa kitte no

What is your hobby?
—Golf.
Are there any golf courses in Japan?
—Yes, there are many. There are about 800.
Really! That's a lot.
Where are you a member?
—Hakone Country Club.
About how many yards is it?
—7,500.
Big, isn't it?
About how many caddies are there?
—About 150.
They are all good caddies.
Are all of them male caddies?
—No. Caddies are usually women in Japan.
By the way, is your hobby golf too?
No, my hobby is stamp-collecting.

語句

1 shumi hobby
2 *gorufu* 'golf'
3 *gorufu*-jō golf course
4 hap-pyaku 800
-pyaku=-hyaku, -byaku hundred
5 Hohō I see
6 ō・i many; much
7 *menbā* 'member'
8 Hakone (a place name)
9 *kantori kurabu* 'country club'
10 *yādo* 'yard'
11 nana-sen-go-hyaku 7,500
-sen=-zen thousand
12 *kyadi* 'caddie'
13 hyaku-go-jū-nin 150 persons
14 mina=minna (N/Adv) all
15 ii=yo・i good
16 de in, at
17 taitei (N/Adv) mostly

3

shūshū[19] desu.

—Watashi no imōto no shumi mo kitte desu. Uchi niwa kirei-na kitte ya mezurashii[20] kitte ga iroiro[21] arimasu.

Sō desu ka. Tokorode, imōto-san wa iku-tsu desu ka?

—Jū-roku-sai[22] desu. Kōkō-sei[23] desu. Kore wa imōto no shashin desu.

Hō[24]..., kirei-na imōto-san desu ne....

—Iyā[25]... sore hodo[26] demo arimasen. Anata nimo[27] imōto-san ga imasu ka?

Iie, otōto ga futa-ri imasu.

Watashi-tachi wa san-nin kyōdai[28] desu.

Watashi no tsugi no otōto wa ni-jū-go-sai[29] desu.

Shita no otōto wa mada[30] gakusei desu.

—Doko no daigaku desu ka?

Rondon Daigaku desu.

Kare no shumi wa ongaku[31] desu.

—Stamps are my younger sister's hobby too. We have all kinds of beautiful and rare stamps at home.

Is that so? By the way, how old is your younger sister?

—Sixteen. She is a high school student. This is a picture of my younger sister.

My, what a pretty sister!

—No, not really. Do you have a younger sister too?

No, I have two younger brothers.

We are three brothers.

My immediately younger brother is 25 years old.

My youngest brother is still a student.

—What university (is he going to)?

University of London.

His hobby is music.

---

18 tokorode By the way
19 shūshū (Nv) collection
20 mezurashi·i rare
21 iroiro (N/Na/Adv) variety, several kinds
22 jū-roku-sai 16 years old
  -sai age, ...old
23 kōkō-sei high school student kōkō=kōtō-gakkō high school -sei student
24 Hō I see
25 Iyā well, no...
26 ...hodo degree See § 104
  sore hodo to that degree
27 ni with See § 12, § 68
28 kyōdai brothers and/or sisters
29 ni-jū-go-sai 25 years old
30 mada still See § 25
31 ongaku music

カタカナ《KATAKANA》

1. *Katakana* is now used primarily for writing loan words (except Chinese) and foreign names. Its orthographical rules are the same as those mentioned on page 33, except for rule 3. Long vowels are expressed by ー in *katakana*.

'news'	ニュース	(*nyūsu*)
'coffee'	コーヒー	(*kōhī*)
'elevator'	エレベーター	(*erebētā*)

2. Because of the phonetic characters in Japanese, some foreign pronunciations cannot be transliterated properly. Vowels are inserted into consonant clusters and added when a foreign word ends in any consonant except **n**.

'street'	ストリート	(*sutorīto*)
'Christmas'	クリスマス	(*kurisumasu*)

Some sounds which are different in a foreign language, **l** and **r** for example, are expressed as the same sound in Japanese.

'locker'	ロッカー	(*rokkā*)
'rocket'	ロケット	(*roketto*)
'ballet'	バレー	(*barē*)
'volley ball'	バレーボール	(*barēbōru*)
'bus' / 'bath'	バス	(*basu*)

3. Long words are often abbreviated.

'television'	テレビ	(*terebi*)
'building'	ビル	(*biru*)
'demonstration'	デモ	(*demo*)
'strike' (walkout)	スト	(*suto*)
'mass communication'	マスコミ	(*masukomi*)

* * *

ラジオ radio
タクシー taxi
レコード record, disc
カメラ camera
マッチ matches
ミシン sewing machine
フォーク fork, folk
プレゼント present, gift
ピンポン ping-pong
ギター guitar
ピアノ piano

パン bread
ビール beer
ジュース juice
サンドイッチ sandwich
ノート notebook
ボールペン ball-point pen
ワイシャツ white shirt
タイプライター typewriter
テープレコーダー tape recorder
バイオリン violin
デパート department store

* * *

アジア Asia
アメリカ America
タイ Thailand
インド India
マレーシア Malaysia
フランス France
イギリス England
カナダ Canada
オーストラリア Australia
メキシコ Mexico
モスクワ Moscow
ロンドン London
ノーベル Nobel
ショパン Chopin
ゲーテ Goethe

アフリカ Africa
ヨーロッパ Europe
ビルマ Burma
インドネシア Indonesia
フィリピン Philippines
ドイツ Germany
スウェーデン Sweden
ニュージーランド New Zealand
アルゼンチン Argentina
ブラジル Brazil
ワシントン Washington
ミュンヘン Munich
ミケランジェロ Michelangelo
プラトン Plato
トルストイ Tolstoy

第 4 課

わたしの 一日[1]

TAPE
No. 1
Side 2

❶ わたしは 毎朝(まいあさ)[2] 六時(ろくじ)[3]半(はん)[4]に[5] 起(お)きます[6]。 そして[7] ラジオ[8]の 中国語(ちゅうごくご)[9]の 勉強(べんきょう)[10]を[11] 始(はじ)めます[12]。 中国語(ちゅうごくご)の 発音(はつおん)[13]は たいへん むずかしいです。 七時半(しちじはん)ごろ[14] 朝(あさ)ご飯(はん)[15]を 食(た)べます[16]。

❷ わたしの 家(いえ)は 郊外(こうがい)[17]に あります。 会社(かいしゃ)は 町(まち)の まん中(なか)に あります。 家(いえ)から[18] 駅(えき)まで[19] 十分(じゅっぷん)[20]あまり[21] 歩(ある)きます。 そして 電車(でんしゃ)[22]で[23] 会社(かいしゃ)へ[24] 行(い)きます[25]。 家(いえ)から 会社(かいしゃ)まで 五十五分(ごじゅうごふん) かかります[26]。 電車(でんしゃ)は いつも たいへん こみます[27]。

❸ 会社(かいしゃ)は 九時(くじ)に 始(はじ)まります[28]。 仕事(しごと)は たいてい[29] 六時(ろくじ)に 終(お)わります[30]。

ときどき[31] 駅(えき)から タクシー[32]で 帰(かえ)ります[33]。 三分(さんぷん)ぐらいです。 百七十円(ひゃくななじゅうえん)[34] かかります。

語句

1 -nichi day
2 mai-asa every morning
  mai- every
  asa (N/Adv) morning
3 -ji o'clock 4 -han half
5 ni at See §18
6 oki·ru get up
7 soshite and; and then
8 *rajio* 'radio'
9 Chūgoku-go Chinese (language)
  Chūgoku China
10 benkyō (Nv) study
11 o See §17
12 hajime·ru (Vt) begin, start
13 hatsuon (Nv) pronunciation
14 ...goro about (for time) See §23
15 asa-gohan breakfast
  gohan meal; boiled rice
16 tabe·ru eat 17 kōgai suburb
18 kara from See §20
19 made till, to See §20
20 -pun=-fun minutes
21 ...amari a little over...
22 densha tramcar
23 de with See §21
24 e to, toward See §19
25 ik·u go
26 kakar·u (Vi) take; cost
27 kom·u get crowded
28 hajimar·u (Vi) begin
29 taitei (Adv) usually
30 owar·u (Vi) end
31 tokidoki sometimes, now and then
32 *takushi* 'taxi'
33 kaer·u (Vi) go/come home
34 -en yen
35 ryokō-sha travel agency
  ryokō (Nv) travel -sha company

❹ わたしの　会社(かいしゃ)は　旅行社(りょこうしゃ)[35]です。　わたしは　本社(ほんしゃ)[36]に　います。　支店(してん)[37]は　全国(ぜんこく)[38]に　八(はち)か所(しょ)[39]　あります。　仕事(しごと)は　たいへん　おもしろいです。

わたしたちは　よく[40]　出張(しゅっちょう)[41]します。　来週(らいしゅう)[42]は　九州(きゅうしゅう)[43]へ　行(い)きます。　しかし[44]、　出張(しゅっちょう)は　とても[45]　つかれます[46]。

❺ 日曜日(にちようび)[47]は　ほとんど[48]の　会社(かいしゃ)は　休(やす)みます[49]。　しかし、　わたしの　会社(かいしゃ)は　めったに[50]　休(やす)みません。　社員(しゃいん)[51]は　こうたい[52]で　休(やす)みます。

休(やす)み[53]の　日(ひ)[54]は　一(いっ)か月(げつ)[55]に[56]　四回(よんかい)[57]ほど[58]です。　その　日(ひ)は　昼(ひる)[59]ごろに　起(お)きます。　あまり　外出(がいしゅつ)[60]しません。　うちで[61]　ゆっくり[62]　小説(しょうせつ)を　読(よ)みます[63]。　夜(よる)[64]は　ビール[65]を　少(すこ)し[66]　飲(の)みます[67]。　そして　ステレオ[68]で　音楽(おんがく)を　聞(き)きます[69]。　ときどき　テレビも　見(み)ます[70]。

---

36 hon-sha　head office
37 shi-ten　branch office
38 zenkoku　the whole country
39 -ka-sho　(number of) places
40 yoku　often; well
41 shutchō　(Nv) business trip
42 rai-shū　next week
　rai-　next, coming　shū　week
43 Kyūshū　(the southern island of Japan)
44 shikashi　but, however
45 totemo＝tottemo　very much
46 tsukare·ru　get tired; tiring
47 Nichi-yōbi　Sunday
　-yōbi　day of the week　-bi　day
48 hotondo　(N/Adv) most, almost
49 yasum·u　rest, have a holiday; be absent
50 mettani...nai　seldom...
51 sha-in　member of a firm
52 kōtai　(Nv) shift, change
　kōtai de　by turns, alternately
53 yasumi　holiday; absence
54 hi　day
55 -ka-getsu　(number of) months
56 ni　in, per　57 -kai　...times
58 ...hodo　about, approximately
59 hiru　(N/Adv) noon, daytime
60 gaishutsu　(Nv) going out
61 de　at, in　See §29
62 yukkuri　leisurely; slowly
63 yom·u　read
64 yoru　(N/Adv) night
65 *biru*　'beer'
66 sukoshi　(N/Adv) a little, some
67 nom·u　drink　68 *sutereo*　'stereo'
69 kik·u　listen, hear
70 mi·ru　see, watch

Dai 4-ka
Watashi no Ichi-nichi

1 Watashi wa mai-asa roku-ji-han ni okimasu. Soshite *rajio* no Chūgoku-go no benkyō o hajimemasu. Chūgoku-go no hatsuon wa taihen muzukashii desu. Shichi-ji-han goro asa-gohan o tabemasu.

2 Watashi no ie wa kōgai ni arimasu. Kaisha wa machi no man-naka ni arimasu. Ie kara eki made jup-pun amari arukimasu. Soshite densha de kaisha e ikimasu. Ie kara kaisha made go-jū-go-fun kakarimasu. Densha wa itsumo taihen komimasu.

3 Kaisha wa ku-ji ni hajimarimasu. Shigoto wa taitei roku-ji ni owarimasu.

Tokidoki eki kara *takushī* de kaerimasu. San-pun gurai desu. Hyaku-nana-jū-en kakarimasu.

4 Watashi no kaisha wa ryokō-sha desu. Watashi wa hon-sha ni imasu. Shi-ten wa zenkoku ni hachi-ka-sho arimasu. Shigoto wa taihen omoshiroi desu.

Watashi-tachi wa yoku shutchō-shimasu. Rai-shū wa Kyūshū e ikimasu. Shikashi, shutchō wa totemo tsukaremasu.

5 Nichi-yōbi wa hotondo no kaisha wa yasumimasu. Shikashi, watashi no kaisha wa mettani yasumimasen. Sha-in wa kōtai de yasumimasu.

Yasumi no hi wa ik-ka-getsu ni yon-kai hodo desu. Sono hi wa hiru goro ni okimasu. Amari gaishutsu-shimasen. Uchi de yukkuri shōsetsu o yomimasu. Yoru wa *bīru* o sukoshi nomimasu. Soshite *sutereo* de ongaku o kikimasu. Tokidoki *terebi* mo mimasu.

Lesson 4

My Day

4

1 I get up at 6:30 every morning. Then I (begin to) study Chinese over the radio. Chinese pronunciation is very difficult. I have breakfast around 7:30.

2 My house is in the suburbs. Where I work is in the middle of town. It is about a ten-minute walk from my house to the train station. Then I take a train to my office. It takes about 55 minutes from my house to the office. The train is always very crowded.

3 My workday begins at 9:00. I usually finish work around 6:00.

Sometimes I go home from the station by cab. It takes about 3 minutes. It costs ¥170.

4 I work for a travel bureau. I am in the main office. We have eight branches throughout the nation. My work is very interesting.

We make a lot of business trips. Next week I will go to Kyushu. But business trips are very tiring.

5 Most companies have Sundays off. But we seldom take the day off where I work. The employees take turns taking days off.

We have about four days off a month. On those days, I get up around noon. I do not go out much. I read stories leisurely at home. In the evening, I have a little beer. Then I listen to music on my stereo. Sometimes I watch television too.

ANSWERS 〈pp. 52, 53〉

I. Watashi wa mai-nichi 1. roku-ji jū-go-fun ni asa-gohan o tabemasu. 2. roku-ji-han ni shinbun o yomimasu. 3. ku-ji jup-pun mae ni kaisha e/ni ikimasu. 4. ku-ji ni shigoto o hajimemasu. 5. go-ji ni shigoto o owarimasu. 6. shichi-ji ni ie e/ni kaerimasu. 7. shichi-ji jū-go-fun ni *terebi* o mimasu. 8. jū-ji ni *rajio* o kikimasu. 9. jū-ichi-ji ni nemasu.

III. 1. de 2. ni;e/ni 3. o;o/wa;de;o 4. ni;ni;e/ni;kara;made;de

IV. 1. Rai-shū watashi wa (watashi no) itoko no ie e/ni ikimasu. Kare no ie wa Tōkyō no kōgai ni arimasu. Watashi no ie kara kare no ie made densha de ichi-jikan gurai desu/kakarimasu. Kare no ie no atari wa shizuka desu. 2. Kyūshū ni watashi no kaisha no shi-ten ga arimasu. Desukara watashi wa ni-ka-getsu ni ik-kai Kyūshū e shutchō-shimasu. Rai-shū watashi wa Kyūshū e ikimasu. Watashi wa itsumo Fukuoka e hikōki de ikimasu. Ichi-jikan-han hodo/gurai kakarimasu.

●文法

§ 16 Expressing Actions or Events—Verbal Predicates

N wa/ga (Time) (Place) (Direction) (Object) **V-masu.**

Question: N wa . . . **V-masu ka?**

Negation: N wa . . . **V-masen.**

In ordinary polite speech, the present affirmative form of all Verbs ('V') ends with **-masu**: e.g. okimasu 'get up,' ikimasu 'go.' 'V-masu' expresses actions or events which regularly or repeatedly take place, or which are to take place in the future. (There is no 'future tense' as such in Japanese.) It may also express the speaker's will when N (ga/wa) is a first person Noun.

e.g. Watashi wa mai-asa 6-ji ni okimasu. 'I get up at 6:00 every morning.'

Anata wa rai-shū Hokkaidō e ikimasu ka? 'Will you go to Hokkaido next week?' 'Are you going to go to Hokkaido next week?'

→(affirmative answer) Hai, ikimasu. 'Yes, I will/am.'

→(negative answer) Iie, ikimasen. 'No, I won't/am not.'

Object, Direction, Place, Time, etc., are expressed, in any order, in the form 'N+P' as shown in the following sections. 'N **ga**' indicates that N is the performer of an action or that which exists or undergoes a change ('Subject'). 'N ga' or 'N o' ('Direct Object') changes to 'N **wa**' when N is the Topic. **Wa** may be attached to other 'N+P' or Adverbs when that part of the sentence is being contrasted with something else.

§ 17 Direct Object: N **o** (+Vt) (Vt: 'Transitive Verb')

e.g. Watashi wa hon o yomimasu. 'I read books.'
(Watashi = I, hon = book, yomimasu = read)

Anata wa nani o tabemasu ka. 'What will you have (to eat)?'

—Tenpura o tabemasu. 'I'll have *tempura*.'

§ 18 Point of Time: **N ni** 'at (6:00),' 'on (Sunday)'

e.g. Watashi wa roku-ji ni okimasu. 'I get up at 6:00.'

NB: Some N or N-Phrases expressing time, period, or frequency do not require -ni because of their Adverbial character.

e.g. kyō 'today,' kon-shū 'this week'

§ 19 Direction: **N e** 'to...,' 'toward...'

e.g. Tōkyō e ikimasu 'go to Tokyo'

Ashita koko e kimasu. 'I'll come here tomorrow.'

§ 20 Starting Point: **N kara** 'from...'

Ending Point: **N made** 'till...,' 'up to...,' 'as far as...'

e.g. Kyōto kara Ōsaka made hashirimasu Kyōtō → Ōsaka

ku-ji kara jū-ji made hashirimasu 9:00 10:00

NB: 'N made' is different from 'N e' in that 'N made+V' implies that the action or event expressed by V continues up to the point of N, while 'N e' merely shows a physical direction in which something moves. Thus 'e' cannot be attached to N expressing time. 'From 6 till (to) 10' ×6-ji kara 10-ji e

§ 21 Instrument or Means: **N de** 'with...,' 'by...'

e.g. *naifu* de kirimasu 'cut with a knife'

Tōkyō e hikōki de ikimasu 'go to Tokyo by plane'

§ 22 Conjunctions

Soshite... 'And...' **Sore kara...** 'And then...'

Shikashi... 'But...' **Keredomo...** 'However, ...'

§ 23 Approximation: goro, hodo, and gurai

N (point of time) goro e.g. jū-ji goro '(at) about 10:00'

N (length of time or quantity) hodo/gurai e.g. jup-pun hodo/gurai '(for) about 10 minutes' sen-en hodo/gurai 'about 1,000 yen'

●練習

ANSWERS→p. 49

I. Make sentences to suit the chart.

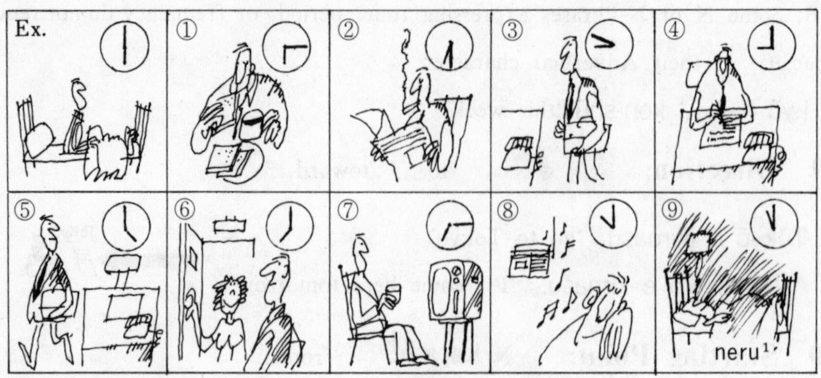

Ex. (6-ji)→Watashi wa mai-nichi[2] roku-ji ni okimasu.

1. (6-ji 15-fun)
2. (6-ji-han)
3. (9-ji 10-pun mae[3])
4. (9-ji)
5. (5-ji)
6. (7-ji)
7. (7-ji 15-fun)
8. (10-ji)
9. (11-ji)

II. Make dialogs as shown in the examples.

(A) Ex. Q: (*pan*[4] o tabemasu) (mai-nichi)

Anata wa mai-nichi *pan* o tabemasu ka?

A: (Hai) Hai, mai-nichi *pan* o tabemasu.

(Iie) Iie, mai-nichi wa tabemasen. Tokidoki tabemasu.

1. Q: (sanpo[5]-shimasu) (mai-asa) A: (Iie)
2. Q: (denwa o kakemasu[6]) (yoku) A: (Hai)

語句

1 ne·ru sleep
2 mai-nichi every day
3 mae before
4 *pan* bread
5 sanpo (Nv) stroll, walk
6 denwa o kake·ru make a telephone call
7 tegami letter, mail
8 kak·u write; draw
9 mai-shū every week
10 mai-ban every night
ban (N/Adv) night
11 su·u inhale
tabako o su·u smoke

3. Q: (tegami[7] o kakimasu[8]) (mai-shū[9]) A: (Iie)

4. Q: (sake o nomimasu) (mai-ban[10]) A: (Iie)

(B) Ex. Q: (*terebi* o mimasu) (yoku) Anata wa yoku *terebi* o mimasu ka?

A: (mettani) Iie, mettani mimasen.

1. Q: (*tabako* o suimasu[11]) (yoku) A: (mettani)
2. Q: (shōsetsu o yomimasu) (yoku) A: (amari)
3. Q: (shutchō-shimasu) (yoku) A: (mettani)

III. Fill in the blanks.

Ex. Watashi wa mai-asa shinbun (o) yomimasu.

1. Watashi wa itsumo *bōru-pen* (   ) tegami o kakimasu.
2. Watashi wa mai-nichi shichi-ji (   ) ie (   ) kaerimasu.
3. Watashi wa yoku *terebi* (   ) mimasu. Amari *rajio* (   ) kikimasen. Shikashi tokidoki *rajio* (   ) ongaku (   ) kikimasu.
4. Watashi wa Tōkyō no kaisha (   ) imasu. Kōbe[12] (   ) kaisha no shi-ten ga arimasu. Desukara[13] watashi wa yoku Kōbe (   ) ikimasu. Tōkyō (   ) Ōsaka[14] (   ) Shin-kansen[15] (   ) ikimasu.

IV. Put the following into Japanese.

1. Next week I am going to my cousins'. His house is in the suburbs of Tokyo. It takes about an hour[16] by train from my house to his. It is quiet around his house.
2. My company has a branch office in Kyushu. So I make a business trip to Kyushu every two months. Next week I am going to Kyushu. I always go to Fukuoka[17] by plane.[18] It takes about an hour and a half.

---

12 Kōbe (a place name)
13 desukara thus, and so
14 Ōsaka (the second biggest city in Japan)
15 Shin-kansen New Trunk Line
16 -jikan hour -kan for, during
17 Fukuoka (a place name)
18 hikōki airplane

●会話

IKURA?

—Irasshaimase.[1]

Fuirumu[2] wa arimasu ka?

—Hai, gozaimasu. *Karā*[3] desu ka?

Ē, san-jū-roku-mai-dori[4] desu.

—*Nega-karā*[5] desu ka, *poji*[6] desu ka?

Nega desu. Ikura[7] desu ka?

—Yon-hyaku-ni-jū-en desu.

Zūmu renzu[8] wa arimasu ka?

—Hai, san-shurui[9] arimasu ga....

Shōto[10] *zūmu*, arimasu ka?

—*Shōto zūmu* desu ne.

Chotto o-machi-kudasai.[11]

Hai, o-matase-shimashita.[12] Kore desu.

Naruhodo[13].... Karui desu ne.

Nan-*miri*[14] kara nan-*miri* no *zūmu* desu ka?

—Ē....to, yon-jū-san kara hachi-jū-roku-*miri* desu.

Benri desu yo.

—Can I help you?
Do you have film?
—Yes, we do. Color?
Yes, with 36 exposures.
—Negative color film (for prints) or positive (for slides)?
Negative. How much is it?
—420 yen.
Do you have zoom lenses?
—Yes, we have three different kinds.
Do you have the short zoom?
—Short zoom, is it?
Wait a minute, please.
Sorry to have kept you waiting. This is it.
I see.
Light, isn't it? From how many millimeters to how many millimeters (does this zoom lens work)?
—Well, let me see. From 43 to 86 millimeters.
It's very convenient.

語句

1 Irasshaimase (Cph: greeting of welcome)
irasshar•u (Honorific) be; come; go See §118
2 *fuirumu* 'film'
3 *karā* 'color'
4 -mai-dori ...exposures (photo)
-mai (Count. for paper, etc.) See §14
dori ←tor•u (take)
5 *nega karā* 'negative color,' film for prints
6 *poji* 'positive,' slides
7 ikura how much
8 *zūmu renzu* 'zoom lens'
9 shurui kinds
10 *shōto* 'short'
11 O-machi-kudasai (Cph)
mats•u wait
o-...-kudasai please
kudasai please give/do...to/for me.
See § 43

How much is it?
—The list price is 34,000 yen, but (do you want to buy it) tax-free?
Yes, tax-free.
Here is my passport.
—Well, in that case, it is 29,000 yen.
OK, I'll take it.
Here are three 10,000 yen bills.
—Thank you.
Wait a minute, please.
Here is your 1,000 yen change. And this is your guarantee.
Thank you.

←kudasar·u
12 O-matase-shimashita (Cph)
o-...-suru (Polite form of suru)
-ase·ru See § 72
13 naruhodo Oh, I see
14 *-miri* 'millimeter'
15 teika fixed/list price
16 -man ten thousands
17 menzei (N) tax-free
zei tax
18 *pasupōto* 'passport'
19 Jā Then
20 satsu bank note
21 shibaraku for a while
22 tsuri change, money given back for balance
23 sore kara and then, after that
24 hoshō-sho warranty card
hoshō (Nv) guarantee
-sho document

Ikura desu ka?

—Teika[15] wa san-man[16]-yon-sen-en desu ga, menzei[17] desu ka?

Ē, menzei desu.

Watashi no *pasupōto*[18] wa koko ni arimasu.

—Soredewa..., ni-man-kyū-sen-en desu.

Jā,[19] sore o kudasai.

Hai, ichi-man-en-satsu[20] san-mai desu.

—Arigatō gozaimasu.

Shibaraku[21] o-machi-kudasai.

Hai, sen-en no o-tsuri[22] desu.

Sore kara,[23] kore wa hoshō-sho[24] desu.

Dōmo arigatō gozaimashita.

あなたと　わたし

❶あなたは　学生（がくせい）です。　会社員（かいしゃいん）ではありません。　わたしも　会社員（かいしゃいん）ではありません。　学生（がくせい）です。

❷あの　人は　ジョーンズ[1]さんです。　医者（いしゃ）です。

❸あなたは　何人（なにじん）[2]ですか。

――わたしは　中国人（ちゅうごくじん）[3]です。　名（な）まえは　ウー[4]です。

❹ジョーンズさんは　今（いま）　日本（にっぽん）に　います。　かれの　家族（かぞく）は　ニューヨーク[5]に　います。

❺それは　なんですか。

――これは　字引（じび）[6]きです。

英語（えいご）[7]の　字引（じび）きですか。

――いいえ、　そうではありません。

スペイン語（ご）[8]の　字引（じび）きです。

❻あした[9]は　五月（ごがつ）[10]　三日（みっか）[11]です。

けんぽう記念日（きねんび）[12]です。

Names of the MONTHS			
一月（いちがつ）	Jan.	七月（しちがつ）	July
二月（にがつ）	Feb.	八月（はちがつ）	Aug.
三月（さんがつ）	Mar.	九月（くがつ）	Sept.
四月（しがつ）	Apr.	十月（じゅうがつ）	Oct.
五月（ごがつ）	May	十一月（じゅういちがつ）	Nov.
六月（ろくがつ）	June	十二月（じゅうにがつ）	Dec.

語句

1 *Jōnzu* 'Jones'
2 nani-jin What nationality...
  nani=nan what
3 Chūgoku-jin Chinese (person)
4 *Ū* (a Chinese name)
5 *Nyū Yōku* 'New York'
6 jibiki=jisho dictionary
7 Ei-go English (language)
  cf. Ei-koku (England)
8 *Supein*-go Spanish (language)
  Supein 'Spain'
9 ashita=asu tomorrow
10 Go-gatsu May
11 mik-ka the third day (of the month)
12 Kenpō-kinen-bi Constitution Memorial Day
  kenpō Constitution
  kinen (Nv) commemoration
13 *basu* 'bus'
14 gakkō school
15 *tabako*-ya tobacco shop
  -ya shop
16 hako box
17 -pon=-hon, -bon See §14
18 *Itaria* 'Italy'
19 *Rōma* 'Rome'
20 *Doitsu*-jin German (person)
  Doitsu Germany
21 *Furansu*-jin French (person)
  Furansu 'France'
22 budō-shu wine
  budō grapes -shu liquor

❼あなたの　自動車(じどうしゃ)は　大(おお)きいですか。

——いいえ、大(おお)きくないです。小(ちい)さいです。

❽あなたは　バス[13]で　学校(がっこう)[14]へ　行(い)きますか。

——いいえ、電車(でんしゃ)で　行きます。

❾たばこ屋(や)[15]は　どこに　ありますか。

——あの　ビルの　うしろに　あります。

❿はこ[16]の　中(なか)に　えんぴつが　二本(にほん)と　ボールペンが　六本(ろっぽん)[17]　あります。

⓫イタリア[18]の　首都(しゅと)は　ローマ[19]です。ローマには　古(ふる)い　建物(たてもの)が　たくさん　あります。

⓬ドイツ人(じん)[20]は　ビールを　よく　飲(の)みます。フランス人(じん)[21]は　ぶどう酒(しゅ)[22]を　たくさん　飲(の)みます。

Names of the DAYS

1 日	tsuitachi
2 日	futsu-ka
3 日	mik-ka
4 日	yok-ka
5 日	itsu-ka
6 日	mui-ka
7 日	nano-ka
8 日	yō-ka
9 日	kokono-ka
10 日	tō-ka
11 日	jū-ichi-nichi
12 日	jū-ni-nichi
13 日	jū-san-nichi
14 日	jū-yok-ka
15 日	jū-go-nichi
16 日	jū-roku-nichi
17 日	jū-shichi-nichi
18 日	jū-hachi-nichi
19 日	jū-ku-nichi
20 日	hatsu-ka
21 日	ni-jū-ichi-nichi
24 日	ni-jū-yok-ka
30 日	san-jū-nichi

Translation: **1** You are a student. You are not a company employee. I am not a company employee either. I am a student.
2 That man is Mr. Jones. He is a doctor.
3 What nationality are you?—I am Chinese. My name is Wu.
4 Mr. Jones is in Japan now. His family is in New York.
5 What is that?—This is a dictionary.
Is it an English dictionary?—No, it is not. It is a Spanish dictionary.
6 Tomorrow is the third day of May. It is Constitution Day.
7 Is your car big?—No, it is not big. It is small.
8 Do you go to school by bus? —No, I go by train.
9 Where is a tobacco shop?—There is one behind that building.
10 There are two pencils and six ball-point pens in the box.
11 The capital of Italy is Rome. There are a lot of old buildings in Rome.
12 Germans drink much beer. French drink a lot of wine.

第 5 課

食堂で

TAPE
No. 2
Side 1

❶木村(きむら)[1]さん、あなたは　もう[2]　昼(ひる)ご飯(はん)[3]を　食(た)べましたか[4]。

——いいえ、まだです。

それでは　いっしょに[5]　地下(ちか)[6]の　食堂(しょくどう)[7]で　食(た)べませんか。

❷——大野(おおの)[8]さんは　木村(きむら)さんと[9]　ろうか[10]を[11]　歩(ある)きました。そして　エレベーター[12]に[13]　乗(の)り[14]ました。食堂(しょくどう)の　入(い)り口(ぐち)[15]で　木村(きむら)さんは　たばこを　買(か)い[16]ました。——

❸——わたしは　カレーライス[17]を　食(た)べます。大野(おおの)さんは　何(なに)を　食(た)べますか。

ぼく[18]は　きのう[19]も　おととい[20]も　カレーライスを　食(た)べました。

それで[21]、きょう[22]は　すし[23]に　します[24]。

木村(きむら)さんは　ゆうべ[25]の　三(さん)チャンネル[26]の　コメディー[27]を　見(み)ましたか。

——いいえ、わたしは　見(み)ませんでした。

うちでは　みんな[28]　よく　テレビを　見(み)ます。ゆうべも　八(はち)

語句

1 Kimura (a family name)
2 mō already　3 hiru-gohan lunch
4 -mashita See §24
5 issho (N) the same, together
　issho-ni (Adv) together
6 chika underground
7 shokudō restaurant, dining hall
8 Ōno (a family name)
9 to See §33　10 rōka corridor, hall
11 o See §28
12 *erebētā* 'elevator'
13 ni See §27　14 nor·u ride, get on
15 iri-guchi entrance　16 ka·u buy
17 *karē-raisu* 'curried rice'
18 boku I (male)　19 kinō yesterday
20 ototoi the day before yesterday
21 sorede therefore
22 kyō today
23 sushi (a Japanese food of vinegared rice and raw fish)
24 ...ni suru will take/decide on
25 yūbe last night
26 *channeru* 'channel'
27 *komedi* 'comedy'
28 minna =mina (N/Adv) all
29 hayaku early; quick, fast←haya·i

時から　九時半まで　家族で　見ました。木村さんは　あまり見ませんか。

——はい、あまり　見ません。いつも　晩　早く[29]　寝ます。

その　かわり[30]、朝は　六時ごろ　起きます。

そうですか。早起き[31]ですね。

❹ところで、出張旅行[32]の　切符[33]を　もう　買いましたか。

——はい、きのう　駅前[34]の　交通公社[35]で　買いました。

わたしは　まだです。きょう　帰り[36]に　買います。座席指定券[37]は　まだ　ありましたか。

——はい、ありました。しかし、寝台券[38]は　もう　ありませんでした。

しかた[39]が　ありません。行き[40]は　指定席[41]ですね。

❺——二人は　食堂を[42]　出[43]ました。そして、隣の　喫茶店[44]にはいり[45]ました。大野さんは　コーヒー[46]を　飲みました。木村さんは　紅茶[47]を　飲みました。それから　エレベーターに乗りました。五階[48]で　二人は　降り[49]ました。午後[50]の　仕事が始まります。——

---

30 kawari　substitute ←kawar·u (change)
　sono kawari　instead
31 haya-oki　early rising/riser
32 shutchō-ryokō　business trip
33 kippu　ticket
34 eki-mae　in front of the station
35 Kōtsū-kōsha　(Japan Travel Bureau)
　kōtsū　traffic　kōsha　corporation
36 kaeri ni　on the way home ←kaer·u
37 zaseki-shitei-ken　reserved seat ticket
　zaseki　seat (in trains, theaters, etc.)
　shitei　(Nv) designation, specification　ken　ticket
38 shindai-ken　sleeping-car ticket
　shindai　bed, berth
39 shikata　means, way, method
　shikata ga nai　can't be helped
40 iki　going ←ik·u (go)
41 shitei-seki　reserved seat　seki seat
42 o　See §26
43 de·ru　leave, go out; graduate
44 kissa-ten　teahouse, coffee shop
45 hair·u　enter　46 *kōhi*　'coffee'
47 kōcha　black tea　48 -kai　floor
49 ori·ru　get off; descend
50 gogo　afternoon, p.m.

Dai 5-ka
Shokudō de

1 Kimura-san, anata wa mō hiru-gohan o tabemashita ka?

——Iie, mada desu.

Soredewa issho-ni chika no shokudō de tabemasen ka?

2 ——Ōno-san wa Kimura-san to rōka o arukimashita. Soshite *erebētā* ni norimashita. Shokudō no iri-guchi de Kimura-san wa *tabako* o kaimashita.——

3 ——Watashi wa *karē-raisu* o tabemasu. Ōno-san wa nani o tabemasu ka? Boku wa kinō mo ototoi mo *karē-raisu* o tabemashita. Sorede kyō wa sushi ni shimasu. Kimura-san wa yūbe no san-*channeru* no *komedī* o mimashita ka?

——Iie, watashi wa mimasen deshita.

Uchi dewa minna yoku *terebi* o mimasu. Yūbe mo hachi-ji kara ku-ji-han made kazoku de mimashita. Kimura-san wa amari mimasen ka?

——Hai, amari mimasen. Itsumo ban hayaku nemasu.

Sono kawari, asa wa roku-ji goro okimasu.

Sō desu ka. Haya-oki desu ne.

4 Tokorode, shutchō-ryokō no kippu o mō kaimashita ka?

——Hai, kinō eki-mae no Kōtsū-kōsha de kaimashita.

Watashi wa mada desu. Kyō kaeri ni kaimasu. Zaseki-shitei-ken wa mada arimashita ka?

——Hai, arimashita. Shikashi, shindai-ken wa mō arimasen deshita.

Shikata ga arimasen. Iki wa shitei-seki desu ne.

5 ——Futa-ri wa shokudō o demashita. Soshite, tonari no kissa-ten ni hairimashita. Ōno-san wa *kōhī* o nomimashita. Kimura-san wa kōcha o nomimashita. Sore kara *erebētā* ni norimashita. Go-kai de futa-ri wa orimashita. Gogo no shigoto ga hajimarimasu.——

Lesson 5

At the Restaurant

5

1 Kimura, have you had lunch already?

——Not yet.

Then let's eat at the restaurant in the basement.

2 ——Ono walked down the hall with Kimura. They got in the elevator. Kimura bought some cigarettes at the entrance to the restaurant.——

3 ——I'll have the curried rice. What will you have, Ono?

I had curried rice yesterday and the day before yesterday. So I'll have *sushi* today. Did you see the comedy on channel three last night, Kimura?

——No, I didn't see it.

We watch a lot of television at my house. Last night the whole family watched from 8:00 to 9:30. Don't you watch television very much, Kimura?

——No, I don't watch much. I always go to bed early. But I get up around 6:00 in the morning instead.

Is that so? An early-riser, are you?

4 Say, did you buy the ticket for your business trip yet?

——Yes, I got it yesterday at the JTB office in front of the station.

I haven't gotten mine yet. I'm going to get it on my way home today. Did they still have some reserved seat tickets left?

——Yes, they did. But they didn't have any more sleeping car tickets.

It can't be helped. I'll have to go by reserved seat, won't I?

5 ——They left the dining hall. Then they went into the coffee shop next door. Ono had coffee. Kimura had tea. After that they got in the elevator. They got off at the fifth floor. The afternoon's work begins.——

ANSWERS 〈pp. 64, 65〉

III Kesa watashi wa 6-ji-han (ni/goro) okimashita. Soshite 7-ji goro (kara) 8-ji goro (made) kōen (o) sanpo-shimashita. Kyō wa Do-yōbi desu. Desukara watashi wa 9-ji (kara) 12-ji (made) kaisha (de) shigoto o shimashita. 12-ji-han ni kaisha (o) demashita. Soshite Shinjuku (e) ikimashita. Shinjuku (de) ***Furansu*** (no) eiga (o) mimashita. Eiga wa 4-ji (ni/goro) owarimashita. Eiga-kan (kara) chika-tetsu no eki (made) arukimashita. Chika-tetsu no eki (de) tomodachi ni aimashita. Watashi wa tomodachi to issho-ni chika-tetsu (ni) norimashita. Tomodachi wa Ginza (de) chika-tetsu (o) orimashita. Watashi wa massugu ie (ni/e) kaerimashita.

IV. Q: (Anata wa) itsu (***depāto*** e) ikimashita ka? A: (Watashi wa) kono mae no Nichi-yōbi ni (***depāto*** e) ikimashita. Q: (Anata wa) dare to ikimashita ka? A: (Watashi wa) imōto to ikimashita. Q: Nani o kaimashita ka? A: (Fuku ya kutsu ya shita-gi o kaimashita.) Q: 7-kai no shokudō e ikimashita ka? A: Hai, ikimashita. Q: Nani o tabemashita ka? A: Sushi o tabemashita. Q: Nani o nomimashita ka? A: ***Kōhi*** o nomimashita.

V. 1. Hai, hairimashita. (Iie, hairimasen deshita.) 2. Hai, norimashita. (Iie, norimasen deshita). 3. Hai, (mō) yomimashita. (Iie, mada desu). 4. Watashi wa ____ Daigaku o demashita.

●文法

§ 24 Action or Event in the Past

N wa . . . V-mashita.

Negation: **N wa . . . V-masen deshita.**

e.g. Watashi wa kyō Kyōto e ikimasu. 'I (will) go to Kyoto today.'

Watashi wa kinō Kyōto e ikimashita. 'I went to Kyoto yesterday.'

Kinō shinbun o yomimashita ka? 'Did you read the paper yesterday?'

—Hai, yomimashita. 'Yes, I did.'

—Iie, yomimasen deshita. 'No, I didn't.'

NB: 'V-mashita' indicates either (1) that an action or event took place in the past (='past tense' in English), or (2) that it has been finished at the time of speech (='present perfect' in English). This difference is shown often by Adverbs such as kinō ('yesterday'), mō ('already, yet'), etc., but sometimes only by context. When (1) is intended in a question of the form '...mashita ka?,' the negative answer to it is '...masen deshita,' as seen above, whereas when (2) is intended, it should be 'mada...masen,' or simply 'mada desu.'

e.g. (Mō) hiru-gohan o tabemashita ka? 'Have you eaten lunch yet?

—Iie, mada tabemasen. 'No, I haven't eaten yet.'

—Iie, mada desu. 'No, not yet.'

§ 25 Adverbs (2)

	+Aff. Predicate	+Neg. Predicate
mō . . .	'already'	'(no) more; (no) longer...'
mada . . .	'still'	'(not) yet'
mettani . . .		'seldom,' 'rarely'

§ 26 Movement Out of: N o+V

ie o demasu

'home' 'leave'

'leave home'

densha o orimasu

'train' 'get down'

'get off the train'

§ 27 Movement Into: N ni+V

o-furo ni hairimasu

'bath' 'enter'

'get into the bath'

densha ni norimasu

'train' 'get on'

'get on the train'

NB: This ni is also sometimes used in place of e (See § 19).

§ 28 Walking, Flying, Passing, etc.: N o+V

kōen o sanpo-shimasu

'park' 'stroll'

'walk in the park'

Honkon o tōrimasu

'Hong Kong' 'pass'

'go by way of Hong Kong'

§ 29 General Expression of Place of Action: N de+V

e.g. shokudō de gohan o tabemasu 'eat at the dining room'

Kyōto de densha ni norimashita 'got on the train in Kyoto'

§ 30 Nominal Use of the Conjunctive Form

The form to which -masu is attached is called the 'Conjunctive form.' This form can be used as a Noun (like the '-ing form' in English).

e.g. Kyōto e ikimasu 'go to Kyoto'

→Iki wa densha desu. 'Going is by train.'

→Kyōto-iki no densha 'Kyoto-going train,' 'train for Kyoto'

hajimarimasu 'begin'

→Hajimari wa 6-ji desu. 'Beginning (time) is 6:00.'

●練習

ANSWERS→p. 61

I. Use the chart on page 52 to make dialogs as shown in the example.

Ex. Q: Anata wa kinō nan-ji[1] ni okimashita ka?

A: Watashi wa kinō 6-ji ni okimashita.

II. Make dialogs as shown in the example.

Ex. Q: (hiru-gohan) (tabemasu) (mō)

Anata wa mō hiru-gohan o tabemashita ka?

A: (hai) Hai, mō tabemashita.

(iie) (kore kara[2]) Iie, mada desu. Kore kara tabemasu.

1. Q: (shigoto) (owarimasu) (mō) A: (Hai)
2. Q: (kono hon) (yomimasu) (mō) A: (Hai)
3. Q: (hōkoku-sho[3]) (kakimasu) (mō) A: (Iie) (kore kara)
4. Q: (ginkō) (ikimasu) (mō) A: (Iie) (kore kara)
5. Q: (ano eiga[4]) (mimasu) (mō) A: (Iie) (rai-shū)

III. Fill in the blanks.

Kesa[5] watashi wa 6-ji-han ( ) okimashita. Soshite 7-ji goro ( ) 8-ji goro ( ) kōen ( ) sanpo-shimashita. Kyō wa Do-yōbi[6] desu. Desukara watashi wa 9-ji ( ) 12-ji ( ) kaisha ( ) shigoto o shimashita.[7] 12-ji-han ni kaisha ( ) demashita. Soshite Shinjuku ( ) ikimashita. Shinjuku ( ) *Furansu* ( ) eiga ( ) mimashita. Eiga wa 4-ji ( ) owarimashita. Eiga-kan[8] ( ) chika-tetsu[9] no eki ( ) arukimashita. Chika-tetsu no eki ( ) tomodachi[10] ni aimashita.[11] Watashi wa tomodachi to issho-ni

語句

1 nan-ji what time
2 kore kara from now
3 hōkoku-sho written report
hōkoku report
4 eiga movies 5 kesa this morning
6 Do-yōbi Saturday 7 suru do
8 eiga-kan movie theater
9 chika-tetsu subway
chika underground
-tetsu←tetsudō (railway)

chika-tetsu ( ) norimashita. Tomodachi wa Ginza[12] ( ) chika-tetsu ( ) orimashita. Watashi wa massugu[13] ie ( ) kaerimashita.

5

IV. Continue the following dialog, using the words in parentheses.

Q: Anata wa yoku *depāto*[14] e ikimasu ka?

A: (amari) Iie, watashi wa amari *depāto* e ikimasen.

Q: (itsu[15])?

A: (kono mae no[16] Nichi-yōbi)

Q: (dare to)?

A: (imōto to)

Q: (nani) (kaimasu)?

A: Fuku[17] ya kutsu[18] ya shita-gi[19] o kaimashita.

Q: (7(nana)-kai no shokudō) (ikimasu)?

A: (Hai)

Q: (nani) (tabemasu)?

A: (sushi)

Q: (nani) (nomimasu)?

A: (*kōhī*)

V. Answer the following questions.

1. Kyō anata wa kissa-ten ni hairimashita ka?
2. Kyō anata wa *takushī* ni norimashita ka?
3. Anata wa mō kyō no shinbun o yomimashita ka?
4. Anata wa dono[20] daigaku o demashita ka?

---

10 tomodachi friend 11 a·u meet
12 Ginza (a shopping street in Tokyo)
13 massugu (Na/Adv) straight
14 *depāto* 'department store'
15 itsu when
16 kono mae no last, previous
17 fuku clothes, suit 18 kutsu shoes
19 shita-gi underwear
-gi clothes cf. fudan-gi
20 dono which, what See § 5

●会話

TSUKAREMASU!

O-taku kara kaisha made dore gurai[1] kakarimasu ka?

—Sō desu ne. . . .

Ichi-jikan-han gurai desu.

Taihen[2] desu nē.

Mai-asa nan-ji ni okimasu ka?

—Roku-ji desu.

Soto[3] wa mada kurai[4] desu.

Uchi kara eki made ichi-*kiro*[5] hodo arukimasu.

Shichi-ji no kyūkō[6] ni norimasu.

Itsumo man'in[7] desu.

Sore wa tsukaremasu ne.

Kaeri no densha mo man'in desu ka?

—Ē, asa mo ban mo man'in desu.

Hiru-gohan wa doko de tabemasu ka?

—Taitei kaisha no shokudō de tabemasu.

Kaisha wa nan-ji ni owarimasu ka?

—Go-ji desu ga,

How long does it take from your house to your company?

—Well, let me see....

About an hour and a half.

It must be very hard for you.

What time do you get up every morning?

—Six o'clock.

It's still dark outside.

I walk about one kilometer from my house to the station.

I take the seven o'clock express.

It's always crowded.

It must be very tiring for you.

Is the train home crowded too?

—Yes, the trains are crowded in the mornings and in the evenings.

Where do you have lunch?

—I usually eat in the company cafeteria.

What time does your office close?

—It closes at five, but I

語句

1 dore gurai about how much/long dore which
2 taihen (Na) no easy task, lots of trouble
3 soto (N) outside
4 kura·i dark
5 *-kiro* 'kilometer/kilogram'
6 kyūkō express
7 man'in (N) full (of people)
8 nokor·u remain

usually stay on at the office until about eight.
Oh, you are so busy.
Do you get a good salary?
—So-so.
I entered this company the year before last.
My current salary is about 80,000 yen.
Is that so?
By the way,
when did you get married?
—Last spring.
Do you have any children?
—Yes, one born in February this year. A boy.
Does he walk yet?
—Not yet.

taitei hachi-ji goro made kaisha ni nokorimasu.[8]
Isogashii[9] desu ne.
Kyūryō[10] wa ii desu ka?
—Māmā[11] desu.
Kono kaisha ni ototoshi[12] hairimashita.
Ima no kyūryō wa hachi-man-en gurai desu.
Sō desu ka.
Tokorode,
itsu kekkon[13]-shimashita ka?
—Kyo-nen[14] no haru[15] desu.
Kodomo-san wa imasu ka?
—Ē, kotoshi[16] no Ni-gatsu ni umaremashita.[17] Otoko no ko desu.
Mō arukimasu ka?
—Mada desu.

9 isogashi·i busy
10 kyūryō salary, wages
11 māmā moderate, so-so
12 ototoshi the year before last
13 kekkon (Nv) marriage
14 kyo-nen last year
-nen year
15 haru spring
16 kotoshi this year
17 umare·ru be born

▼A wedding ceremony

日本

日本は　島国[1]　です。　おもな[2]　島は　北海道[3]と、　本州[4]と、　四国[5]と、　九州です。　その　ほか[6]　小さい　島が　たくさん　あります。　大きさ[7]は　だいたい[8]　370,000 km²（三十七万平方[9]　キロメートル[10]）です。　これは　インド[11]の　$\frac{1}{9}$（九分[12]の一）、アメリカ[13]の　$\frac{1}{25}$（二十五分の一）、　ソ連[14]の　$\frac{1}{60}$（六十分の一）です。　しかし、　人口[15]は　多いです。　だいたい　100,000,000人（一億人[16]）います。人口密度[17]は　1km²に　280人（二百八十人）ぐらいです。

全体[18]に　山が　多いです。　火山[19]も　たくさん　あります。　そして、　平野[20]が　少[21]ないです。　長い　川[22]も　あまり　ありません。

北海道では、　冬[23]　雪[24]が　降[25]ります。　しかし、　九州では、　めったに　雪が　降りません。

六月には　よく　雨[26]が　降ります。夏[27]には　いつも　台風[28]が　来[29]ます。　春、　さくら[30]が　さきます。　たいへん　きれいです。　秋[31]の　もみじ[32]も　美しい[33]です。

北海道
Hokkaidō
本州
Honshū
Tōkyō
Ōsaka
四国
Shikoku
九州
Kyūshū
沖縄
Okinawa
0　200km
0　100km

Japan

Japan is an island country. The main islands are Hokkaido, Honshu, Shikoku, and Kyushu. Besides these, there are many small islands.

Japan is about 370,000 km^2 in size. This is 1/9 of India, 1/25 of the U. S. A., and 1/60 of the U. S. S. R. But Japan has a large population, about 100,000,000. The population density is about 280 people per km^2.

As a whole, Japan has many mountains, including many volcanos, but few plains. There are not many long rivers either.

In winter, it often snows in Hokkaido, but seldom in Kyushu. It rains a lot in June. There are typhoons every summer. In spring, the cherry blossoms come out. They are very pretty. The maple leaves in autumn are beautiful too.

▶Asamayama

語句

1 shima-guni island country
  shima island
  -guni =kuni country, nation
2 omo (Na) main
3 Hokkaidō (the northern-most island of Japan)
4 Honshū (the main Japanese island)
5 Shikoku (a southern Japanese island)
6 hoka other
  sono hoka besides that
7 ōki-sa size ←ōki・i (large)
8 daitai about, approximately
9 heihō- the square (of a number)
10 *mētoru* 'meter'
11 *Indo* 'India'
12 (x)bun-no-(y) y/x
13 *Amerika* 'America'
14 So-ren the Soviet Union
15 jinkō population
16 oku hundred million
17 jinkō-mitsudo population density
  mitsudo density
18 zentai (N) whole
  zentai ni as a whole
19 kazan volcano
20 heiya plain, open field
21 sukuna・i few, little (quantity), scarce
22 kawa river
23 fuyu winter
24 yuki snow
25 fur・u fall (rain, snow, etc.)
26 ame rain
27 natsu summer
28 taifū typhoon
29 kuru come
30 sak・u bloom
31 aki autumn, fall
32 momiji maple
33 utsukushi・i beautiful

第 6 課

ハイキング

TAPE
No. 2
Side 1

❶ きのうは 日曜日でした。[1] さいわい[2] 朝から たいへん いい 天気[3]でしたから[4]、 わたしは 五人の 友だちと ハイキング[5]に 行き[6]ました。 大阪から 京都まで 電車で 行きました。 京都駅[7]から バスに 乗りました。 電車も バスも 人で いっぱい[8]でした。 バスは 山の 中を 走り[9]ました。

❷ 高雄[10]に 着き[11]ました。 まず[12] 高山寺[13]へ 有名な 鳥獣戯画[14]を 見に 行きました。 たいへん おもしろかったです[15]。 わたしたちは 近く[16]の 茶店[17]に 昼ご飯を 食べに はいりました。

▼*Choju-giga*

語句

1 deshita See § 31
2 saiwai (Na/Adv) luckily, fortunately
3 tenki (N) weather; good weather
4 kara (Conj) as, since, because
 See § 36
5 *haikingu* 'hiking'
6 ...ni ik·u go (for...) See § 34
7 Kyōto-eki Kyoto station
8 ippai (N) full
 ...de ippai filled with...
9 hashir·u run
10 Takao (a place name)
11 tsuk·u arrive
12 mazu firstly, before anything else
13 Kōzan-ji (a temple in Kyoto)
 -ji (Buddhist) temple
14 Chōjū-giga (an ink sketch of birds and beasts at play)
15 -katta desu See § 32
16 chikaku neighborhood←chika·i (near)

❸ そこから 山道(やまみち)[18]を 三(さん)キロほど 歩(ある)きました。 道(みち)は あまり 急(きゅう)[19]ではありませんでした。 山(やま)の 空気(くうき)は たいへん きれいでした。 空(そら)[20]は とても 青(あお)[21]かったです。 山(やま)の みどり[22]も 美(うつく)しかったです。

▲Arashiyama

❹ やがて[23] 清滝(きよたき)[24]に 着(つ)きました。 むかし[25] 芭蕉(ばしょう)[26]は ここで 有名(ゆうめい)な 俳句(はいく)[27]を つくり[28]ました。 滝(たき)の 水(みず)は たいへん 冷(つめ)たかった[29]です。 友(とも)だちは 写真(しゃしん)を たくさん とり[30]ました。

❺ わたしたちは 午後四時(ごごよじ)ごろ 嵐山(あらしやま)[31]に 着(つ)きました。 友(とも)だちは とても つかれましたが、 わたしは あまり つかれませんでした。 足(あし)[32]も いたく[33]なかったです。 たいへん 楽(たの)しい[34] ハイキングでした。

* * *

---

17 cha-mise old-fashioned tea house
  cha tea mise shop
18 yama-michi mountain path
  michi way, road
19 kyū (Na) steep; sudden; urgent
20 sora sky 21 ao·i blue; green
22 midori green
23 yagate presently, soon
24 Kiyo-taki (a place name)
  taki waterfall
25 mukashi olden times
26 Bashō (a haiku poet: 1644-94)
27 haiku (a 5-7-5 syllabled poem)
28 tsukur·u make, produce, compose
29 tsumeta·i cold
30 tor·u take
31 Arashi-yama (a place name)
32 ashi foot; leg
33 ita·i painful, hurt
34 tanoshi·i pleasant

Dai 6-ka
Haikingu

1 Kinō wa Nichi-yōbi deshita. Saiwai asa kara taihen ii tenki deshita kara, watashi wa go-nin no tomodachi to *haikingu* ni ikimashita. Ōsaka kara Kyōto made densha de ikimashita. Kyōto-eki kara *basu* ni norimashita. Densha mo *basu* mo hito de ippai deshita. *Basu* wa yama no naka o hashirimashita.

2 Takao ni tsukimashita. Mazu Kōzan-ji e yūmei-na Chōjū-giga o mi ni ikimashita. Taihen omoshirokatta desu. Watashi-tachi wa chikaku no cha-mise ni hiru-gohan o tabe ni hairimashita.

3 Soko kara yama-michi o san-*kiro* hodo arukimashita. Michi wa amari kyū dewa arimasen deshita. Yama no kūki wa taihen kirei deshita. Sora wa totemo aokatta desu. Yama no midori mo utsukushikatta desu.

4 Yagate Kiyo-taki ni tsukimashita. Mukashi Bashō wa koko de yūmei-na haiku o tsukurimashita. Taki no mizu wa taihen tsumetakatta desu. Tomodachi wa shashin o takusan torimashita.

5 Watashi-tachi wa gogo yo-ji goro Arashi-yama ni tsukimashita. Tomodachi wa totemo tsukaremashita ga, watashi wa amari tsukaremasen deshita. Ashi mo itaku nakatta desu. Taihen tanoshii *haikingu* deshita.

▼*Haiku* by Basho at Kiyotaki

清滝や
波に散りこむ
青松葉
芭蕉

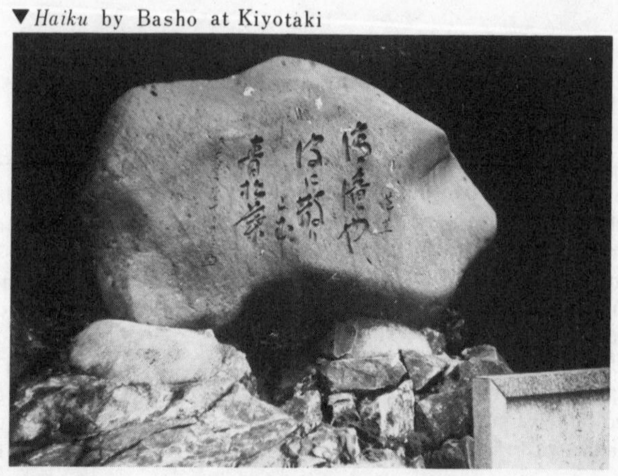

Lesson 6

Hiking

6

1 Yesterday was Sunday. Happily, it was a very nice day since morning, so I went hiking with five of my friends. We took the train from Osaka to Kyoto. From Kyoto station, we took a bus. Both the train and the bus were filled with people. The bus ran through the mountains.

2 We got to Takao. First we went to Kozan-ji Temple to see the famous "Choju-giga." It was very interesting. We went into a nearby tea house to have lunch.

3 After that we walked the mountain paths for some three kilometers. The paths were not very steep. The mountain air was very clear. The sky was very blue. The mountain greenery was very beautiful too.

4 Soon we came to Kiyotaki. A long time ago, Basho composed a famous *haiku* here. The water in the waterfall was very cold. My friends took a lot of pictures.

5 We got to Arashiyama around 4:00 in the afternoon. My friends were very tired, but I was not very tired. My feet did not hurt either. It was a very enjoyable outing.

ANSWERS 〈pp. 76, 77〉

I. 1. ...4-gatsu 3(mik)-ka, Do-yōbi deshita. 2. 4-gatsu 6(mui)-ka, Ka-yōbi desu. 3. ... Moku (-yōbi deshita.) 4. ...Kin-yōbi desu. 5. ...Sui-yōbi deshita. 6. ...3-gatsu 28-nichi (deshita.) 7. ...4-gatsu 8(yō)-ka desu.

II. 1. Q: Kare no hanashi wa nagakatta desu ka? A: Iie, nagaku nakatta desu. Mijikakatta desu. 2. Q: Kono *terebi* wa yasukatta desu ka? A: Iie, yasuku nakatta desu. Takakatta desu. 3. Q: Kono mae no shiken wa muzukashikatta desu ka? A: Iie, muzukashiku nakatta desu. Yasashikatta desu. 4. Q: Shutchō no tetsuzuki wa kantan deshita ka? A: Iie, kantan dewa arimasen deshita. Fukuzatsu deshita. 5. Q: Sono ryokō-sha no hito wa shinsetsu deshita ka? A: Iie, shinsetsu dewa arimasen deshita. Fu-shinsetsu deshita.

III. Kinō wa ii tenki deshita. Sora ga taihen aokatta desu. Niwa no bara no hana mo taihen kirei deshita. Kinō watashi no kaisha wa yasumi deshita. Watashi wa hima deshita. Ototoi made totemo isogashikatta desu. Kinō watashi wa yukkuri yasumimashita. Uchi ni imashita. Ototoi kara watashi no kodomo wa byōki deshita. Shikashi kinō wa sukoshi genki deshita. Watashi wa gogo isha ni ai ni ikimashita.

IV. (B) 1. ...amari shizuka dewa arimasen deshita. 2. ...totemo shizuka deshita. 3. ... sukoshi shizuka deshita. 4. ...sukoshi mo shizuka dewa arimasen deshita. (D) 1. ...zutto byōki deshita. 2. ...kyō mo mada byōki desu. 3. ...kinō made byōki deshita.

V. Watashi wa kotoshi no 4-gatsu ni Nippon-go no benkyō o hajimemashita. Hajime wa Nippon-go wa taihen muzukashikatta desu. Shikashi ima wa amari muzukashiku nai desu. Nippon-go no hatsuon mo muzukashiku nai desu. Watashi wa mai-shū Ka-yōbi to Kin-yōbi ni Nippon-go o benkyō-shimasu. Kyō Nippon-go no jugyō ga arimashita. Kyō no jugyō wa omoshirokatta desu. Atarashii kotoba o takusan naraimashita.

●文法

§ 31 Past Tense Form of the Nominal Predicate

N_1 wa N_2 deshita. 'N_1 was N_2.'

Negation: **N_1 wa N_2 dewa arimasen deshita.** 'N_1 was not N_2.'

e.g. Kyō wa Nichi-yōbi desu. 'Today is Sunday.'

Kinō wa Do-yōbi deshita. 'Yesterday was Saturday.'

Kinō wa yasumi deshita ka? 'Was yesterday a holiday?'

—Iie, yasumi dewa arimasen deshita. 'No, it wasn't a holiday.'

§ 32 Past Tense Forms of A and Na

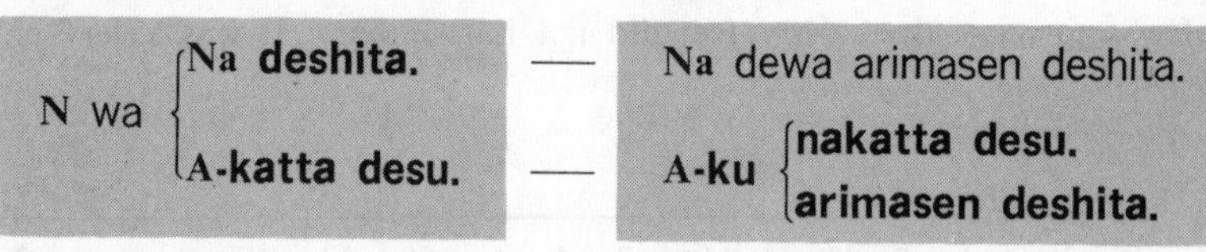

			Negation:
N wa	Na **deshita.**	—	Na dewa arimasen deshita.
	A-**katta desu.**	—	A-ku **nakatta desu.** / **arimasen deshita.**

e.g. Hanako-san wa kirei desu ne. 'Hanako is pretty, isn't she?'

Mukashi mo anna-ni kirei deshita ka? 'Was she that pretty before too?'

—Iie, mukashi wa anna-ni kirei dewa arimasen deshita.

'No, she wasn't that pretty a long time ago.'

Ano eiga wa omoshirokatta desu ka? 'Was the movie interesting?'

—Iie, amari omoshiroku nakatta desu. 'No, it wasn't very interesting.'

§ 33 Joint Actions: N to (V) '(do...) with N'

e.g. Tomodachi to eiga ni ikimashita. 'I went to a movie with a friend.'

Watashi to *pinpon* o shimasen ka? 'Won't you play ping-pong with me?'

NB: This N must be Animate, typically Human.

§ 34 Purpose

N V (Conj. form)	+ **ni**	**ikimasu.** **kimasu.** **kaerimasu.**	'go 'come 'go home	for...' in order to...'

e.g. *haikingu* ni ikimasu 'go hiking (go for a hike)'

Gohan o tabe ni kaerimasu. 'I go home to eat.'

NB: This expression of purpose is possible only when the main (following) Verb is iku, kuru, or kaeru. For all other Verbs, another pattern is necessary. (See § 103)

§ 35 Predicative vs. Prenominal Uses of Adjectives

Most of the 'i Adjectives' can be used as Prenominal modifiers for N as well as sentence predicates as seen in § 6 and § 7.

There are, however, a few Adjectives which take different forms depending upon whether they are used as Predicates or as Prenominal modifiers.

e.g. Sono mise wa chikai desu. 'That shop is near.'

Chikaku no mise de kaimashita. 'I bought it at a nearby shop.'

tōku no machi 'a faraway town' (cf. tōi desu. '...is far.')

ōku no hito 'many people' (cf. ōi desu. '...are many/much.')

There is also a group of words that are only used as Prenominal modifiers for N (abbreviated as 'PreN').

e.g. tonda 'awful' sugureta eiga 'an excellent movie'

§ 36 Conjunctive Particles

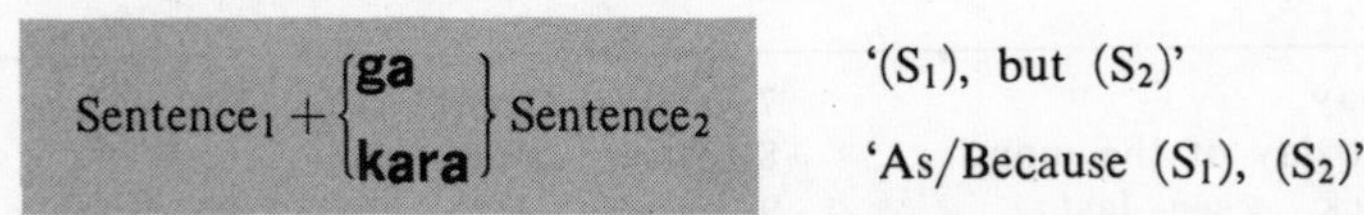

Sentence$_1$ + {**ga** / **kara**} Sentence$_2$

'(S_1), but (S_2)'

'As/Because (S_1), (S_2)'

e.g. Ii tenki deshita kara, *haikingu* ni ikimashita.

'As the weather was fine, I went hiking.'

●練習

ANSWERS→p. 73

I. Complete the sentences.

Kyō wa 4(shi)-gatsu 5(itsu)-ka, Getsu-yōbi[1] desu.

Kinō wa 4-gatsu 4(yok)-ka, Nichi-yōbi deshita.

1. Ototoi wa ____________________
2. Ashita wa ____________________
3. 4-gatsu tsuitachi[2] wa ____ -yōbi deshita.
4. 4-gatsu 9(kokono)-ka wa ____________________
5. 3-gatsu 31(san-jū-ichi)-nichi wa ____________________
6. Sen-shū[3] no Nichi-yōbi wa ____________ deshita.
7. Kon-shū[4] no Moku-yōbi wa ____________________

Days of the Week
Nichi-yōbi ……Sunday
Getsu-yōbi ……Monday
Ka-yōbi ……Tuesday
Sui-yōbi ……Wednesday
Moku-yōbi ……Thursday
Kin-yōbi ……Friday
Do-yōbi ……Saturday

II. Make dialogs as shown in the example.

Ex. Q: (kinō no *pāti*[5]) (omoshiroi)

Kinō no *pāti* wa omoshirokatta desu ka?

A: (iie) (tsumaranai)

Iie, omoshiroku nakatta desu. Tsumaranakatta desu.

1. Q: (kare no hanashi[6]) (nagai) A: (iie) (mijikai[7])
2. Q: (kono *terebi*) (yasui) A: (iie) (takai)
3. Q: (kono mae no shiken[8]) (muzukashii) A: (iie) (yasashii)
4. Q: (shutchō no tetsuzuki[9]) (kantan[10]) A: (iie) (fukuzatsu[11])
5. Q: (sono ryokō-sha no hito) (shinsetsu) A: (iie) (fu-shinsetsu[12])

III. Substituting kinō for kyō, change the entire passage to suit.

Kyō wa ii tenki desu. Sora ga taihen aoi desu. Niwa[13] no bara no hana

語句

1 Getsu-yōbi Monday
2 tsuitachi the 1st day of the month
3 sen-shū last week sen- last
4 kon-shū this week kon- this
5 *pāti* 'party'
6 hanashi story; talk ←hanas·u
7 mijika·i short
8 shiken examination
9 tetsuzuki procedure, formalities
10 kantan (Na) not complicated, simple
11 fukuzatsu (Na) complicated
12 fu-shinsetsu (N/Na) unkind

mo taihen kirei desu. Kyō watashi no kaisha wa yasumi desu. Watashi wa hima[14] desu. Kinō made totemo isogashikatta desu. Kyō watashi wa yukkuri yasumimasu. Uchi ni imasu. Kinō kara watashi no kodomo wa byōki[15] desu. Shikashi kyō wa sukoshi genki[16] desu. Watashi wa gogo isha ni ai ni ikimasu.

6

IV. Make sentences as shown in the examples.

(A) Ex. (omoshiroi)→Ano eiga wa omoshirokatta desu.

1. (nagai) 2. (furui) 3. (tsumaranai)

(B) Ex. (taihen)→Sono heya wa taihen shizuka deshita.

1. (amari) 2. (totemo)

3. (sukoshi) 4. (sukoshi mo[17])

(C) Ex. (totemo)→Watashi wa kinō totemo isogashikatta desu.

1. (sukoshi) 2. (amari)

3. (sukoshi mo) 4. (taihen)

(D) Ex. (kinō)→Watashi wa kinō byōki deshita.

1. (zutto[18]) 2. (kyō mo mada) 3. (kinō made)

V. Put the following into Japanese.

I began to study Japanese this April. At first,[19] Japanese was very difficult. But now it is not so difficult. Japanese pronunciation is not difficult either. I study Japanese every Tuesday and Friday. I had Japanese lessons[20] today. Today's lessons were interesting. I learned[21] many new words.[22]

---

fu- non- (Pref. expressing negative)
13 niwa garden
14 hima (Na) leisure; not busy
15 byōki (N) sick, sickness
16 genki (Na) healthy
17 sukoshi mo...nai not...at all
18 zutto (Adv) all the time
19 hajime beginning ←hajime·ru
hajime wa at first
20 jugyō class (lesson)
21 nara·u learn
22 kotoba language; word

●会話

OMOSHIROKATTA?

—Kono mae no Nichi-yōbi doko e ikimashita ka?

Kyōto e ikimashita.

—Kyōto kenbutsu[1] wa omoshirokatta desu ka?

Ē, omoshirokatta desu.

—Kyōto wa furui machi desu. Yūmei-na o-tera[2] ya niwa ga takusan arimasu. Kyōto no doko e ikimashita?

Heian-jingū,[3] Nanzen-ji,[4] Nijō-jō[5] nado[6] e ikimashita.

—Doko ga yokatta[7] desu ka?

Nijō-jō no niwa ga utsukushikatta desu.

—Hito wa sukunakatta desu ka?

Iie, taihen ōkatta desu.

—Sō deshō.[8] Kyōto no meisho[9] wa itsumo hito ga ōi desu. Jū-nen[10] gurai mae wa motto[11] shizuka-

—Where did you go last Sunday?

I went to Kyoto.

—Was it interesting sightseeing in Kyoto?

Yes, it was interesting.

—Kyoto is an old town. There are many famous temples and gardens. Where did you go in Kyoto?

I went to Heian Shrine, Nanzen-ji Temple, Nijo Castle, and so on.

—Where did you enjoy most?

The garden at Nijo Castle was beautiful.

—Wasn't it crowded? (←Were there few people?)

Yes, it was crowded. (←No, there were many.)

—That's what I expected. Famous places in Kyoto are always crowded.

語句

1 kenbutsu (Nv) sight-seeing
2 tera (Buddhist) temple
3 Heian-jingū (a Shinto shrine in Kyoto)
　-jingū (Shinto) shrine
4 Nanzen-ji (a temple in Kyoto)
5 Nijō-jō (a castle in Kyoto) -jō castle
6 ...nado ...and some others, et cetera
7 yo・i=ii good, satisfactory
8 deshō (Future or Presumptive form of desu)
9 meisho famous place
10 -nen ...year(s)

6

na machi deshita.

Kyōto de nani o kaimashita ka?

E-hagaki[12] o takusan kaimashita.

Kirei-na e-hagaki desu.

Shashin mo takusan torimashita.

—Nara[13] e mo ikimashita ka?

Ē, ikimashita.

Daibutsu[14] wa taihen ōkikatta desu.

Kasuga-taisha[15] mo totemo kirei deshita.

—Shika[16] ga imasen deshita ka?

Takusan imashita.

Ko-jika[17] ga kawairashikatta[18] desu.

Ko-jika no shashin o takusan torimashita.

Kuni no imōto ni okurimasu.[19]

It was a much quieter town about ten years ago.

What did you buy in Kyoto?

I bought a lot of picture postcards.

They are beautiful.

I also took a lot of pictures.

—Did you go to Nara too?

Yes, I did.

The Great Buddha was very big.

Kasuga Shrine was also very beautiful.

—Weren't the deer there?

There were many.

The fawns were quite cute.

I took many pictures of the fawns. I'll send them to my younger sister at home.

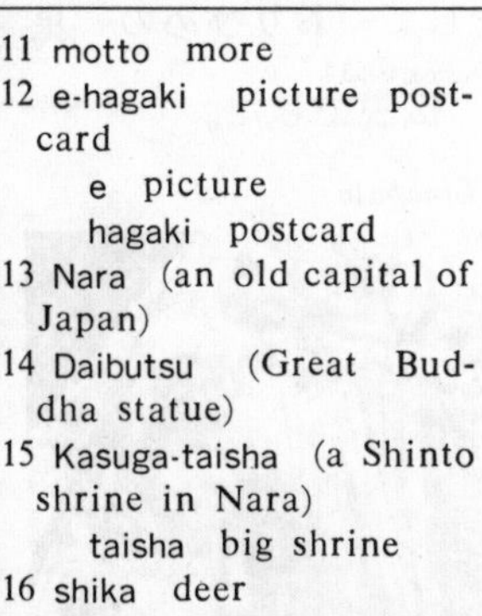

11 motto more

12 e-hagaki picture postcard

  e picture

  hagaki postcard

13 Nara (an old capital of Japan)

14 Daibutsu (Great Buddha statue)

15 Kasuga-taisha (a Shinto shrine in Nara)

  taisha big shrine

16 shika deer

17 ko-jika young deer

  ko- child

  -jika=shika deer

18 kawairashi·i cute

19 okur·u send

▼Nara Park

日本の　行事—1

日本の　行事は[1]　たいてい　中国から　来ました。　その　中の[2]　いくつかは　もう　なくなりました[3]。　しかし、　今でも[4]　まだ　ほとんどの　家庭で[5]　いろいろな　行事を　します。

まず　一月には　正月の[6]　行事が　あります。　家の　入り口に　門松や[7]　しめなわを[8]　かざります[9]。　朝は　おもちを[10]　食べます。　たくさんの　人が　お寺や　神社に[11]　参ります[12]。

二月の　初めに[13]　節分が[14]　あります。　長い　冬の　終わりです[15]。　節分の　晩には　まめを[16]　まきます[17]。　まめで　おにを[18]　追い出します[19]。　そして　福の　神を[20]　家の　中へ　招きます[21]。

三月三日は　ひな祭りです[22]。　女の子は　ひな人形を[23]　へやの　中に　かざります。　五月五日の　たんごの　節句は[24]　男の子の　祭りです。　こいのぼりを[25]　立てます[26]。

七月には　たなばたが[27]　あります。　星の[28]　祭りです。　牛かいの[29]　星が　一年に[30]　一度[31]　この　夜だけ[32]　天の川を[33]　わたります[34]。　そして　おりひめの[35]　星に　会います。　この　ロマンチックな[36]　話は　中国の　伝説でした[37]。

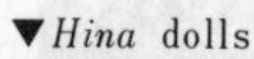

▼*Hina* dolls　▼Carp streamers　▼*Tanabata*

Ceremonial Events—1

Most of Japan's ceremonial events came from China. Some of them have since disappeared, but some are still celebrated in most families.

January begins with New Year's Day. People decorate the gates to their houses with pine branches and sacred ropes. They eat rice cakes for breakfast. Many go to the temples and shrines to worship.

Setsubun at the beginning of February means the end of the long winter. On that night, the people scatter beans to drive away the evil spirits and to invite in good luck.

Girls exhibit their *Hina* dolls on the Doll's Festival, March 3. May 5 is the Boy's Festival when boys put up their carp streamers.

Tanabata is in July. It is the Stars' Festival. According to a romantic Chinese legend, this is the one night of the year when the Cowherd Star is able to cross the Milky Way and meet the Weaver Star.

6

語句

1 gyōji ceremonial event
2 ikutsu ka some, several
3 naku-nar•u vanish, be lost; die
4 ima demo even now
5 katei family, home
6 Shō-gatsu New Year's Day(s)
7 kado-matsu (pine branches as New Year's gate decorations)
  matsu pine
8 shime-nawa (sacred rope)
  nawa rope
9 kazar•u decorate
10 mochi (rice cake)
11 jinja shrine
12 mair•u go to worship
13 ...no hajime the beginning of...
14 Setsubun (the day before the beginning of spring in the lunar calendar)
15 owari end ←owar•u (end)
16 mame beans, peas
17 mak•u scatter
18 oni ogre
19 oidas•u drive away
20 Fuku no kami God/Goddess of Luck
  kami god
21 manek•u invite
22 Hina-matsuri (Girl's Festival)
  matsuri festival
23 Hina-ningyō (Girl's Festival dolls)
  ningyō doll
24 Tango no Sekku (Boy's Festival)
25 koi-nobori carp streamer
  koi crap
  nobori streamer, flag ←nobor•u (rise, climb)
26 tate•ru hoist, make...stand; build
27 Tanabata (Stars' Festival)
28 hoshi star
29 ushi-kai cowherd
  ushi cow
  kai ←ka•u (keep animals)
30 ichi-nen one year
31 ichi-do once
  -do times (frequency)
32 ...dake only
33 Ama no gawa the Milky Way
  gawa←kawa (river)
34 watar•u cross
35 Ori-hime Weaver Princess
  ori ←or•u (weave) hime princess
36 *romanchikku* (Na) 'romantic'
37 densetsu legend

第 7 課

公園

TAPE
No. 2
Side 2

❶ 公園(こうえん)には たくさん 花(はな)が さいています[1]。 木(き)も たくさん あります。 子(こ)どもが おおぜい[2] 遊(あそ)んで[3]います。 小鳥(ことり)[4]が 木(き)の 上(うえ)で 歌(うた)って[5]います。 池(いけ)[6]には 橋(はし)[7]が かかって[8]います。 こいが およいで[9]います。 赤(あか)い こいも 黒(くろ)い[10] こいも います。

❷ 向(む)こうで 中学生(ちゅうがくせい)[11]が 写生(しゃせい)[12]を しています。 男(おとこ)の子(こ)と 女(おんな)の子(こ)が ぶらんこ[13]に 乗(の)っています。 女(おんな)の人(ひと)が そばで 見(み)ています。 こかげ[14]で 若(わか)い 男女(だんじょ)[15]が 話(はな)して[16]います。 公園(こうえん)の 中(なか)は 明(あか)るい[17] 光(ひかり)[18]で いっぱいです。

❸ わたしたちは 先週(せんしゅう)の 土曜日(どようび)、 お弁当(べんとう)[19]を もって[20]、 公園(こうえん)へ

語句

1 -te-i-ru =-de-i-ru See §37
2 ōzei a large number of people
3 asob·u play
4 ko-tori little bird
5 uta·u sing 6 ike pond
7 hashi bridge
8 kakar·u span; be built over
9 oyog·u swim 10 kuro·i black
11 chūgaku-sei junior high school student chūgaku=chū-gakkō junior high school
12 shasei (Nv) sketching
13 buranko swing
14 ko-kage shade of a tree
kage shade; shadow; silhouette; image; reflection
15 dan-jo man and woman
16 hanas·u speak, tell, talk
17 akaru·i bright, light; cheerful
18 hikari light, ray
19 bentō lunch (to take out)
20 mots·u have, hold
21 kadan flower bed
22 -te kara after...ing See §40
23 mawar·u (Vi) go round; (make a) detour

行きました。 花壇[21]の 美しい 花を 見てから、[22] 池を 回っ[23]て、 ベンチ[24]で 休みました。 わたしは 本を 読みました。 妹は 写生を しました。 それから こかげで 歌[25]を 歌ったり[26]、 ハーモニカ[27]を ふいたり[28]しました。 小学生[29]が ボール[30]を 投げ[31]たり、 すもう[32]を とったりして 遊んでいました。 わたしたちは うしろの 丘[33]に 上って[34]、 町を 見おろしました[35]。 汽車[36]が 走っていました。 遠く[37]に 川が 光って[38]いました。

❹ わたしたちは 川の 近くに 住んで[39]います。 わたしは 川の こちらの 町は よく 知って[40]います。 しかし、 川の 向こうがわ[41]の 町の こと[42]は あまり 知りません。

---

24 *benchi* 'bench'
25 uta song
26 -tari=-dari See § 39
27 *hāmonika* 'harmonica'
28 fuk·u (Vt) blow
29 shōgaku-sei primary school pupil
  shōgaku=shō-gakkō primary school
30 *bōru* 'ball'
31 nage·ru throw
32 sumō (Japanese traditional wrestling)
  sumō o tor·u do *sumo*
33 oka hill
34 nobor·u climb; rise
35 mi-oros·u look down
36 kisha (steam-powered) train
37 tōku (N/Adv) faraway place ←tō·i (far)
38 hikar·u shine, glitter
39 sunde-i·ru live, reside
  sum·u (live) See § 37 NB
40 shitte-i·ru know
  shir·u get to know See § 37 NB
41 mukō-gawa that side, the other side
  -gawa side
42 koto thing; matter; fact; situation

Dai 7-ka
Kōen

1 Kōen niwa takusan hana ga saite-imasu. Ki mo takusan arimasu. Kodomo ga ōzei asonde-imasu. Ko-tori ga ki no ue de utatte-imasu. Ike niwa hashi ga kakatte-imasu. Koi ga oyoide-imasu. Akai koi mo kuroi koi mo imasu.

2 Mukō de chūgaku-sei ga shasei o shite-imasu. Otoko no ko to onna no ko ga buranko ni notte-imasu. Onna no hito ga soba de mite-imasu. Ko-kage de wakai dan-jo ga hanashite-imasu. Kōen no naka wa akarui hikari de ippai desu.

3 Watashi-tachi wa sen-shū no Do-yōbi, o-bentō o motte, kōen e ikimashita. Kadan no utsukushii hana o mite kara, ike o mawatte, *benchi* de yasumimashita. Watashi wa hon o yomimashita. Imōto wa shasei o shimashita. Sore kara ko-kage de uta o utattari, *hāmonika* o fuitari shimashita. Shōgaku-sei ga *bōru* o nagetari, sumō o tottari shite asonde-imashita. Watashi-tachi wa ushiro no oka ni nobotte, machi o mi-oroshimashita. Kisha ga hashitte-imashita. Tōku ni kawa ga hikatte-imashita.

4 Watashi-tachi wa kawa no chikaku ni sunde-imasu. Watashi wa kawa no kochira no machi wa yoku shitte-imasu. Shikashi, kawa no mukō-gawa no machi no koto wa amari shirimasen.

▼ Shinjuku-gyoen

Lesson 7
The Park

7

1 There are many flowers blooming in the park. There are many trees too. Many children are playing there. The birds are singing in the trees. There is a bridge over the pond. The carp are swimming. There are red carp and black carp.

2 Over there, some junior high school students are sketching. A boy and a girl are swinging on the swings. A woman is watching nearby. A young man and woman are talking in the shade of the trees. The park is filled with bright sunshine.

3 We took our lunches to the park last Saturday. Looking at the beautiful flowers in the flower beds, we went around the lake and rested on the benches. I read a book. My younger sister drew some sketches. Then we sang and played our harmonicas in the shade. Grade school children were throwing balls, wrestling, and playing other games. We climbed up the hill behind the park and looked down on the town. A train was going by. The river glittered in the distance.

4 We live near the river. I know the town on this side of the river very well. But I do not know the town on the other side of the river very well.

ANSWERS <pp. 88, 89>

I. A: Kono hito wa ima: 1. *piano* o hiite-imasu. 2. hanashite-imasu. 3. (uta o) utatte-imasu. 4. *terebi* o mite-imasu. 5. shashin o totte-imasu. 6. oyoide-imasu. 7. hon o yonde-imasu. 8. asonde-imasu. 9. *basu* o matte-imasu.

II. (A) 1. Watashi wa yoku *piano* o hiitari, utattari shimasu. 2. Watashi wa yoku tomodachi to hanashitari, asondari shimasu. 3. Watashi wa kinō hon o yondari, *terebi* o mitari, shashin o tottari shimashita. 4. Watashi wa kinō oyoidari, hon o yondari shimashita.

III. (A) 1. Watashi wa kesa 7-ji ni okite sanpo-shimashita. 2. Watashi wa yūbe eiga o mite, ban-gohan o tabete kaerimashita. 3. Watashi wa kinō tomodachi ni atte, *bīru* o nonde hanashimashita. 4. Watashi wa yūbe ie ni kaette *rajio* o kiite, hon o yonde nemashita.

IV. 1. Kare wa kutsu o nuide heya ni hairimashita. 2. Anata wa ima ikura o-kane o motte-imasu ka? 3. "Anata wa kaisha no chikaku ni sunde-imasu ka?" "Iie, watashi no ie wa kaisha kara totemo/taihen tōi desu." "Sore wa fu-ben desu ne." "Iie, watashi wa kuruma o motte-imasu. Mai-nichi kuruma de kaisha e ikimasu." 4. "Anata wa kare no atarashii ie no denwa-bangō o shitte-imasu ka?" "Iie, furui bangō wa shitte-imasu ga, atarashii bangō/no wa shirimasen." 5. "Kyō *depāto*/hyakka-ten wa aite-imasu ka?" "Iie, shimatte-imasu. Kyō wa Getsu-yōbi desu." 6. Kinō watashi wa ginkō e ittari, denwa o kaketari, tegami o kaitari shite totemo/taihen isogashikatta desu.

●文法

§ 37 Progressive (or Continuous) Form of Verbs

. . . V-te-imasu.

This form indicates:

1. An action or event in progress (for V expressing continuous, durative actions or events, such as walking, eating, raining, etc.)

e.g. Kodomo ga asonde-imasu. 'Children are playing.'

Anata wa nani o shite-imasu ka? 'What are you doing?'

—Shasei o shite-imasu. '(I am) sketching.'

2. A state resulting from a previous action or event (for V expressing instantaneous or momentary events or actions, such as beginning or arriving)

e.g. Matsuri wa mō hajimatte-imasu. (hajimatte←hajimaru 'to begin')

'The festival has already started (and is now going on).' (*not* 'is beginning')

Ginkō wa mada aite-imasu ka? 'Is the bank still open?'

—Iie, mō shimatte-imasu. 'No, it is already closed.'

3. A particular quality, state, condition, or manner of something

e.g. Ike ni hashi ga kakatte-imasu. (kakatte←kakaru 'to hang')

'There is (hanging) a bridge over the pond.'

Michi ga magatte-imasu. 'The road is curved.'

Tanaka-san wa futotte (yasete)-imasu. 'Tanaka is fat (thin).'

NB: (1) The 'V-te-imashita form' is the past counterpart of the 'V-te-imasu.'

e.g. Kodomo ga asonde-imashita. 'Children were playing.'

Matsuri wa hajimatte-imashita. 'The festival had already started.'

(2) Remember that some events or actions may be seen as continuous in English but instantaneous in Japanese, and vice versa.

e.g. shinde-imasu (shinde←shinu 'to die') 'is dead,' not '(someone) is dying'

Hankachi ga ochite-imasu. (ochite←ochiru 'to fall') 'A handkerchief is lying on the ground.'

(3) Some verbs such as the following are 'Stative verbs' in English, hence their equivalents must take the '-te-imasu form' in Japanese.

'know'→shitte-imasu 'have'→motte-imasu

'live (in Kyoto)'→(Kyōto ni) sunde-imasu

(4) For the formation of 'V-te,' see Appendix.

(5) The '-te-imasu form' of V is often used to express the speaker's immediate reaction to a particular state of affairs, and in that case, the Subject takes the Particle ga, and not wa.

7

§ 38 Succession of Two or More Actions or Events

. . . V-te, (. . . V-te,) . . . shimasu/shimashita.

e.g. Oka ni nobotte, machi o mimashita.

'We climbed the hill, and looked at the town.'

§ 39 Alternative (or Indefinite Number of) Actions or Events

. . . V-tari, . . . V-tari, . . . V-masu/-mashita.

e.g. Oka ni nobottari, machi o mitari shimashita.

'We did such things as climbing the hill, looking at the town (and maybe some other things, not necessarily in this order).'

§ 40 'After doing . . .'

. . . V-te kara . . .

e.g. Hana o mite kara, oka ni noborimashita.

'After looking at the flowers, we climbed the hill.'

NB: '-te, …-te' also indicates the order in which the series of actions or events takes place, but '-te kara' makes it clearer.

●練習

ANSWERS→p. 85

I. Use the chart to make dialogs as shown in the example.

Ex. Q: Kono hito wa ima nani o shite-imasu ka?

A: Kono hito wa ima ongaku o kiite-imasu.

II. Use the chart to make sentences as shown in the examples.

(A) Ex. (Ex)+1 (yoku) Watashi wa yoku ongaku o kiitari, *piano* o hiitari shimasu.

1. 1+3 (yoku)
2. 2+8 (yoku) (tomodachi to)
3. 7+4+5 (kinō)
4. 6+7 (kinō)

(B) Ex. (Ex)+3 (kyō) Kyō watashi wa ongaku o kiite kara uta o utaimashita.

1. 4+3 (yūbe)
2. 1+7 (itsumo)
3. 7+8 (itsumo)
4. 3+5 (kinō) (watashi-tachi)
5. 2+8 (kyō) (tomodachi to)
6. 6+3 (kono mae no Nichi-yōbi)
7. 8+4 (kinō) (watashi-tachi)

語句

1 *piano* 'piano'
2 hik•u play (musical instrument); pull
3 mats•u wait
4 ban-gohan supper
5 furo bath
6 furo ni hair•u take a bath
7 yam•u stop (rain, snow, etc.)
8 nug•u take off (clothes, shoes, socks, etc.)
9 kane money (=o-kane); metal

III. Combine the sentences.

(A) Ex. (kyō) (Yūbin-kyoku e ikimasu.) (Kitte o kaimasu.)

Watashi wa kyō yūbin-kyoku e itte kitte o kaimasu.

1. (kesa) (7-ji ni okimasu.) (Sanpo-shimasu.)
2. (yūbe) (Eiga o mimasu.) (Ban-gohan[4] o tabemasu.) (Kaerimasu.)
3. (kinō) (Tomodachi ni aimasu.) (*Bīru* o nomimasu.) (Hanashimasu.)
4. (yūbe) (Ie ni kaerimasu.) (*Rajio* o kikimasu.) (Hon o yomimasu.) (Nemasu.)

(B) Ex. (mai-asa) (Sanpo-shimasu.) (Asa-gohan o tabemasu.)

Watashi wa mai-asa sanpo-shite kara asa-gohan o tabemasu.

1. (kyō) (Shigoto ga owarimasu.) (Tomodachi ni aimasu.)
2. (mai-ban) (O-furo[5] ni hairimasu.[6]) (Nemasu.)
3. (yūbe) (Ame ga yamimasu.[7]) (Gaishutsu-shimasu.)

IV. Put the following into Japanese.

1. He took off[8] his shoes and entered the room.
2. How much money[9] do you have now?
3. "Do you live near your office?"

   "No, I don't. My house is very far from my office."

   "It is inconvenient,[10] isn't it?"

   "No. I have a car.[11] I go to work by car every day."
4. "Do you know the telephone number[12] at his new house?"

   "No. I knew his old number, but I don't know his new one."
5. "Is the department store[13] open[14] today?" "No. It's closed.[15] Today is Monday."
6. Yesterday I was very busy, going to the bank, making phone calls, and writing letters.

---

10 fu-ben (Na) inconvenient
  ben ←benri (Na) convenient; useful
11 kuruma car; wheel
12 denwa-bangō telephone number
  bangō number
13 hyakka-ten=*depāto* department store
14 ak·u (Vi) open; become available
15 shimar·u (Vi) close

●会話

GOMEN-KUDASAI

Gomen-kudasai.[1]

Taeko[2]-san wa irasshaimasu ka?

—Hai, orimasu.[3]

Dochira-sama[4] deshō ka?

Rinda[5] desu.

—Ā, *Rinda*-san! O-machi-shite-imashita.

Dōzo, kochira e.

O-jama[6] shimasu.

—Ara[7]! Irasshai!

Konnichi wa.

—O-kā-san,[8] kochira ga *Rinda*-san.

Rinda-san, watashi no haha[9] desu.

Rinda desu. Yoroshiku.

Kono atari wa totemo shizuka desu ne.

—Ē, kuruma mo amari tōrimasen[10] kara.

O-tō-san[11] wa?

—Chichi[12] wa ima ni-kai de hon o yonde-imasu.

Excuse me.
Is Taeko at home?
—Yes, she is.
May I ask your name?
Linda.
—Ah, Linda! We have been waiting for you. Please come this way.
Thank you very much. (←I'm sorry to intrude on you like this.)

—Hey! Come on in!
It's nice to see you.
—Mother, this is Linda.
Linda, this is my mother.
I am Linda. Glad to meet you.
This neighborhood is quiet indeed, isn't it?
—Yes, and we don't have very many cars passing by here either.
Your father is...?
—Father is upstairs reading a book now.

語句

1 Gomen-kudasai (Cph) Anybody home?
2 Taeko (a given name (f))
3 or·u =i·ru be staying/in
4 dochira-sama who (very polite) dochira which -sama (politer than -san)
5 *Rinda* 'Linda'
6 jama (Na/Nv) obstacle, interruption, something in the way
7 Ara Hey (fem.)
8 o-kā-san mother (Polite)
9 haha mother
10 tōr·u pass
11 o-tō-san father (Polite)
12 chichi father
13 ato de later
14 go-....-suru (Polite form of suru)

I'll introduce you later.
Your mother is a tea ceremony teacher, isn't she?
—Yes, on Sunday afternoons she teaches tea ceremony and flower arrangement.
How many students does she have?
—About thirty.
Taeko, do you make tea yourself?
—No, I can't.
I make very good coffee though.
Oh, that's interesting.

—This is my room.
There are so many books, aren't there?
—On holidays, I read books or listen to records here.
You've got a lot of records too.
—I collect modern jazz records.

Ato de[13] go-shōkai-shimasu.[14]

O-kā-san wa o-cha[15] no sensei desu ne?

—Hai, Nichi-yōbi no gogo o-cha to ikebana[16] o oshiete[17]-imasu.

O-deshi[18]-san wa nan-nin imasu ka?

—San-jū-nin gurai desu.

Taeko-san, anata mo o-cha o tatemasu[19] ka?

—Watashi wa dame[20] desu.

Kōhī wa jōzu[21]-ni iremasu[22] ga....

Mā,[23] omoshiroi desu ne.

—Koko ga watashi no heya desu.

Hon ga takusan arimasu ne.

—Yasumi no hi wa, koko de hon o yondari *rekōdo*[24] o kiitari shimasu.

Rekōdo mo takusan arimasu ne.

—*Modan*[25] *jazu*[26] no *rekōdo* o atsumete[27]-imasu.

7

---

go- See § 118
shōkai (Nv) introduction
15 o-cha tea ceremony; tea
16 ikebana flower arrangement
17 oshie·ru teach; show; tell
18 deshi (personal) student
19 o-cha o tate·ru make tea
20 dame (Na) no good
21 jōzu (Na) skillful, be good at...
22 *kōhī* o ire·ru make coffee
ire·ru (Vt) put...in
23 Mā Oh (female)
24 *rekōdo* 'record,' disc
25 *modan* (Na) 'modern'
26 *jazu* 'jazz'
27 atsume·ru (Vt) collect, gather

日本の 行事—2

関東[1]では 七月、 関西[2]では 八月に おぼん[3]が あります。 おぼんには 先祖[4]の たましい[5]が 帰ります。 おぼんの 最初[6]の 日に 先祖の たましいを むかえ[7]ます。 最後[8]の 日には 火[9]を つけて[10]、たましいを 送り[11]ます。有名な 京都の 大文字[12]も その 行事の 一つ[13]です。

秋は 空も すんで[14]いて 月[15]も たいへん きれいです。 九月の 満月[16]の 日に お月見[17]を します。

十月は スポーツ[18]の シーズン[19]です。学校では 運動会[20]が あります。 また[21] 人びと[22]は ハイキングに 行ったり、サイクリング[23]を したりします。

お米[24]の 取り入れ[25]も 始まります。 そして 十月、 十一月には 豊作[26]を 祝って[27]、 村[28]や 町で 秋祭り[29]が あります。

十一月 十五日は 七五三[30] です。 親[31]が 三歳と 五歳と 七歳の 子どもを 連れて[32]、 神社に 参ります。

年[33]の くれ[34]は みんな たいへん いそがしいです。大そうじ[35]を したり、おもち[36]を ついたりします。 大みそか[37]には 夜中[38]の 十二時から 除夜の かね[39]を 聞いて 新しい 年を むかえます。

▼*Daimonji* ▼Harvest Festival ▼*Joya no kane*

Ceremonial Events—2

We have the "*Bon* Festival" in July in the Kanto District and in August in Kansai. Our ancestors' souls come back to this world during *Bon*. We welcome them on the first day and see them off on the last day, lighting the way back. The famous *Daimonji* in Kyoto is one of these events.

In the autumn, the sky is clear and the moon is beautiful. We enjoy viewing the full moon in September. October is a good season for sports. Schools hold athletic events, and many people go hiking and cycling.

Autumn is also the season for harvest. Many villages and towns have festivals celebrating good crops in October and November.

November 15 is *Shichi-go-san*, when parents take their children aged three, five, and seven years old to the shrines.

Everyone is very busy at the end of the year, cleaning house and pounding rice for rice cakes. We welcome the new year with the bells of the temples at midnight on New Year's Eve.

7

語句

1 Kantō (Tokyo and the surrounding prefectures)
2 Kansai (Osaka, Kyoto, Kobe, and the surrounding prefectures)
3 (o-)bon (*Bon* Festival: Buddhist)
4 senzo ancestors
5 tamashii spirit, soul
6 saisho (N/Adv) the first
7 mukae•ru welcome, receive
8 saigo (N) the last
9 hi fire
10 tsuke•ru attach; turn on (light, TV, etc.) hi o tsuke•ru set fire
11 okur•u see off; send
12 Dai-monji (the mountain bonfire shaped like the character 大)
  dai- big, great
13 ...no hito-tsu one of...
14 sunde-i•ru be clear ←sum•u (get clear)
15 tsuki moon; month
16 man-getsu full moon
  man- full -getsu moon; month
17 tsuki-mi moon-viewing (ceremonially) cf. hana-mi (flower-viewing)
18 *supōtsu* 'sports'
19 *shizun* 'season'
20 undō-kai athletic meeting
  undō physical exercise
  kai meeting
21 mata and also; again
22 hito-bito people
23 *saikuringu* 'cycling'
24 kome rice
25 tori-ire harvest, crop ←tori-ire•ru (take...in; harvest)
26 hōsaku abundant harvest
27 iwa•u celebrate
28 mura village
29 aki-matsuri harvest festival
30 Shichi-go-san (festival for children three, five, and seven years old)
31 oya parent
32 tsure•ru accompany, take
33 toshi year; age
34 kure (N) toward the end
35 ō-sōji general cleaning
  ō- big; large-scale
  sōji (Nv) cleaning, sweeping
36 mochi o tsuk•u pound boiled rice into paste
37 Ō-misoka New Year's Eve
38 yonaka midnight; (during) the night
39 joya no kane temple bells to ring out the old year and ring in the new year (Buddhist) kane bell

第 8 課

夏休みの 日記[1]

TAPE No. 2 Side 2

七月十日（雨）

❶ きのうも 雨だった[2]。きょうも また[3] 雨だ[4]。一週間[5] 一度[6]も 晴れ[7]なかった[8]。ことしは つゆ明け[9]が おそい[10]。

あすから[11] 夏休み[12]が 始まる。去年の 夏は 山に 登った[13]。夏山[14]は ほんとうに[15] すばらしかった[16]。雪も 高山植物[17]も 美しかった。空も 雲[18]も きれいだった。

❷ ことしの 夏休みには 北海道へ 行く。北海道では、札幌[19]の 町や 摩周湖[20]や 知床半島[21]などを 回る。わたしは 北海道の ことは あまり 知らない[22]。ときどき ガイド・ブック[23]を 開いて[24]、旅行の ことを 考えて[25]いる。

▲Shiretoko National Park

語句

1 nikki diary
2 datta See §41 -ta See §41
3 mata again; also
4 da (Plain form of desu) See §41
5 is-shū-kan a week
 -kan during, between
6 ichi-do mo...nai never, not once
7 hare·ru clear up
8 -nakatta See §41
9 tsuyu-ake end of the rainy season
 tsuyu rainy season ake ←ake·ru (end and begin anew)
 cf. yo-ake (dawn)
10 oso·i late; slow
11 asu=ashita tomorrow
12 natsu-yasumi summer vacation
13 nobor·u climb
14 natsu-yama summer mountains
15 hontō (N) true, real
 hontō-ni truly, really, indeed
16 subarashi·i wonderful
17 kōzan-shokubutsu alpine plants
 kōzan high mountain
 shokubutsu plants, vegetation
18 kumo cloud
19 Sapporo (the biggest city in Hokkaido)
20 Mashū-ko Lake Mashu
 -ko lake
21 Shiretoko-hantō Shiretoko Peninsula
 hantō peninsula
22 -nai See §41

八月九日(はちがつここのか) (晴(は)れ[26])

❸ ゆうべ 北海道(ほっかいどう)から 帰(かえ)った。 北海道(ほっかいどう)は 実(じつ)に[27] よかった。 札幌(さっぽろ)は 北海道(ほっかいどう)の 文化(ぶんか)[28]と 政治(せいじ)[29]と 産業(さんぎょう)[30]の 中心(ちゅうしん)[31]である[32]。 しかし 古(ふる)い 町(まち)ではない[33]。 新(あたら)しい ユニーク[34]な 町(まち)である。

わたしは 北海道(ほっかいどう)の 自然(しぜん)[35]に 感動(かんどう)[36]した。 青(あお)い 湖(みずうみ)[37]、 広(ひろ)い[38] 野原(のはら)[39]、 地平線(ちへいせん)[40]の 夕日(ゆうひ)[41]……

❹ 毎日毎日(まいにちまいにち)が 充実(じゅうじつ)[42]していた。 わたしは 少(すこ)しも つかれ[43]を 感(かん)[44]じなかった。 今度(こんど)[45]の 旅行(りょこう)の 収穫(しゅうかく)[46]は けっして[47] 小(ちい)さな[48] もの[49]ではない。

▲Akan National Park

---

23 *gaido-bukku* 'guidebook'
24 hirak・u (Vi/Vt) open
25 kangae・ru think, consider
26 hare fine weather ←hare・ru
27 jitsu-ni really, truly, indeed
28 bunka culture
29 seiji politics
30 sangyō industry
31 chūshin center
32 de aru=da, desu
33 dewa nai See §41
34 *yuniku* (Na) 'unique'
35 shizen nature
36 kandō (Nv) being impressed/moved
37 mizuumi lake
38 hiro・i spacious, vast; broad
39 nohara field, plain (smaller than heiya)
40 chihei-sen horizon
 sen line
41 yū-hi setting sun cf. asa-hi
 yū- evening hi sun
42 jūjitsu (Nv) fullness, completeness; be full/fulfilled
43 tsukare tiredness, fatigue
 ←tsukare・ru (get tired)
44 kanji・ru feel
45 kondo (N/Adv) this time; next time
46 shūkaku (Nv) harvest, yield
47 kesshite...nai never
48 chiisa-na=chiisa・i small See §7
49 mono thing

Dai 8-ka
Natsu-yasumi no Nikki

Shichi-gatsu tō-ka (Ame)

1 Kinō mo ame datta. Kyō mo mata ame da. Is-shū-kan ichi-do mo hare-nakatta. Kotoshi wa tsuyu-ake ga osoi.

Asu kara natsu-yasumi ga hajimaru. Kyo-nen no natsu wa yama ni nobotta. Natsu-yama wa hontō-ni subarashikatta. Yuki mo kōzan-shoku-butsu mo utsukushikatta. Sora mo kumo mo kirei datta.

2 Kotoshi no natsu-yasumi niwa Hokkaidō e iku. Hokkaidō dewa, Sapporo no machi ya Mashū-ko ya Shiretoko-hantō nado o mawaru. Watashi wa Hokkaidō no koto wa amari shiranai. Tokidoki *gaido-bukku* o hiraite, ryokō no koto o kangaete-iru.

Hachi-gatsu kokono-ka (Hare)

3 Yūbe Hokkaidō kara kaetta. Hokkaidō wa jitsu-ni yokatta. Sapporo wa Hokkaidō no bunka to seiji to sangyō no chūshin de aru. Shikashi furui machi dewa nai. Atarashii *yunīku*-na machi de aru.

Watashi wa Hokkaidō no shizen ni kandō-shita. Aoi mizuumi, hiroi nohara, chihei-sen no yūhi. . . .

4 Mai-nichi-mai-nichi ga jūjitsu-shite-ita. Watashi wa sukoshi mo tsukare o kanjinakatta. Kondo no ryokō no shūkaku wa kesshite chiisa-na mono dewa nai.

▶ Akan National Park

Lesson 8

Summer Vacation Diary

July 10 (Rainy)

1 It was rainy yesterday too. And it is rainy again today. It hasn't been clear once all week. The rainy season is late ending this year.

The summer vacation starts tomorrow. Last summer I went mountain climbing. The summer mountains were just fabulous. The snow and the alpine plants were beautiful. The sky and the clouds were beautiful too.

2 This summer vacation I'm going to go to Hokkaido. In Hokkaido, I'm going to go to Sapporo, Lake Mashu, the Shiretoko Peninsula, and lots of other places. I don't know much about Hokkaido. Sometimes I open my guidebooks and think about my trip.

August 9 (Clear)

3 I got home from Hokkaido last night. Hokkaido was really great. Sapporo is the center of Hokkaido culture, politics, and industry. But it is not an old city. It is a new and unique city.

I was impressed by Hokkaido's nature. The blue lakes, vast plains, and the sun setting on the horizon....

4 Every day was full. I didn't feel tired in the least. I got a lot out of this trip.

ANSWERS ⟨pp. 100, 101⟩

I. (A) 1. ...kōen o sanpo-suru. 2. ...o-sake o nomu. 3. ...kuni e kaeru. 4. ...kōen ga aru. 5. ...Nippon-go o hanasu. 6. ...*pan* o kau. 7. ...sakana o takusan taberu. (B) 1. ...eiga o minai. 2. ...doko e mo ikanai. 3. ...chikaku o tōranai. 4. ...dare mo inai. 5. ...denwa ga nai. (C) 1. ...hon o katta. 2. ...eki made aruita. 3. ...jiko o shitta. 4. ...yoku oyoida. 5. ...4-gatsu ni shinda. (D) 1. ...*pāti* ni ikanakatta. 2. ...*depāto* e itta ga, nani mo kawanakatta. 3. ...*basu* o matta ga, ...sonna-ni matanakatta. 4. ...kaze ga fuita. Sorede hikōki wa tobanakatta.

II. 1. (omoi; omoku nai; omokatta; omoku nakatta) 2. (karui; karuku nai; karukatta; karuku nakatta) 3. (yasui; yasuku nai; yasukatta; yasuku nakatta) 4. (takai; takaku nai; takakatta; takaku nakatta) 5. (benri da; benri dewa nai; benri datta; benri dewa nakatta) 6. (kirei da; kirei dewa nai; kirei datta; kirei dewa nakatta) 7. (*Oranda*-sei da; *Oranda*-sei dewa nai; *Oranda*-sei datta; *Oranda*-sei dewa nakatta)

III. 1. (nai) 2. (shizuka dewa nai) 3. (datta); (da) 4. (datta); (kirei dewa nai) 5. (da); (da/hon da); (dewa nai/hon dewa nai)

IV. Watashi wa kyo-nen Nippon e kita. Ima Kyōto ni sunde-iru ga, amari Kyōto no koto o shiranai. Tokidoki yūmei-na o-tera o tazuneru. Sen-shū Koke-dera e itta. Yūmei-na niwa o mita. O-chaseki ga atta ga, watashi wa hairanakatta. Taitei watashi wa o-tera de e-hagaki o kau ga, sono hi wa ii e-hagaki ga nakatta. Sorede, nani mo kawanakatta.

●文法

§ 41 Two Levels of Speech: Polite Style vs. Plain Style

All the Predicates have at least two forms ('styles') corresponding to the speaker's degree of politeness toward the listener. The forms we have been using so far in this book are examples of the Polite style, which is used most commonly in daily conversation between adults who are not close friends. The Plain style, on the other hand, is used between members of a family, classmates, or between people in similar relationships. It is also used in writing, such as books, theses, newspapers, diaries, etc. In writing letters, however, the Polite style is more common, since it is a more or less faithful copy of the spoken language.

			Polite style	Plain style
V	present	aff.	tabemasu 'eat'	taberu
		neg.	tabemasen	tabenai
	past	aff.	tabemashita	tabeta
		neg.	tabemasen deshita	tabenakatta
A	present	aff.	osoi desu 'be late'	osoi
		neg.	osoku nai desu osoku arimasen	osoku nai
	past	aff.	osokatta desu	osokatta
		neg.	osoku nakatta desu osoku arimasen deshita	osoku nakatta
N/Na + Copula	present	aff.	ame desu 'be rainy'	ame da/de aru
		neg.	ame dewa arimasen	ame de(wa) nai
	past	aff.	ame deshita	ame datta/de atta
		neg.	ame dewa arimasen deshita (ame dewa nakatta desu)	ame de(wa) nakatta

NB: dewa is sometimes contracted as ja or jā.

§ 42 Conjugation of Verbs: 3 Kinds of V

The Verb forms which we have been using so far, such as ikimasu, nomimasu, norimasu, tabemasu, mimasu, shimasu, etc., are composed of two parts: '-masu,' an Auxiliary expressing the Polite style, and the part that precedes it. The part preceding '-masu' is called the 'Conjunctive form,' and is used in various ways (besides being used as the 'base' for the 'V-masu form') as we will see later. The forms of V or A you find in the dictionary (called the 'Dictionary form') are the present affirmative forms in the Plain style of V or A. The Dictionary form of V or A is conjugated for Past, Negative, Past Negative, Imperative, Volitional, etc., just as the 'V-masu form' is conjugated for Negative, Past, etc., as we have seen in the preceding lessons.

8

Japanese Verbs are divided, in terms of conjugation pattern, into '1st Group' Verbs, '2nd Group' Verbs, and two 'Irregular' Verbs (suru 'do' and kuru 'come'). 1st Group V are those whose 'STEMS' (capitalized in the table below) end in consonants, and 2nd Group V are those whose STEMS end in vowels (e or i).

	Conj.+masu	Dict. form	Negative	'te'	'ta' (past)
1st Group	KAKimasu	KAKu	KAKanai	KAIte	KAIta
	OYOGimasu	OYOGu	OYOGanai	OYOIde	OYOIda
	HANAShimasu	HANASu	HANASanai	HANASHIte	HANASHIta
	YOMimasu	YOMu	YOManai	YONde	YONda
	SHINimasu	SHINu	SHINanai	SHINde	SHINda
	TOBimasu	TOBu	TOBanai	TONde	TONda
	MAChimasu	MATsu	MATanai	MATte	MATta
	NORimasu	NORu	NORanai	NOTte	NOTta
	KAimasu	KA(W)u	KAWanai	KATte	KATta
2nd Group	TABEmasu	TABEru	TABEnai	TABEte	TABEta
	MImasu	MIru	MInai	MIte	MIta
Irreg.	Shimasu	Suru	Shinai	Shite	Shita
	Kimasu	Kuru	Konai	Kite	Kita

NB: Certain sound changes occur at the final part of the STEM of 1st Group V in forming the '-te' or '-ta' form.

●練習

ANSWERS→p. 97

I. Rewrite the following sentences in the Plain style.

(A) 1. Watashi wa mai-nichi kōen o sanpo-shimasu.

2. Watashi wa mai-ban o-sake o nomimasu.

3. Watashi wa rai-nen[1] kuni e kaerimasu.

4. Kono machi niwa kirei-na kōen ga arimasu.

5. Kare wa jōzu-ni Nippon-go o hanashimasu.

6. Watashi wa itsumo kono mise de *pan* o kaimasu.

7. Nippon-jin wa sakana[2] o takusan tabemasu.

(B) 1. Watashi wa amari eiga o mimasen.

2. Kotoshi no natsu wa doko e mo ikimasen.

3. Kono *basu* wa watashi no ie no chikaku o tōrimasen.

4. Ano heya niwa dare mo imasen.

5. Kono heya niwa denwa ga arimasen.

(C) 1. Kinō *depāto* de hon o kaimashita.

2. Kesa eki made arukimashita.

3. *Terebi* de sono jiko[3] o shirimashita.

4. Kyo-nen no natsu wa yoku oyogimashita.

5. Watashi no haha wa kotoshi no 4-gatsu ni shinimashita.[4]

(D) 1. Watashi wa kinō no *pāti* ni ikimasen deshita.

2. Kinō *depāto* e ikimashita ga, nani mo kaimasen deshita.

3. Kinō wa teiryū-jo[5] de 10-pun hodo *basu* o machimashita ga, kyō wa sonna-ni machimasen deshita.

4. Yūbe tsuyoi kaze[6] ga fukimashita.[7] Sorede hikōki wa tobimasen[8] deshita.

語句

1 rai-nen next year
2 sakana fish 3 jiko accident
4 shin·u die
5 teiryū-jo streetcar/bus stop
-jo=-sho place
6 kaze wind 7 fuku (Vi) blow
8 tob·u fly; jump
9 *Oranda*-sei made in Holland

II. Replace the underlined words by the words in parentheses, and make sentences as shown in the examples.

Ex. Kanojo no jitensha wa atarashii desu.

a. Kanojo no jitensha wa atarashii.

b. Kanojo no jitensha wa atarashiku nai.

c. Kanojo no jitensha wa atarashikatta.

d. Kanojo no jitensha wa atarashiku nakatta.

1. (omoi) 2. (karui) 3. (yasui) 4. (takai)
5. (benri-na) 6. (kirei-na) 7. (*Oranda*-sei[9])

III. Fill in the blanks using Plain style verbs.

1. Kono machi niwa tosho-kan wa aru ga, bijutsu-kan wa ( ).
2. Kyōto wa shizuka-na machi da. Shikashi Tōkyō wa amari ( ).
3. Kinō made kare wa byōki ( ). Shikashi kyō wa mō genki ( ).
4. Mukashi kono kawa no mizu wa kirei ( ) ga, ima wa mō amari ( ).
5. Kore wa watashi no hon ( ). Are mo watashi no ( ). Shikashi sono ōkii hon wa watashi no ( ).

IV. Rewrite the following in the Plain style.

Watashi wa kyo-nen Nippon e kimashita. Ima Kyōto ni sunde-imasu ga, amari Kyōto no koto o shirimasen. Tokidoki yūmei-na o-tera o tazune-masu.[10] Sen-shū Koke-dera[11] e ikimashita. Yūmei-na niwa o mimashita. O-cha-seki[12] ga arimashita ga, watashi wa hairimasen deshita. Taitei watashi wa o-tera de e-hagaki o kaimasu ga, sono hi wa ii e-hagaki ga arimasen deshita. Sorede, nani mo kaimasen deshita.

Oranda 'Holland'
-sei made in... e.g. Nippon-sei
10 tazune·ru visit; ask
11 Koke-dera (a Kyoto temple famous for its moss garden)
koke moss -dera=tera temple
12 (o-)cha-seki tea ceremony; place where tea ceremony is performed

●会話

GENKI KAI?

Tarō: Yā, genki kai[1]?

Hanako[2]: Ē, genki yo.

Anata mo kuroku natta[3] wa ne.[4]

Oyogi[5] ni itta no[6]?

T: Iya,[7] yama e itta yo.

H: Doko no yama e itta no?

Hodaka[8]? Soretomo,[9] Norikura[10]?

T: Iya, Minami-*Arupusu*[11] ni nobotta.

Kita-dake[12] ga yūdai[13] de

taihen yokatta.

H: Nan-nichi hodo itta no?

T: Is-shū-kan da.

Yama-goya[14] ni tomattari[15] *tento*[16] o

hattari[17] shite tanoshikatta yo.

Kimi[18] wa doko e itta?

T: Hi, you OK?
H: Yes, I'm OK.
You look so tan.
Did you go swimming?
T: No, I went to the mountains.
H: What mountain did you go to?
Hodaka, or Norikura?
T: No, I went climbing in the Southern Alps.
Kita-dake was majestic and very exciting.
H: How many days were you there?
T: One week.
We had a fantastic time staying in mountain huts and sometimes in a tent. Where did you go?

語句

1 kai See §65
2 Hanako (a given name (f))
3 kuroku naru get sunburnt
  nar·u become
4 wa ne See §65
5 oyogi swimming
  ←oyog·u (swim)
6 no (Ps. indicating a question (Familiar))
7 Iya No, not that
8 Hodaka (name of a mountain)
9 soretomo or else
10 Norikura (name of a mountain)
11 Minami-*Arupusu* Southern Alps (in Japan)
  minami south
  Arupusu 'Alps'
12 Kita-dake (name of a mountain)
  kita north
  -dake high mountain

H: I went to Shonan Beach and had a nice time swimming, playing games, and singing songs around the campfire at night; it was great.
T: How many people were there in your group?
H: There were four of us. This same group is going to go again to a swimming pool.
T: Always having fun, aren't you?
What about your studies?
H: Of course. They're OK.
T: Well, see you again, then.

H: Shōnan-kaigan[19] de asonda wa.
Oyoidari *gēmu*[20] o shitari,
yoru wa *kyanpu-faiyā*[21] o kakonde[22]
uta o utattari shite
tanoshikatta wa.
T: Nan-nin hodo no *gurūpu*[23] datta?
H: Yo-nin de itta no.[24]
Onaji[25] *gurūpu* de mata *pūru*[26] ni iku no.
T: Asonde bakari[27] da ne.
Benkyō wa daijōbu[28] kai?
H: Mochiron[29] yo.
T: Jā, mata ne.

8

13 yūdai (Na) majestic
14 yama-goya mountain hut
-goya=koya hut, small house
15 tomar·u (Vi) stay (overnight); stop
16 *tento* 'tent'
17 har·u stretch, pitch (a tent)
18 kimi you (sing. Friendly)
19 Shōnan-kaigan Shonan Beach
kaigan beach
20 *gēmu* 'game'
21 *kyanpu-faiyā* 'campfire'
22 kakom·u surround
23 *gurūpu* 'group'
24 no ..., you know (fem.)
25 onaji same
26 *pūru* 'pool' swimming pool
27 ...bakari only, just
28 daijōbu all right
29 mochiron of course

日本の　着物

三世紀[1]ごろの　中国の　歴史[2]の　本は、　日本の　着物[3]について　書いて[4]いる。　日本人は　当時[5]　大きい　布[6]に　あな[7]を　あけて[8]　頭[9]から　かぶって[10]いた。　三世紀から　七世紀ごろの　古墳[11]の　はにわ[12]の　人形は　いろいろな　着物を　着[13]ている。　これが　当時の　日本の　服装[14]であった。　この　ころ[15]は、　ワンピース[16]から　ツーピース[17]に　かわって[18]いて、　男女[19]とも　はかま[20]を　はいた[21]。

八世紀の　初めの　法律[22]では　役人[23]の　服装が　決まって[24]いた。　だいたい　中国や　朝鮮[25]の　服装と　にて[26]いた。

平安時代[27]、　宮廷[28]の　婦人[29]は　きれいな　着物を　たくさん　重ねて[30]　着ていた。　これが　十二ひとえ[31]である。

▲*Junihitoe*（井筒雅風考証・所蔵）

鎌倉時代[32]ごろから　下着の　小そで[33]を　ふだん着[34]として[35]　着た。　次の　室町時代[36]では　婦人は　正式[37]な　服装としても　小そでを　着た。　それが　今の　着物に　発達[38]した。

着物は　日本人の　スタイル[39]にも　日本の　気候[40]にも　適して[41]いる。　しかし　そでや　すそ[42]が　長いから　活動[43]には　適していない。　若い　人は　いつも　洋服[44]を　着ていて、　お正月や　結婚式[45]などの　特別[46]な　機会[47]に　しか[48]　着物を　着ない。

▲A modern *kimono*

Kimono

A Chinese history book written in the 3rd century says that the Japanese cut holes in large pieces of cloth and wore them at that time. The clay images found in the old tombs made from the 3rd to the 7th centuries show the costume of the people in those days. Around that time they began to wear two-piece clothes, an upper garment and a skirt.

In the early 8th century, there was a law regulating the government officials' costumes, which resembled those in China and Korea.

In the Heian Period the court ladies wore *Junihitoe*, several beautiful *kimonos* one over another. People started wearing *kosode*, which they used to wear as undergarments, as home wear in the Kamakura Period, and ladies wore *kosode* even as formal clothing in the following, the Muromachi, period. This has developed into the *kimono* which we wear today.

Kimono is suitable both for the Japanese build and climate. But it limits a person's movement, since it has long sleeves and is ankle-length. Young people wear Western clothes in every day life and *kimonos* only on special occasions such as New Year's Day and weddings.

8

語句

1 seiki century 2 rekishi history
3 kimono (traditional Japanese clothing)
4 ...ni tsuite about, concerning...
5 tōji at that time, those days
6 nuno cloth 7 ana hole
8 ake•ru (Vt) open
9 atama (upper part of) head
10 kabur•u put on (hat, pullover sweater, etc.) put...over one's head
11 kofun old mound
12 haniwa clay image
13 ki•ru wear (shirts, dress)
14 fukusō style of dress, costume
15 ...no koro the time/age/days of...
16 *wanpīsu* 'one-piece'
17 *tsūpīsu* 'two-piece'
18 kawar•u (Vi) change
19 ...tomo both/all...together
20 hakama (a formal *kimono* skirt)
21 hak•u put on, wear (trousers, skirt, socks, shoes)
22 hōritsu law
23 yakunin government worker, official
24 kimar•u (Vi) get fixed/decided cf. kime•ru (Vt)
25 Chōsen Korea
26 nite-iru resemble ←ni•ru
27 Heian-jidai Heian Period (794-1192)
jidai period, age
28 kyūtei imperial court
29 fujin lady
30 kasane•ru fold, put one on top of another
31 jū-ni-hitoe (a special kind of *kimono*)
32 Kamakura-jidai Kamakura Period (1192-1333) Kamakura (a place name)
33 kosode (a kind of *kimono*)
sode sleeve
34 fudan-gi everyday clothes
fudan everyday, usual
35 ...to shite as...
36 Muromachi-jidai Muromachi Period (1338-1573)
37 seishiki (N/Na) formal
38 hattatsu (Nv) develop
39 *sutairu* 'style' 40 kikō climate
41 teki-suru be suitable for, suit
42 suso hem of clothes/skirt/trousers
43 katsudō (Nv) activity
44 yō-fuku Western clothes
yō- Western cf. yō-shiki (Western style) yō-sho (imported book)
45 kekkon-shiki wedding ceremony
shiki ceremony
46 tokubetsu (N/Na/Adv) special
47 kikai occasion, opportunity
48 shika...nai only

第 9 課

町の中

TAPE
No. 3
Side 1

❶車(くるま)が　たくさん　通(とお)りますね。

——はい、この　へん[1]は　いつも　自動車(じどうしゃ)や　バイク[2]で　いっぱいですから、気(き)[3]を　つけて[4]　歩(ある)いてください[5]。この前(まえ)の　日曜日(にちようび)にも　すぐ[6]　そこで　事故(じこ)が　ありました。

信号(しんごう)[7]は　どこに　ありますか。

——百(ひゃく)メートル　先(さき)[8]の　交差点(こうさてん)[9]まで　ありません。あの　交差点(こうさてん)で　あちら側(がわ)[10]へ　渡(わた)りましょう[11]。この　へんは　むかしは　静(しず)かな　いい　町(まち)でしたが、今(いま)は　すっかり[12]　変(か)わりました。

空気(くうき)も　よく　ないですね。

——子(こ)どもは　いつも　家(いえ)の　中(なか)で　遊(あそ)ばなければなりません[13]から、かわいそう[14]です。

❷——今(いま)　信号(しんごう)は　青(あお)[15]ですが、もう　赤(あか)[16]に　変(か)わります。

今(いま)から　渡(わた)らない　ほうが　いい[17]ですね。待(ま)ちましょうか。

——ええ、ちょっと　待(ま)った　ほうが　いいです。次(つぎ)の　青(あお)

語句

1 hen　the area of; around
2 *baiku*　'bike,' motorcycle
3 ki　mind; care
4 ki o tsuke·ru　be careful
5 -te-kudasai　See § 43
6 sugu　(Adv) soon; near
　sugu soko　right over there
7 shingō　signal; traffic light
8 saki　(N) ahead, away; tip; future
9 kōsa-ten　intersection
　kōsa　cross　ten　point
10 achira-gawa　that side
　achira　there, yonder
11 -mashō　let us　See § 49
12 sukkari　completely, quite
13 -nakereba narana·i　have to　See § 45
14 kawaisō　(Na) pitiful
15 ao　(N) blue; green ←ao·i
16 aka　(N) red ←aka·i
17 hō ga ii　had better　See § 48
18 ao-shingō　green light
19 ...ni nar·u　become...
20 Sā　Now, Well
21 tōri　street

信号(しんごう)[18]まで　待(ま)ちましょう。

ああ、　青(あお)に　[19]なりました。　さあ、[20]　渡(わた)りましょう。

この　通(とお)り[21]は　だいぶん[22]　静(しず)かですね。　お宅(たく)は　もう　すぐですね。

——はい、　あと[23]　二百(にひゃく)メートルほどです。　ああ、　向(む)こうから　一郎(いちろう)[24]が　来(き)ました。

❸——おとうさん、　お帰(かえ)り[25]。　公園(こうえん)へ　遊(あそ)びに　行(い)っても　いい[26]。

——お客(きゃく)[27]さんに　あいさつ[28]を　しなさい[29]。

——おじさん[30]、　今日(こんにち)は。

やあ、　今日(こんにち)は。

——もう　おそいから　いっしょに　帰(かえ)ろう。

これこれ[31]、　そんなに　道(みち)の　まん中(なか)に　出(で)ては　いけません[32]。　さあ、　もっと　右(みぎ)の　ほう[33]を　歩(ある)きなさい。

❹ああ、　ちょっと　待(ま)ってください。　いい　店(みせ)が　ありました。　ケーキ[34]を　買(か)いましょう。……一郎(いちろう)くん[35]、　はい[36]。

——おじさん、　ありがとう。

——どうも　ありがとうございます。　しかし、　この　次(つぎ)[37]からは　そんなに　気(き)を　つかわ[38]ないでください。

---

22 daibun =daibu　fairly, largely
23 ato　the rest; after
24 Ichirō　(a given name (m))
25 O-kaeri　(Cph) Welcome home.
26 -temo ii　may, can, be allowed to See § 47
27 kyaku　guest, visitor; customer
28 aisatsu　(Nv) greeting
29 -nasai　See § 44
30 oji-san　Sir!, Mister!; uncle
31 Kore-kore!　Here, here.
32 -tewa ikenai　should not, ought not See § 46
33 hō　side; direction
34 *kēki*　'cake'
35 -kun　Mr. (Suf. used by men, usually to men of equal or lower status/age)
36 Hai　Here it is; Yes
37 kono tsugi　next time
38 tsuka·u　use
ki o tsuka·u　be attentive/considerate

Dai 9-ka
Machi no Naka

1 Kuruma ga takusan tōrimasu ne.

——Hai, kono hen wa itsumo jidōsha ya *baiku* de ippai desu kara, ki o tsukete aruite-kudasai. Kono mae no Nichi-yōbi nimo sugu soko de jiko ga arimashita.

Shingō wa doko ni arimasu ka?

——Hyaku-*mētoru* saki no kōsa-ten made arimasen. Ano kōsa-ten de achira-gawa e watarimashō. Kono hen wa mukashi wa shizuka-na ii machi deshita ga, ima wa sukkari kawarimashita.

Kūki mo yoku nai desu ne.

——Kodomo wa itsumo ie no naka de asobanakereba narimasen kara, kawaisō desu.

2 ——Ima shingō wa ao desu ga, mō aka ni kawarimasu.

Ima kara wataranai hō ga ii desu ne. Machimashō ka?

——Ē, chotto matta hō ga ii desu. Tsugi no ao-shingō made machimashō.

Ā, ao ni narimashita. Sā, watarimashō.

Kono tōri wa daibun shizuka desu ne. O-taku wa mō sugu desu ne.

——Hai, ato ni-hyaku-*mētoru* hodo desu. Ā, mukō kara Ichirō ga kimashita.

3 ———O-tō-san, o-kaeri. Kōen e asobi ni ittemo ii?

——O-kyaku-san ni aisatsu o shi-nasai.

———Oji-san, konnichi wa!

Yā, konnichi wa!

——Mō osoi kara issho-ni kaerō. Kore-kore, sonna-ni michi no man-naka ni detewa ikemasen. Sā, motto migi no hō o aruki-nasai.

4 Ā, chotto matte-kudasai. Ii mise ga arimashita. *Kēki* o kaimashō...... Ichirō-kun, hai.

———Oji-san, arigatō.

——Dōmo arigatō gozaimasu. Shikashi, kono tsugi kara wa sonna-ni ki o tsukawanaide-kudasai.

Lesson 9

In the Town

1 There sure are a lot of cars, aren't there?

——Yes. Watch where you're walking, since this area is always filled with cars and motorcycles. Last Sunday there was an accident right over there.

Where's the traffic light?

——There isn't one until that intersection 100 meters on up.

Let's cross over that way at that intersection. This area used to be a nice quiet neighborhood, but it sure has changed.

The air isn't very good either.

——I feel sorry for the children, because they always have to play inside.

2 ——The light is green now, but it's changing to red.

We'd better not cross the street now. Let's wait, shall we?

——Yes, it's better to wait a bit. Let's wait for the next green light.

It's green. Well, let's go. This street is pretty quiet. It's only a little way more to your house, right?

——Right. It's about 200 meters more. Here comes Ichiro.

3 ———Welcome home, Father. Can I go to the park to play?

——Say hello to our guest.

———Hello, sir.

Hello.

——It's late, so let's go home together. Hey, don't walk out into the middle of the street like that. Walk more on the right-hand side.

4 Wait up a minute, please. There was a very nice shop. Let's buy some cake.

......Here you are, Ichiro.

———Thank you.

——Thank you very much. But please don't worry about things like that next time.

ANSWERS 〈pp. 112, 113〉

II. 1. ...made hataraite Nichi-yōbi ni yasumimasu. 2. ...nete asa hayaku... 3. ...yoru nenaide benkyō-shimasu. 4. ...yomanaide *terebi* bakari... 5. ...benkyō-shinaide itsumo... 6. ...matanaide *takushi* de... 7. ...kawanaide *biru*...

III. 1. (ikanakutemo ii desu). 2. (nottewa ikemasen). 3. (katta hō ga ii desu). 4. (mamoranakereba narimasen). 5. "(konakereba narimasen ka)?" "(kite-kudasai)." 6. "(kaettemo ii desu ka)?" "(kaettewa ikemasen). (ite-kudasai)." 7. (utawanaide-kudasai). 8. (suttewa ikemasen). 9. (ikanai hō ga ii desu). 10. (*doa* o shime-nasai).

IV. 1. Ashita watashi-tachi wa *haikingu* ni ikimasu. Watashi-tachi wa asa kara ban made arukanakereba narimasen. Asa hayaku shuppatsu-shimasu kara, kon'ya wa hayaku nemashō. 2. Ashita wa kaisha e konakutemo ii desu ga, asatte wa kanarazu kite-kudasai. 3. Kodomo wa o-sake o nondari, *tabako* o suttari shitewa ikemasen.

●文法

§ 43 Requesting a Thing or Action

N o	kudasai.	'Please give me....'
... V-te		'Please do...(for me).'
Neg: V-(a)naide		'Please do not....'

e.g. Mizu o kudasai. 'Give me water, please.'

Matte-kudasai. 'Please wait.' (matte ←matsu 'wait')

Matanaide-kudasai. 'Please do not wait.'

NB: matanaide is the '-te form' of matanai, which is the negative form of matsu 'wait.' For the formation of the Plain negative forms of the 3 kinds of V, see the table in § 42.

§ 44 Order or Command

V(Conj. form)-**nasai.**

e.g. Machi-nasai. 'Wait!'

Koko ni namae o kaki-nasai. 'Write your name here.'

NB: This is a more straightforward way of ordering someone to do something, but still the style is polite. Its plain variation, which is a more blunt and harsh expression, is mate, kake, tabero, miro, etc. (formed by adding an 'e' to 1st Group V stems and 'ro' to 2nd Group V stems). The Irregular Plain imperatives are shiro (←suru) and koi (←kuru).

§ 45 Duty or Obligation

V-(a)**nakereba narimasen.** '...have to do....' 'must do....'

e.g. Watashi wa Nara e ikanakereba narimasen. 'I have to go to Nara.'

Anata wa isoganakereba narimasen. 'You have to hurry.'

NB: Literally, this means, 'if...do not do..., it won't work out.'

§ 46 Prohibition

V-tewa ikemasen. '...must not do....'

e.g. Koko de *tabako* o suttewa ikemasen. 'You may not smoke here.'

Koko o watattewa ikemasen. 'You must not cross the street here.'

§ 47 Permission

V-temo ii desu. 'It will be all right to do....'
'You may do....'

e.g. Koko de *tabako* o suttemo ii desu ka? 'May I smoke here?'

—Hai, (suttemo) ii desu. 'Yes, you may (smoke).'

—Iie, (suttewa) ikemasen. 'No, you may not (smoke).'

§ 48 Advice

V-ta hō ga ii desu. 'It would be better if you did....'
'You'd better do....'

Negation: **V-(a)nai hō ga ii desu.** 'It would be better not to do....'

NB: 'hō' is used in a sentence almost like any other Noun, although it never occurs without being modified by other words or phrases. Such Nouns are called Pseudo Nouns.

§ 49 Expressions of Will, Offering, or Inviting

V-mashō. 'Let us do....'; 'I will do....'
V-mashō ka? 'Shall we do...?'; 'Shall I do...?'

e.g. *Bīru* o nomimashō ka? 'Shall we have some beer?'

—Hai, nomimashō. —'Yes, let's (have some).'

Anata o machimashō ka? 'Shall I wait for you?'

—Hai, matte-kudasai. —'Yes, please (wait).'

●練習

ANSWERS→p. 109

I. Transform the sentences as shown in the examples.

Ex. *Pen*[1] de kakimasu.

(A) Q: *Pen* de kakanakereba narimasen ka?

A: *Pen* de kakanakutemo ii desu ga, *pen* de kaita hō ga ii desu.

(B) Q: *Pen* de kaitemo ii desu ka?

A: Iie, *pen* de kaitewa ikemasen. *Pen* de kakanaide-kudasai.

(C) Q: *Pen* de kakimashō ka?

A: Hai, *pen* de kaite-kudasai.

(D) *Pen* de kaki-nasai.

1. Kyō Nagoya[2] e ikimasu.
2. Ashita koko e kimasu.
3. Kono hon o yomimasu.
4. Mado o shimemasu.[3]
5. Kono fuku o sentaku[4]-shimasu.
6. Kare o machimasu.
7. Ima o-kane o haraimasu.[5]
8. Nippon-go de hanashimasu.

II. Combine the sentences.

1. Watashi-tachi wa Getsu-yōbi kara Do-yōbi made hatarakimasu.[6] Soshite Nichi-yōbi ni yasumimasu.
2. Yoru hayaku ne-nasai. Soshite asa hayaku oki-nasai.
3. Kare wa tokidoki yoru nemasen. Soshite benkyō-shimasu.
4. Kare wa mettani shinbun o yomimasen. *Terebi* bakari mite-imasu.
5. Sono kodomo wa benkyō-shimasen deshita. Itsumo asonde-imashita.
6. Watashi-tachi wa *basu* o machimasen deshita. *Takushī* de ikimashita.
7. Watashi wa sono o-kane de hon o kaimasen deshita. (Sono o-kane de) *bīru* o nomimashita.

語句

1 *pen* 'pen'
2 Nagoya (a name of a city between Tokyo and Osaka)
3 shime•ru (Vt) close, shut
4 sentaku (Nv) washing (clothes)
5 hara•u pay
6 hatarak•u work
7 tomar•u stop
8 jisho＝jibiki dictionary
9 kisoku regulations, rules

III. Complete the sentences.

1. Kyō wa Nichi-yōbi desu kara, kaisha e (need not go).
2. Kono densha wa anata no eki niwa tomarimasen[7] kara, (should not get on it).
3. Kono jisho[8] wa taihen ii jisho desu kara, (better buy it).
4. Watashi-tachi wa iroiro-na kisoku[9] o (should observe[10]).
5. "Ashita nan-ji ni koko e (have to come)?"

   "Kanarazu[11] 9-ji ni koko e (please come)."
6. "Kyō wa tsukaremashita. Mō (may I go home)?" "Iie, (please don't go home). Mō sukoshi koko ni (please stay)."
7. Kodomo ga nete-imasu. Sonna-ni ōkii koe[12] de (please do not sing).
8. Eiga-kan dewa *tabako* o (should not smoke).
9. Netsu[13] ga arimasu kara, kyō wa kaisha e (better not go).
10. Samui[14] kara (shut the door).

IV. Put the following into Japanese.

1. Tomorrow we are going on a hike. We'll have to walk from morning till evening. We'll start[15] early in the morning, so let's go to bed early tonight.[16]
2. You don't have to come to work tomorrow, but be sure to come the day after tomorrow.[17]
3. Children must neither drink nor smoke.

---

10 mamor·u keep (a promise); observe (the rules); obey; protect
11 kanarazu (Adv) without fail
12 koe voice
13 netsu fever
netsu ga aru feverish
14 samu·i cold (for weather only)
15 shuppatsu (Nv) departure, start
16 kon'ya tonight
17 asatte the day after tomorrow

●会話

OISHII!

—Shokuji[1] ni ikimashō ka?

Ē, oishii[2] mise ni tsurete-itte[3]-kudasai.

—Nani ga ii desu ka?

Wa-shoku[4]? Soretomo, Chūka-ryōri[5]?

Wa-shoku ga ii desu.

—Jā, sushi-ya[6] e ikimashō.

Koko wa kirei-na sushi-ya deshō?

Tokidoki kimasu. Sonna-ni takaku nakute, oishii desu yo.

Sate,[7] nani ni shimasu ka?

Tekka[8] ni shimasu. Anata wa?

—Watashi wa moriawase[9] desu.

Akadashi[10] wa ikaga[11] desu?

Miso[12] *sūpu*[13] desu ne.

Chūmon[14]-shite-kudasai.

—Chotto...Tekka to moriawase, sore ni[15] akadashi futa-tsu kudasai.

—Shall we go to eat?

Yes, please take me to someplace good.

—What would you like? Japanese food or Chinese food?

I prefer Japanese food.

—OK, let's go to a *sushi* shop.

This is a good *sushi* shop, isn't it?

I come here sometimes. It isn't so expensive and the food is delicious.

Well, what'll you have?

I'll take *tekka.* How about you?

—I'll have *moriawase.*

Don't you want *akadashi*?

That's 'miso' soup, isn't it?

Please order.

—Say! Can we have one *tekka* and one *moriawase*, and two *akadashi*?

語句

1 shokuji (Nv) meal, eating
2 oishi・i delicious
3 tsurete-iku take (a person) to, accompany
4 Wa-shoku Japanese food
5 Chūka-ryōri Chinese food
   ryōri (Nv) cooking
6 sushi-ya sushi shop
7 Sate Well, ...
8 tekka (a kind of *sushi*)
9 moriawase (a kind of *sushi*)
10 akadashi (a kind of soup)

——What will you have to drink, sir?

—One bottle of beer, please.

——Sorry to have kept you waiting.

Well, beautiful, isn't it? Japanese cooking is always arranged so beautifully. It's just..., it's never served warm.

—That's so. Soup and rice are better served hot, but *sushi* and *sashimi* are better cold.

—How is it? Is it good? Yes, very.

——O-nomimono[16] wa?

—*Bīru* ip-pon kudasai.

——Hai, o-machidō-sama.[17]

Hō, kirei desu ne. Nippon no ryōri wa mina taihen kirei desu.

Tada,[18] amari atatakaku[19] nai desu ne.

—Sō desu ne. *Sūpu* ya gohan wa atsui[20] hō ga ii desu ga, sushi ya sashimi[21] wa tsumetai hō ga ii desu.

—Ikaga desu? Oishii desu ka?

Ē, totemo totemo.

9

11 ikaga? How do you like ...?; What about...?
12 miso bean paste
13 *sūpu* 'soup'
14 chūmon (Nv) order (a thing)
15 sore ni besides; moreover
16 nomimono something to drink
17 o-machidō-sama (Cph)
18 tada only
19 atataka·i warm
20 atsu·i hot
21 sashimi (raw fish)

産　業—1

日本は　もともと[1]　農業国[2]だったが、　戦後[3]　工業[4]が　急速[5]に　発達して、今では　世界[6]の　おもな　工業国[7]の　一つである。　労働人口[8]の　うち[9]　約[10]19%[11]が　農業や　水産業[12]などの　第一次産業[13]、　34%ぐらいが　工業などの第二次産業[14]、　約47%が　サービス業[15]などの　第三次産業[16]で　働いている。

農業人口は　この　20年間に　約半分[17]に　減った[18]。　農業でも　機械化[19]がずいぶん[20]　進んで[21]いる。　むかしから　農業生産物[22]の　おもな　ものは　米だ。日本は　まわり[23]が　海だから、むかしから　水産業が　さかんだ[24]。　沿岸[25]では　工場の　廃水[26]で　水が　よごれて[27]いて、　さかなが　減っているから、遠洋漁業[28]が　ふえて[29]いる。

木材[30]の　需要[31]は　年々[32]　ふえている。　しかし　国内[33]の　木材の　供給[34]はあまり　多くないから、　木材を　外国[35]から　輸入[36]しなければならない。

日本には　鉄[37]や　銅[38]などの　鉱物[39]は　ほとんど[40]　ない。　石油[41]も　ほとんどない。　石炭[42]は　むかしは　たくさん　あったが、　今では　たいへん　少ない。これら[43]の　ものは　ほとんど　外国から　輸入している。

Employment by industrial sector

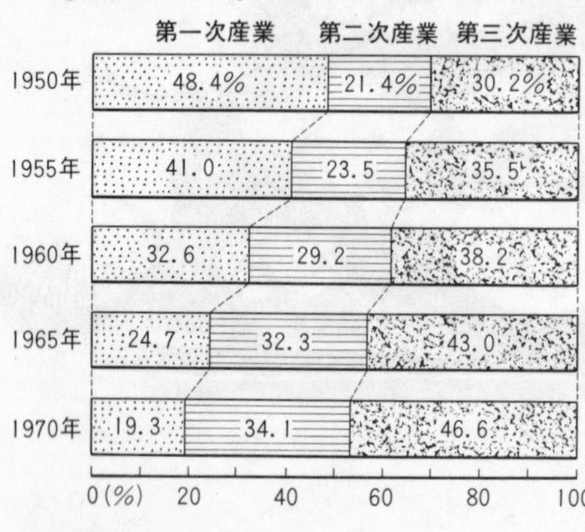

Industry—1

Japan was originally an agricultural country, but the rapid industrial development since World War II has made her one of the world's main industrial countries. About 19% of the working population is engaged in primary industries such as agriculture and fishing, about 34% in secondary industries such as manufacturing, and about 47% in tertiary industries such as service.

The farming population has fallen to about half what it was twenty years ago. Agriculture has also been mechanized considerably. Rice has been the main crop for many years.

Fishing has flourished for a long time in Japan, surrounded as it is by the sea. Lately, deep-sea fishing has been increasing because the coastal seas are polluted by foul drainage from factories, and this has cut catches there.

The demand for timber is increasing every year, but timber must be imported because the domestic supply is so small. Nor is Japan rich in mineral resources such as iron and copper. There is not much petroleum either. Japan used to have a lot of coal but she has only a little now. Thus Japan imports almost all of these raw materials.

9

語句

1 motomoto originally
2 nō-gyō-koku agricultural country
  nō-gyō agriculture
  -gyō vocation, profession
  -koku country, nation
3 sen-go postwar
4 kō-gyō engineering industry
5 kyūsoku (Na) rapid
  kyūsoku-ni rapidly
6 sekai world
7 kō-gyō-koku industrial nation
8 rōdō-jinkō working population
  rōdō (Nv) labor
9 ...no uchi among...
10 yaku about, approximately
11 *pāsento* 'percent'
12 suisan-gyō fisheries industry
13 dai-ichi-ji-sangyō primary industry
  dai- (Pref. expressing ordinal numbers) dai-...-ji the ...-th
14 dai-ni-ji-sangyō secondary industry
15 *sābisu*-gyō service industry
  sābisu (Nv) 'service'
16 dai-san-ji-sangyō tertiary industry
17 hanbun half
18 her•u (Vi) decrease, be reduced
19 kikai-ka (Nv) mechanization, automatization -ka (Nv) -ization
20 zuibun extremely; quite
21 susum•u advance, progress, go on to the next step
22 nō-gyō-seisan-butsu agricultural products
  seisan-butsu product
  seisan (Nv) production
23 mawari surroundings
24 sakan (Na) flourishing
25 engan (N) coast along...
26 haisui (Nv) drainage, sewage
27 yogore•ru become dirty
28 en'yō-gyo-gyō deep-sea fishery
  en'yō deep-sea gyo-gyō fishery
29 fue•ru (Vi) increase
30 mokuzai timber, wood
31 juyō (N) demand
32 nen-nen year after year
33 koku-nai (N) within the country, domestic -nai within
34 kyōkyū (Nv) supply
35 gaikoku foreign country
36 yunyū (Nv) import
  cf. yushutsu (export)
37 tetsu iron
38 dō copper
39 kōbutsu mineral
40 hotondo almost
41 sekiyu petroleum
42 sekitan coal
43 kore-ra these
  -ra (Suf. expressing plural)

第 10 課

夏の 手紙

TAPE
No. 3
Side 1

❶ マリアさん[1]、 毎日 暑い[2] 日が 続き[3]ますが、 お元気ですか。 きょうは 八月七日で[4]、 立秋[5]です。 しかし、「秋の始まり[6]」も 名まえだけで、 まだ 真夏[7]の 暑さ[8]ですね。

❷ 休みが 始まってから、 もう 一か月 たち[9]ました。 この前 わたしが あなたの 家へ 行ってから、 半月[10]に なり[11]ますね。 この 半月の あいだ[12]、 わたしは 山に 登ったり、 海水浴[13]に 行ったりして、 よく 遊びました。 中部地方[14]の 山山[15]は 高くて きれいでした。 山の 上には まだ 雪が 残っていました。 わたしたちが 山に 登っている あいだは ずっと よい 天気でしたが、 海へ 行っている あいだは よく 雨が 降りました。 その のち[16]は 毎日 むし暑く[17]て[18] たいへんです。

❸ わたしは このごろ[19] 毎朝 六時に 起きて、 すずしい[20] あいだに 二時間 フランス語[21]の 勉強を します。 夜は 暑

語句

1 *Maria* 'Maria'
2 atsu·i hot
3 tsuzuk·u (Vi) continue
  cf. tsuzuke·ru (Vt)
4 de See § 54
5 Risshū (the first day of autumn on the lunar calendar)
6 hajimari beginning ←hajimar·u
7 ma-natsu midsummer
  ma- at the height/center of
8 atsu-sa heat ←atsu·i
9 tats·u elapse
10 han-tsuki half a month
11 …ni naru amount to…
12 …no aida during… See § 51
13 kaisuiyoku swimming at the beach
  kaisui sea water -yoku bathing
14 Chūbu-chihō (Nagoya and the surrounding prefectures)
  chihō district, locality
15 yama-yama many mountains
  cf. hito-bito, ie-ie (many houses)
16 nochi later, after
17 mushi-atsu·i sultry, hot and stuffy
  mushi- ←mus·u (steam)
18 -kute See § 54
19 kono-goro these days, recently
20 suzushi·i cool

い　とき[22]は　まどを　あけ[23]たまま[24]　寝(ね)ます。

❹　八月二十二日(はちがつにじゅうににち)は　土曜日(どようび)で、　ぼんおどり[25]の　日(ひ)です。　町(まち)の　人々(ひとびと)は　みな　夜通し(よどおし)[26]　おどります[27]。　いつも　晩(ばん)は　静(しず)かで　さびしい[28]　町(まち)も、　その　夜(よる)だけは　さわがしくて[29]　にぎやかな[30]　町(まち)に　なります。　歌(うた)や　わらい声(ごえ)[31]が　町(まち)じゅう[32]に　流(なが)れます[33]。　みんな　歌(うた)いながら[34]　おどります。　見物人(けんぶつにん)[35]も　おどりの　輪(わ)[36]を　見(み)ながら　いっしょに　歌(うた)います。　ぼんおどりは　たいへん　おもしろいですから、　マリアさん、　土曜(どよう)[37]の　夕方(ゆうがた)[38]から　ぜひ[39]　来(き)てください。　いっしょに　おどりましょう。　ごちそう[40]を　作(つく)って[41]　待(ま)っています。

❺　まだ　暑(あつ)さが　続(つづ)きますから、　どうぞ　おからだ[42]に　気(き)を　つけてください。　さようなら。

八月七日(はちがつなのか)

友子(ともこ)[43]

---

21 *Furansu*-go　French (language)
22 toki　time, occasion　See § 50
23 ake・ru　open (Vt)
24 -ta mama　See § 53
25 Bon-odori　Bon Festival Dance
　odori　dance ←odor・u
26 yo-dōshi　all night
27 odor・u　dance
28 sabishi・i　lonely, forlorn, desolate
29 sawagashi・i　noisy
30 nigiyaka　(Na) lively, animated
31 warai-goe　sounds of laughter
　warai←wara・u　(laugh)
　-goe＝koe　voice
32 machi-jū　the whole town
　-jū　the whole, throughout
33 nagare・ru　flow
34 -nagara　while …ing See § 52
35 kenbutsu-nin　onlooker
36 wa　circle, ring
37 Do-yō＝Do-yōbi　Saturday
38 yūgata　evening
39 zehi　by all means, without fail
40 gochisō　good food, feast
41 tsukur・u　make
42 karada　body; health
43 Tomoko　(a given name (f))

Dai 10-ka
Natsu no Tegami

1 *Maria*-san, mai-nichi atsui hi ga tsuzukimasu ga, o-genki desu ka? Kyō wa Hachi-gatsu nano-ka de, Risshū desu. Shikashi, 'aki no hajimari' mo namae dake de, mada ma-natsu no atsu-sa desu ne.

2 Yasumi ga hajimatte kara, mō ik-ka-getsu tachimashita. Kono mae watashi ga anata no ie e itte kara, han-tsuki ni narimasu ne. Kono han-tsuki no aida, watashi wa yama ni nobottari, kaisuiyoku ni ittari shite, yoku asobimashita. Chūbu-chihō no yama-yama wa takakute kirei deshita. Yama no ue niwa mada yuki ga nokotte-imashita. Watashi-tachi ga yama ni nobotte-iru aida wa zutto yoi tenki deshita ga, umi e itte-iru aida wa yoku ame ga furimashita. Sono nochi wa mai-nichi mushi-atsukute taihen desu.

3 Watashi wa kono-goro mai-asa roku-ji ni okite, suzushii aida ni ni-jikan *Furansu*-go no benkyō o shimasu. Yoru wa atsui toki wa mado o aketa mama nemasu.

4 Hachi-gatsu ni-jū-ni-nichi wa Do-yōbi de, bon-odori no hi desu. Machi no hito-bito wa mina yodōshi odorimasu. Itsumo ban wa shizuka de sabishii machi mo, sono yoru dake wa sawagashikute nigiyaka-na machi ni narimasu. Uta ya warai-goe ga machi-jū ni nagaremasu. Minna utainagara odorimasu. Kenbutsu-nin mo odori no wa o minagara issho-ni utaimasu. Bon-odori wa taihen omoshiroi desu kara, *Maria*-san, Do-yō no yūgata kara zehi kite-kudasai. Issho-ni odorimashō. Gochisō o tsukutte matte-imasu.

5 Mada atsu-sa ga tsuzukimasu kara, dōzo o-karada ni ki o tsukete-kudasai. Sayōnara!

Hachi-gatsu nano-ka

Tomoko

Lesson 10

A Summer Letter

10

August 7

1 Dear Maria,

The days continue hot, but I hope you are in good health. Today is August 7, *Risshu*. But it is "the beginning of fall" in name only, and it is still as hot as midsummer.

2 It is already a month since our vacation started. And it is half a month since I went to your house, isn't it? During this half-month, I have been having a lot of fun, climbing mountains, going swimming in the ocean, and everything. The mountains in the Chubu area are high and beautiful. There was still some snow left on the mountain tops. All the time I was mountain climbing, the weather was good, but it rained a lot while I was at the beach. Since then, it has been terribly muggy every day.

3 Recently, I have been getting up every morning at 6:00 and studying French for two hours while it is still cool. At night when it is hot I sleep with my bedroom window open.

4 August 22 is a Saturday and the day of the *bon* dance. The people in our town dance all night. Even towns which are always quiet and lonely at night become noisy and lively that one night. The town rings with song and laughter. Everyone sings and dances. Even the spectators sing along while watching the circle of dancers. The *bon* dancing is very interesting, so I hope you will please come on Saturday evening. Let's dance together. I'll fix a big supper and be waiting for you.

5 The hot days are continuing yet, so please take care of your health. Goodbye.

Tomoko

ANSWERS 〈pp. 124, 125〉

I. (A) 1. (Rai-nen *Yōroppa* e) iku toki (tomodachi to issho-ni ikimasu). 2. (...ga) kita toki (watashi...). 3. (...ga) nai toki (tomodachi...). 4. (...ga) ii toki (yoku...).
(B) 1. (...ga) futte-iru aida (kissa-ten...). 2. (...) watashi ga Nippon ni inai aida (anata...). 3. (...ga) byōki no aida (watashi...).
(C) 1. (...o) tabenagara (*terebi*...). 2. (...o) abinagara (uta...). 3. (...o) kangaenagara (kōen ...). 4. (Hiru) hatarakinagara (yoru...).
(D) 1. (...o) haita mama (ie...). 2. (...o) aketa mama (asa...). 3. (...hayaku) dekaketa mama (mada...). 4. (...ni) suwatta mama (nagai...).
(E) 1. a. Shūshoku-shite kara (kekkon...). b. Shūshoku-suru mae ni (kekkon...). 2. a. (...e) itte kara (*Biru*...). b. (...e) iku mae ni (*Biru*...). 3. a. (...ni) atte kara (shokuji...). b. (...ni) au mae ni (shokuji...).

II. 1. toki 2. toki 3. aida 4. tsuketa mama 5. utainagara 6. neru mae ni

III. (A) 1. Nippon no dōro wa semakute abunai desu. 2. Kyōto wa shizuka de kirei desu. 3. Kare no ie wa eki kara tōkute fu-ben desu. (B) 1. Kanojo wa watashi no imōto de, namae wa *An* desu. 2. Kyō wa Nichi-yōbi de, kaisha wa yasumi desu.

●文法

§ 50 Phrases and Clauses Expressing Time

kono/sono/ano	+ **toki** (**ni**)	'(at) this/that time'
N **no**		'(at) the time of...'
Na-**na**		'(at) a...time'
A (Dict. form)		'(at) a...time'
V (Dict. form)		'When...,'
V-ta		'When...has/had done...,'
V-te-iru		'When...is/was doing...,'

Toki by itself means 'time,' but it is mostly used as a Pseudo Noun (See § 48), and it functions something like the conjunction 'when' in English. The Particle **ni** can be omitted because of toki's Adverbial character.

e.g. ame no toki '(at) a time of rain'='when it rains'

hima-na toki '(at) a leisurely time'='when one is not busy'

samui toki '(at) a cold time'='when it is cold'

unten-suru toki '(at) a driving time'='when one drives'

Politeness (style) or Past (tense) need not be observed in the phrase or clause preceding toki, because it is a subordinate (or dependent) clause, and style and tense are expressed by the form of the Predicate at the end of the whole sentence. Thus when the main Predicate expresses the Past tense, then the V or A preceding toki may or may not take the Past tense form ('-ta form'). The '-ta form' of V usually shows that the action or event is finished at the time expressed by the main Predicate. Compare the following:

Nippon e kuru toki, kare ga kūkō made kite-kuremashita.

'When I came to Japan, he came to the airport (to see me off).'

Nippon e kita toki, kare ga kūkō made kite-kuremashita.

'When I came to Japan, he came to the airport to meet me.'

§ 51 Other Expressions of Temporal Relations

N no V-te-iru } + **aida**	'while...'; 'during the time of...'

N no V (Dict.) } + **mae (ni)**	'before...'

N no V-ta } + **ato (de)**	'after...'

10

§ 52 Two Simultaneous Actions

V_1 (Conj. form) + **-nagara** V_2	'do(V_2) while doing(V_1)'

e.g. *terebi* o minagara gohan o taberu 'eat while watching TV'

§ 53 'as...is'

V_1-ta + mama V_2

This presupposes that the Subject is already in a certain state (expressed by V-ta, A, or some other modifier) and performs some action (V_2) while maintaining the original state.

e.g. Watashi wa tatta (<tatsu 'stand') mama *kōhī* o nomimashita.

'(I had been standing and) I drank my coffee standing.'

§ 54 Conjoining Adjectival or Nominal Predicates

... A-**kute**, ... Na **de**, ... N **de**, ...	'..., and...'

e.g. Kanojo wa wakakute, kirei desu. 'She is young and pretty.'

●練習

ANSWERS→p.121

I. Combine the following sentences.

(A) using 'toki'

1. (Rai-nen *Yōroppa*[1] e ikimasu.) (Tomodachi to issho-ni ikimasu.)
2. (Kare ga kimashita.) (Watashi wa mada nete-imashita.)
3. (O-kane ga arimasen.) (Tomodachi ni karimasu.[2])
4. (Tenki ga ii desu.) (Yoku kōen de asobimasu.)

(B) using 'aida'

1. (Ame ga futte-imashita.) (Kissa-ten ni imashita.)
2. (Kotoshi no natsu watashi wa Nippon ni imasen.) (Anata wa watashi no ie o tsukattemo[3] ii desu.)
3. (Kodomo ga byōki desu.) (Watashi wa kaisha o yasumanakereba narimasen.)

(C) using 'nagara'

1. (Gohan o tabemasu.) (*Terebi* o mimasu.)
2. (*Shawā*[4] o abimasu.[5]) (Uta o utaimasu.)
3. (Iroiro-na koto o kangaemasu.) (Kōen o sanpo-shimasu.)
4. (Hiru hatarakimasu.) (Yoru daigaku de benkyō-shimasu.)

(D) using 'mama'

1. (Kutsu o hakimasu.) (Ie ni haittewa ikemasen.)
2. (Mado o akemashita.) (Asa made nemutte[6]-imashita.)
3. (Kanojo wa asa hayaku dekakemashita.[7]) (Mada kaerimasen.)
4. (Kare wa sono isu ni suwarimashita.[8]) (Nagai aida ugokimasen[9] deshita.)

語句

1 *Yōroppa* 'Europe'
2 kari·ru borrow cf. kas·u (lend)
3 tsuka·u spend, use
4 *shawā* 'shower'
5 abi·ru pour/dash (water, etc.) over oneself
6 nemur·u sleep cf. ne·ru (go to bed, lie down, sleep)
7 dekake·ru go out
8 suwar·u sit
9 ugok·u (Vi) move
10 mae ni See § 51

(E) using '-te kara,' and then '...mae ni[10]'

1. (Shūshoku[11]-shimasu.) (Kekkon-shimasu.)
2. (Anata no ie e ikimasu.) (*Biru*[12] ni denwa o kakemasu.)
3. (Kare ni aimasu.) (Shokuji-shimashō.)

II. Choose the correct word.

1. Watashi ga *hōmu*[13] ni tsuita (aida, toki), densha no *doa* ga shimarimashita.
2. Watashi ga sono mise de kaimono[14] o shite-iru (aida, toki), kare ga mise no mae o tōrimashita.
3. Watashi ga sono mise de kaimono o shite-iru (aida, toki), kare wa watashi o matte-imashita.
4. *Rajio* o (tsuketa[15] mama, tsukenagara) asa made nemutte-imashita.
5. Minna de uta o (utatta mama, utainagara) yama ni noborimashita.
6. Yoru (neru mae ni, nete kara) ha[16] o migakimasu.[17]

III. Make sentences using the key phrases.

(A) Ex. (kono tatemono) (ōkii) (atarashii)

→Kono tatemono wa ōkikute atarashii desu.

1. (Nippon no dōro) (semai[18]) (abunai[19])
2. (Kyōto) (shizuka) (kirei)
3. (kare no ie) (eki kara tōi) (fu-ben)

(B) Ex. (kore) (tosho-kan) (are) (bijutsu-kan)

→Kore wa tosho-kan de, are wa bijutsu-kan desu.

1. (kanojo) (watashi no imōto) (namae) (*An*[20])
2. (kyō) (Nichi-yōbi) (kaisha) (yasumi)

---

11 shūshoku (Nv) get/find employment
12 *Biru* 'Bill'
13 *hōmu* 'platform'
14 kaimono shopping
15 tsuke·ru turn on
16 ha tooth
17 migak·u polish, brush
18 sema·i small and narrow cf. hiro·i
19 abuna·i dangerous
20 *An* 'Ann'

●会話

II TENKI DESU NE

Tsutomu[1]: Ii tenki desu ne.
Dō desu,[2] *tenisu*[3] o shimasen ka?

Emiko[4]: Ē, ii wa yo.[5]
Kigae[6] o shite kara iku wa.
Sukoshi matte-ite ne.

T: Un,[7] jā boku wa *raketto*[8] to *bōru* o karite-kimashō.[9]

E: O-negai ne.[10] Sugu kuru wa.

E: O-machidō-sama.

T: Sā, ikimashō.

E: Mā, takusan no hito ne.
Kōto[11] ga hito-tsu mo[12] aite[13]-inai wa.

T: Do-yōbi no gogo desu kara, hito ga ōi desu.

E: Dō shimashō?

T: Kono *benchi* ni kakete[14] sukoshi machimashō.
Honto[15]-ni ii o-tenki desu nē....

T: It's a nice day, isn't it?
How about a game of tennis?

E: Yes, fine with me.
I'll go after I change clothes.
Wait a minute, will you?

T: Sure. I'll go borrow some rackets and balls.

E: Please.
I'll be right back.

E: Sorry to have kept you waiting.

T: Let's go.

E: My, there are so many people here. There is not a single court available.

T: It's because it's Saturday afternoon that there are so many people.

E: What shall we do?

T: Let's sit down on this bench and wait a bit. It really is a nice day, isn't it?

語句

1 Tsutomu (a given name (m))
2 Dō desu (Cph) What do you say to ...ing?
3 *tenisu* 'tennis'
4 Emiko (a given name (f))
5 ii wa yo Fine with me. (fem.)
6 kigae changing (clothes)
7 Un=Hai Ok (Familiar)
8 *raketto* 'racket'
9 karite-kuru borrow...and come -te-kuru See § 87
10 O-negai ne (Cph: short for 'O-negai-shimasu' and used when asking a favor) negai wishes, hopes ←nega·u (wish)
11 *kōto* 'court'

E: Shall we have some juice while we are waiting?
T: I'll go buy it.

E: It's cold and delicious. They are playing volley ball and basketball here too.
T: They are even playing baseball over there.
E: Autumn really is the season for sports, isn't it?
T: Look, there is a court free now. Let's begin.
E: Yes, let's go.
Oh dear, I've left my tennis shoes behind.
Is it all right to play in these shoes?
T: No, you can't go onto the court with those shoes on.
I'll go get your tennis shoes.
Can you wait here a moment?
E: I'm sorry, really.

---

12 hito-tsu mo...nai not a single
13 ak·u be vacant; open
14 kake·ru (on a chair)
15 honto=hontō
16 *jūsu* 'juice'
17 ...demo ...or something
18 *barē-bōru* 'volleyball'
19 *basuketto-bōru* 'basketball'
20 yakyū baseball
21 yar·u =suru do; play (sport)
22 *tenisu-shūzu* 'tennis shoes,
23 wasure·ru forget
24 kashira I wonder
25 totte-kuru go (and) get
26 Gomen-nasai (Cph: apologizing)

E: Matte-iru aida, *jūsu*[16] demo[17] nomimasen ka?

T: Boku ga katte-kimashō.

E: Tsumetakute oishii wa.
Barē-bōru[18] ya *basuketto-bōru*[19] mo shite-imasu ne?

T: Mukō dewa yakyū[20] mo yatte[21]-imasu.

E: *Supōtsu* no aki ne.

T: Ā, *kōto* ga akimashita.
Hajimemashō ka?

E: Ē, hajimemashō.
Ara, *tenisu-shūzu*[22] o wasurete[23]-kita wa.
Kono kutsu de shitemo ii kashira[24]?

T: Iya, sono kutsu de *kōto* ni haittewa ikemasen.
Boku ga *tenisu-shūzu* o totte-kimashō.[25]
Koko de matte-ite-kudasai.

E: Gomen-nasai[26] ne.

10

日本の　歴史—1

わが国[1]の　いちばん　[2]古い　歴史の　本は　「古事記[3]」である。　それより[4]　前の　ことは　考古学[5]の　資料[6]からしか　わからない[7]。　そのころ　日本には　「縄文文化[8]」と　「弥生文化[9]」　が　あって、　「弥生時代[10]」　には　農業が　発達してきた。　次の　「古墳時代[11]」　は　いわゆる[12]氏姓制度[13]の　時代で、　天皇家[14]も　氏族[15]の　一つであった。

▲Jomon pottery

聖徳太子[16]は　七世紀の　初め、　わが国　最初の　憲法を　作った。　太子は　たいへん　かしこくて[17]、　一度[18]に　十人の　うったえを[19]　聞きながら　判断[20]を　下した[21]。　太子は　法隆寺[22]など　たくさんの　お寺を　建てた[23]。　この　時代から　710年に　奈良に　都[24]が　移る[25]　前までの　あいだが、　「飛鳥時代[26]」である。　太子は　また　留学生[27]を　中国へ　送った。　[28]かれらは　日本に帰って、中国の　政治制度[29]を　伝えた[30]。

645年の　「大化の改新[31]」や　672年の「壬申の乱[32]」の　のち、天皇中心[33]の政治体制[34]が　確立[35]した。

「奈良時代[36]」に　中央政府[37]は　都や地方[38]に　たくさんの　寺を　作って、それらを　人々の　精神的[39]　中心に[40]した。　しかし、　それで　財政的[41]に困った[42]。　その　あいだに　藤原氏[43]の勢力[44]が　[45]のびた。

▲Shotoku Taishi

Japanese History—1

The oldest Japanese history book is *Kojiki.* Only archeological data can give us information on the ages before this, during which the Jomon and Yayoi cultures flourished. Agriculture was developed in the Yayoi Period. The Kofun Age was called the age of the clan system, the Imperial family being one of these clans.

Shotoku Taishi wrote the first Japanese Constitution at the beginning of the 7th century. He was clever enough to pass judgment on cases while listening to ten people's appeals at the same time. He built Horyu-ji and many other temples. The period from his rule until the capital was moved to Nara in 710 is called the Asuka Period. Taishi sent some students to China. They came back and introduced the Chinese political system. The emperor-centered political structure was strengthened after the Taika Restoration of 645 and the Jinshin Revolt of 672.

The central government built many temples in the Nara capital and in the countryside, making them the spiritual centers of the nation. But this also created financial difficulties. During this period, the Fujiwaras gained power.

10

語句

1 waga our; my
  waga kuni our country
2 ichiban the most; first See § 60
3 Kojiki (the oldest Japanese chronicle, compiled in 712)
4 ...yori than... See § 59
5 kōko-gaku archaeology
  -gaku -ology; learning
6 shiryō data, information resource
7 wakar•u understandable; understand
8 Jōmon-bunka Jomon Culture (8~7000-300 B.C.)
9 Yayoi-bunka Yayoi Culture (300 B.C.-300 A.D.)
10 Yayoi-jidai Yayoi Period
11 Kofun-jidai Kofun Period
12 iwayuru so-called
13 shisei-seido clan system
  shisei clan, family seido system
14 Tennō-ke Imperial family
  Tennō Emperor of Japan
  -ke family
15 shizoku clan
16 Shōtoku Taishi Prince Shotoku (574-622) taishi prince
17 kashiko•i wise, clever
18 ichi-do ni at once, at the same time
19 uttae appeal ←uttae•ru (appeal, sue)
20 handan (Nv) judgment
21 handan o kudas•u pass judgment; judge
22 Hōryū-ji (a temple in Nara)
23 tate•ru build
24 miyako capital city, governmental site
25 utsur•u (Vi) transfer, move
26 Asuka-jidai Asuka Period (593-710)
27 ryūgaku-sei foreign student, student studying abroad
  ryūgaku (Nv) studying abroad
28 kare-ra they
29 seiji-seido political system
30 tsutae•ru convey (ideas, information)
31 Taika-no-kaishin Taika Restoration
32 Jinshin-no-ran Jinshin Revolt
  ran revolt, turmoil
33 -chūshin centered on/in...
34 seiji-taisei political structure
  taisei structure, establishment
35 kakuritsu (Nv) establishing
36 Nara-jidai Nara Period (710-794)
37 chūō-seifu central government
  chūō center seifu government
38 chihō local places
39 seishin-teki (Na) spiritual
  seishin spirit
  -teki having the quality of...
40 ...ni suru make (something)...
41 zaisei-teki (Na) financial
  zaisei finance
42 komar•u be in trouble, be at a loss
43 Fujiwara-shi Fujiwara family
  -shi=-uji ...family; clan
44 seiryoku power, influence
45 nobi•ru extend, expand; increase

第 11 課

教室[1]で

TAPE
No. 3
Side 2

❶ ブラウンさんが 立って[2] 本を 読みます。日本人は ご飯を 食べる 前に、「いただきます[3]」と 言います[4]。食べおわった[5] とき[6]に、「ごちそうさま[7]」と 言います。朝 人に 会った ときには、「おはようございます」と 言います。昼間[8] 人に 会った ときは、「こんにちは」と 言って、日が くれて[9]からは、「こんばんは」と 言います。また、人と 別れる[10] ときは「さようなら」と 言います。手紙の 終わりにも よく「さようなら」と 書きます。晩 寝る 前には、「おやすみなさい」と 言います。

❷ 「はい、けっこう[11]です。」と 先生が 言いました。そのとき「先生、質問[12]があります。」と 一人が 言いました。ビルという[13] 学生です。「何ですか。どうぞ。」と 先生は 答え[14]ました。「英語の **greetings** は、日本語で 何と 言いますか。」と ビルは たずね[15]ました。「あいさつと 言います。」「おはようございますという ことばは どんな 意味[16]ですか。」

語句

1 kyōshitsu classroom
  -shitsu room
2 tats·u stand (up); start
3 Itadakimasu (Cph)
  itadak·u receive (things, food, drink, etc.) (Humble, hence polite, expression of mora·u)
4 i·u say
  ...to i·u say that...
5 -owar·u finish ...ing
6 ...toki (ni) when... See § 50
7 Gochisō-sama (Cph)
8 hiru-ma during the day
9 kure·ru get dark; come to the end (of a day, year, etc.)
10 wakare·ru (Vi) part, separate

「It's very early! という　意味(いみ)です。英語(えいご)では Good Morning! と　言(い)いますね。」「よく　わかりました。」

❸　「日本人(にっぽんじん)は　あいさつの　中(なか)に、よく　天気(てんき)や　季節(きせつ)[17]の　ことばを　使(つか)います。これは　日本人(にっぽんじん)の　国民性(こくみんせい)[18]だと　思(おも)[19]います。」

▲A scene from Hiroshige's "Fifty-three stages of the Tokaido"

---

11 kekkō (Na) satisfactory, good, fine
12 shitsumon (Nv) question
13 ...to i・u called/named... See § 58
14 kotae・ru answer, reply
15 tazune・ru inquire; call on/at
16 imi (Nv) meaning
17 kisetsu season
18 kokumin-sei national character
kokumin citizens of a nation, people
-sei character
19 ...to omo・u think See § 56

Dai 11-ka
Kyōshitsu de

1 *Buraun*-san ga tatte hon o yomimasu.

Nippon-jin wa gohan o taberu mae ni, "Itadakimasu" to iimasu. Tabe-owatta toki ni, "Gochisō-sama" to iimasu. Asa hito ni atta toki niwa, "Ohayō gozaimasu" to iimasu. Hiru-ma hito ni atta toki wa, "Kon-nichi wa" to itte, hi ga kurete kara wa, "Konban wa" to iimasu. Mata, hito to wakareru toki wa "Sayōnara" to iimasu. Tegami no owari nimo yoku "Sayōnara" to kakimasu. Ban neru mae niwa, "O-yasumi-nasai" to iimasu.

2 "Hai, kekkō desu." to sensei ga iimashita. Sono toki "Sensei, shitsumon ga arimasu." to hito-ri ga iimashita. *Biru* to iu gakusei desu. "Nan desu ka? Dōzo." to sensei wa kotaemashita. "Ei-go no 'greetings' wa, Nippon-go de nan to iimasu ka?" to *Biru* wa tazunemashita. "Aisatsu to iimasu." "O-hayō gozaimasu to iu kotoba wa donna imi desu ka?" "'It's very early!' to iu imi desu. Ei-go dewa 'Good morning!' to iimasu ne." "Yoku wakarimashita."

3 "Nippon-jin wa aisatsu no naka ni, yoku tenki ya kisetsu no kotoba o tsukaimasu. Kore wa Nippon-jin no kokumin-sei da to omoimasu."

▶A scene from Hiroshige's "Fifty-three stages of the Tokaido"

Lesson 11

In the Classroom

1 Mr. Brown stands up and reads from his text.

"Japanese say 'Itadakimasu' before they eat. After they have finished eating, they say 'Gochisosama.' When they meet someone in the morning, they say 'Ohayo gozaimasu.' When meeting in the afternoon, they say 'Konnichi wa,' and after sundown they say 'Konban wa.' When parting with someone, they say 'Sayonara.' They often write 'Sayonara' at the end of letters too. Before going to bed they say 'Oyasuminasai'."

2 The teacher said, "Yes, that's fine." Then one student said, "Sir, I have a question." It is a student named Bill. The teacher responded, "Yes, what is it?" Bill asked, "What is the Japanese for the English word 'greetings'?" "It is 'aisatsu'." "What does the phrase 'Ohayo gozaimasu' mean?" "It means 'It's very early.' But in English it translates as 'Good morning'." "I see."

3 "The Japanese also often use weather or seasonal expressions in their greetings. I think this is part of the Japanese national character."

▶A scene from Hiroshige's "Fifty-three stages of the Tokaido"

ANSWERS 〈pp. 136, 137〉

II. 1. Kare wa Takahashi to iu Nippon no *pianisuto* desu.
2. Ano hito wa Yamada to iu Nippon-go no sensei desu.
3. Watashi wa Tachikawa to iu Tōkyō no chikaku no machi ni sunde-imasu.
4. Ima 'Kokoro' to iu shōsetsu o yonde-imasu.
5. Watashi wa kono aida Tōkyō de Shinjuku-gyoen to iu kirei-na niwa o mimashita.
6. Kokutetsu de Hakone e iku toki Odawara to iu eki de densha o norikaenakereba narimasen.

III. 1. hana 2. hon/kyōka-sho 3. hito

V. 1. 'Ball-point pen' wa Nippon-go de nan to iimasu ka? —*Bōru-pen* to iimasu.
2. 'Newspaper' wa Nippon-go de nan to iimasu ka? —Shinbun to iimasu.
3. 'To introduce' wa Nippon-go de nan to iimasu ka? —Shōkai-suru to iimasu.

VI. 1. Kare wa ashita koko e konai to omoimasu. 2. Kaigi wa mō owatta to omoimasu. 3. *Tomu*-san wa byōki da to omoimasu. 4. Sono eiga wa omoshiroi to omoimasu. 5. Kono kasa wa *Sumisu*-san no da to omoimasu.

●文法

§ 55 Quoting

N wa/ga ... to iimasu. 'N says....'

e.g. Tarō wa ohayō gozaimasu to iimashita. 'Taro said, "Good morning."'
=Ohayō gozaimasu to Tarō wa iimashita.

The Verbs of Saying, besides i(w)-u, include: kotae-ru 'answer, reply'; hanas-u 'tell, talk'; kak-u 'write'; happyō-suru 'announce, make public'; etc.

NB: When N is a third person, it is better to use '-te-iru form' instead of the simple Present form. The Past form can be used for any person.

e.g. Tarō wa kaeru (kaerimasu) to itte-imasu. 'Taro says he is going home.'
Rajio wa taifū ga kuru to itte-imasu.
'The radio says a typhoon is on its way.'

§ 56 Telling What Someone Thinks

N wa ... to omoimasu. 'N thinks that....'

e.g. Watashi wa kare wa/ga Nippon-jin da to omoimasu.
'I think (that) he is a Japanese.'

NB: (1) The Predicate expressing the thought content (the Predicate preceding 'to') normally takes the Plain style, unlike the part quoted by the Verbs of Saying.

(2) When the sentence is in the Present tense, the N, unless otherwise specified, is assumed to be the speaker himself in a statement and the addressee in a question. Thus, a sentence like

Yamada-san wa ma ni au to omoimasu.

means only, 'I think Mr. Yamada will be in time.' and not, 'Yamada thinks....' In other tenses, however, it is often necessary to specify.

§ 57 Calling or Naming

(N wa) X o Y to iimasu. '(N) calls X Y.'

e.g. Nippon-jin wa kore o hashi to iimasu.

'Japanese people call these "*hashi*" ('chopsticks').'

When the N is an unspecified and indefinite number of people, 'N wa' is omitted, and 'X o' changes to 'X wa,' X becoming the Topic of the sentence.

e.g. Kore wa 'hashi' to iimasu. 'These are called "*hashi*".'

When one introduces himself, he says, 'Watashi wa . . .to iimasu (or mōshimasu, a Humble form of iimasu).' instead of saying, 'Watashi no namae wa . . . desu.'

e.g. Watashi wa *Sumisu* to mōshimasu. 'I am called "Smith".'

11

§ 58 Changing the above pattern into a Nominal Construction

Y to iu X 'X (which is) called Y'

e.g. *Sumisu* to iu hito 'a man called/named Smith'

o-hashi to iu mono 'something called *o-hashi*'

'*Pīsu*' to iu *tabako* 'cigarettes named "Peace"'

Question: Kore wa nan to iu mono desu ka? 'What is this called?'

You will find that some such constructions are equivalent to the 'Appositive construction' in English. Compare the following.

Kinō (watashi wa) Tarō ga kekkon-shita to iu shirase o kikimashita.

'Yesterday I heard *the news that* Taro got married.'

Watashi wa Nippon-go o Rōma-ji-ka shita hō ga ii to iu iken o motte-imasu (or, . . .to iu iken desu). 'I have *the opinion* (or, I am of *the opinion*) *that* it is better to Romanize Japanese.'

Kare wa sensō ga owatta to iu koto o shiranakatta.

'He did not know *the fact that* the war had ended.'

●練習

ANSWERS→p. 133

I. Make dialogs as shown in the example.

Ex. (kore) (tabemono[1]) (sushi) Q: Kore wa nan to iu tabemono desu ka?

A: Sushi to iu tabemono desu.

1. (kore) (kudamono[2]) (kaki[3])
2. (kore) (gakki[4]) (koto[5])
3. (kore) (tori) (uguisu[6])
4. (koko) (o-tera) (Koke-dera)
5. (koko) (eki) (Kanda[7])
6. (koko) (tokoro[8]) (Ueno[9])

II. Combine the sentences.

Ex. (Kore wa Nippon no gakki desu.) (Namae wa koto desu.)

→Kore wa koto to iu Nippon no gakki desu.

1. (Kare wa Nippon no *pianisuto*[10] desu.) (Namae wa Takahashi[11] desu.)
2. (Ano hito wa Nippon-go no sensei desu.) (Namae wa Yamada desu.)
3. (Watashi wa Tōkyō no chikaku no machi ni sunde-imasu.) (Machi no namae wa Tachikawa[12] desu.)
4. (Ima shōsetsu o yonde-imasu.) (Shōsetsu no namae wa 'Kokoro'[13] desu.)
5. (Watashi wa kono aida[14] Tōkyō de kirei-na niwa o mimashita.) (Niwa no namae wa Shinjuku-gyoen[15] desu.)
6. (Koku-tetsu[16] de Hakone e iku toki, sono eki de densha o norikaenake-[17] reba narimasen.) (Eki no namae wa Odawara[18] desu.)

語句

1 tabemono food
2 kudamono fruit
3 kaki persimmon
4 gakki musical instrument
5 koto (a Japanese musical instrument)
6 uguisu nightingale
7 Kanda (a place name)
8 tokoro place
9 Ueno (a place name)
10 *pianisuto* 'pianist'
11 Takahashi (a family name)
12 Tachikawa (a place name)
13 Kokoro (the title of a novel by Natsume Soseki)
kokoro heart, mind
14 kono aida the other day
15 Shinjuku-gyoen Shinjuku Royal Garden
16 Koku-tetsu Japan National Railways

III. Fill in the blanks.

1. Sakura to iu ( ) wa haru ni sakimasu.
2. Watashi-tachi no Nippon-go no kyōka-sho[19] wa 'Atarashii Nippon-go' to iu ( ) desu.
3. Kinō anata no rusu[20] no aida ni *Sumisu*[21]-san to iu ( ) kara anata ni denwa ga arimashita.[22]

IV. Answer the following questions.

1. Nippon-jin wa hito to wakareru toki, 'Sayōnara' to iimasu. Anata no kuni dewa nan to iimasu ka?
2. Nippon-go de denwa o kakeru toki, hajime ni 'Moshi-moshi'[23] to iimasu. Anata no kuni dewa nan to iimasu ka?
3. Nippon-jin wa ie o hōmon[24]-suru toki, genkan[25] de 'Gomen-kudasai' to iimasu. Anata no kuni dewa nan to iimasu ka?
4. Nippon-go de o-iwai[26] o iu toki, 'Omedetō'[27] to iimasu. Anata no kuni dewa nan to iimasu ka?

V. Practice the following pattern.

Ex. "Stamp" wa Nippon-go de nan to iimasu ka? —Kitte to iimasu.

1. "ball-point pen" 2. "newspaper" 3. "to introduce"

VI. Expand the following sentences with "to omoimasu."

1. Kare wa ashita koko e kimasen.
2. Kaigi[28] wa mō owarimashita.
3. *Tomu*-san wa byōki desu.
4. Sono eiga wa omoshiroi desu.
5. Kono kasa wa *Sumisu*-san no desu.

←Nihon Kokuyū Tetsudō
kokuyū national, owned by the state tetsudō railway
17 norikae·ru change cars/trains/planes
18 Odawara (a place name)
19 kyōka-sho textbook -sho book
20 rusu being away from home/office; absent
21 *Sumisu* 'Smith'
22 denwa ga ar·u get a phone call
23 Moshi-moshi (Cph) Hello (telephone)
24 hōmon (Nv) visit
25 genkan entrance of a house
26 iwai celebration, congratulations ←iwa·u (congratulate, celebrate)
27 Omedetō (Cph) Congratulations!
28 kaigi meeting, conference

11

●会話

SHUPPATSU-SHIMASU

Katō[1]: Suzuki[2]-san, *Furansu* e iku to iu hanashi desu nē.

Suzuki: Ē, Go-gatsu no sue[3] ni shuppatsu-shimasu.

K: Oku-san[4] mo issho desu ka?

S: Hai, tsuma[5] mo kodomo mo tsurete-ikimasu.

K: Chō-kikan[6] no taizai[7] desu ka?

S: Ē, ni-nen gurai desu.

K: O-kā-san wa?

S: Sono aida, haha wa ane[8] no ie de kurashimasu.[9]

K: O-kā-san wa hantai[10] dewa arimasen deshita ka?

S: Ē, iku-na[11] to iimashita ga, shigoto desu kara shikata ga arimasen. Tokorode, anata no oji-san wa mada *Yōroppa* desu ka? Tashika[12] *Furansu* desu ne?

K: Mr. Suzuki, I hear you are going to France, is that right?
S: Yes, I'm leaving at the end of May.
K: Is your wife going with you?
S: Yes, I'm taking both my wife and my children.
K: Are you going to stay long?
S: Yes, about two years.
K: What about your mother?
S: During that time, my mother will be living with my elder sister.
K: Didn't your mother object?
S: Yes, she said I should not go, but since it's my job, there's nothing I can do about it. By the way, is your uncle still in Europe? If I remember right, he is in France, isn't he?

語句

1 Katō (a family name)
2 Suzuki (a family name)
3 sue end of a term
4 oku-san wife (Polite)
5 tsuma wife
6 chō-kikan (for) a long term/time chō- long kikan term, period of time
7 taizai (Nv) stay
8 ane elder sister cf. imōto (younger sister)
9 kuras•u live; spend time
10 hantai (Nv) objection
11 -na don't (Prohibition)
12 tashika (Na) quite surely, if I remember right
13 gaikoku-sei foreign-made

K: He came home last October.
Since he uses only foreign goods, all his relatives call him by the nickname "Jean Gabin."
He always says Paris is so wonderful.
S: Then, is it all right if I go to listen to his stories about when he was abroad?
K: Of course it is. I am sure he will be pleased. My uncle was working for a company in Paris called NKK.
S: If I remember right, it's near the Champs Elysées.
I'll be living in the same area, because my company's Paris branch is near Etoile.

K: Kyo-nen no Jū-gatsu ni kaette-kimashita.
Gaikoku-sei[13] no mono bakari[14] tsukaimasu kara, shinrui[15] no mono[16] wa *Jan Gyaban*[17] to iu adana[18] de yonde-[19] imasu.
Itsumo *Pari*[20] wa subarashii to itteimasu.
S: Sorejā,[21] mukō no o-hanashi o kiki ni ittemo ii desu ka?
K: Ii desu tomo.[22]
Kitto[23] yorokobimasu[24] yo.
Oji[25] wa *Pari* no *NKK* to iu kaisha ni tsutomete[26]-imashita.
S: Tashika, *Shanzerize*[27] no chikaku desu ne. Watashi mo ano atari ni sumu to omoimasu.
Watashi no kaisha no *Pari*-shiten wa *Etowāru*[28] no chikaku desu kara.

14 ...bakari only, exclusively, nothing but...
15 shinrui relatives
16 mono person
17 *Jan Gyaban* 'Jean Gabin'
18 adana nickname
19 yob·u call
20 *Pari* 'Paris'
21 sorejā then
22 ...tomo for sure; of course (Emphatic)
23 kitto surely, certainly
24 yorokob·u be glad
25 oji uncle cf. oba (aunt)
26 tsutome·ru work for (a company)
27 *Shanzerize* 'Champs Elysées'
28 *Etowāru* 'Etoile'

11

マスコミ

（読売新聞提供）

新聞や ざっし[1]、 ラジオ、 テレビでの 情報活動[2]を マスコミ[3]と 言います。 日本では 近年[4] マスコミが 非常[5]に 発達しています。

新聞には 四つの おもな 全国紙[6]、 多く[7]の 地方紙[8]、 専門紙[9]が あります。 1970年の 調査[10]では 日本の 日刊新聞[11]の 発行部数[12]は 人口 1,000人あたり[13] 511部[14]で、 これは スウェーデン[15]の 534部に ついで[16] 世界第二位[17]です。

テレビの 普及率[18]は 人口 1,000人あたり 223台で、 たいていの 家庭に 一台は あります。「オリンピック[19]を カラーで 見よう[20]。」とか[21]、「月での 散歩を カラーで 見よう。」という 広告[22]で 電機メーカー[23]は カラーテレビ[24]を たくさん 売り[25]ました。 その 結果[26]、 今では カラーテレビも かなり[27] 普及しています。

マスコミ、 とくに[28] テレビは 子どもに 大きな[29] 影響[30]を 与え[31]ています。 子どもたち[32]は 夜 おそくまで[33] テレビの 前を 離れ[34]ないので、 親[35]は 困っています。 こんな[36] 子どもを 「テレビっ子[37]」と 言います。 「テレビっ子」は だんだん[38] ふえています。 また、 ラジオを 聞きながら、 あるいは[39] テレビを 見ながら 勉強します。 こんな 人を 「ながら族[40]」と 言います。 もちろん、 おとなの 中[41]にも 「ながら族」は たくさん います。

Mass Media

Radio, television, and press information activities are called "mass communication." Mass communication has recently shown great development in Japan.

There are four main nation-wide newspapers and many local and specialized ones. According to a 1970 survey, 511 daily newspapers are published per 1,000 people every day in Japan, a figure led internationally only by Sweden's 534.

The television ownership ratio is up to 223 sets per 1,000 people, and almost all families have at least one set. Electrical appliance manufacturers sold many color sets with advertisements saying "Let's watch the Olympics in color," and "Let's watch the moon walk in color." As a result, color television is pretty widely diffused.

Mass media, especially television, have a great influence on children. Yet many parents are worried that their children stay up late at night watching television. We call such children "TV children." The number of "TV children" is gradually increasing. Many students study while listening to the radio or watching television. We call these people the "∼ing crowd," although of course this also includes many adults.

11

語句

1 zasshi magazine
2 jōhō-katsudō information activities
 jōhō information
3 *masu-komi* 'mass communication,' mass media
4 kin-nen (in) recent years
5 hijō-ni=taihen very, greatly
6 zenkoku-shi nation-wide paper
 -shi newspaper
7 ōku no many, most cf. ō•i See § 35
8 chihō-shi local paper
9 senmon-shi specialty newspaper
 senmon specialty
10 chōsa (Nv) investigation, survey
11 nik-kan-shinbun daily newspaper
 nik-kan published daily cf. shū-kan (weekly), gek-kan (monthly), nen-kan (annual)
12 hakkō-busū number of copies printed, circulation
 hakkō (Nv) issue
 busū number of copies
13 ...atari per...
14 -bu ...copies
15 *Suēden* 'Sweden'
16 ...ni tsuide next/second to...
 ←tsug•u succeed to; follow...
17 sekai-dai-...-i the ...-th in the world
18 fukyū-ritsu diffusion ratio
 fukyū (Nv) diffusion, spread
 -ritsu ratio, proportion, percentage
19 *Orinpikku* 'Olympic Games'
20 miyō (Plain style of mimashō)
21 ...toka such as...
22 kōkoku (Nv) publicity, advertisement
23 denki-*mēkā* electric appliance maker
 denki electrical appliance
 mēkā 'maker,' manufacturer
24 *karā-terebi* 'color television'
25 ur•u sell
26 kekka result
 sono kekka as a result, consequently
27 kanari quite, fairly
28 tokuni especially
29 ōki-na=ōki•i large See § 7
30 eikyō (Nv) influence, effect
31 atae•ru give
32 kodomo-tachi children
33 yoru osoku late at night
34 hanare•ru (Vi) detach, leave
35 ...node since, as
36 konna like this See § 8
37 *Terebik*-ko 'TV' child
38 dandan gradually, step by step
39 aruiwa or else
40 Nagara-zoku people who do two things at once See § 52 -zoku tribe
41 otona adult

第 12 課

東京(とうきょう)・京都(きょうと)・大阪(おおさか)

TAPE
No. 3
Side 2

❶東京(とうきょう)は 日本(にっぽん)の 首都(しゅと)です。 京都(きょうと)は むかし 日本(にっぽん)の 首都(しゅと)でした。 東京(とうきょう)という 名(な)まえは 東(ひがし)[1]の みやこという 意味(いみ)です。 東京(とうきょう)は 京都(きょうと)より[2] ずっと[3] 大(おお)きいです。 人口(じんこう)も 京都(きょうと)より ずっと 多(おお)いです。

❷——東京(とうきょう)と 京都(きょうと)と どちら[4]が 古(ふる)いですか。

京都(きょうと)の ほう[5]が 東京(とうきょう)より 古(ふる)いです。 東京(とうきょう)は 京都(きょうと)ほど[6] 古(ふる)くは ありません。 東京(とうきょう)は 京都(きょうと)より 新(あたら)しい 町(まち)です。

——東京(とうきょう)と 京都(きょうと)と どちらが 静(しず)かですか。

もちろん 京都(きょうと)の ほうが 東京(とうきょう)より 静(しず)かです。 東京(とうきょう)の 町(まち)は 車(くるま)で いっぱいで、 たいへん さわがしいです。

——では[7]、 どちらが きれいですか。

京都(きょうと)です。 町(まち)が あまり 大(おお)きくなくて、 まわりに 山(やま)が あります。 それで 町全体(まちぜんたい)が 落(お)ち着(つ)い[8]ています。

❸——商業(しょうぎょう)[9]や 工業(こうぎょう)は どちらが さかんですか。

もちろん どちらも[10] 東京(とうきょう)の ほうが さかんです。 東京(とうきょう)は 日本(にっぽん)の 政治(せいじ)・経済(けいざい)[11]の 中心(ちゅうしん)です。 会社(かいしゃ)も 工場(こうじょう)も 東京(とうきょう)に

語句

1 higashi　east
2 …yori　than…　See §59
3 zutto　much, by far; all the time
4 dochira　which
5 …no hō ga　…is more…　See §59
6 …hodo　to the extent of…　See §62
7 dewa　Well, then…
8 ochitsuk·u　become calm/settled
9 shō-gyō　commerce
10 dochira mo　both
11 keizai　economy
12 shūchū　(Nv) concentration
13 dentō-sangyō　traditional industry
　dentō　tradition
14 kankō　tourism; sightseeing
15 haya·i　fast, quick
16 Hikari　super-express *Hikari*
　hikari　light

集中[12]しています。 京都は 伝統産業[13]と 観光[14]の 町です。

——東京と 京都と 大阪の 中で、 どこが いちばん 大きいですか。

東京が いちばん 大きいです。人口も 東京が いちばん 多いです。

❹——東京から 大阪へは 何で 行きますか。

たいてい 新幹線で 行きます。新幹線は たいへん 速い[15]です。 新幹線の「ひかり」[16]は 東京から 大阪まで 三時間十分で 走ります。 「こだま」[17]は 四時間十分で 走ります。東海道線[18]の 列車[19]は 七時間以上[20] かかります。「ひかり」が いちばん 速くて 便利です。 東京と 大阪の 間には 飛行機も 飛んでいます。飛行機は 五十分ぐらいしか かかりません。 飛行機の ほうが 「ひかり」 より 三倍[21]以上 速いです。 しかし、 東京都心[22]から 羽田空港[23]までと 大阪市内[24]から 伊丹空港[25]までが 不便です。 ですから、多くの 人が 飛行機よりも 新幹線の ほうを よく 利用[26]しています。料金[27]は 飛行機の ほうが 二倍ぐらい かかります。

---

17 Kodama limited express *Kodama*
kodama echo
18 Tōkaidō-sen Tokaido Line
19 ressha train
20 ...ijō more than...
21 -bai ...times, -fold See § 62
22 toshin the center of a city
23 Haneda-kūkō Haneda Airport
Haneda (a place name)
kūkō airport
24 shinai (N) in the city
25 Itami-kūkō Itami Airport
Itami (a place name)
26 riyō (Nv) utilizing, use
27 ryōkin fee, fare, charge

Dai 12-ka
Tōkyō, Kyōto, Ōsaka

1 Tōkyō wa Nippon no shuto desu. Kyōto wa mukashi Nippon no shuto deshita. Tōkyō to iu namae wa higashi no miyako to iu imi desu. Tōkyō wa Kyōto yori zutto ōkii desu. Jinkō mo Kyōto yori zutto ōi desu.

2 ——Tōkyō to Kyōto to dochira ga furui desu ka?

Kyōto no hō ga Tōkyō yori furui desu. Tōkyō wa Kyōto hodo furuku wa arimasen. Tōkyō wa Kyōto yori atarashii machi desu.

——Tōkyō to Kyōto to dochira ga shizuka desu ka?

Mochiron Kyōto no hō ga Tōkyō yori shizuka desu. Tōkyō no machi wa kuruma de ippai de, taihen sawagashii desu.

——Dewa, dochira ga kirei desu ka?

Kyōto desu. Machi ga amari ōkiku nakute, mawari ni yama ga arimasu. Sorede machi zentai ga ochitsuite-imasu.

3 ——Shō-gyō ya kō-gyō wa dochira ga sakan desu ka?

Mochiron dochira mo Tōkyō no hō ga sakan desu. Tōkyō wa Nippon no seiji, keizai no chūshin desu. Kaisha mo kōjō mo Tōkyō ni shūchū-shite-imasu. Kyōto wa dentō-sangyō to kankō no machi desu.

——Tōkyō to Kyōto to Ōsaka no naka de, doko ga ichiban ōkii desu ka?

Tōkyō ga ichiban ōkii desu. Jinkō mo Tōkyō ga ichiban ōi desu.

4 ——Tōkyō kara Ōsaka e wa nani de ikimasu ka?

Taitei Shinkan-sen de ikimasu. Shinkan-sen wa taihen hayai desu. Shinkan-sen no 'Hikari' wa Tōkyō kara Ōsaka made san-jikan jup-pun de hashirimasu. 'Kodama' wa yo-jikan jup-pun de hashirimasu. Tōkaidō-sen no ressha wa shichi-jikan ijō kakarimasu. 'Hikari' ga ichiban hayakute benri desu. Tōkyō to Ōsaka no aida niwa hikōki mo tonde-imasu. Hikōki wa go-jup-pun gurai shika kakarimasen. Hikōki no hō ga 'Hikari' yori san-bai ijō hayai desu. Shikashi, Tōkyō-toshin kara Haneda-kūkō made to Ōsaka-shinai kara Itami-kūkō made ga fu-ben desu. Desukara, ōku no hito ga hikōki yori mo Shinkan-sen no hō o yoku riyō-shite-imasu. Ryōkin wa hikōki no hō ga ni-bai gurai kakarimasu.

Lesson 12

Tokyo, Kyoto, and Osaka

1 Tokyo is the capital of Japan. Kyoto is an ancient capital of Japan. The name Tokyo means "Eastern Capital." Tokyo is much bigger than Kyoto. Its population is also much larger than Kyoto's.

2 ——Which is older, Tokyo or Kyoto?

Kyoto is older than Tokyo. Tokyo is not as old as Kyoto. Tokyo is a newer town than Kyoto.

——Which is quieter, Tokyo or Kyoto?

Kyoto is quieter than Tokyo, of course. Tokyo is filled with cars and is very noisy.

——Then which is prettier?

Kyoto. It is not a very big town and it is surrounded by mountains. Thus the entire town seems calm and settled.

3 ——Which has more business and industry?

Of course, Tokyo has more of both. Tokyo is the political and economic center of Japan. Companies and factories are also concentrated in Tokyo. Kyoto is a town of traditional industries and tourism.

——Which is the biggest, Tokyo, Kyoto, or Osaka?

Tokyo is the biggest. Tokyo has the most people too.

4 ——How do you get from Tokyo to Osaka?

You usually go by New Tokaido Line. The New Tokaido Line is very fast. The New Tokaido Line super-express *Hikari* runs from Tokyo to Osaka in three hours and ten minutes. The *Kodama* takes four hours and ten minutes. The old Tokaido Line takes over seven hours. The *Hikari* is the fastest and most convenient. There are also airplanes flying between Tokyo and Osaka. The airplane takes only about fifty minutes. The airplane is more than three times as fast as the *Hikari* express. But it is very inconvenient to go from downtown Tokyo to Haneda Airport or from central Osaka to Itami Airport. So most people use the New Tokaido Line rather than go by airplane. The airplane is about twice as expensive.

ANSWERS 〈pp. 148, 149〉

II. 1. takai 2. samui 3. wakai 4. atsui

IV. (A) 1. Q: ...no naka de doko ga ichiban ōkii desu ka? A: Chūgoku ga ichiban ōkii desu. 2. Q: ...no naka de dore ga ichiban takai desu ka? A: *Eberesuto* ga ichiban takai desu. 3. Q: ...no naka de dore/nani ga ichiban muzukashii desu ka? A: ...... 4. Q: ...no naka de dare ga ichiban se ga takai desu ka? A: ...... 5. Q: ...no naka de doko ga ichiban furui desu ka? A: *Rōma* ga ichiban furui desu. 6. Q: ...no naka de dore/nani ga ichiban hayai desu ka? A: Hikōki ga ichiban hayai desu. 7. Q: ...no naka de dore/nani ga ichiban kantan desu ka? A: ...... (B) 1. Q: ...no naka de nani ga ichiban oishii desu ka? 2. Q: ...no naka de nani ga ichiban tanoshikatta desu ka? 3. Q: ...no naka de nani ga ichiban omoshiroi desu ka? 4. Q: ...no naka de dare ga ichiban hima desu ka? 5. Q: ...no naka de doko ga ichiban kirei desu ka?

V. 1. Tōkyō-*tawā* (Tokyo Tower) desu. 2. Fuyu desu. 3. Nara ni arimasu.

●文法

§ 59 Comparing Two Things ('Comparative')

N_1 wa N_2 yori {A / Na} desu. 'N_1 is more...than N_2.'

e.g. Tōkyō wa Ōsaka yori ōkii desu. 'Tokyo is larger than Osaka.'

Question and Answer:

N_1 to N_2 to dochira ga {A / Na} desu ka? 'Which is more..., N_1 or N_2?'

N_1 no hō ga {A / Na} desu. 'N_1 is more....'

e.g. Chika-tetsu to *basu* to dochira ga benri desu ka?

'Which is more convenient, the subway or the bus?'

Chika-tetsu no hō ga benri desu. 'The subway is more convenient.'

§ 60 Comparing Three or More Things ('Superlative')

{N_1 to N_2 to N_3 to ... N_n / X} no {naka / uchi} de N_1 ga ichiban {A / Na} desu.

'N_1 is the most... {among N_1 N_2 N_3...N_n.' / in X.'}

(X: a set including N_1, N_2, N_3, ...N_n)

e.g. {A-san to B-san to C-san no naka de / Kono san-nin no naka de / Kono *kurasu* (no naka) de} dare ga ichiban wakai desu ka?

'Who is the youngest {Mr. A, Mr. B, or Mr. C?' / of these three?' / in this class?'}

A-san ga ichiban wakai desu. 'Mr. A is the youngest.'

§ 61 Scope or Limit: N de

e.g. Fuji-san wa Nippon de ichiban takai desu.

'Mt. Fuji is the highest mountain in Japan.'

Kono mikan wa ikura desu ka? 'How much are these tangerines?'

—Zenbu de hyaku-en desu. 'One hundred yen (for the whole lot).'

Ichi-nen-jū de ichiban samui tsuki wa itsu desu ka?

'Which is the coldest month of the year?'

§ 62 Some More Expressions of Comparison

onaji 'the same'

e.g. A-san to B-san to dochira ga se ga takai desu ka?

'Who is taller, Mr. A or Mr. B?'

—Onaji (gurai) desu. 'They are (about) the same.'

A wa B to onaji gurai se ga takai desu.

'A is about as tall as B.'

...hodo '(to) the extent'

e.g. A wa B hodo se ga takaku nai desu. 'A is not as tall as B.'

cf. B wa A yori se ga takai desu. 'B is taller than A.'

Kon-shū wa sen-shū hodo isogashiku arimasen.

'I am not as busy this week as I was last week.'

A-**bai** 'A times as...as...'

e.g. Ōsaka no jinkō to Kyōto no jinkō to dochira ga ōi desu ka?

'Which is larger, the population of Osaka or the population of Kyoto?'

—Ōsaka no jinkō no hō ga ōi desu. Ni-bai gurai desu.

'The population of Osaka is larger. It's about twice as large.'

Chikyū no chokkei wa tsuki (no chokkei) no yon-bai desu.

'The diameter of the earth is 4 times that of the moon.'

A-**bun no** B $\frac{B}{A}$

e.g. ni-bun no ichi '1/2'=han-bun 'half' yon-bun no san '3/4'

Tsuki wa chikyū no yon-bun no ichi (no ōki-sa) desu.

'The moon is one fourth (the size) of the earth.'

●練習

ANSWERS→p. 145

I. Make dialogs as shown in the example.

Ex. (Tōkyō) (Kyōto) (ōkii) Q: Tōkyō to Kyōto to dochira ga ōkii desu ka?
A: Tōkyō no hō ga ōkii desu.

1. (kono jisho) (ano jisho) (benri)
2. (Shinkan-sen) (hikōki) (hayai)
3. (sake) (*bīru*) (oishii)
4. (Nippon no jitensha) (*Oranda* no jitensha) (jōbu[1])
5. (Nippon no eiga) (gaikoku no eiga) (yoku mimasu)

II. Fill in the blanks with a suitable word from among those given below.

atsui, samui, ōkii, takai, wakai, ōi

Ex. Tōkyō no jinkō wa Kyōto no jinkō yori (ōi) desu.

1. *Eberesuto*[2] wa Fuji-san[3] yori ( ) desu.
2. Hokkaidō no fuyu wa Tōkyō no fuyu yori ( ) desu.
3. Haha wa chichi yori ( ) desu.
4. *Karukatta*[4] wa Ōsaka yori ( ) desu.

III. Make sentences as shown in the example.

Ex. (Tōkyō) (Kyōto) (furui) Tōkyō wa Kyōto hodo furuku nai desu.

1. (soroban[5]) (keisan-ki) (benri)
2. (kotoshi no fuyu) (kyo-nen no fuyu) (samui)
3. (Shugakuin-rikyū[6]) (Katsura-rikyū[7]) (yūmei)

語句

1 jōbu (Na) strong, stout, solid; healthy
2 *Eberesuto* 'Everest'
3 Fuji-san Mt. Fuji
-san mountain
4 *Karukatta* 'Calcutta'
5 soroban Japanese abacus
6 Shugakuin-rikyū Shugakuin Detached Palace (Kyoto)
7 Katsura-rikyū Katsura Detached Palace (Kyoto)
8 *Ōsutoraria* 'Australia'

IV. Make questions and answer them.

(A) Ex. (Tōkyō) (Ōsaka) (Nagoya) (ōkii)

Q: Tōkyō to Ōsaka to Nagoya no naka de doko ga ichiban ōkii desu ka?

A: Tōkyō ga ichiban ōkii desu.

1. (*Kanada*) (*Ōsutoraria*[8]) (Chūgoku) (ōkii)
2. (*Eberesuto*) (*Mattāhorun*[9]) (Fuji-san) (takai)
3. (*Furansu*-go) (*Roshia*-go[10]) (Nippon-go) (muzukashii)
4. (anata) (o-tō-san) (o-kā-san) (se ga takai[11])
5. (*Rōma*) (*Nyū Yōku*) (*Pari*) (furui)
6. (Shinkan-sen) (hikōki) (jidōsha) (hayai)
7. (*tenisu*) (*pinpon*[12]) (*bōringu*[13]) (kantan)

(B) Ex. (ichi-nen) (atsui)

Q: Ichi-nen no naka de itsu ga ichiban atsui desu ka?

A: Hachi-gatsu ga ichiban atsui desu.

1. (Nippon no tabemono) (oishii)
2. (gakusei-jidai[14] no omoide[15]) (tanoshikatta)
3. (*supōtsu*) (omoshiroi)
4. (anata-gata) (hima)
5. (Nippon no toshi[16]) (kirei)

V. Answer the following questions.

1. Tōkyō de ichiban takai tatemono wa nan desu ka?
2. Nippon de ichiban samui kisetsu[17] wa itsu desu ka?
3. Nippon de ichiban furui o-tera wa doko ni arimasu ka?

---

9 *Mattāhorun* 'Matterhorn'
10 *Roshia*-go Russian (language)
Roshia 'Russia'
11 se ga takai tall
12 *pinpon* 'ping-pong,' table tennis
13 *bōringu* 'bowling'
14 gakusei-jidai when one is/was a student
15 omoide memory, recollection
16 toshi city, urban
17 kisetsu season

●会話

RYOKAN WA ARIMASU KA?

Hoteru-annai-sho[1] wa doko desu ka?

—Sono kaidan[2] o nobotte-kudasai.

Hidari-te[3] ni arimasu.

Arigatō.

Sumimasen ga,

watashi wa *hoteru* o sagashite[4]-imasu.

Ii *hoteru* o shōkai-shite-kudasai.

—Kono atari niwa yō-shiki[5] no *hoteru* wa arimasen ga, Nippon no ryokan[6] wa arimasu. Ryokan demo ii desu ka?

Ryokan no hō ga ii desu.

Nippon no *mūdo*[7] ga aru to omoimasu.

—Jā, Asahi Ryokan ni shimasu ka?

Kono atari de mottomo[8] rippa-na[9] ryokan desu.

Takaku nai desu ka?

—Ē, kanari takai desu yo.

Ni-shoku-tsuki[10] de, ip-paku[11] roku-sen-en desu.

Where is the hotel information office?

—Go up those stairs. It's on the left-hand side.

Thanks.

Excuse me, I'm looking for a hotel.

Can you recommend a good hotel?

—There are no Western style hotels around here, but there are some Japanese inns. Is a Japanese inn all right?

A Japanese inn is even better.

I think it has a Japanese atmosphere.

—Well, how about the Asahi Inn? It's the finest inn around here.

Isn't it expensive?

—Well, it's rather expensive. It's 6,000 yen a night, including two meals.

語句

1 *hoteru*-annai-sho hotel information
 annai-sho information bureau
 annai (Nv) guide
 -sho＝-jo office
2 kaidan stairs
3 hidari-te the left-hand side cf. migi-te
4 sagas·u look for, search
5 yō-shiki Western style
 -shiki style
6 ryokan inn
7 *mūdo* 'mood,' atmosphere
8 mottomo the most
9 rippa (Na) excellent
10 -shoku-tsuki with... meals
 -tsuki including, at-

On top of that, there is a 10% tax and a 5% service charge.
A cheaper one would be better.
—It's a little far from here, but what about the Momiji Inn?
It's quieter and cheaper.
How long does it take to walk there?
—Let me see.... Over twenty minutes, I think.
Fine, I'll go there.
—I'll draw you a map.
Thanks. Sorry to have troubled you.
How much do I owe you?
—What? For the information? It's free.
Well, then, this is for you.
—No, thank you.
We don't accept tips in Japan.
Oh, is that so?
Thanks, really.

Soreni, zeikin[12] ga jup-*pāsento*,

Sābisu-ryō[13] ga go-*pāsento* desu.

Motto yasui hō ga ii desu ga....

—Koko kara sukoshi tōi desu ga,

Momiji Ryokan wa ikaga deshō?

Koko yori shizuka de, nedan[14] mo yasui desu yo.

Aruite nan-pun kakarimasu ka?

—Sō desu ne..., ni-jup-pun ijō kakaru to omoimasu.

Ii desu. Sono ryokan ni shimasu.

—Dewa, chizu[15] o kakimashō.

Arigatō.

Dōmo o-sewa[16] ni narimashita.

Ikura desu ka?

—Hā?[17] Tesū-ryō[18] desu ka?

Mu-ryō[19] desu.

Sorejā, kore wa *chippu*[20] desu.

—Iie, kekkō[21] desu.

Nippon niwa *chippu* no shūkan[22] wa arimasen.

Sō desu ka.

Hontō-ni arigatō.

12

tached with...
11 -paku =-haku...overnight stay
12 zeikin tax
13 *sābisu*-ryō service charge
-ryō=ryōkin fee
14 nedan price
15 chizu map
16 sewa (Nv) care
(o)-sewa ni nar·u receive kindness/care
17 Hā? What?
18 tesū-ryō commission
19 mu-ryō no charge, free
20 *chippu* 'tip'
21 kekkō desu (Cph: for either accepting or declining)
22 shūkan habit, custom

教　育

日本の　教育制度は[1]　6・3・3・4制[2]、　つまり[3]　小学校[4]6年、中学校[5]3年、　高等学校[6]　3年、　大学　4年です。　そして　最初の　9年間は　義務教育[7]です。　この　期間[8]の　就学率[9]は　100%に　近い[10]ですから、　日本では　文盲[11]の　人が　ほとんど　いません。　文盲率[12]は　約[13]0.7%　です。

高等学校への　進学率[14]は　87%ぐらいですが　年々　増加[15]の　傾向[16]に　あります。　その　率は　地方より　都会[17]の　ほうが　高いです。　高等学校の　卒業者[18]の　30%ぐらいが　大学へ　進学しますが、　入学試験[19]を　受け[20]なければなりません。

大学は　全国に　約890校[21]　あります。その　うち[22]　国公立[23]が　約180校で　あと[24]は　全部　私立[25]です。　大学の　数[26]は　アメリカが　いちばん　多いですが、　日本は　その　次ぐらいです。しかし　有名な　大学に　志願者[27]が　集中しますから、　その　入学試験の　競争率[28]は　たいへん　高いです。入学試験に　落ち[29]て、　多くの　学生が　一年か　二年　浪人生活[30]を　送り[31]ます。

大学は　ふつう[32]　4年ですが、　医学部[33]は　6年です。　大学の　上に　大学院[34]が　あります。　修士課程[35]が　2年、　博士課程[36]が　3年です。

Distribution of students

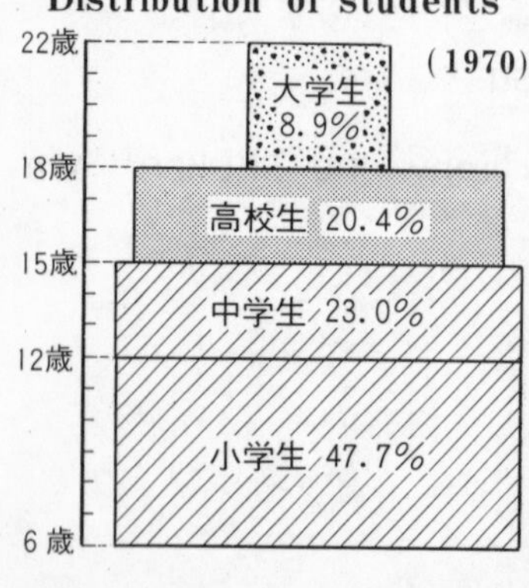

▲An entrance examination

Education

The educational system in Japan is a 6-3-3-4 system, that is, 6 years of elementary school, 3 of junior high school, 3 of senior high school, and 4 of college. The first nine years are compulsory. The percentage of school attendance during this period is almost 100%, and illiteracy is very low, about 0.7%.

About 87% of all junior high school graduates go on to senior high school, although this percentage is increasing every year and the figure is higher for urban areas than for rural areas. About 30% of the senior high school graduates go to college, but they have to take entrance examinations.

There are about 890 colleges and universities in Japan. About 180 of them are national or public, and the others are all private. The U. S. A. has more colleges and universities than any other country, but Japan is probably in second place. However, because everybody wants to go to the "name schools," there is keen competition in the entrance examinations. Many students, having failed in the examinations, stay out of school for one or two years rather than go to a second-choice college.

12

Most colleges and universities are for four years, but medical school is six. After a student finishes his undergraduate work, there is graduate school, which has a two-year master's course and a three-year doctorate course.

語句

1 kyōiku-seido educational system
kyōiku education
2 Roku-san-san-yon-sei 6-3-3-4 system
-sei=seido system
3 tsumari namely, in other words
4 shō-gakkō elementary school
5 chū-gakkō junior high school
6 kōtō-gakkō (senior) high school
7 gimu-kyōiku compulsory education
gimu duty, obligation
8 kikan period of time
9 shūgaku-ritsu school attendance rate
shūgaku (Nv) going to school
10 ...ni chika•i almost..., nearly
11 monmō (N) illiterate; illiteracy
12 monmō-ritsu illiteracy rate
13 rei-ten-nana 0.7
rei zero ten point
14 shingaku-ritsu percentage of students going on to higher education
shingaku (Nv) going on to a higher school
15 zōka (Nv) increase
16 keikō tendency
17 tokai urban area
18 sotsugyō-sha graduate (person)
sotsugyō (Nv) graduation
-sha person, -er
19 nyūgaku-shiken=nyū-shi entrance examination nyūgaku (Nv) entering school
20 uke•ru take, receive
shiken o uke•ru sit for/take an exam
21 -kō =gakkō school
22 sono uchi among them
23 kok-kō-ritsu national and public
←koku-ritsu (state-supported),
kō-ritsu (public-supported)
24 ato the rest
25 shi-ritsu private (school, institute)
26 kazu number
27 shigan-sha applicant
shigan (Nv) apply, volunteer
28 kyōsō-ritsu competition ratio
kyōsō (Nv) competition
29 ochi•ru (Vi) drop, fall; fail (in the exam)
30 rōnin-seikatsu life away from school
rōnin masterless *samurai*; unsuccessful examinee who stays out of school to study for the next year's exam
seikatsu (Nv) life, daily life
31 okur•u spend (time); send
32 futsū (N) usually, ordinary
33 igaku-bu medical science department
i-gaku medical science
-bu department
-gaku-bu department (university)
34 daigaku-in graduate school
35 shūshi-katei master's course
shūshi master of arts/science
katei course
36 hakushi-katei doctorate course
hakushi=hakase doctorate, Ph.D

第 13 課

日本語の 勉強

TAPE
No. 4
Side 1

❶ わたしは 三か月 前から 日本語の 勉強を しています。それで、いつも いい 辞書が ほしい[1]と 思っています。英和辞典[2]だけで なく[3]、和英辞典[4]も ほしいです。しかし、外国人用[5]の いい 辞書が なかなか[6] 見つからなくて[7]、困っています。

❷ わたしの 教科書の 索引[8]には、単語[9]が 千三百[10]しか ありませんから、とても 不便です。あと 二千語[11]か 三千語[12]あった ほうが いいです。わたしの 友だちも いい 辞書を ほしがって[13]います。みんなが「正しい[14] 日本語を 書きたい。[15]」「美しい 日本語を 話したい。」と 言っています。

❸ 先週 わたしたちは、教室で 日本の 歌の テープ[16]を 聞きました。「さくら さくら」[17]「赤とんぼ」[18]などでした。わたしは 前から 日本の 歌が 好き[19]でしたが、日本語の 勉強を 始めてから、日本語で 歌いたいと 思いはじめま[20]

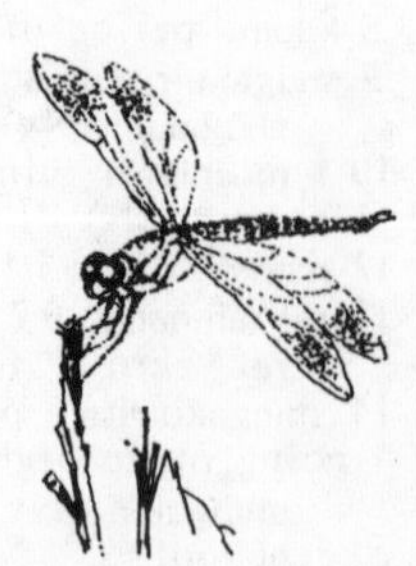

語句

1 hoshi·i (A) desirable, want See §63
2 Ei-Wa-jiten English-Japanese dictionary
   jiten =jisho dictionary
3 ...dake de naku not only...but
4 Wa-Ei-jiten Japanese-English dictionary
5 gaikoku-jin-yō for foreigners
   gaikoku-jin foreigner
   -yō for
6 nakanaka (not) easily, very; considerably
7 mitsukar·u (Vi) be found
8 sakuin index
9 tango word
10 -byaku =-hyaku, -pyaku hundred

した。 みんなは 何度も[21] 「赤とんぼ」を 聞きたがりました。 あんな[22] 美しい メロディー[23]が きらい[24]な 人は いないと わたしは 思います。

赤とんぼ

三木露風作詞
山田耕筰作曲

---

11 -go (Count. for words)
12 -zen =-sen thousand
13 -gar・u show signs of... See § 63
14 tadashi・i correct, right
15 -ta・i want to See § 63
16 *tēpu* 'tape'
17 Sakura Sakura (title of a song)
18 Aka-tonbo (title of a song)
  tonbo dragonfly
19 suki (Na) like, favorite See § 64
20 -hajime・ru begin to...
21 nan-do mo many times
22 anna like that See § 8
23 *merodī* 'melody'
24 kirai (Na) dislike

Dai 13-ka
Nippon-go no Benkyō

1 Watashi wa san-ka-getsu mae kara Nippon-go no benkyō o shite-imasu. Sorede, itsumo ii jisho ga hoshii to omotte-imasu. Ei-Wa-jiten dake de naku, Wa-Ei-jiten mo hoshii desu. Shikashi, gaikoku-jin-yō no ii jisho ga nakanaka mitsukaranakute, komatte-imasu.

2 Watashi no kyōka-sho no sakuin niwa, tango ga sen-san-byaku shika arimasen kara, totemo fu-ben desu. Ato ni-sen-go ka san-zen-go atta hō ga ii desu. Watashi no tomodachi mo ii jisho o hoshi-gatte-imasu. Minna ga "Tadashii Nippon-go o kakitai." "Utsukushii Nippon-go o hanashitai." to itte-imasu.

3 Sen-shū watashi-tachi wa, kyōshitsu de Nippon no uta no *tēpu* o kiki-mashita. 'Sakura Sakura,' 'Aka-tonbo' nado deshita. Watashi wa mae kara Nippon no uta ga suki deshita ga, Nippon-go no benkyō o hajimete kara, Nippon-go de utaitai to omoi-hajimemashita. Minna wa nan-do mo 'Aka-tonbo' o kikita-garimashita. Anna utsukushii *merodī* ga kirai-na hito wa inai to watashi wa omoimasu.

Lesson 13

Studying Japanese

1 I have been studying Japanese for the last three months. So I have always wished I had a good dictionary. I want not only an English-Japanese dictionary but also a Japanese-English dictionary. But I am having trouble because it is hard to find a good dictionary for foreigners.

2 Since there are only 1,300 words in the index in my textbook, it is very inconvenient. It would be nice if there were 2,000 or 3,000 words more. My friends also want good dictionaries. They all say, "I want to write correct Japanese," and "I want to speak good Japanese."

3 Last week we heard a tape of Japanese songs in the classroom. There were *Sakura Sakura*, *Akatonbo*, and others. I have liked Japanese songs for a long time, but since I have started studying Japanese I have begun to want to sing them in Japanese. Everyone wanted to hear *Akatonbo* over and over. I do not think there is anyone who does not like that beautiful melody.

13

ANSWERS 〈pp. 160, 161〉

I. (D) 1. Q: Anata no suki-na sak-ka wa dare desu ka? 2. Q: Anata no suki-na iro wa nan desu ka? 3. Q: Anata no suki-na Nippon no machi wa doko desu ka? 4. Q: Anata no kirai-na kisetsu wa itsu desu ka? 5. Q: Anata no kirai-na *terebi* no bangumi wa nan desu ka?
II. (A) 1. Kono hon ga/o karitai desu. 2. Kōcha ga/o nomitai desu. 3. Nippon no koto ga/o motto shiritai desu. 4. Mai-nichi Nippon-go ga/o benkyō-shitai desu. 5. Fuji-san ni noboritai desu.
(B) 1. Hikōki ni noritaku nai desu. 2. Tōkyō ni sumitaku nai desu. 3. Ima dare nimo aitaku nai desu.
(C) 1. Benri-na jisho ga hoshii desu. 2. Atsui *kōhī* ga hoshii desu. 3. Nagai kyūka ga hoshii desu.
III. Ex. 1 Nodo ga kawakimashita kara, (*jūsu* ga hoshii desu.) 2. Onaka ga sukimashita kara, (sushi ga tabetai desu.) 3. Atama ga itai desu kara, (dare nimo aitaku nai desu.) 4. Nippon-go o benkyō-shite-imasu kara, (ii jisho ga hoshii desu.) 5. Ii tenki desu kara, (*haikingu* ni ikitai desu.) 6. Tsukaremashita kara, (yasumitai desu.) 7. Kinō tetsuya o shimashita kara, (kyō ichi-nichi netai desu.)

●文法

§ 63 Expressions of Desire or Hope

N_1 **wa**	N_2 **ga hoshii desu.**	'N_1 wants N_2.'
	(N_2 **ga/o**) **V-tai desu.**	'N_1 wants to do...(N_2).'

e.g. Watashi wa *kamera* ga hoshii desu. 'I want a camera.'

Watashi wa *kamera* ga kai-tai desu. 'I want to buy a camera.'

NB: Hoshii is an A. '-tai' (want to) is attached to the Conj. form of V, and the V is then used as an A.

e.g. Anata wa *kamera* ga hoshii/kai-tai desu ka?

'Do you want (to buy) a camera?'

—Iie, hoshiku nai/kai-taku nai desu. 'No, I don't want (to buy) one.'

Watashi wa sono *kamera* ga hoshikatta desu ga, o-kane ga arimasen deshita. 'I wanted that camera, but I did not have any money.'

Iki-taku nakatta desu ga, ikimashita.

'I didn't want to go, but I went.'

NB: These Predicates, like many other Adjectives expressing emotion or feeling, are basically to express the feelings of the speaker (and those of a second person in a question). When you want to use them for a third person, some modifications are necessary, such as the following. It is not enough to simply substitute Topics.

e.g. Watashi wa *kamera* ga hoshii desu.

×Tarō wa *kamera* ga hoshii desu.

Tarō wa *kamera* ga hoshii to itte-imasu.

'Taro says he wants a camera.'

Tarō wa *kamera* o hoshi-gatte-imasu. (Literally, 'Taro is showing signs of wanting a camera.')

Tarō wa *kamera* ga hoshii no desu.

The 'Adjectives of emotion' include: ureshii 'glad, happy'; kanashii 'sad'; kowai 'afraid'; sabishii 'lonely.'

NB: The object of V-tai (N_2) may be indicated with either o or ga.

§ 64 Expressions of Like or Dislike

N_1 **wa** N_2 **ga** { **suki** / **kirai** } **desu.** 'N_1 { likes / dislikes } N_2.'

NB: Both suki and kirai are Na. When they are used as prenominal modifiers they take the '-na' form.

e.g. suki-na tabemono 'food that one likes' 'one's favorite food'

To express 'like/dislike...very much,' the prefix **dai-** is attached.

e.g. Anata wa *kōhī* ga suki desu ka? 'Do you like coffee?'

—Hai, dai-suki desu. 'Yes, I like it very much.'

Anata no kirai-na tabemono wa nan desu ka?

'What food don't you like?'

—Sashimi desu. '*Sashimi*.'

NB: 'N_2 ga' in the above pattern changes to 'N_2 wa' in negative answers, and also when N_2 is contrasted with some other thing.

e.g. Anata wa kōcha ga suki desu ka? 'Do you like (black) tea?'

—Iie, kōcha wa suki dewa arimasen. 'No, I don't like tea.'

Watashi wa *bīru* wa suki desu ga, o-sake wa suki dewa arimasen.

'I like beer, but I don't like *sake*.'

In all the 'N_1 wa N_2 ga....' constructions, the substitution of 'N_2 wa' for 'N_2 ga' has the same effect.

e.g. Anata wa *kamera* ga hoshii desu ka? 'Do yo want a camera?'

—Iie, *kamera* wa hoshiku nai desu. 'No, I don't want a camera.'

Watashi wa *tēpu-rekōdā* wa hoshii desu ga, *kamera* wa hoshiku nai desu.

'I want a tape recorder, but I don't want a camera.'

§ 65 Expressions of Intimacy in the Sentence-final Forms

In conversations between intimate friends, a variety of Sentence-final forms (mostly Sentence-final Particles) are used. Most commonly used are:

... **no?** (Question, mostly by women); ... **wa.** (Confirmation, by women only); and ... **kai?**/... **dai?** (Question, by men only)

●練習

ANSWERS→p. 157

I. Make dialogs as shown in the examples.

(A) Ex. (Nihon-ryōri[1]) Q: Anata wa Nihon-ryōri ga suki desu ka?

A: Iie, suki dewa arimasen. Kirai desu.

1. (*bōringu*) 2. (*uisukī*[2]) 3. (neko) 4. (*gurūpu*-ryokō[3])

(B) Ex. Q: (*supōtsu*) Anata wa *supōtsu* no naka de nani ga ichiban suki desu ka?

A: (*tenisu*) *Tenisu* ga ichiban suki desu.

1. Q: (*Furansu* no shōsetsu-ka[4]) A: (*Roman Roran*[5])
2. Q: (*Yōroppa* no toshi) A: (*Junēbu*[6])
3. Q: (Nippon no shiki[7]) A: (aki)

(C) Ex. Q: (tabemono) Anata wa donna tabemono ga suki desu ka?

A: (*sarada*[8]) *Sarada* ga suki desu.

1. Q: (nomimono) A: (*tomato-jūsu*[9])
2. Q: (ongaku) A: (*jazu*)
3. Q: (josei[10]) A: (kawairashii josei)

(D) Ex. Q: (suki) (shōsetsu) Anata no suki-na shōsetsu wa nan desu ka?

A: (*S.F.*[11] shōsetsu) *S.F.* shōsetsu desu.

1. Q: (suki) (sak-ka[12]) A: (Matsumoto Seichō[13])
2. Q: (suki) (iro[14]) A: (ao to midori)
3. Q: (suki) (Nippon no machi) A: (Kurashiki[15])
4. Q: (kirai) (kisetsu) A: (fuyu)
5. Q: (kirai) (*terebi* no bangumi[16]) A: (manga[17] no bangumi)

語句

1 Nihon-ryōri Japanese cooking
2 *uisukī* 'whisky'
3 *gurūpu*-ryokō 'group' travel
4 shōsetsu-ka novelist
5 *Roman Roran* 'Romain Rolland'
6 *Junēbu* 'Geneva'
7 shiki four seasons
 -ki season (←kisetsu)
8 *sarada* 'salad'
9 *tomato-jūsu* 'tomato juice'
10 josei female, woman
 cf. dansei (male)
11 *S.F.* 'science fiction'
12 sak-ka writer
13 Matsumoto Seichō (a contemporary writer; 1909-)

II. Change the sentences as shown in the examples.

(A) Ex. (Kyō no shinbun o yomimasu.) Kyō no shinbun ga/o yomitai desu.

1. (Kono hon o karimasu.)
2. (Kōcha o nomimasu.)
3. (Nippon no koto o motto shirimasu.)
4. (Mai-nichi Nippon-go o benkyō-shimasu.)
5. (Fuji-san ni noborimasu.)

(B) Ex. (Kyō wa doko e mo ikimasen.) Kyō wa doko e mo ikitaku nai desu.

1. (Hikōki ni norimasen.)
2. (Tōkyō ni sumimasu.)
3. (Ima dare nimo aimasen.)

(C) Ex. (Kono mizu wa tsumetai desu.) Tsumetai mizu ga hoshii desu.

1. (Kono jisho wa benri desu.)
2. (Kono *kōhī* wa atsui desu.)
3. (Kondo no kyūka[18] wa nagai desu.)

III. Complete the following sentences.

1. Nodo[19] ga kawakimashita[20] kara,
2. Onaka[21] ga sukimashita[22] kara,
3. Atama ga itai[23] desu kara,
4. Nippon-go o benkyō-shite-imasu kara,
5. Ii tenki desu kara,
6. Tsukaremashita kara,
7. Kinō tetsuya[24] o shimashita kara,

---

14 iro color
15 Kurashiki (a place name)
16 bangumi program (radio or TV)
17 manga cartoon
18 kyūka=yasumi vacation
19 nodo throat
20 kawak·u get dry
nodo ga kawak·u get thirsty
21 onaka stomach, belly
22 suk·u become empty/vacant
onaka ga suk·u get hungry
23 ita·i hurt, painful
atama ga ita·i have a headache
24 tetsuya (Nv) sitting/staying up all night

13

●会話

DŌ SHIMAHSITA?

—Kao-iro[1] ga warui[2] desu ne.

Dō shimashita?

Ni-san-nichi mae kara

atama ga itai desu.

Soreni, sukoshi netsu ga arimasu.

—Sore wa ikemasen[3] ne.

Tabun[4] kaze[5] deshō.

Isha e ikitai to omoimasu ga,

ii o-isha-san o oshiete-kudasai.

—Watashi no kakari-tsuke[6] no

o-isha-san o shōkai-shimashō.

Arigatō.

Kyō no gogo sassoku[7] ittemo ii desu ka?

—Ii desu yo. Soretomo,

ima kara issho-ni ikimasen ka?

Soredewa o-negai-shimasu.[8]

—Watashi mo sukoshi atama ga itakute,

soreni netsu mo arimasu.

Issho-ni ikimashō.

—You don't look very well.
What's the matter?
I've had a headache for the last 2 or 3 days.
Moreover, I've got a slight fever.
—That will never do.
It's probably a cold.
I think I ought to go see a doctor. Could you recommend a good one?
—I'll give you the name of the doctor I always go to.
Thanks.
Would it be all right to go right away this afternoon?
—Of course. Or, why don't we go together right now?
If that's all right with you, please, let's go.
—I've got a bit of a headache and a slight fever myself.
Let's go together, then.

語句

1 kao-iro facial color, complexion kao face
2 waru·i bad
3 ikenai not good
4 tabun probably
5 kaze a cold
6 kakari-tsuke a doctor one always consults
kakari ←kakar·u (see a doctor)
-tsuke ←tsuke·ru (habitually do...)
7 sassoku right now, without delay
8 O-negai-shimasu (Cph: used when asking a favor)
9 daru·i dull, lethargic

—Please sit down.
What's the matter with you?
I've got a bad headache and feel run down.
—That's too bad.
Open your mouth, please.
Hmmm...
Please take off your shirt.
....
It's a cold.
It's all right. No need to worry.
I'll give you a shot, but are you allergic to anything?
No, it's all right.
But I'm not very fond of shots....

—Take two of these tablets after every meal and before you go to bed.
I see.
Thank you very much.
—Take care of yourself.

—Dōzo koko ni suwatte-kudasai.

Dō shimashita?

Totemo atama ga itakute karada ga darui[9] desu.

—Sore wa ikemasen nē.

Chotto kuchi[10] o akete-kudasai.

Hahān[11]....

Shatsu[12] o nuide-kudasai.

....

Kaze desu.

Daijōbu desu. Shinpai[13] irimasen.[14]

Chūsha[15] o shimasu ga,

arerugi[16] wa arimasen ka?

Hai, daijōbu desu.

Demo,[17] chūsha wa amari suki dewa nai desu....

—Kono kusuri[18] o, shokuji no ato to neru mae ni, ni-jō[19]-zutsu nonde[20]-kudasai.

Hai, wakarimashita.

Dōmo arigatō gazaimashita.

—O-daiji-ni.[21]

13

---

karada ga daru·i feel run down
10 kuchi mouth
11 Hahān Hm..., I see
12 *shatsu* 'shirt'
13 shinpai (Nv) worry
14 ir·u need, be necessary
15 chūsha (Nv) injection
16 *arerugī* 'allergy'
17 demo although, but
18 kusuri medicine
19 -jō (Count. for tablets)
20 nom·u take (medicine); drink
21 O-daiji-ni (Cph) Take good care (of yourself) (to a sick person).

手紙

みんな　ときどき　友だちに　会って　話が　したいです。　友だちが　遠くに　いる　ときも　ようすが　知り[1]たいです。　だから　そんな[2]　ときは　手紙[3]を　書きます。

たいていの　手紙は　前文[4]、　本文[5]、　結び[6]の　部分[7]から　できています[8]。前文は　「拝啓[9]」、「お手紙　ありがとうございました。」などの　あいさつで　始めます。　次[10]に　季節の　あいさつを　述べます[11]。「もう　春です。」とか「きびしい[12]　寒さ[13]の　おり[14]……」とか　書きます。　それから　相手[15]の　ようすを　聞いたり、　自分[16]の　ようすを　書いたりします。　前文を　省き[17]たい　ときは、「前略[18]」と　書いて、　すぐ　本文に　はいります。

本文は　自然[19]な　ことばで　書いた　ほうが　いいです。　ていねい[20]な　口語体[21]を　よく　使います。

結びには　「おからだを　たいせつに[22]」などの　別れ[23]の　あいさつや　「皆さま[24]に　よろしく[25]」などの　ことづて[26]の　あいさつを　書きます。　その　あとに「さようなら」、「では　また[27]」　などの　結びの　ことばを　書いて　手紙を　終わります。　そして　日付[28]、　自分の　名まえ、　相手の　名まえを　書きます。

若い　人は　こんな　形式[29]に　あまり　従い[30]たがりません。　簡単な　用事[31]の　ときは　手紙よりも　はがきを　よく　書きます。お正月に　たくさん　年賀状[32]を　出し[33]ますが、　これも　はがきです。　夏の　暑い　間には　暑中見舞い[34]の　はがきを　書きます。

Letters

Everyone wants to see and talk with friends once in a while. When our friends live far away, we want to ask them how they are. Thus we write letters.

Most letters include a salutation, body, and closing remarks. The salutation begins with "Haikei." After this comes "Thank you for your letter" and the compliments of the season such as "Already it is spring" or "During this severe cold...." Then we inquire about the addressee's health and tell about ours. When we want to omit the salutation, we write "Zenryaku" and start with the body.

The body is best written in natural language, and polite colloquial is often used in letters.

In closing we write "Please take care" and "Please give my best to everybody," and then "Good-bye." Then we write the date, our name, and the addressee's name.

Young people do not want to follow this format as strictly. When there is not much to say, we use postcards rather than letters. Postcards are also used for New Year's Cards and Summer's Greetings.

語句

1 yōsu manner, condition, state of things
2 dakara =desukara therefore, so
3 sonna such, like that See § 8
4 zenbun preface
5 honbùn main text, body
6 musubi closing ←musub·u (conclude; tie)
7 bubun part
8 ...kara dekite-iru consist of...
9 Haikei Dear... (letter)
10 tsugi ni next
11 nobe·ru state, mention, note
12 kibishi·i severe, harsh, rigid
13 samu-sa (N) cold ←samu·i
14 ori occasion
15 aite the other side (when two persons or groups are involved); partner; opponent
16 jibun oneself
17 habuk·u omit
18 Zen-ryaku Omitting the greeting (letter)
19 shizen (N/Na) nature, natural
20 teinei (Na) polite; detailed
21 kōgo-tai colloquial style
kōgo colloquial speech
cf. bungo (literary speech)
-tai style
22 taisetsu (Na) =daiji important
23 wakare parting ←wakare·ru (part with, separate from)
24 mina-sama everybody (Polite)
25 ...ni yoroshiku give best regards to...
26 kotozute message
27 Dewa mata Will write again
28 hi-zuke date
29 keishiki form, fomality
30 shitaga·u follow, obey
31 yōji errand, business
32 Nenga-jō New Year's Card
nenga New Year's Day greetings
-jō letter
33 das·u put out; send (letter)
34 Shochū-mimai Summer's Greetings
shochū during the hot season
mimai inquiring after (a sick person) ←mima·u (inquire after)

第 14 課

姉と 音楽

TAPE
No. 4
Side 1

❶ わたしの 姉(あね)は 音楽大学(おんがくだいがく)[1]の 一年生(いちねんせい)[2]で、ことしの 春(はる) 大学(だいがく)に 入学(にゅうがく)した ときから イタリア語(ご)[3]を 勉強(べんきょう)しています。それで、今(いま)では イタリア語(ご)が 少(すこ)し わかります。イタリア語(ご)で「サンタ・ルチア」[4]や「帰(かえ)れ ソレントへ」[5]を 歌(うた)う ことが[6] できます。姉(あね)の 専門(せんもん)は ピアノですが、最近(さいきん)[7]は 声楽(せいがく)[8]も 好(す)きだと 言(い)っています。ピアノは 小学生(しょうがくせい)の ときから 習(なら)いはじめたので、たいへん じょうずです。

❷ わたしの 家(いえ)では 父(ちち)も 母(はは)も 歌(うた)を 歌(うた)う ことが 好(す)きですが、二人(ふたり)とも あまり じょうずではありません。楽器(がっき)も 二人(ふたり) そろって[9] へた[10]です。わたしも ハーモニカと アコーディオン[11]だけは できますが、その ほか[12]の 楽器(がっき)は みな にがて[13]です。第一(だいいち)[14]、楽譜(がくふ)[15]を 見(み)て 歌(うた)う ことが できません。近(ちか)ごろ[16]の 小学生(しょうがくせい)は ほとんど みな 楽譜(がくふ)だけで 歌(うた)う ことが できますから、外国(がいこく)の 人(ひと)は よく「日本(にっぽん)の 音楽教(おんがくきょう)

語句

1 ongaku-daigaku music college
2 -nen-sei ...-th grader of school
3 *Itaria*-go Italian (language)
4 *Santa Ruchia* 'Santa Lucia'
5 Kaere *Sorento* e (title of an Italian song)
  Kaere (Imperative form of kaer·u)
  Sorento 'Surriento'
6 deki·ru be possible/able See § 66
  ...koto ga deki·ru can...
7 saikin (N/Adv) recently, of late
8 seigaku vocal music
9 sorotte all together ←soro·u (all the members being present)
10 heta (Na) unskillful
11 *akōdion* 'accordion'
12 hoka (N) the others/rest
  sono hoka other than that
13 nigate (Na) weak point
14 dai-ichi (the) first; primarily, before anything else
15 gakufu sheet music, score
16 chika-goro (N/Adv) recent, these days
17 ongaku-kyōiku musical education
18 reigai exception
19 shōtai (Nv) invitation

育[17]は　すばらしいです。」と　言います。　わたしは　たぶん　例外[18]だと　思います。

❸　姉は　よく　パーティーから　招待[19]を　受けます。　知り合い[20]から　よく　電話が　かかってきます[21]。「道子[22]さんの　歌と　ピアノを　パーティーで　聞きたい。」という　注文や、「土曜の　晩に　市民会館[23]へ　来ることが　できますか。」という　問い合わせ[24]です。　姉は　ピアノ演奏[25]も　歌も　好きですから、たいてい　引き受け[26]ますが、　近ごろは、「わたしは　時間[27]が　なくて　勉強できない。」と　言いはじめました。　しかし、わたしは　うらやましくて[28]　しかたが　ありません。　なぜなら[29]、姉は　好きな　ことに　時間を　使って　いそがしがっているからです。

❹　わたしの　ほう[30]は　大学の　入学試験の　準備[31]で、一つも[32]　好きな　スポーツが　できません。　毎日毎日　きらいな　数学[33]や　英語の　勉強を　しなければなりません。　大学では、のびのびと[34]　好きな　研究[35]が　できる　ことが　いちばん　すばらしいと　思いながら、　いやな[36]　勉強を　続け[37]ています。

---

20 shiriai　acquaintance
　←shiria·u (become acquainted with)
21 denwa ga kakar·u =denwa ga ar·u get a phone call　cf. denwa o kake·ru/suru (make a phone call)
22 Michiko (a given name (f))
23 shimin-kaikan　citizens' hall
　shimin　citizen (of a city/town)
　kai-kan　assembly hall
24 toi-awase　inquiry for information
25 *piano*-ensō　piano recital
　ensō (Nv) musical performance
26 hiki-uke·ru　accept (an offer of work)
27 jikan　time
28 urayamashi·i　envious; enviable
29 naze nara　because
　naze　why　…nara　if
30 …no hō　…side, direction
31 junbi (Nv) preparation
32 hito-tsu mo…nai　not a single…, not at all
33 sūgaku　mathematics
34 nobi-nobi to　in an relaxed manner
35 kenkyū (Nv) research, study
36 iya (Na) unfavorable, distasteful, nasty
37 tsuzuke·ru (Vt) continue

Dai 14-ka
Ane to Ongaku

1 Watashi no ane wa ongaku-daigaku no ichi-nen-sei de, kotoshi no haru daigaku ni nyūgaku-shita toki kara *Itaria*-go o benkyō-shite-imasu. Sorede, ima dewa *Itaria*-go ga sukoshi wakarimasu. *Itaria*-go de '*Santa Ruchia*' ya 'Kaere *Sorento* e' o utau koto ga dekimasu. Ane no senmon wa *piano* desu ga, saikin wa seigaku mo suki da to itte-imasu. *Piano* wa shōgaku-sei no toki kara narai-hajimeta node, taihen jōzu desu.

2 Watashi no ie dewa chichi mo haha mo uta o utau koto ga suki desu ga, futa-ri tomo amari jōzu dewa arimasen. Gakki mo futa-ri sorotte heta desu. Watashi mo *hāmonika* to *akōdion* dake wa dekimasu ga, sono hoka no gakki wa mina nigate desu. Dai-ichi, gakufu o mite utau koto ga dekimasen. Chika-goro no shōgaku-sei wa hotondo mina gakufu dake de utau koto ga dekimasu kara, gaikoku no hito wa yoku "Nippon no ongaku-kyōiku wa subarashii desu." to iimasu. Watashi wa tabun reigai da to omoimasu.

3 Ane wa yoku *pātī* kara shōtai o ukemasu. Shiriai kara yoku denwa ga kakatte-kimasu. "Michiko-san no uta to *piano* o *pātī* de kikitai." to iu chūmon ya, "Do-yō no ban ni shimin-kaikan e kuru koto ga dekimasu ka?" to iu toi-awase desu. Ane wa *piano*-ensō mo uta mo suki desu kara taitei hiki-ukemasu ga, chika-goro wa, "Watashi wa jikan ga nakute ben-kyō dekinai." to ii-hajimemashita. Shikashi, watashi wa urayamashikute shikata ga arimasen. Naze nara, ane wa suki-na koto ni jikan o tsukatte isogashi-gatte-iru kara desu.

4 Watashi no hō wa daigaku no nyūgaku-shiken no junbi de, hito-tsu mo suki-na *supōtsu* ga dekimasen. Mai-nichi-mai-nichi kirai-na sūgaku ya Ei-go no benkyō o shinakereba narimasen. Daigaku dewa, nobi-nobi to suki-na kenkyū ga dekiru koto ga ichiban subarashii to omoinagara, iya-na ben-kyō o tsuzukete-imasu.

Lesson 14

My Sister and Music

1 My elder sister is a freshman at a college of music, and since she entered the college this spring she has been studying Italian. So now she understands a little Italian. She can sing *Santa Lucia* and *Torna a Surriento* in Italian. Although her major is piano, she has recently said she likes vocal music as well. Since she has been taking piano lessons since she was in primary school, she is very good.
2 At my house, both my father and mother like to sing too, but they are not very good singers. And they are both poor musicians too. I can play only the harmonica and the accordion, but I am no good at any other instruments. In the first place, I can not read sheet music for singing. Nowadays, almost all grade school children can sing with just the sheet music, so foreigners say that Japanese musical education is very good. I think maybe I am an exception.
3 My sister gets invited to a lot of parties. She gets a lot of phone calls from people she knows. They say, "Michiko, please play the piano and sing for us at the party," or ask her "Can you come to the civic auditorium on Saturday evening?" Since she likes to play the piano and to sing, she usually says she can, but lately she has begun to complain of not having enough time to study. Still, I envy her no end. She is busy using her time with something that she enjoys doing.
4 I am busy getting ready for my college entrance exams and can not play any of my favorite sports. Every day I have to study hateful math and English. But I continue this distasteful studying, thinking how wonderful it would be to be able to do research you like leisurely at the university.

14

ANSWERS 〈pp. 172, 173〉

I. (A) 1. Q: Anata wa jidōsha no unten ga dekimasu ka? 2. Q: Anata wa *Furansu*-go ga dekimasu ka? 3. Q: Anata wa *gorufu* ga dekimasu ka? 4. Q: Anata wa ryōri ga dekimasu ka? 5. Q: Anata wa koto ga dekimasu ka? (B) 1. Q: Anata wa jidōsha no unten ga jōzu desu ka? 2. Q: Anata wa *Furansu*-go ga jōzu desu ka? 3. Q: Anata wa *gorufu* ga jōzu desu ka? 4. Q: Anata wa ryōri ga jōzu desu ka? 5. Q: Anata wa koto ga jōzu desu ka?
IV. 1. Kare wa Nippon-go no kaiwa ga jōzu desu. 2. Kanojo wa *Itaria*-go o taihen jōzu-ni hanasu koto ga dekimasu. 3. Watashi wa mada Nippon/Nippon-go no shinbun o yomu koto ga dekimasen. 4. "Anata wa kare no kōen ga wakarimashita ka?" "Iie, zenzen wakarimasen deshita." 5. "Ashita/Asu watashi-tachi wa watashi no ie de *pāti* o shimasu. Kimasen ka?" "Zannen desu ga, watashi wa odoru koto ga dekimasen." "Odoru koto ga dekinakutemo ii desu. Hanashi o shi ni kite-kudasai." 6. "Kondo no Nichi-yōbi watashi wa tomodachi to (issho-ni) *saikuringu* ni ikimasu." "Watashi mo ikitai desu. Otōto wa itsumo *saikuringu* ni ikitai to itte-imasu. Kare o tsurete-ittemo ii desu ka?" "Mochiron. Dare demo watashi-tachi to issho-ni iku koto ga dekimasu. Shikashi, (anata no) otōto-san wa nagai jikan jitensha ni noru koto ga dekimasu ka? Watashi-tachi wa asa kara ban made (jitensha ni) noranakereba narimasen."

●文法

§ 66 Ability

N_1 **wa** N_2 **ga**	**dekimasu.**	'N$_1$	can do N_2	
	jōzu desu.		is good at	
	heta desu.		is poor at	
	tokui desu.		is good at (and likes)	N$_2$.'
	nigate desu.		is poor at (and dislikes)	
	wakarimasu.		(can) understand	

e.g. Anata wa *tenisu* ga dekimasu ka? 'Can you play tennis?'

—Hai, dekimasu. 'Yes, I can.'

Watashi wa *tenisu* ga tokui desu. 'Tennis is my favorite sport.'
(or, *Tenisu* wa tokui desu.)

—Iie, dekimasen. 'No, I can't.'

Watashi wa *tenisu* ga nigate desu. 'I seldom play tennis, and when
(or, *Tenisu* wa nigate desu.) I do, I am awful.'

Yamada-san wa *Tai*-go ga dekimasu ka? 'Can Yamada speak Thai?'

—Hai, kare wa *Tai*-go ga taihen jōzu desu. 'Yes, he speaks Thai very well.'

NB: (1) Dekimasu (<deki·ru 'be possible') is conjugated just like any other V, but it belongs to a special class of V which have many other features in common with A or Na. This class of V includes: ar-u 'exist, there is'; i-ru 'there is (for people), stay'; ir-u 'need, necessary'; etc. These verbs are called 'Stative Verbs.' Since they express states, they have no '-te-iru form' (See § 37), and all of them except i-ru ('stay') lack the imperative form.

(2) Jōzu and heta are 'Na adjectives'; tokui and nigate are used either as N or Na.

Tai-go ga jōzu-na hito 'a person (who is) good at Thai'

Tokui no/na *supōtsu* '(one's) favorite sport'

§ 67 Nominalizing a Verb: the Use of koto

When it is necessary to use a V in a position that is reserved for an N, the V must be given an N-like quality. The commonest way is to use the Pseudo Noun koto after the V.

e.g. Eiga wa omoshiroi desu. 'Movies are interesting.'
(N)

Eiga o tsukuru koto wa omoshiroi desu. 'To make movies is interesting.'
(V)
(N)

Watashi wa shi ni kyōmi o motte-imasu. 'I am interested in poetry.'
(N)

Watashi wa shi o kaku koto ni kyōmi o.... 'I am interested in writing poetry.'
(V)
(N)

Thus it is possible now to expand the patterns introduced so far, for instance:

§ 64→ N_1 **wa** (N_2 o) V (Dict.) **koto ga suki/kirai desu.**

e.g. Watashi wa yama ni noboru koto ga suki desu.

'I like to climb mountains.'

§ 59→ (N **o**) V (Dict.) **koto wa** (N **o**) V (Dict.) **koto yori** A/Na **desu.**

e.g. *Bokushingu* o miru koto wa (*bokushingu* o) suru koto yori omoshiroi desu.

'To watch a boxing match is more fun than to box.' 'It is more fun to watch a boxing match than (it is) to box.'

§ 66→ N_1 **wa** (N_2 **o**) V (Dict.) **koto ga dekimasu (jōzu desu,** etc.).

e.g. Watashi wa Chūgoku-go o yomu koto ga dekimasu. Shikashi, hanasu koto wa dekimasen.

'I can read Chinese, but I can't speak it.'

14

●練習

ANSWERS→p. 169

I. Make dialogs using the chart.

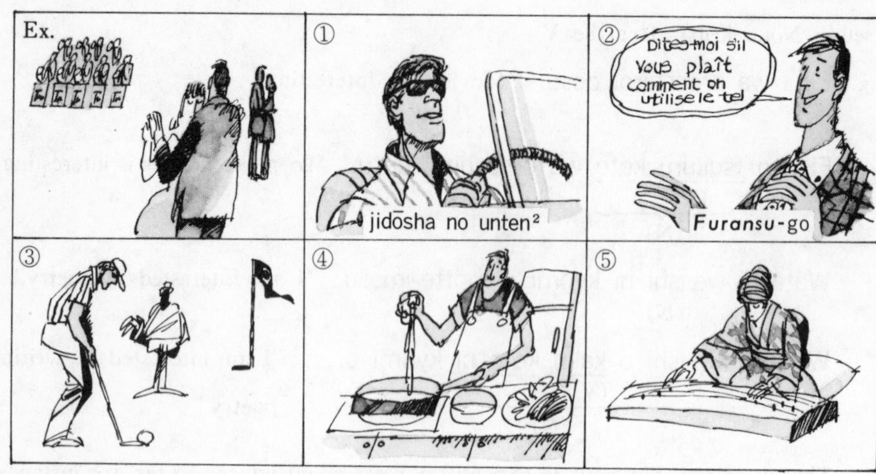

(A) Ex. Q: Anata wa *dansu*[1] ga dekimasu ka?

A: (Hai) Hai, dekimasu.

(Iie) Iie, *dansu* wa dekimasen.

(B) Ex. Q: Anata wa *dansu* ga jōzu desu ka?

A: (Hai) Hai, jōzu desu.

(Iie) Iie, amari jōzu dewa arimasen. Heta desu.

II. Change the sentences as shown in the example.

Ex. (Nippon-go o hanashimasu)

Watashi wa Nippon-go o hanasu koto ga dekimasu.

1. (Kan-ji[3] o kakimasu.)
2. (Jidōsha o kumitatemasu.[4])
3. (Tatta mama nemasu.)
4. (*Taipu*[5] o uchimasu.[6])
5. (Kono kikai no kōzō[7] o setsumei[8]-shimasu.)

語句

1 *dansu* (Nv) 'dance'
2 unten (Nv) driving, operating (car/train/machine)
3 kan-ji Chinese character/letter
4 kumitate·ru assemble, put together
5 *taipu* 'typewriter'; typing
6 uts·u strike, hit
taipu o uts·u type (V)
7 kōzō structure, construction
8 setsumei (Nv) explanation
9 tokui (Na) (something) which one is good at See §66

III. Answer the following questions.

1. Anata no kazoku wa minna Nippon-go ga dekimasu ka?
2. Anata no tomodachi wa minna *gorufu* ga dekimasu ka?
3. Anata wa kaimono ga jōzu desu ka?
4. Anata no o-kā-san wa ryōri ga jōzu desu ka?
5. Anata no ichiban tokui[9]-na ryōri wa nan desu ka?
6. Anata no tokui-na gaikoku-go[10] wa nan desu ka?
7. Anata no tokui-na *supōtsu* wa nan desu ka?
8. Anata no suki-na haiyū[11] wa dare desu ka?

IV. Put the following into Japanese.

1. He is good at Japanese conversation.[12]
2. She can speak Italian very well.
3. I can't read Japanese newspapers yet.
4. "Did you understand his lecture[13]?"

   "No, I didn't understand it at all.[14]"
5. "Tomorrow we are going to have a party at my house. Would you please come?"

   "I'm sorry,[15] but I can't dance."

   "It doesn't matter if you can't dance. Come and talk."
6. "Next Sunday I am going bicycling with my friends."

   "I want to go too. My brother always says that he wants to go bicycling. Do you mind if I take him?"

   "No, anybody[16] can go with us. But can your brother ride a bicycle for a long time? We have to ride from morning till evening."

---

10 gaikoku-go foreign language
11 haiyū actor, actress
12 kaiwa (Nv) conversation
13 kōen (Nv) lecture (to a large audience) cf. kōgi (university lecture)
14 zenzen...nai not at all
15 zannen (Na) regrettable
16 dare demo anybody, anyone, whoever

●会話

$1 = ¥?

Koko de *toraberāzu chekku*[1] o en ni kaeru[2] koto ga dekimasu ka?

—Hai, dekimasu.

Doko no ginkō no kogitte[3] desu ka?

'Bank of America' desu.

Hyaku-hachi-jū-*doru*[4] o-negai-shimasu.

—*Pasupōto* o misete[5]-kudasai.

Shibaraku o-machi-kudasai ne.

Ichi-*doru* wa en de ikura desu ka?

—Kyō wa ni-hyaku-roku-jū-hachi-en desu.

Koko de kitte o kau koto mo dekimasu ka?

—Iie, koko wa ginkō desu kara, kitte wa utte-imasen.

Yūbin-kyoku e itte-kudasai.

Ā, sō desu ka.

Yūbin-kyoku wa chikai desu ka?

—Hai, sugu tonari desu.

Kono o-kane o kuni no kazoku ni okuritai no desu ga. . . .

Can I cash traveler's checks here, please?

—Yes, you can.

Which bank issued the checks?

Bank of America.

180 dollars, please.

—Please show me your passport.

Wait a minute, please.

How much is one dollar in yen?

—Today, it is 268 yen.

Can I buy stamps here too?

—No, this is a bank.

We don't sell stamps.

Please go to the post office.

Oh, I see.

Is the post office near here?

—Yes, it is right next door.

I'd like to send this money to my family back home.

語句

1 *toraberāzu chekku* 'traveler's check'

2 kae•ru change, exchange; cash (check) cf. kawar•u (Vi)

3 kogitte check (bank or personal)

4 *doru* 'dollar'

5 mise•ru show (Vt), let... see

6 yōshi form, paper used

—Kono yōshi[6] ni atesaki[7] to

anata no jūsho[8] o kinyū[9]-shite-kudasai.

Zenbu de go-man-en desu ne?

Hai.

Watashi wa kan-ji ya hira-gana[10] ga heta desu kara, sumimasen ga, kawari ni[11] kaite-kudasaimasen ka?

—Ē, ii desu yo. Demo, Nippon-go wa totemo o-jōzu desu ne.

Iyā, hanasu koto wa dekimasu ga, kan-ji ya hira-gana wa sukoshi shika kaku koto ga dekimasen.

Nippon-go wa yondari kaitari suru koto ga, totemo muzukashii desu.

—Omoshiroi desu ne.

Watashi-tachi Nippon-jin wa Ei-go o yondari kaitari suru koto wa dekimasu ga, hanasu koto ga nakanaka dekimasen.

—Would you fill out this form with the address of the recipient and your own address, please?

Altogether that's 50,000 yen, isn't it?

Yes.

I don't know *kanji* or *hiragana* very well, so could you write them for me?

—OK. But your Japanese is very good.

Not really. I can speak Japanese, but I can't write *kanji* or *hiragana* very well.

I find it very difficult to read and write Japanese.

—It's interesting, isn't it? We Japanese can read and write English, but we have difficulty speaking it.

14

for a specific purpose

7 atesaki mailing address

8 jūsho address

9 kinyū (Nv) filling out (form), fill in (blanks)

10 hira-gana (Japanese characters) cf. kata-kana, kan-ji

11 kawari ni instead, in place (of)

▶ Bank of Tokyo

産　業 —2

日本の 工業生産高[1]は アメリカに ついで、 ソ連と かた[2]を 並べて[3]いる。 戦後 まず 繊維[4]工業などの 軽工業[5]が 発達した。 そして、 日本製品[6]は 急速に 世界市場[7]へ 進出[8]する ことが できたが、 それは おもに[9] 日本の 労働者[10]の 勤勉[11]な 努力[12]と 低賃金[13]に よって[14]いた。 1960年ごろからは 重工業[15]、化学[16] 工業が 日本の 工業の 中心になった。

すぐれた[17] 技術[18]が 日本の 工業を ささえて[19]いる。 造船[20]、 自動車工業は 特に 有名だ。 化学繊維[21]、 合成繊維[22]の 技術も 非常に進んでいる。

日本にとって[23] 貿易[24]は きわめて[25] 重要[26]である。 日本は 資源[27]が 少ないから 原料[28]を 外国から 輸入している。 それを 加工[29]して、 輸出[30]する。 つまり 加工貿易[31]と いう ことが できる。 近年 輸出額[32]が 輸入額よりも 多い。 これからは 輸出と 輸入の バランス[33]を とる ことが 必要[34]だ。

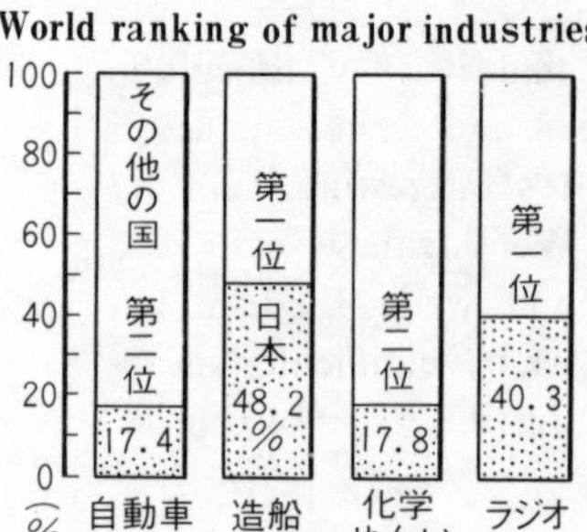

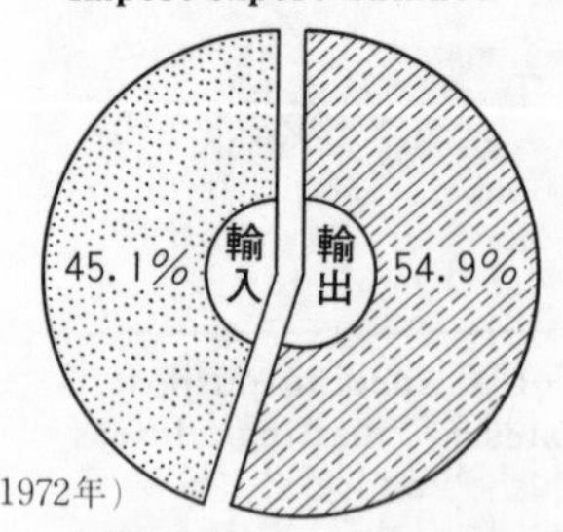

貿易の 相手国[35]では アメリカが 一番である。 アメリカは 日本の 輸入・輸出額の 約$\frac{1}{3}$を 占めて[36]いる。 以前[37]は 綿花[38]、 羊毛[39]が 輸入の 中心で、 綿織物[40]、 おもちゃ[41]が 輸出の 中心であった。 しかし 今日[42]では 石油、 鉄が 輸入の 中心である。 輸出品[43]の おもな ものは 船舶[44]、自動車、 テレビ、 ラジオなどである。 カメラや とけいなどの 精密[45] 製品は 評判[46]が いい。 日本人は 手先[47]が 器用[48]で、 細かい[49] 仕事が じょうずである。

Industry —2

Japan is led by the U.S.A. but ranks with the U.S.S.R. in industrial production. After World War II, light industry developed first and Japanese products were able to advance rapidly into world markets, supported by Japanese labor's diligent efforts and low wages. Since around 1960, the heavy and chemical industries have been the center of Japanese industry.

Superior technology also supports Japan's industry. Japanese shipbuilding and automobile engineering are especially well-known. Chemical and synthetic fibers are advanced too.

Trade is very important to Japan, which imports raw materials and processes them for export. Recently, exports have come to exceed imports, and it is necessary for Japan to strike a balance between the two.

The U.S.A. is Japan's biggest trading partner, accounting for about 1/3 of Japan's total trade. While cotton and wool used to be the main import items and cotton textiles and toys used to be the main exports, today petroleum and iron are the prime imports and the main exports are ships, automobiles, television sets, radios, etc. Precision products like cameras and watches are also highly regarded, as the Japanese are skillful with their hands and good at detailed work.

語句

1 seisan-daka amount of production
-daka=-taka amount
2 kata shoulder
3 narabe•ru put...side by side, arrange; rank kata o narabe•ru rank with
4 sen'i fiber, textile
5 kei-kōgyō light industry
6 seihin product cf. -sei
7 shijō market
8 shinshutsu (Nv) advance, launch
9 omo-ni mainly
10 rōdō-sha laborer
11 kinben (Na) diligent
12 doryoku (Nv) efforts
13 tei-chingin low wages
tei- low chingin wages, salary
14 ...ni yor•u depend upon...
15 jū-kō-gyō heavy industry
16 kagaku chemistry
17 sugureta (PreN) superior, excellent ←sugure•ru (excel)
18 gijutsu techniques
19 sasae•ru support
20 zōsen shipbuilding
21 kagaku-sen'i chemical fibers
22 gōsei-sen'i synthetic fibers
gōsei (Nv) synthesize
23 ...ni totte for...
24 bōeki foreign trade
25 kiwamete extremely
26 jūyō (Na) important
27 shigen resource
28 genryō raw material
29 kakō (Nv) processing, process
30 yushutsu (Nv) export
31 kakō-bōeki manufacturing trade
32 -gaku amount (finance) cf. -daka
33 *baransu* 'balance'
baransu o tor•u 'balance' (V)
34 hitsuyō (Na) necessary
35 aite-koku the other country (in a relation involving two countries)
36 shime•ru occupy
37 izen before, the past
38 menka=men cotton
39 yōmō wool
40 men-orimono cotton textile
orimono textile ←or•u (weave)
41 omocha toy
42 konnichi today, nowadays
43 yushutsu-hin export product
-hin article, goods
44 senpaku ship, vessel
45 seimitsu (Na) precision, fine
46 hyōban reputation
47 tesaki fingers
48 kiyō (Na) skillful, dextrous, handy
49 komaka•i small and fine; detailed

第 15 課

ドライブ

TAPE
No. 4
Side 2

❶あさっての　日曜日(にちようび)、あなたは　ひまが　ありますか。

——はい、ありますが、何(なん)でしょうか。

友(とも)だちの　車(くるま)が　あいていますから、ドライブ[1]に　行(い)きたいと　思(おも)います。わたしは　日本(にっぽん)の　運転免許(うんてんめんきょ)[2]が　ありませんが、あなたは　持(も)っていますか。

——はい、わたしは　去年(きょねん)　免許(めんきょ)を　取(と)りました。

では、日光(にっこう)[3]へ　いっしょに　ドライブを　しませんか。

❷——いいですね。この　車(くるま)は　クーラー[4]も　ありますね。いちばん　新(あたら)しい　型(かた)[5]ですね。この　型(かた)は　デザイン[6]が　よくて　馬力(ばりき)[7]も　ありますから、とても　人気(にんき)[8]が　あります。よく　知(し)っていますね。

——わたしは　まだ　車(くるま)が　ありませんから、一台(いちだい)　買(か)いたいと　思(おも)っています。

あまり[9]　安(やす)いのは、故障(こしょう)[10]する　ことが　[11]ありますから、だめ

語句

1 *doraibu* (Nv) 'drive'
2 unten-menkyo　driver's license
　menkyo　license
3 Nikkō　(a place name)
4 *kūrā* 'cooler,' air conditioner
5 kata＝katachi　model, style, type
6 *dezain* 'design'
7 bariki　horsepower
8 ninki　popularity
　ninki ga ar·u　be popular

ですよ。

❸この　辺(へん)の　景色(けしき)[12]は　すばらしいですね。

——わたしは　この　近(ちか)くまで　二(に)、三回(さんかい)[13]　用事(ようじ)で　来(き)た　ことが　あります[14]。

わたしは　東京(とうきょう)から　北(きた)の　方(ほう)へ　来(き)た　ことが　ありませんから、何(なん)でも[15]　めずらしいです。

——向(む)こうの　山(やま)が　赤城山(あかぎさん)[16]です。

そうですか。名(な)まえを　聞(き)いた　ことが　あります。

14

▲Mt. Akagi

---

9 amari　extremely, too
10 koshō　(Nv) breakdown, being out of order
11 …koto ga ar·u　occasionally　See § 69
12 keshiki　view, scenery
13 ni-san-kai　two or three times
14 -ta koto ga ar·u　See § 69
15 nan demo　anything, whatever
16 Akagi-san　(name of a mountain)

Dai 15-ka

Doraibu

1 Asatte no Nichi-yōbi, anata wa hima ga arimasu ka?

——Hai, arimasu ga, nan deshō ka?

Tomodachi no kuruma ga aite-imasu kara, *doraibu* ni ikitai to omoimasu. Watashi wa Nippon no unten-menkyo ga arimasen ga, anata wa motte-imasu ka?

——Hai, watashi wa kyo-nen menkyo o torimashita.

Dewa, Nikkō e issho-ni *doraibu* o shimasen ka?

2 ——Ii desu ne. Kono kuruma wa *kūrā* mo arimasu ne. Ichiban atarashii kata desu ne. Kono kata wa *dezain* ga yokute bariki mo arimasu kara, totemo ninki ga arimasu.

Yoku shitte-imasu ne.

——Watashi wa mada kuruma ga arimasen kara, ichi-dai kaitai to omotte-imasu.

Amari yasui no wa, koshō-suru koto ga arimasu kara, dame desu yo.

3 Kono hen no keshiki wa subarashii desu ne.

——Watashi wa kono chikaku made ni-san-kai yōji de kita koto ga arimasu.

Watashi wa Tōkyō kara kita no hō e kita koto ga arimasen kara, nan demo mezurashii desu.

——Mukō no yama ga Akagi-san desu.

Sō desu ka. Namae o kiita koto ga arimasu.

Lesson 15
A Drive

1 Are you free the day after tomorrow, Sunday?

——Yes, but what?

My friend's car is available, so I thought it would be nice to go for a drive.

I don't have a Japanese driver's license, but do you have one?

——Yes, I got a license last year.

Then why don't we go for a drive to Nikko?

2 ——This is nice. This car even has air conditioning too, doesn't it?

It's the latest model. This is a very popular model, since it is good-looking and has lots of horsepower.

You know a lot about cars, don't you?

——I don't have a car yet, but I want to buy one.

The very cheap ones break down, and so they're no good.

3 Isn't the scenery along here beautiful?

——I've been near here two or three times on business.

I've never been north of Tokyo before, so it's all new to me.

——That mountain over there is Mt. Akagi.

Is that so? I've heard the name.

15

ANSWERS 〈pp. 184, 185〉

I. 1. Q: ...hōmon-shita koto ga arimasu ka? A: Iie, ichi-do mo hōmon-shita koto ga arimasen. 2. Q: ...okureta koto ga arimasu ka? A: Hai, ichi-do dake okureta koto ga arimasu. 3. Q: ...kita koto ga arimasu ka? A: Hai, nan-do mo kita koto ga arimasu. 4. Q: ...yonda koto ga arimasu ka? A: Iie, mada yonda koto ga arimasen. 5. Q: ...itta koto ga arimasu ka? A: Iie, ik-kai mo itta koto ga arimasen. 6. Q: ...atta koto ga arimasu ka? A: Hai, ni-do dake atta koto ga arimasu. 7. Q: ...mita koto ga arimasu ka? A: Hai, ik-kai dake mita koto ga arimasu. 8. Q: ...hanashita koto ga arimasu ka? A: Hai, san-do hodo hanashita koto ga arimasu. 9. Q: ...kiita koto ga arimasu ka? A: Hai, nan-do mo kiita koto ga arimasu.

II. 1. omoidashimasu→omoidasu koto ga arimasu. 2. mimasu→miru koto ga arimasu. 3. shimasu→suru koto ga arimasu. 4. kimasu→kuru koto ga arimasu. 5. kakemasu→kakeru koto ga arimasu.

III. Kono kaisha wa... 1. heya ga yaku 300 arimasu. 2. kaigi-shitsu ga ōkii desu. 3. setsubi ga ii desu. 4. sha-in ga sukunai desu. 5. kinmu-jikan ga gozen 9-ji kara gogo 5-ji made desu. 6. kyūryō ga ii desu.

IV. 1. Watashi wa atama ga itai desu. 2. Watashi no kaisha wa *Yōroppa* ni shi-ten ga itsu-tsu arimasu. 3. Watashi wa Fuji-san ni nobotta koto ga arimasu ga, ima demo sono utsukushii hi-no-de o omoidasu koto ga arimasu. 4. Anata wa Nippon-go de tegami o kaita koto ga arimasu ka?

●文法

§ 68 Expressions of Possession

N_1 {wa / niwa} N_2 ga {arimasu. / ōi desu. / sukunai desu.}　'N_1 {has / has many/much / has few/little} N_2.'

e.g. Anata wa kyōdai ga arimasu ka? 'Do you have any brothers or sisters?'

—Hai, ani ga hito-ri to imōto ga futa-ri arimasu.

'Yes, I have one elder brother and two younger sisters.'

Kyōto wa o-tera ga ōi desu. Shikashi kōjō wa sukunai desu.

'Kyoto has many temples, but few factories.'

NB: This pattern looks almost like the pattern expressing existence or location introduced in § 12, but is different in several ways.

(1) This pattern expresses that somebody or something (N_1) possesses something (N_2), rather than 'there is something at a certain place.' N_1 here may or may not be an N of place as in § 12; it can be a person or an abstract being.

(2) This pattern allows arimasu to be used for Animate N. Compare:

Anata wa oku-san ga arimasu ka? 'Do you have a wife? (=Are you married?)'

×Ima uchi ni oku-san ga arimasu ka? 'Is (your) wife at home now?'

Possession can be expressed by the Verbal Predicate '(...o) motte-imasu' (motte being the -te form of the verb motsu 'to hold'), which may be closer to the English 'have.' However, this expression is not commonly used in daily conversation, and is limited to instances in which N_2 is an inanimate object.

e.g. Anata wa ima o-kane o ikura motte-imasu ka?

(=Anata wa ima o-kane ga ikura arimasu ka?)

'How much money do you have now?'

×Anata wa oku-san o motte-imasu ka?

§ 69 Expressions of Experience

N_1 wa . . . V-ta koto ga arimasu. 'N_1 has had the experience of V-ing.'

e.g. Anata wa Hokkaidō e itta koto ga arimasu ka? —Iie, arimasen.

'Have you ever been to Hokkaido?' —'No, I have never been there.'

NB: If the Present form (iku, taberu, etc.) is used in this pattern in place of V-ta, it means 'It sometimes happens that...' or 'There are cases in which...'

e.g. Kono tokei wa (tokidoki) susumu koto ga arimasu.

'This watch sometimes runs fast.'

§ 70 The 'Whole' and its 'Part'

When one selects something (N_1) as the Topic, and then wants to make some comment on a part of N_1 or something belonging to or closely related to N_1 (N_2) the following pattern is used. The Predicate is typically (but not necessarily) Adjectival.

N_1 wa N_2 ga . . . .

e.g.

Mearī wa
- me ga { ōkii desu. / aoi desu. } 'As for Mary, her eyes are { large.' / blue.' }
- kami no ke ga { nagai desu. / kirei desu. } 'Mary has { long hair.' / beautiful hair.' }
- o-tō-san ga byōki desu. 'Mary's father is ill.'

Zō wa
- hana ga nagai desu. 'As for elephants, their trunks are long.'
- ashi ga futoi desu. 'Elephants have fat legs.'

Kono machi wa kōgai ga hidoi desu. 'This town has awful pollution.'

Ano hito wa o-jii-san ga yūmei-na seiji-ka deshita.

'That person, his grandfather was a famous politician.'

Kono jidōsha wa katachi wa ii desu ga, *enjin* wa warui desu.

'This car looks nice, but the engine is no good.'

15

 ANSWERS→p. 181

I. Make dialogs as shown in the example.

Ex. Q: (hikōki ni noru) Anata wa hikōki ni notta koto ga arimasu ka?

A: (ichi-do mo) Iie, ichi-do mo notta koto ga arimasen.

1. Q: (Nippon no katei o hōmon-suru) A: (ichi-do mo[1])
2. Q: (kaigi ni okureru[2]) A: (ichi-do dake)
3. Q: (kimono o kiru) A: (nan-do mo)
4. Q: (Kawabata Yasunari[3] no shōsetsu o yomu) A: (mada)
5. Q: (Hokkaidō e iku) A: (ik-kai mo[4])
6. Q: (sha-chō[5] ni au) A: (ni-do dake)
7. Q: (Kabuki[6] o miru) A: (ik-kai dake)
8. Q: (Nippon no *sararī-man*[7] to hanasu) A: (san-do hodo)
9. Q: (Nippon no dentō-ongaku[8] o kiku) A: (nan-do mo)

II. Rewrite the sentences using '...koto ga arimasu.'

Nagasaki[9] wa watashi no furusato[10] desu ga, 15(jū-go)-nen mae ni Tōkyō e dete-kimashita.[11] Ima wa watashi no kazoku wa dare mo imasen.

Ex. Ima demo tokidoki Nagasaki e ikimasu.

→Ima demo Nagasaki e iku koto ga arimasu.

1. Ima demo tokidoki sono fūkei[12] o omoidashimasu.[13]
2. Ima demo tokidoki furusato no yume[14] o mimasu.
3. Ima demo tokidoki omoide-banashi[15] o shimasu.
4. Ima demo tokidoki tomodachi kara tegami ga kimasu.
5. Ima demo tokidoki tomodachi ni denwa o kakemasu.

語句

1 ichi-do mo...nai never
2 okure·ru be delayed/late/slow
3 Kawabata Yasunari (a novelist and 1968 Nobel prize winner; 1899-1972)
4 ik-kai =ichi-do once
5 sha-chō president (of a company)
6 Kabuki (traditional Japanese drama)
7 *sararī-man* 'salaried man'
8 dentō-ongaku traditional music
9 Nagasaki (a place name in Kyushu)
10 furusato birthplace, home town
11 dete-kuru come out
-te-kuru ...and come; come ...ing
See § 87
12 fūkei =keshiki landscape, scene
13 omoidas·u recall cf. omoide
14 yume dream
yume o mi·ru dream (V)

III. Read the following and then write about the company, using the '...wa... ga' construction.

Watashi-tachi no kaisha wa furukute, taihen yūmei desu. Tatemono mo furukatta node kyo-nen atarashii *biru* ga dekimashita.[16] Naka wa taihen hirokute, heya ga yaku 300 arimasu. Ōki-na kaigi-shitsu[17] mo arimasu. Mata, atarashikute benri-na jimu-kikai[18] ya *konpyūtā*[19] nado mo saikin hairimashita. Desukara, sha-in no kazu wa sukunai desu. Kinmu-jikan[20] wa gozen[21] 9 (ku)-ji kara gogo 5 (go)-ji made desu. Kyūryō ga ii node minna yoku hatarakimasu.

Ex. (tatemono) →Kono kaisha wa tatemono ga atarashii desu.

1. (heya)
2. (kaigi-shitsu)
3. (setsubi[22])
4. (sha-in)
5. (kinmu-jikan)
6. (kyūryō)

IV. Put the following into Japanese.

1. I have a headache.
2. My company has 5 branch offices in Europe.
3. I have climbed Mt. Fuji and I still sometimes recall the beautiful sunrise.[23]
4. Have you ever written a letter in Japanese?

---

15 omoide-banashi talking about the old days -banashi=hanashi story
16 deki·ru be completed, come into existence
17 kaigi-shitsu meeting/conference room
18 jimu-kikai office machine
jimu office work
19 *konpyūtā* 'computer'
20 kinmu-jikan on-duty hours
kinmu (Nv) work, duty, service (office/company)
21 gozen in the morning, a. m. cf. gogo
22 setsubi equipment, facilities
23 hi-no-de sunrise

15

●会話

ODOROKIMASHITA!

Nippon niwa shūkan-shi[1] ga takusan arimasu ne.

—Ē, zenkoku-teki[2]-na kibo[3] no shūkan-shi dake de, sō...,

nana-jus-shurui gurai arimasu.

Hō.... Kore wa odorokimashita.[4]

Gekkan[5] no zasshi mo ōi desu ka?

—Totemo ōi desu.

Sōgō-zasshi[6] ya bungaku,[7] geijutsu[8] no zasshi, soreni shumi no zasshi, tatoeba,[9] *gorufu*, shashin, tsuri[10] no zasshi, ongaku no zasshi; ryokō no zasshi ni[11] jūtaku[12] zasshi; mikon[13] no josei muke[14] no zasshi ni, shufu[15] muke no zasshi; otoko no ko, onna no ko, sore-zore[16] no tame no zasshi....

Sorewa-sorewa[17] takusan arimasu yo.

Zenbu de sen-shurui ijō arimasu.

You have many weekly magazines in Japan, don't you?

—Yes, counting only national weeklies, well..., there are about 70.

Oh, that's quite a surprise.
Are there many monthly magazines too?

—There are lots.
There are very general magazines; literary and artistic magazines; and then magazines on various hobbies; for example, golf, photography, fishing, and music; magazines on travel and on housing; magazines for unmarried women and for housewives; magazines for boys and magazines for girls....
Yes, there are a lot, really.
Altogether there are more than 1,000 of them.

語句

1 shūkan-shi weekly magazine
  shūkan published weekly
  -shi magazine
2 zenkoku-teki (Na) national
3 kibo scale, scope
4 odorok·u be surprised
5 gekkan published monthly
6 sōgō-zasshi general magazine
  sōgō- general, all-round
7 bungaku literature
8 geijutsu art
9 tatoeba for example
10 tsuri fishing, angling← tsur·u (fish, angle, hang)
11 ...ni adding to...
12 jūtaku house, residence

Ippan-ni,[18] Nippon-jin wa
yoku hon o yomimasu ne.
Man'in no densha no naka demo
mina kanarazu nani ka[19] yonde-imasu ne.
Are niwa odorokimashita.
Soreni ōki-na hon-ya[20] ga takusan arimasu shi[21]....
Kinō mo Shinjuku no hon-ya ni ikimashita ga, nan demo sorotte-iru node kanshin-shimashita.
—Ano hon-ya wa tokuni yōsho-bu[22] ga yūmei desu.
Watashi wa senmon ga kenchiku desu ga, kōgaku-kankei[23] senmon no hon-ya mo arimasu ka?
—Kanda niwa kitto aru to omoimasu.

In general, the Japanese read a lot of books.
Even in crowded trains everyone's always reading something.
That's quite a surprise.
Moreover, there are lots of big bookshops....
I went to that bookstore in Shinjuku again yesterday, and I was really impressed at the selection they have.
—That bookstore is particularly well-known for its foreign book section.
I'm majoring in architecture, but are there any bookstores specializing in engineering texts?
—I'm sure there are some in Kanda.

15

13 mikon unmarried cf. kekkon (marriage)
14 ...muke=...muki intended for
15 shufu housewife
16 sore-zore (N/Adv) each, respectively
17 sorewa-sorewa really; so much
18 ippan-ni in general
ippan general
19 nani ka something
20 hon-ya bookshop
21 ...shi ...and also
22 yōsho-bu foreign book section
yōsho books from Western countries
23 kōgaku-kankei on engineering
kōgaku engineering
kankei (Nv) relation

日本の 文字

日本の 文字[1]には 漢字と かな[2]が あります。 かなには、 ひらがなと カタカナ[3]とが あります。 むかし、 日本には 文字が なかったので、 おとなりの 中国から 借りました。 古代[4]の 中国は、 漢時代[5]が 有名でしたので、 中国の 文字を 漢字、 中国の 文章[6]を 漢文[7]と いいます。

漢字は、 画数[8]が 多いので、 書くときに 時間が かかりました。 そこで[9]、 日本人は ひらがなと カタカナを 作りました。 ひらがなの 「あ」は 漢字の 「安」を 簡単に した もので、 カタカナの 「ア」は 漢字「阿」の 一部[10]です。

日本の 文化は、 平安時代まで、 中国の 影響が 強く、 公式[11]の 文章は すべて[12] 漢文でした。

カタカナは 仏教[13]の 僧侶[14]たちが 経典[15]を 読む ときに よみがな[16]として 使いました。 ひらがなは 女性が 使いました。 男性[17]も 私用[18]の 文章では 使う ことも ありました。

その 傾向は 現代日本語[19]の 文体[20]にも 残っています。

漢字には、 中国風[21]の 読み方[22]と 日本風の 読み方が あります。 それを 音[23]と 訓[24]と いいますが、 わたしたちは その どちらをも 勉強する ことが 必要です。

安	あ	あ	阿ア
以	い	い	伊イ
宇	う	う	宇ウ
衣	え	え	江エ
於	お	お	於オ

Japanese Writing

Japanese writing uses both *kanji* and *kana*. *Kana* includes *hiragana* and *katakana.* A long time ago, there was no alphabet in Japan, so the characters for writing were borrowed from neighboring China. As ancient China was then ruled by the Han (Kan) Dynasty, the characters were called *kanji* and the writing *kanbun.*

Because *kanji* has many strokes, it takes a long time to write. Thus the Japanese created *hiragana* and *katakana.* The *hiragana* あ is a simplification of the *kanji* 安, and the *katakana* ア is part of the *kanji* 阿.

Until the Heian Period, Japanese culture was strongly influenced by the Chinese, and all official writings were in *kanbun.*

Katakana was used by Buddhist priests in reading their scriptures. *Hiragana* was used by women. Men also used it in their private writings. This pattern remains even in the present styles of writing Japanese.

Kanji has Chinese readings and Japanese readings. These are called *on* and *kun* readings, but we have to study both of them.

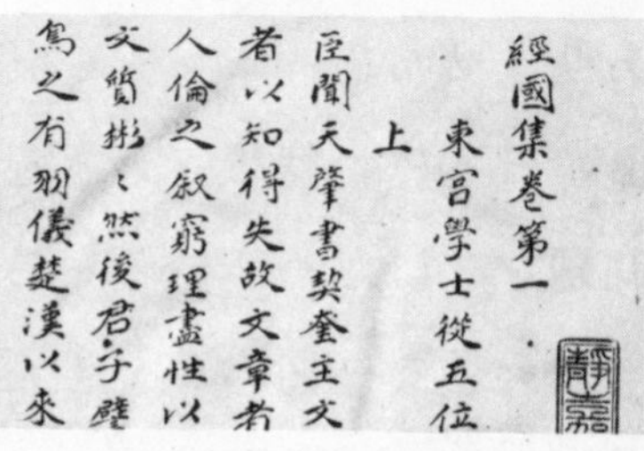
經國集巻第一
東宮學士従五位
上
臣聞天肇書契奎主文
者以知得失故文章者
人倫之叙窮理盡性以
文質彬々然後君子譬
鳥之有羽儀楚漢以來

語句

1 moji letter, script, characters
2 kana (Japanese letters)
3 kata-kana (Japanese letters)
4 kodai ancient times
5 Kan-jidai Han Period
  Kan Han Dynasty (China, 202 B.C.-220 A.D.) cf. kan-ji
6 bunshō sentence
7 kan-bun Chinese writing
8 kaku-sū the number of strokes
  -sū number
9 sokode therefore, so
10 ichi-bu one part
11 kōshiki formal, official
12 subete all
13 Bukkyō Buddhism
14 sōryo monk
15 kyōten Buddhist scriptures, sutra
16 yomi-gana *kana* used as phonetic symbols
17 dan-sei man, male
18 shiyō private use
19 gendai-Nippon-go modern Japanese
  gendai (N) modern (times)
20 buntai writing style
21 Chūgoku-fū Chinese style
  -fū ...style, taste
22 yomi-kata how to read, reading
  -kata how to
23 on (phonetic reading of a Chinese character)
24 kun (Japanese reading of a Chinese character)

第16課

老人問題

TAPE
No. 4
Side 2

❶ 近ごろ「恍惚の人[1]」という ことばが よく 使われ[2]ます。これは 老人[3]という 意味で 言われています。もともとは 小説の 名まえです。この 小説は 有吉佐和子[4]という 作家に よって[5] 書かれました。

❷ 日本には 昔、まずしい[6] 百姓[7]の あいだに[8]「うばすて[9]」という 風習[10]が ありました。まずしくて 老人に ご飯を 食べさせる[11] ことが できないから、山に 老人を すてに[12] 行かせ[13]ました。これも「楢山節考[14]」という 小説に 書かれています。これは 昔の 話で、もちろん 今では こんな ことは ありません。

❸ 日本は 戦後 大きな 発展[15]を しましたが、現在[16] 老人問題[17]を はじめ[18] いろいろな 問題が 生まれ[19]ています。そして 大きな 関心[20]が もたれています。それは 社会保障制度[21]の 問題で あると 同時に[22]、若者[23]をも ふくめて[24] わたした

語句

1 Kōkotsu no Hito (the title of a novel)
  kōkotsu ecstasy
2 -are・ru See §71
3 rōjin old man/woman, the aged
4 Ariyoshi Sawako (novelist; 1931-)
5 …ni yotte (Passive) by… See §71
6 mazushi・i poor, humble
7 hyakushō peasant, farmer
8 …no aida ni/de among
9 uba-sute discarding old women
  -sute ←sute・ru (discard)
10 fūshū custom
11 -sase・ru See §72
12 sute・ru throw away, dump, discard
13 -ase・ru ＝-sase・ru See §72
14 Narayama-bushi-kō (the title of a novel by Fukazawa Shichiro)
15 hatten (Nv) development
16 genzai (N/Adv) at present, present time
17 rōjin-mondai problems of the aged
  mondai problem
18 …o hajime beginning with…, especially…
19 umare・ru be born
20 kanshin concern
21 shakai-hoshō-seido social security system shakai society

ち　みんなの　生(い)きがい[25]の　問題(もんだい)でも　あるからです。

❹　わたしは　「恍惚(こうこつ)の人(ひと)」を　読(よ)んで　いろいろと　考(かんが)えさせられ[26]ました。　わたしは　友人(ゆうじん)[27]にも　この　小説(しょうせつ)を　買(か)って　読(よ)ませたいと　思(おも)っています。　これからは[28]　若(わか)い　人(ひと)たちも　自分(じぶん)の　問題(もんだい)として　老人問題(ろうじんもんだい)を　考(かんが)えなければならないと　思(おも)います。

うばすての話(はなし)

ある[29]　おばあさん[30]が　むすこ[31]に　せおわれて[32]　山(やま)の　中(なか)へ　すてられに　行(い)く　とき、　何度(なんど)も　木(き)の　えだ[33]を　折(お)って[34]　道(みち)に　すてました。　その　わけ[35]を　むすこに　たずねられて、　おばあさんは　「おまえ[36]が　帰(かえ)る　ときの　道(みち)しるべ[37]だ。」と　言(い)いました。　そう　言(い)われて　むすこは　なみだ[38]を　流(なが)し[39]、　また　おばあさんを　せおって　家(いえ)へ　帰(かえ)りました。

16

---

hoshō　(Nv) security
22 dōji　the same time
　…to dōji ni　at the same time
23 waka-mono　young person
　waka ←waka•i　(young)
24 fukume•ru　include
25 iki-gai　purpose in life, reason for living
26 -rare•ru　See §71
27 yūjin＝tomodachi　friend
28 kore kara wa　from now on, hereafter
29 aru　(PreN) a certain…
30 (o-)bā-san　old woman; grandmother
31 musuko　son　cf. musume (daughter)
32 se-o•u　carry on the back, be burdened with
33 eda　branch, twig
34 or•u　bend; break
35 wake　reason
36 omae　you (sing.) (Familiar or slightly derogatory)
　cf. omae-tachi (pl.)
37 michi-shirube　guidepost, milestone
38 namida　tears
39 nagas•u　(Vt) let flow
　namida o nagas•u　shed tears

Dai 16-ka
Rōjin-mondai

1 Chika-goro 'Kōkotsu no Hito' to iu kotoba ga yoku tsukawaremasu. Kore wa rōjin to iu imi de iwarete-imasu. Motomoto wa shōsetsu no namae desu. Kono shōsetsu wa Ariyoshi Sawako to iu sak-ka ni yotte kakaremashita.

2 Nippon niwa mukashi, mazushii hyakushō no aida ni 'uba-sute' to iu fūshū ga arimashita. Mazushikute rōjin ni gohan o tabesaseru koto ga dekinai kara, yama ni rōjin o sute ni ikasemashita. Kore mo 'Narayama-bushi-kō' to iu shōsetsu ni kakarete-imasu. Kore wa mukashi no hanashi de, mochiron ima dewa konna koto wa arimasen.

3 Nippon wa sen-go ōki-na hatten o shimashita ga, genzai rōjin-mondai o hajime iroiro-na mondai ga umarete-imasu. Soshite ōki-na kanshin ga motarete-imasu. Sore wa shakai-hoshō-seido no mondai de aru to dōji ni, waka-mono o mo fukumete watashi-tachi minna no iki-gai no mondai demo aru kara desu.

4 Watashi wa 'Kōkotsu no Hito' o yonde iroiro to kangaesaseraremashita. Watashi wa yūjin nimo kono shōsetsu o katte yomasetai to omotte-imasu. Kore kara wa wakai hito-tachi mo jibun no mondai to shite rōjin-mondai o kangaenakereba naranai to omoimasu.

Uba-sute no hanashi

Aru o-bā-san ga musuko ni se-owarete yama no naka e suterare ni iku toki, nan-do mo ki no eda o otte michi ni sutemashita. Sono wake o musuko ni tazunerarete, o-bā-san wa "Omae ga kaeru toki no michi-shirube da." to iimashita. Sō iwarete musuko wa namida o nagashi, mata o-bā-san o se-otte ie e kaerimashita.

Lesson 16

Problems of the Aged

1 The term "*kokotsu no hito*" has recently come into wide-spread use. This is used to refer to the aged. Originally, it was the title of a novel. The novel was written by an authoress named Ariyoshi Sawako.

2 A long time ago in Japan, there was a custom of "*ubasute*" among impoverished farmers. Because they were too poor to feed their old people, they took them out and abandoned them in the mountains. This is described in the novel *Narayama Bushiko*. Yet this is an ancient story and such things are no longer done.

3 Although Japan has made great progress since the War, the present situation has given rise to the problem of the aged and a diversity of other problems. There is great concern over these issues. At the same time as this is a problem for the social security system, it is also a question of life values for all of us, including even the young.

4 Reading *Kokotsu no Hito* made me think about many things. I would like to buy this book for my friends to read too. I feel that young people must think about the problems of the aged as their own problems.

16

A Story of *Ubasute*

Once when an old woman was being carried on her son's back into the mountains to be abandoned, she broke off branches from the trees and threw them on the path as they went. When her son asked her why she was doing this, she said, "So you won't get lost on the way home." When the son heard this, he began crying, picked up his mother again, and returned home with her on his back.

ANSWERS 〈pp. 196, 197〉

I. 1. Kono atarashii kyōka-sho wa Tōkyō no shuppan-sha kara hakkō-sarete-iru. (sarete-imasu) 2. Kyō michi de watashi wa kirei-na onna no hito ni hanashi-kakerareta. (hanashi-kakeraremashita) 3. Kare wa minna kara gichō ni erabareta. (erabaremashita) 4. Kōgai-mondai wa ōku no kuni no gaku-sha ni yotte kenkyū-sarete-iru. (sarete-imasu) 5. Ano ko-domo wa haha-oya ni shikarareta koto ga nai. (shikarareta koto ga arimasen) 6. ***Supein***-go wa yaku 20-ka-koku no hito-bito ni yotte hanasarete-iru. (hanasarete-imasu) 7. 'Genji Monogatari' wa Murasaki Shikibu to iu onna no hito ni yotte kakareta to ōku no gaku-sha ni iwarete-iru. (iwarete-imasu)

II. 1. Sensei wa watashi o yobimashita. 2. Watashi no kaban wa dare ka ni akeraremashita. 3. Kono hanashi wa mada dare nimo shirarete-imasen. 4. Sono dorobō wa dare ni tsuka-maeraremashita ka? 5. Sono ko-inu wa shinsetsu-na hito ni hirowaremashita.

IV. 1. sanpo-sase 2. nomase 3. tabesase 4. yasumase 5. sase/yarase 6. nesase

V. 1. Watashi wa kare ni 2-jikan matas(er)aremashita. (I was made to wait for him for 2 hours.) 2. Watashi wa mai-asa haha ni ***pan*** o kai ni ikas(er)aremasu. (I am made to go to buy bread every morning by my mother.) 3. Sono gakusei wa sensei ni onaji koto o nan-do mo iwas(er)aremashita. (That student was made to say the same thing again and again.)

VI. 1. Watashi wa imōto ni/o yūbin-kyoku e ikasemashita. 2. Kono jisho wa Nippon de hiroku tsukawarete-imasu. 3. Dōzo watashi ni/o ikasete-kudasai. 4. Kono kaisha wa 1920-nen ni tateraremashita. 5. Kyo-nen yaku 200-man-bon no kasa ga kono kōjō de tsukurare-mashita ga, sono hanbun ga omo-ni ***Amerika*** ni yushutu-saremashita. 6. Watashi wa nomitaku arimasen deshita ga, ***tomato-jūsu*** o nomas(er)aremashita.

●文法

§ 71 Passive Construction

N_1 **wa** N_2 {**ni** / **ni yotte** / **kara**} V-(r)**are-ru.** 'N₁ is V-ed by N₂.'

e.g. Dorobō wa keikan ni tsukamae-rare-ta.
'thief' 'policeman' 'was caught'
'The thief was caught by the policeman.'

cf. Keikan ga dorobō o tsukamae-ta. 'The policeman caught the thief.'

NB: (1) This pattern indicates that N_1 is affected by N_2's action expressed by V.

(2) The Passive form of V is obtained by attaching the Auxiliary -are- or -rare- to the Stem of V, the former for 1st Group V (e.g. koros-u 'kill' →koros-are-ru; kak-u 'write'→kak-are-ru), and the latter for 2nd Group V (e.g. tabe-ru 'eat'→tabe-rare-ru; mi-ru 'see'→mi-rare-ru). Other Auxiliary elements such as masu, nai, etc. are carried over unchanged.

(3) The 'agent' (performer of the action) (N_2 above) takes ni, ni yotte, or kara, depending upon the kind of V. Roughly speaking, ni is for the verbs expressing actions directly affecting an object, such as killing, pushing, breaking, chasing, etc.; kara for verbs expressing directed movement (kara showing origin), such as sending, giving, receiving, ordering, etc.; and ni yotte for most other verbs. However, when the agent is clear, Active sentences are more common than Passive sentences.

(4) In addition to this Passive construction, which is essentially the same as the passive construction in English, there is also a peculiarly Japanese passive which involves the intransitive verbs.

e.g. Watashi wa kinō kaeri ni ame ni furareta.
(literally 'I was rained on yesterday on my way home.')

Kanojo wa kodomo no toki chichi ni shinarete kurō-shimashita.

(literally 'She was died on by her father when she was a child and had a hard time.')

Such expressions are used when the subject suffered some loss or trouble because of an event, and hence this has been called the 'passive of suffering (or misfortune).' Although they look like the ordinary passive, they can not be converted into 'active' sentences.

§ 72 Causative Construction

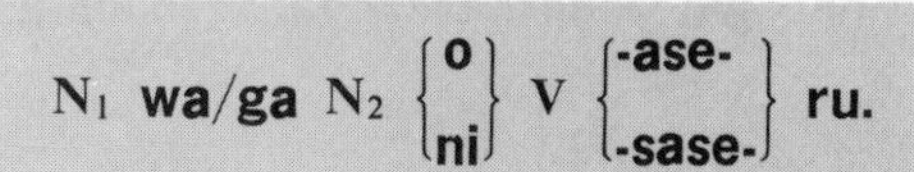
N_1 wa/ga N_2 {o / ni} V {-ase- / -sase-} ru.

'N_1 makes (lets) N_2 do....'
'N_1 causes N_2 to do....'

e.g. Watashi wa otōto o Tōkyō e ik-ase-mashita.

'I made (let) my brother go to Tokyo.'

Kare wa kodomo ni gohan o tabe-sasete-imasu.

'He is letting the child eat.' (He is feeding the child.)

Watashi o ikasete-kudasai. 'Please let me go.'

NB: (1) The Causative form is obtained by attaching -ase- to the stems of 1st Group V and -sase- to 2nd Group V. Suru becomes saseru and kuru becomes kosaseru.

(2) The Object N_2 takes ni when the V is transitive, and either ni or o when it is intransitive.

(3) The Causative is used only when N_2 is lower than N_1 in status or age, or it is inanimate. cf. -te-morau (See § 74)

(4) The Causative form may be combined with the Passive form.

e.g. Otōto wa chichi ni Tōkyō e ik-ase-rare-mashita (or, ik-asare-mashita)

'My brother was made to go to Tokyo by my father.'

The Passive form of the Causative form usually implies that the subject is forced to do something against his will.

16

●練習

ANSWERS→p. 193

I. Rewrite the following in the Passive form, and then in the Polite style.

1. Tōkyō no shuppan-sha[1] ga kono atarashii kyōka-sho o hakkō[2]-shite-iru.
2. Kyō michi de kirei-na onna no hito ga watashi ni hanashi-kaketa.[3]
3. Minna ga kare o gichō[4] ni eranda.[5]
4. Ōku no kuni no gaku-sha[6] ga kōgai[7]-mondai o kenkyū-shite-iru.
5. Ano haha-oya[8] wa kodomo o shikatta[9] koto ga nai.
6. Yaku 20(ni-juk)-ka-koku[10] no hito-bito ga *Supein*-go o hanashite-iru.
7. Murasaki Shikibu[11] to iu onna no hito ga 'Genji Monogatari'[12] o kaita to ōku no gaku-sha ga itte-iru.

II. Change the voice: (Active to Passive and Passive to Active)

1. Watashi wa sensei ni yobaremashita.[13]
2. Dare ka[14] ga watashi no kaban[15] o akemashita.
3. Dare mo mada kono hanashi o shitte-imasen.
4. Dare ga sono dorobō[16] o tsukamaemashita[17] ka?
5. Shinsetsu-na hito ga sono ko-inu[18] o hiroimashita.[19]

III. Answer the following questions.

1. Anata no kuni dewa donna uta ga yoku utawarete-imasu ka?
2. Anata no kuni dewa dono shinbun ga ichiban ōku no hito ni yomarete-imasu ka?
3. Anata no kuni dewa donna mono ga yushutu-sarete-imasu ka?

語句

1 shuppan-sha publisher (company)
2 hakkō (Nv) publication
3 hanashi-kake•ru speak to, address
4 gichō chairman (of meeting, conference)
5 erab•u elect; choose, select
6 gaku-sha scholar
7 kōgai environmental pollution
8 haha-oya mother cf. chichi-oya (father)
9 shikar•u scold
10 -ka-koku (number of) countries
11 Murasaki Shikibu (the authoress of *Genji-Monogatari*; 978-1016?)
12 Genji Monogatari *The Tale of Genji* (the oldest novel in Japan, written by

4. Anata no kuni dewa donna mono ga yunyū-sarete-imasu ka?

5. Anata no daigaku wa nan-nen gurai mae ni tateraremashita ka?

IV. Fill in the blanks using the Causative forms.

Watashi no kodomo wa karada ga yowai[20] node, mai-asa (1. (take a walk))masu. Asa-gohan niwa gyūnyū[21] o (2. (drink))te, yasai[22] to kudamono o takusan (3. (eat))masu. Kodomo ga gakkō kara kaette kara wa, sukoshi (4. (take a rest))te, sono ato de karui undō o (5. (do))[23]masu. Yoru wa hayaku (6. (go to bed))masu.

V. Rewrite the following sentences in the Passive form and tell what they mean.

1. Kare wa watashi o 2-jikan matasemashita.
2. Haha wa mai-asa watashi ni *pan* o kai ni ikasemasu.
3. Sensei wa sono gakusei ni onaji koto o nan-do mo iwasemashita.

VI. Put the following into Japanese.

1. I let my younger sister to go to the post office.
2. This dictionary is widely[24] used in Japan.
3. Please let me go.
4. This company was established in 1920.
5. About two million umbrellas were produced in this factory last year, and half of them were exported, mainly to the U.S.
6. I didn't want to, but I was forced to drink the tomato juice.

---

a court lady Murasaki Shikibu)
monogatari tale
13 yob·u call, summon; invite
14 dare ka somebody, anybody
15 kaban bag, briefcase, suitcase
16 dorobō thief, robber
17 tsukamae·ru catch hold of
18 ko-inu small dog, puppy
19 hiro·u pick up cf. sute·ru
20 yowa·i weak
21 gyūnyū (cow's) milk
22 yasai vegetables
23 sase·ru make (someone) do See § 72
24 hiroku widely, by many people ← hiro·i

●会話

KARĀ-TEREBI?

Kono *terebi* wa *dezain* ga totemo ii desu ne. *Karā* desu ka?

—Hai, saishin-gata[1] no *karā-terebi* desu.

Toranjisutā[2] desu kara

denki-dai[3] ga sonna-ni kakarimasen.

Hito-tsu ikaga desu ka?

Hoshii desu nē....

Demo, takai deshō ne?

—*Rōn*[4] demo ii desu yo.

Kakari[5] no mono ni tetsuzuki-sase-mashō ka?

Ni-juk-kai-barai[6] de *OK* desu.

* * *

—Rei no[7] *haijakku*[8] no hannin[9] ga tsukamaeraremashita ne.

Sō desu ka. Shinbun de hōdō[10]-sare-mashita ka?

—Iie, saki-hodo[11] no *rajio* no *nyūsu*[12] de hōsō[13]-saremashita.

Terebi o tsukete-goran[14]-nasai.

The design of this television is very good. Is it color?

—Yes, it is the newest model color TV. Since it is transistorized, your electricity bills are not so high. Wouldn't you like to have one?

Yes, I would....

But it's probably expensive, isn't it?

—Loans are available. Shall I get our man in charge to fill out the forms for you? Twenty installments would be OK.

* * *

—That hijacker was caught, you know.

Is that so? Was it reported in the newspaper?

—No, it was broadcast over the last radio news. Switch on the TV.

語句

1 saishin-gata the newest model
 saishin (N) the newest, the latest

2 *toranjisutā* 'transistor'

3 denki-dai electricity charges, power rates
 -dai charge, fee

4 *rōn* 'loan,' easy payment plan

5 kakari (N) (a clerk) in charge

6 -kai-barai ...times installment, payments
 -barai payment
 ←hara·u

7 rei no that...in question

8 *haijakku* 'highjack'

9 hannin criminal

It's just time for the noon news, so this incident will certainly be broadcast.

* * *

My TV is out of order.
—That's inconvenient, isn't it? Shall I have my younger brother fix it? His major is electrical engineering, and so he can easily fix it.
Oh, that would be very nice.
I'd really appreciate it.
Can he fix it here, or shall I take it to your brother's place?
—No, my brother can come here. This is his summer vacation, so he's free now.

Chōdo[15] ima o-hiru no *nyūsu* no jikan[16] desu kara, kitto kono jiken[17] no koto ga hōsō-saremasu yo.

* * *

Terebi, koshō na n desu.[18]
—Sore wa fu-ben desu ne.
Watashi no otōto ni naosasemashō[19] ka? Otōto wa denki-kōgaku[20] ga senmon desu kara, kantan-ni shūri[21]-shimasu yo.
Sore wa arigatai[22] desu ne.
Zehi o-negai-shitai desu.
Koko de shūri ga dekimasu ka, soretomo, kono *terebi* o otōto-san no o-taku e motte-ikasemashō[23] ka?
—Iya, otōto ni koko e kosasemasu.
Ima natsu-yasumi de, otōto wa hima desu kara.

16

10 hōdō (Nv) report (news)
11 saki-hodo a while ago
12 *nyūsu* 'news'
13 hōsō (Nv) broadcast
14 -te goran(-nasai) Why don't you...?; Just do...
15 chōdo just
16 ...no jikan time for...
17 jiken incident, happening, affair
18 ...n desu =...no desu The fact is that See § 101
19 naos•u mend, fix
20 denki-kōgaku electrical engineering
21 shūri (Nv) mend, fix
22 arigata•i convenient, gracious, kind
23 motte-ik•u take, bring

日本の 歴史—2

「大化の改新」では 土地[1]の 私有[2]が 許[3]されなかった。 これが 「公地公民[4]」の 土地制度と よばれている。 しかし、 例外として、 寺や 神社や 高い 位[5]の 人々は、 特別に 土地が 与えられた。 また、 八世紀の 中ごろ[6]、 新しく 土地が 開か[7]れ、 その 土地の 私有が 許された。 その 結果、 だんだん 私有地[8]が ふえ、 奈良時代から 平安時代に かけて[9]、 土地制度は 徐々[10]に くずされて[11]いった。

藤原氏は 多くの 私有地を もち、 中央政府の 高い 官職[12]を 独占[13]し、 自分たちの むすめを 天皇と 結婚させた。 そして その 皇后[14]の 男の 子を 天皇にし、 政治を 自由[15]に あやつった[16]。

藤原氏以外[17]の 人々は 地方の 役人に なった。 これが 武士[18] 階級[19]である。 初め 平家[20]が、 のちに 源氏[21]が 勢力を 得[22]た。 1192年 源 頼朝[23]に よって 鎌倉[24]に 幕府[25]が 開かれ、 武家[26] 政治が 始められた。 1338年 足利氏[27]によって、 京都に 室町[28] 幕府が 開かれ、 16世紀まで 続いた。

この間[29] 1274年と 1281年に モンゴル[30]の 大軍[31]が 北九州[32]に 攻め[33]てきたが、 台風が 吹いて 多くの 船[34]が しずんだ[35]。 これを 「神風[36]」と 言う。 これ以後[37] 九州や 瀬戸内海[38] 沿岸の 漁民[39]は 朝鮮半島や 中国大陸[40]まで 行って 貿易を した。 彼らは 武装[41]していたので、 「倭寇[42]」と 言われて、 おそれられた[43]。

一方[44]、 ポルトガル・スペイン[45]などから 貿易船[46]が 来て、 鉄砲[47]や キリスト教[48]などが 伝えられた。 織田信長[49]や 豊臣秀吉[50]は キリスト教を 保護[51]したが、 徳川[52] 幕府は これを 禁止[53]した。 それから 開国[54]まで 約二百年間 鎖国[55] 政策[56]が とられる。 この間 わが国の 文化は 西欧[57]の 近代[58] 文明[59]から おくれるが、 独自[60]の 文化が 栄え[61]た。

Japanese History—2

The Taika reforms prohibited private ownership of land and instituted a system of public ownership. However, temples, shrines, and high-ranking people were allowed to own land, these regulations becoming still laxer as new land was opened later. As a result, private landholdings were gradually expanded and the restrictions on landownership fell into disuse in the Nara and Heian periods.

The Fujiwara family had extensive landholdings, monopolized official positions within the central government, and married its daughters into the Imperial family. They then installed those offspring as Emperor to gain a free hand. The non-Fujiwara's were officials in outlying districts, constituting a warrior class. First the Heike and then the Genji clans took control. In 1192, Minamoto no Yoritomo established the Kamakura Shogunate. The Muromachi Shogunate established in Kyoto in 1338 lasted into the 16th century.

After Mongol forces attacking Japan in 1274 and 1281 had their fleets destroyed by "Divine Winds," Japanese journeyed to Korea and China for trade. Being armed, however, they were called "Wako" and were much feared. At the same time, traders from Portugal and Spain brought firearms and Christianity to Japan. Christianity was first protected by some lords, but it was banned by the Tokugawa Shogunate. During Japan's nearly 200 years of isolation, modernization lagged behind the West while a uniquely Japanese culture was developed.

16

語句

1 tochi land, estate
2 shi-yū private ownership
3 yurus•u allow, permit, forgive
4 Kōchi-kōmin public-land-public-people
5 kurai rank, status
6 naka-goro around the middle (of...)
7 hirak•u (Vi/Vt) cultivate; open
8 shiyū-chi private land/estate
9 ...kara...ni kakete from...through/as far as...
10 jojo-ni gradually
11 kuzus•u destroy, pull down
12 kanshoku government post
13 dokusen (Nv) monopolize
14 Kōgō Empress cf. Tennō (Emperor)
15 jiyū-ni freely; unrestrictedly
16 ayatsur•u operate
17 ...igai except...
18 bushi warrior, *samurai*
19 kaikyū (social) class
20 Hei-ke the Taira family
21 Genji the Minamoto family
22 e•ru get, obtain
23 Minamoto no Yoritomo (1147-99)
24 Kamakura (a place name)
25 Bakufu Japan's feudal government
26 buke *samurai* family cf. bushi
27 Ashikaga-shi the Ashikaga family
28 Muromachi (a place name)
29 kono-kan during this time, meanwhile
30 *Mongoru* 'Mongol'
31 tai-gun large army/force
gun army, force, military
32 Kita-Kyūshū Northern Kyushu
33 seme•ru attack
34 fune ship 35 shizum•u (Vi) sink
36 Kami-kaze Divine Wind
37 kore-igo after this
38 Seto-naikai Seto Inland Sea
39 gyomin fishermen
40 tairiku continent
41 busō (Nv) armament
42 Wakō Japanese pirates
43 osore•ru fear, be afraid/frightened
44 ip-pō one side; on the other hand
45 *Porutogaru* 'Portugal'
46 -sen ship 47 teppō gun
48 Kirisuto-kyō Christianity
49 Oda Nobunaga (1534-82)
50 Toyotomi Hideyoshi (1536-98)
51 hogo (Nv) protection
52 Tokugawa (a family name)
53 kinshi (Nv) prohibition
54 kaikoku opening of the country
55 sakoku national isolation (policy)
56 seisaku policy
57 Seiō Western Europe
58 kindai modern age cf. gendai
59 bunmei civilization cf. bunka
60 dokuji (N) unique, indigenous
61 sakae•ru flourish, thrive

第 17 課

銀婚式

TAPE
No. 5
Side 1

❶ きょうは　わたしたちの　両親(りょうしん)[1]の　銀婚式(ぎんこんしき)[2]です。　父(ちち)と　母(はは)が　結婚(けっこん)してから　二十五年(にじゅうごねん)　たちました。　わたしたち　子(こ)ども　三人(さんにん)は　心(こころ)から[3]　両親(りょうしん)を　祝(いわ)って[4]あげたいと　思(おも)います。

❷ 弟(おとうと)と　妹(いもうと)は　何(なに)か　すばらしい　おくり物(もの)[5]を　あげる[6]と　言(い)っています。　わたしは　旅行(りょこう)の　切符(きっぷ)を　あげたいと　思(おも)います。

❸ 両親(りょうしん)は　戦争(せんそう)[7]の　直後(ちょくご)[8]に　結婚(けっこん)しました。　苦(くる)しい[9]　生活(せいかつ)[10]の　中(なか)で　わたしたち　三人(さんにん)を　よく　じょうぶに　育(そだ)て[11]てくれ[12]ました。　また　わたしを　大学(だいがく)にまで　行(い)かせてくれました。　両親(りょうしん)の　青春時代(せいしゅんじだい)[13]は　たいへんだったと　よく　聞(き)かされます。　戦(せん)

▼Sitting in a happy circle

語句

1 ryōshin　both parents
2 ginkon-shiki　silver wedding
3 kokoro kara　heartily, from the bottom of one's heart
4 -te-age·ru　See §74
5 okuri-mono　gift, present
6 age·ru　give　See §73
7 sensō　(Nv) war
8 choku-go　(N) immediately after
9 kurushi·i　hard, trying, needy
10 seikatsu　(Nv) living, daily life
11 sodate·ru　(Vt) raise, bring up, grow

争で　十分に[14]　勉強が　できなかった、　外国語なども　教えてもらわなかった[15]と　言います。

*　*　*

❹　きょうの　お祝いは　とても　楽しかったです。　子どもたちから　プレゼント[16]を　もらって[17]、両親は　たいへん　喜びました。　そして　なみだぐんで[18]いました。　父は　みんなに　記念の　せんす[19]を　くれ[20]ました。　それから、　みんなで　いろいろなことを　話したり、　歌を　歌ったり　しました。　めずらしく　母が　ことを　ひいてくれました。

❺　両親の　二十五年の　結婚生活[21]は　たいへん　多くの　ことを　教えてくれました。

▼A *Koto* concert

12 -te-kure•ru　See § 74
13 seishun-jidai　(one's) youthful days
　seishun　youth
14 jūbun　(Na/Adv) enough
15 -te-mora•u　See § 74
16 *purezento*　'present,' gift
17 mora•u　receive, be given　See § 73
18 namida-gum•u　be tearful
19 sensu　fan
20 kure•ru　give　See § 73
21 kekkon-seikatsu　married life

Dai 17-ka
Ginkon-shiki

1 Kyō wa watashi-tachi no ryōshin no ginkon-shiki desu. Chichi to haha ga kekkon-shite kara ni-jū-go-nen tachimashita. Watashi-tachi kodomo san-nin wa kokoro kara ryōshin o iwatte-agetai to omoimasu.

2 Otōto to imōto wa nani ka subarashii okuri-mono o ageru to itte-imasu. Watashi wa ryokō no kippu o agetai to omoimasu.

3 Ryōshin wa sensō no choku-go ni kekkon-shimashita. Kurushii seikatsu no naka de watashi-tachi san-nin o yoku jōbu-ni sodatete-kuremashita. Mata watashi o daigaku ni made ikasete-kuremashita. Ryōshin no seishun-jidai wa taihen datta to yoku kikasaremasu. Sensō de jūbun-ni benkyō ga dekinakatta, gaikoku-go nado mo oshiete-morawanakatta to iimasu.

* * *

4 Kyō no o-iwai wa totemo tanoshikatta desu. Kodomo-tachi kara *purezento* o moratte, ryōshin wa taihen yorokobimashita. Soshite namida-gunde-imashita. Chichi wa minna ni kinen no sensu o kuremashita. Sore kara, minna de iroiro-na koto o hanashitari, uta o utattari shimashita. Mezurashiku haha ga koto o hiite-kuremashita.

5 Ryōshin no ni-jū-go-nen no kekkon-seikatsu wa taihen ōku no koto o oshiete-kuremashita.

Lesson 17

Silver Wedding Anniversary

1 Today is our parents' silver wedding anniversary. It is twenty-five years since my father and mother were married. We three children would heartily like to congratulate them.

2 My younger brother and younger sister say they are going to give them a wonderful present. I think I will give them a travel coupon.

3 My parents were married right after the War. Even though life was hard, they did a good job of bringing the three of us up healthy. They even sent me to college. I have often heard how difficult things were when they were young. Because of the War, people could not study enough. And it is said that foreign languages were not taught at school.

* * *

4 The celebration today was great fun. Our parents were very happy to get presents from their children. They were moved to tears. My father gave all of us commemorative fans. Then we all talked, and sang, and had a good time. Mother even played the *koto* for us.

5 Our parents' twenty-five years of married life has really taught us a lot.

17

ANSWERS 〈pp. 208, 209〉

I. 1. age, age, age 2. kure, moratta 3. kure 4. age, kure
5. kure, kure, kure, age, morat, kure, morai, age

II. (a) Watashi wa tomodachi ni tanjō-bi no *pāti* ni kite-moraimashita. (b) Tomodachi wa watashi ni iroiro-na *purezento* o kuremashita. (c) Tomodachi wa watashi no imōto ni *kakuteru* o tsukutte-moraimashita. (d) Watashi wa tomodachi no hito-ri ni *piano* o hiite-moraimashita. (e) Watashi-tachi wa haha ni oishii gochisō o tsukutte-moraimashita.

III. 1. Watashi wa kanojo kara kirei-na *Kurisumasu-kādo* o (okutte-)moraimashita. (Kanojo wa watashi ni...o (okutte-)kuremashita.) 2. "Kare wa anata ni kippu o kuremashita ka?" "Iie, kuremasen deshita." ("Anata wa kare kara...moraimashita ka?" "Iie, moraimasen deshita.") 3. Kodomo ni michi o oshiete-moraimashita. (Kodomo ga...oshiete-kuremashita.) 4. Sensei ga isha o yonde-kudasaimashita. (Sensei ni...yonde-itadakimashita.) 5. Kyō wa jisho o ni-satsu motte-imasu kara, kore o kashite-agemasu.

●文法

§ 73 Verbs of Giving and Receiving

In Japanese, the verbs expressing giving and receiving depend upon WHO gives to WHOM. Thus, for example, the English verb 'to give' takes entirely different Japanese verbs in the following:

a. I gave the teacher a pen.

b. The teacher gave me a pen.

a′. Watashi wa sensei ni *pen* o **age**mashita. (<age-ru)

b′. Sensei wa watashi ni *pen* o **kure**mashita. (<kure-ru)

Furthermore, an English sentence such as *b* can be converted into:

c. I was given a pen by the teacher. (=I got a pen from the teacher.)

Japanese has still another verb **mora(w)-u** which corresponds to the passive form of the English 'give.'

c′. Watashi wa sensei ni/kara *pen* o **morai**mashita.

The decisive factors in the choice of verbs are the grammatical 'persons' (first, second, or third person) of the giver and the recipient.

The verb **age-ru** is chosen when:

'I/we give something to you/him/her.' (1→2, 3); 'You give to him/her.' (2→3) or; 'He/she gives to him/her.' (3→3)

The verb **mora(w)-u** is chosen when:

'I/we receive from you/him/her.'(1←2, 3); 'You receive from him/her.' (2←3) or; 'He/she receives from him/her.' (3←3)

The verb **kure-ru** is chosen when:

'You/he/she give to me/us.'(2, 3→1) or; He/she gives to you.' (3→2)

These three verbs also have their 'honorific' counterparts which are used to express special respect for the person involved in the relation. **Sashiageru**, instead of ageru, is used when the recipient is notably superior to the giver in age and/or status; **itadaku**, instead of mora(w)u, when the giver is superior to the recipient; and **kudasaru**, instead of kureru, when the giver is obviously superior to the recipient.

The uses of these Verbs of giving may be pictured as follows:

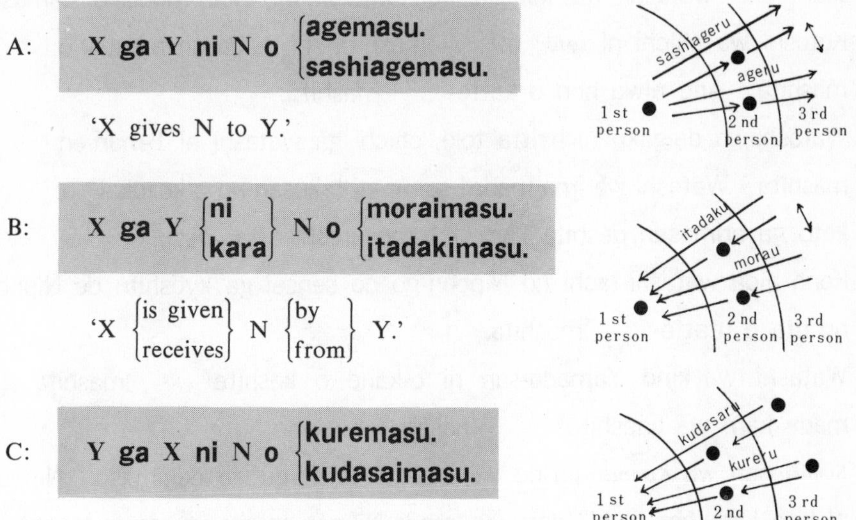

§ 74 Expressions of Benefactive Acts—Giving and Receiving Acts

Doing something for the benefit of someone else is regarded in Japanese as essentially the same as giving a thing to someone. Thus the Verbs expressing giving and receiving are attached (as auxiliaries) to the '-te form' of the Verb expressing the action. The uses of such Compound Verbs follow the same rules as in § 73.

A: **X ga Y ni (. . . o) V-te-agemasu.** 'X does...for Y.'

e.g. Watashi wa Tarō ni Ei-go o oshiete-agemashita.

B: **X ga Y ni (. . . o) V-te-moraimasu.** 'X has Y do...(for X).'

e.g. Watashi wa Tarō ni Nippon-go o oshiete-moraimashita.

C: **Y ga X ni (. . . o) V-te-kuremasu.** 'Y does...for X.'

e.g. Tarō ga watashi ni Nippon-go o oshiete-kuremashita.

●練習

ANSWERS→p. 205

I. Fill in the blanks with 'ageru,' 'morau,' or 'kureru.'

1. Mai-toshi[1] watashi wa kazoku no tanjō-bi[2] ni okuri-mono o shimasu. Kotoshi wa chichi ni *sētā*[3] o (   )mashita shi, haha niwa kutsu o (   ) mashita. Ane niwa hon o katte-(   )mashita.
2. Watashi ga daigaku ni haitta toki, chichi ga watashi ni 1-man-en (   ) mashita. Watashi wa ima made[4] sonna-ni takusan no o-kozukai[5] o (   ) koto ga arimasen deshita kara, totemo ureshikatta[6] desu.
3. Kono aida watashi-tachi no Nippon-go no sensei ga kyōshitu de Nippon no uta o utatte-(   )mashita.
4. Watashi wa kinō Yamada-san ni o-kane o kashite[7]-(   )mashita ga, mada kare wa kaeshite[8]-(   )masen.
5. *Sumisu*-san wa *Kanada*-jin de, *Furansu*-go to Ei-go ga dekimasu. Nippon ni kite kara han-toshi[9] desu ga, mada Nippon-go ga jōzu dewa arimasen. Kono aida *Sumisu*-san ga "Nippon-go o oshiete-(   )masen ka?" to watashi ni tanomimashita.[10] Watashi wa "Hai, ii desu. Sono kawari[11] ni watashi ni *Furansu*-go o oshiete-(   )masen ka?" to iimashita. *Sumisu*-san wa "Ii desu yo." to itte-(   )mashita node, ima watashi wa *Sumisu*-san ni Nippon-go o oshiete-(   )te, sono kawari ni *Furansu*-go o oshiete-(   )te-imasu. *Sumisu*-san wa tokidoki *Kanada* no kirei-na kitte o watashi ni (   )masu. Kyō mo watashi wa kirei-na hana no kitte o kare ni (   )mashita. Desukara, kondo no *Kurisumasu*[12] ni watashi wa nani ka Nippon no mono o kare ni (   )tai to omotte-imasu.

語句

1 mai-toshi every year, yearly
2 tanjō-bi birthday
 tanjō (Nv) birth
3 *sētā* 'sweater'
4 ima made until now, before
5 kozukai pocket money, allowance
6 ureshi・i happy, glad
7 kas・u lend cf. kari・ru (borrow)

II. Read the following and rewrite the underlined sentences to begin with the designated words.

Kinō wa watashi no tanjō-bi deshita. Tomodachi ga tanjō-bi no *pātī* ni kite-kuremashita.(a) Watashi wa tomodachi ni iroiro-na *purezento* o moraimashita.(b) Watashi no imōto wa tomodachi ni *kakuteru*[13] o tsukutte-agemashita.(c) Tomodachi no hito-ri ga watashi ni *piano* o hiite-kuremashita.(d) Watashi-tachi wa minna de utattari odottari shimashita. Ban-gohan ni haha ga watashi-tachi ni oishii gochisō o tsukutte-kuremashita.(e)

(a) Watashi wa

(b) Tomodachi wa

(c) Tomodachi wa

(d) Watashi wa

(e) Watashi-tachi wa

17

III. Put the following into Japanese.

1. I received a beautiful Christmas card[14] from her.
2. "Did he give you the ticket?" "No, he didn't."
3. I had a child show me the way.
4. The teacher called a doctor for me.
5. I have two dictionaries with me today. I will lend this one to you.

---

8 kaes·u return
9 han-toshi half a year
10 tanom·u ask, request, ask a favor of
11 sono kawari (ni) instead of that
12 *Kurisumasu* 'Christmas'
13 *kakuteru* 'cocktail'
14 *kādo* 'card'

●会話

KIREI DESU NĒ!

Pātī no kai-jō[1] ga wakaranai no desu[2] ga, dō shimashō?

—Watashi mo hakkiri[3] wakarimasen ga, daijōbu desu yo. Yamada-san fusai[4] ga kuruma de tsurete-itte-kuremasu kara.

Sore wa arigatai desu ga, wazawaza[5] koko made kite-morau no wa kinodoku[6] desu nē.

—Ii desu yo. Futa-ri wa *doraibu* ga suki na n desu. Soreni, kono aida anata ga Kyōto o annai-shite-ageta deshō? Sono o-rei[7] no tsumori[8] deshō kara, mā[9] ii desu yo.

Sō desu ka...? Sorejā, tsurete-itte-moraimashō.

—Yamada-san wa go-ji goro ni watashi no uchi ni yotte[10]-kuremasu kara, yo-ji-han goro oku-san to issho-ni kite-kudasai.

I don't know where the party is. What can I do?

—I'm not sure myself, but it's all right. Mr. and Mrs. Yamada will take us by car.

That's very good of them, but I'm sorry that they have to come all this way for us.

—That's all right. They both like to drive. Anyway, you showed them around Kyoto the other day, didn't you? Maybe they mean to repay you. Anyway, it's okay.

Really? Then, let's go with them.

—Mr. Yamada will drop over to my house around five, so please come with your wife at about four-thirty.

語句

1 kai-jō meeting place, site
2 ...no desu =...n desu
3 hakkiri (to) clearly, distinctly
4 fusai Mr. and Mrs. ...
5 wazawaza (Adv) going out of one's way (to do something)
6 kinodoku (Na) sorry, sad, pitiful
7 (o-)rei thanks, gratitude
8 tsumori intention, motive See § 77
9 mā perhaps, well
10 yor·u drop in, stop over
11 uketsuke reception

—Please get a rose from the receptionist, and put it at the pocket of your suit.
Yours is a white rose, since you are a special guest.
Will they make me give a speech at the party? I'm no good at making speeches.
—Since it is an informal group, you don't need to worry about it.
Now it's starting.
That person in the grey suit is Mr. Tanaka.
I'll introduce you later.
The girl in the beautiful *kimono* next to him is Tanaka's daughter.
How beautiful!
—Certainly is. The colors on the *kimono* are gorgeous.
No, no, I meant the young lady.

—Uketsuke[11] de bara no hana o moratte-kudasai. Sore o ***sūtsu***[12] no ***poketto***[13] ni sashite[14]-kudasai. Anata wa shiroi bara desu;

tokubetsu no o-kyaku-sama desu kara.

Pāti de ***supichi***[15] o saseraremasu ka? Watashi wa ***supichi*** ga nigate na n desu ga....

—Iya, kiraku[16]-na nakama[17] desu kara, sō ki ni shinakute[18] ii desu yo.

Sā, hajimarimasu yo.

Ano ***gurē***[19] no ***sūtsu*** no hito ga Tanaka-san desu.

Ato de shōkai-shite-agemashō.

Sono tonari no kirei-na kimono no onna no hito wa Tanaka-san no o-jō-san[20] desu.

Kirei desu nē!

—Kirei deshō. Ii iro no kimono desu.

Iya, iya, o-jō-san ga kirei da to itta no desu!

(office/desk) ←uketsuke·ru (accept/take up)
12 ***sūtsu*** 'suit'
13 ***poketto*** 'pocket'
14 sas·u stick, pierce, prick, stab
15 ***supichi*** 'speech'
16 kiraku (Na) easygoing, carefree
17 nakama company, party, colleague, comrade
18 ki ni suru worry about, be concerned over
19 ***gurē*** 'grey'
20 o-jō-san young lady/girl; daughter (Polite)

17

日 本 人

ジャパニーズ・スマイル[1]という[2] ことばが ある。 日本人は、 よく わけの わからない[3] わらいを[4] すると いわれる。 外国人は うす気味悪く[5] 思い、 これについて 悪口[6]を 言うが、 それは 日本人の 気質[7]を 知らないからである。

日本人は 昔から よい、 悪いという 判断を 直接[8]に はっきりと 言う ことを 避ける[9]。 相手の 立場[10]を 考えて、 その人を 傷つける[11] ことを おそれる[12]からである。

日本人は いつも 相手の 立場を 考えて、 ものを 言う[13]。 英語では 自分の 答え[14]が 肯定[15]の ときは、 'Yes'、 否定[16]の ときは、 'No'と 言うが、 日本語の 「はい」や 「いいえ」は 相手の 問い方[17]を 重んじる[18]。 たとえば、「行きませんか。」と 聞かれた ときは、 「はい、 行きません。」とか「いいえ、 行きます。」と 答える。 行かない ことを 相手が 予想[19]して 聞いていると 考えるからである。

人に 物を あげる ときでも、「つまらない 物ですが」と 言う。 人を よんで ごちそうする ときも 「何も ありませんが」と 言う。 理論的[20]には 「つまらない 物を もらっても しかたがない」、 「ない 物は 食べられない」と 考えられる。 しかし、 日本人は 自分で[21] 自分の 物を 「よい 物」とか 「りっぱな 物」 などとは 言わない。 それは 自分の 考え方[22]を 相手に おしつける[23] ことを 避けたいからである。

日本人の 表現[24]は このように いつも 複雑な 日本人の 心理[25]を 反映[26]している。

The Japanese

The Japanese are said to have an inscrutable grin dubbed "the Japanese smile." Uneasy in its presence, foreigners speak ill of this smile, but such criticism simply shows their lack of understanding.

The Japanese people have long avoided making direct and explicit judgments of good or bad. Instead, care is taken to consider the other person's position and not to hurt his feelings, and this has become an ingrained habit. Although English uses "yes" when the respondent's answer is affirmative and "no" when it is negative, the Japanese "*hai*" and "*iie*" depend upon the phrasing of the question. Thus "Don't you want to go?" is answered with "Yes, I don't." or "No, I do." in accordance with the asker's assumption that the person does not want to go.

Even giving someone something is accompanied by the disclaimer that "It's a mere trifle." Although it would not make sense to be giving out mere trifles, the Japanese hesitates to praise his gift to someone, this out of reluctance to impose a value judgment upon the recipient. In such ways does Japanese speech reflect the Japanese psychology.

17

語句

1 *Japanizu* 'Japanese'
2 *sumairu* 'smile'
3 wake no wakaranai inscrutable, impossible to understand
4 warai laughter ←wara·u
5 usu-kimi-waru·i weird, eerie
6 waru-kuchi slander, abuse, "bad mouth"
7 kishitsu disposition
8 chokusetsu (N/Adv) direct
9 sake·ru avoid
10 tachiba standpoint, point of view, position
11 kizu-tsuke·ru injure
12 osore·ru be afraid; worry
13 mono o i·u say something
14 kotae (N) answer ←kotae·ru
15 kōtei (Nv) affirmation
16 hitei (Nv) negation
17 toi-kata how it is asked
toi ←to·u (inquire, ask)
18 omonji·ru make much of, attach importance to
19 yosō (Nv) expectation, forecast
20 riron-teki (Na) theoretical, logical
riron theory, logics
21 jibun de by oneself cf. hitori de (for/by oneself)
22 kangae-kata way of thinking, how one thinks about things
23 oshitsuke·ru press, force
24 hyōgen (Nv) expression
25 shinri state of mind, psychology
26 han'ei (Nv) reflect

第 18 課

論文を　書く

TAPE
No. 5
Side 1

❶　ある　新聞社[1]が　「日本人　および[2]　日本文化[3]」という　タイトル[4]で　論文[5]を　募集[6]しています。　わたしは　日本の　伝統文化[7]に　興味[8]を　もっていますから、　論文を　書こう[9]と　思います。　題[10]は「日本の　伝統文化と　現代」に　しよう[11]と　思います。　たいへん　むずかしい　問題ですが、　以前[12]から　一度[13]　まとめて[14]みよう[15]と　思っていました。　さっそく　資料を　整理[16]したり、　図書館へ　行ったり　して、　勉強しようと　思っています。　外国人の　日本についての　研究書[17]も　もっと　読もうと　考えています。

❷　わたしの　友人の　スミスさんは　貿易の　仕事を　していますが、「日本人の　外国観[18]」という　題で　論文を　書くつ

語句

1 shinbun-sha　newspaper company
2 oyobi　and (Formal)
3 Nippon-bunka　Japanese culture
4 *taitoru*　'title'
5 ronbun　thesis, essay
6 boshū　(Nv) inviting people to apply; recruiting
7 dentō-bunka　traditional culture
8 kyōmi　interest, concern
9 -ō　See § 75
10 dai　title
11 -yō　See § 75
12 izen　(N) before
13 ichi-do　(N/Adv) once
14 matome·ru　(Vt) arrange; complete
15 -te-mir·u　do...and see　See § 89

もりだと[19] 言(い)っています。 彼(かれ)は、 いつか[20] 二人(ふたり)で いろいろ話(はな)し合(あ)おう[21]、 また 図書館(としょかん)へも 行(い)こうと 言(い)っています。

❸ 先日(せんじつ)[22] アメリカの 友人(ゆうじん)から 手紙(てがみ)が 来(き)ました。 その中(なか)で 彼(かれ)は、「わたしは 論文(ろんぶん)を 書(か)く つもりです。 日本(にっぽん)の 映画(えいが)について 考(かんが)えてみる つもりです。」と 書(か)いています。 わたしは 外国人(がいこくじん)の 「日本映画論(にっぽんえいがろん)[23]」は とても おもしろいと 思(おも)いました。 わたしは、 おたがいに[24] よい 論文(ろんぶん)を 書(か)きましょうと 返事(へんじ)[25]を 出(だ)しました。

▼A movie theater in Ueno

18

---

16 seiri (Nv) put things in order, (re-) arrange
17 kenkyū-sho research papers/book
18 -kan view of...
19 tsumori intention See §77
20 itsu ka some time, someday
21 hanashi-a·u talk with each other, discuss
-a·u do something together with somebody else
22 sen-jitsu the other day
23 -ron theory/discussion on/of...
24 (o-)tagai-ni each other, mutually
25 henji (Nv) answer, reply (to a letter), response

Dai 18-ka
Ronbun o Kaku

1 Aru shinbun-sha ga "Nippon-jin oyobi Nippon-bunka" to iu *taitoru* de ronbun o boshū-shite-imasu. Watashi wa Nippon no dentō-bunka ni kyōmi o motte-imasu kara, ronbun o kakō to omoimasu. Dai wa "Nippon no dentō-bunka to gendai" ni shiyō to omoimasu. Taihen muzukashii mondai desu ga, izen kara ichi-do matomete-miyō to omotte-imashita. Sassoku shiryō o seiri-shitari, tosho-kan e ittari shite, benkyō-shiyō to omotte-imasu. Gaikoku-jin no Nippon ni tsuite no kenkyū-sho mo motto yomō to kangaete-imasu.

2 Watashi no yūjin no *Sumisu*-san wa bōeki no shigoto o shite-imasu ga, "Nippon-jin no gaikoku-kan" to iu dai de ronbun o kaku tsumori da to itte-imasu. Kare wa, itsu ka futa-ri de iroiro hanashi-aō, mata tosho-kan e mo ikō to itte-imasu.

3 Sen-jitsu *Amerika* no yūjin kara tegami ga kimashita. Sono naka de kare wa, "Watashi wa ronbun o kaku tsumori desu. Nippon no eiga ni tsuite kangaete-miru tsumori desu." to kaite-imasu. Watashi wa gaikoku-jin no "Nippon-eiga-ron" wa totemo omoshiroi to omoimashita. Watashi wa, o-tagai-ni yoi ronbun o kakimashō to henji o dashimashita.

▲Movie theaters in Shinjuku

Lesson 18
Writing an Essay

1 One of the newpapers is soliciting essays on "The Japanese People and Japanese Culture." Since I am interested in traditional Japanese culture, I think I will write an essay. I think I will call it "Japan's Traditional Culture and the Present." It is a very difficult topic, but I have been wanting to organize my thoughts on this for some time. I think I will start studying it right away, organizing my material, going to the library, and otherwise working on it. I also want to read more of what foreign researchers have written about Japan.

2 A friend of mine named Smith, who is working for a trading company, says he plans to write an essay on "Japanese Views of Foreign Lands." He says we should get together some day to have a long talk and go to the library.

3 A letter came from my American friend the other day. In it, he wrote, "I intend to write an essay. I plan to give some thought to Japanese films." I think a foreigner's views on Japanese films would be very interesting. I wrote back with the hope that we both write good essays.

18

▼A scene from a Japanese film

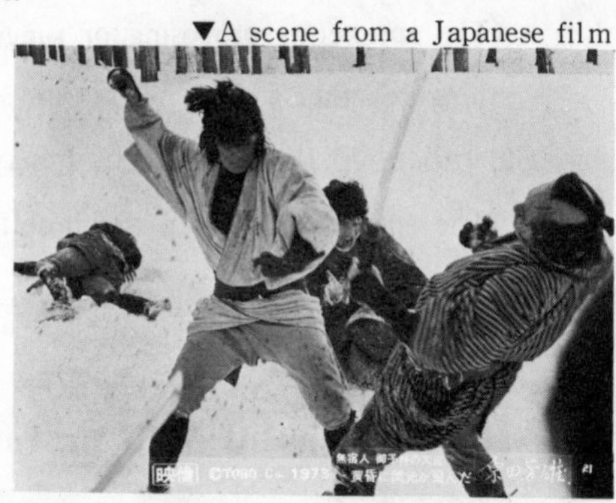

ANSWERS ⟨pp. 220, 221⟩

I. 1. kikimashō/kikō 2. ikimashō/ikō 3. haraimashō/haraō 4. machimashō/matō 5. mimashō/miyō 6. sōji-shimashō/sōji-shiyō 7. kimashō/koyō 8. kimemashō/kimeyō

II. 1. shiyō 2. aō 3. tabeyō 4. narō 5. kaō

IV. 1. A: ...iku tsumori desu. B: ...ikanai tsumori desu. 2. A: ...hanasu... B: ...hanasanai... 3. A: ...kuru... B: ...konai... 4. A: ...yameru... B: ...yamenai... 5. A: ...shūshoku-suru... B: ...shūshoku-shinai...

V. 1. benkyō-suru 2. mi ni ikimashō 3. shiyō 4. ikō 5. tsurete-iku

VI. 1. Rai-getsu kara jidōsha no unten o narau/narai-hajimeru tsumori desu. (...naraō/narai-hajimeyō to omoimasu.) 2. Kare ni riyū o setsumei-suru tsumori deshita ga, wasuremashita. 3. Mō ichi-nen Nippon ni iru tsumori desu. (...iyō to omoimasu.)

●文法

§ 75 Expressions of Will or Intent (1)

The speaker can express his will or intent, or ask the will or intent of the listener, simply by using the Present form of Verbs, affirmative or negative.

e.g. Anata wa ikimasu ka? 'Will you go?' 'Are you going?'
—Hai, ikimasu. 'Yes, I will go.' 'Yes, I am going.'
—Iie, ikimasen. 'No, I won't go.' 'No, I am not going.'

Will or intent can also be expressed by the 'Volitional form' of Verbs: ik-ō, nom-ō, nor-ō (1st Group); tabe-yō, mi-yō (2nd Group); and shiyō, koyō (Irregular). All take the -mashō form in the Polite style.

e.g. Mado o akemashō/akeyō ka? 'Shall I open the window?'
(The speaker is asking the will or desire of the listener about an action to be taken by the speaker.)

Ashita Kyōto e ikimashō/ikō. 'Let's go to Kyoto tomorrow.'
(The speaker is proposing or suggesting to the listener that they do something together.)

Sā, mō neyō (ka). 'Well, I may as well go to bed.'
(The speaker is talking to himself.)

§ 76 Expressions of Will or Intent (2)

(Watashi wa) V(Volitional form) **to omoimasu/omotte-imasu.**

'I think I will do...'; 'I am thinking of doing...'

e.g. (Watashi wa) kaisha o yameyō to omoimasu.
'I think I'll quit my company.'

(Watashi wa) rai-nen kuni e kaerō to omotte-imasu.
'I am thinking of going back to my country next year.'

NB: The difference between omoimasu and omotte-imasu is that omoimasu indicates the speaker's thoughts at the moment of speech, whereas omotte-imasu indicates that he has had that idea or intention over a longer span of time, including the time of speech. The subject of both these Present form Verbs is assumed to be the speaker himself, even if it is not mentioned. The Past form can take a third-person subject.

§ 77 Expressions of Will or Intent (3)

(Watashi wa) V(Dict. form) **tsumori desu.** 'I intend to do...'

e.g. Watashi wa bengoshi ni naru tsumori desu.

'I am going to be (intend to be) a lawyer.'

Watashi wa ano toki kaisha o yameru tsumori deshita.

'At that time I intended to quit the company.'

18

§ 78 Expressions of Will or Intent—Summary and Comparison

All the patterns introduced here are concerned primarily with the will or intent of *the speaker* (or *the listener* in a question). The Present forms and the Volitional forms express the will or intent of the speaker directly and subjectively, while those patterns introduced in § 76 and § 77 express it as a fact and with a more objective attitude. Thus to express past will (of anybody), it is necessary to use the patterns in § 76 and § 77.

In order to express the will or intent of a third person, such forms as '... to itte-imasu' ('he says that...'), '... rashii desu' ('it seems that...'), and so on must be added. (See § 63, § 112)

e.g. Yamada-san wa kuni e kaeru tsumori da to itte-imasu.

'Mr. Yamada says that he intends to go back home.'

●練習

ANSWERS→p. 217

I. Practice the pattern using the key phrases below.

Ex. (shinbun o yomu) Shinbun o yomimashō/yomō.

1. (*nyūsu* o kiku)
2. (kissa-ten e iku)
3. (o-kane o harau)
4. (tomodachi o matsu)
5. (eiga o miru)
6. (heya o sōji-suru)
7. (mō ichi-do kuru)
8. (ryokō no *sukejūru*[1] o kimeru[2])

II. Make dialogs as shown in the example.

Ex. Q: (kondo no Nichi-yōbi) (doko e iku) Anata wa kondo no Nichi-yōbi doko e ikō to omotte-imasu ka?

A: (yama) Yama e ikō to omotte-imasu.

1. Q: (kyō ie e kaette kara) (nani o suru) A: (*tenisu*)
2. Q: (ashita) (dare ni au) A: (tomodachi)
3. Q: (kon-ban[3]) (nani o taberu) A: (o-sushi)
4. Q: (shōrai[4]) (nani ni naru) A: (seiji-ka[5])
5. Q: (*bōnasu*[6] de nani o kau) A: (*sutereo*)

III. Make dialogs using 'tsumori' with the key phrases in II.

Ex. Q: Anata wa kondo no Nichi-yōbi doko e iku tsumori desu ka?

A: Yama e iku tsumori desu.

語句

1 *sukejūru* 'schedule'
2 kime・ru (Vt) decide cf. kimar・u (Vi)
3 kon-ban tonight, this evening
4 shōrai (N/Adv) in the future, time to come
5 seiji-ka politician, statesman
6 *bōnasu* 'bonus'
7 yame・ru stop...ing; quit
8 ichi-nichi-jū all day long
9 ukiyo-e (a kind of "floating-world" art developed in the Edo Period)
10 tenran-kai exhibition

IV. Practice the pattern using the key phrases below.

Ex. (*piano* o kaimasu) A: Watashi wa *piano* o kau tsumori desu.

B: Watashi wa *piano* o kawanai tsumori desu.

1. (ano daigaku ni ikimasu)
2. (kare ni hanashimasu)
3. (ashita daigaku e kimasu)
4. (Nippon-go no benkyō o yamemasu[7])
5. (ano kaisha ni shūshoku-shimasu)

V. Fill in the blanks.

Kinō no Nichi-yōbi, watashi wa ichi-nichi-jū[8] (1. study) tsumori deshita ga, asa tomodachi kara denwa ga atte, "Bijutsu-kan de ukiyo-e[9] no tenran-kai[10] ga arimasu kara (2. let's go to see)." to sasowaremashita.[11] Watashi mo ukiyo-e ga dai-suki[12] desu kara, benkyō wa yoru ni (3. will do) to omotte, tomodachi to issho-ni dekakemashita. Shikashi, hito ga ippai de hairu koto ga dekimasen deshita. Tsugi no Nichi-yōbi niwa asa hayaku (4. will go) to omoimasu. Imōto mo (5. take) tsumori desu.

VI. Put the following into Japanese.

1. I think I will start learning to drive next month.[13]
2. I intended to have explained the reason[14] to him, but I forgot.
3. I am thinking of staying in Japan for one more[15] year.

---

11 saso·u invite, call for, tempt
12 dai-suki (Na) like...very much cf. dai-kirai (hate)
13 rai-getsu next month cf. rai-shū (next week), rai-nen (next year)
14 riyū reason
15 mō more
mō ichi-nen one more year

18

●会話

HIKKOSU TSUMORI

Rippa-na o-uchi desu ne. Niwa mo hiroi shi, heya mo ōkute benri da shi, ii desu ne.

—Ni-nen mae ni tateta n desu ga ne. Chotto komatta koto[1] ga arimashite ne[2]....

Dō shita n desu ka?

—Iya, kōgai desu yo. Kinjo[3] ni kōjō ga dekimashite ne. Kemuri[4] yara[5] sōon[6] yara de, nayamasareru[7] n desu yo.

Sore wa ikemasen nē.... Sekkaku[8] ii o-uchi o tateta noni,[9] zannen desu ne.

—Ē, sorede, ima hikkosō[10] to omotte-iru no desu. Kono ie wa, zannen nagara,[11] uru tsumori desu.

Shikashi, kōgai de kōjō o uttaeru[12] koto ga dekimasen ka?

—Sō shiyō to omotte, kinjo no hito-tachi to sōdan[13]-shita no desu ga,

Lovely house, isn't it? The yard is big, and it's convenient with so many rooms. How nice!

—I built it two years ago, but we've been having some trouble.

What's the trouble?

—Well, it's pollution. A factory has been built in the neighborhood and we're annoyed by the smoke and noise.

That's terrible. After you built such a lovely house, that's too bad.

—Yes, so I'm thinking of moving. I hate to do it, but I'm going to sell this house.

But can't you file a suit against the factory over the pollution?

—I thought of that and talked it over with the

語句

1 komatta koto trouble, difficulty
2 ....-te ne , you know
3 kinjo neighborhood
4 kemuri smoke
5 ...yara=ya for example ...and
6 sōon noise
7 nayamas·u afflict, annoy cf. nayam·u (be vexed)
8 sekkaku...noni with much trouble/effort (in vain)
9 ...noni in spite of the fact that...
10 hikkos·u move (to a different house)
11 zannen nagara While it seems a shame/regret

neighbors, but it appears to be a rather difficult problem ....

Is that so? And where are you going to move to?

—I think I'll live in a really quiet neighborhood this time. Fortunately I found a good apartment.

I'm glad you did.

—Yes. It faces south and has a park right in front of it. It's on the second floor of a five-story apartment building. I like it very much. I'm going to move in next month. Please come and see us there.

Thank you.

nakanaka[14] muzukashii mondai deshite ne....

Sō desu ka. Sorede, doko e hikkosu tsumori desu ka?

—Kondo wa hontō-ni shizuka-na tokoro ni sumō to omotte-iru n desu yo. Saiwai, ii *manshon*[15] ga arimashite ne.

Sore wa yokatta desu ne.

—Ē, minami-muki[16] de chōdo ie no mae ga kōen desu. Go-kai-date[17] no ni-kai de, totemo ki ni itte[18]-iru n desu. Rai-getsu hikkosu tsumori desu. Ichi-do zehi asobi[19] ni kite-kudasai.

Arigatō gozaimasu.

18

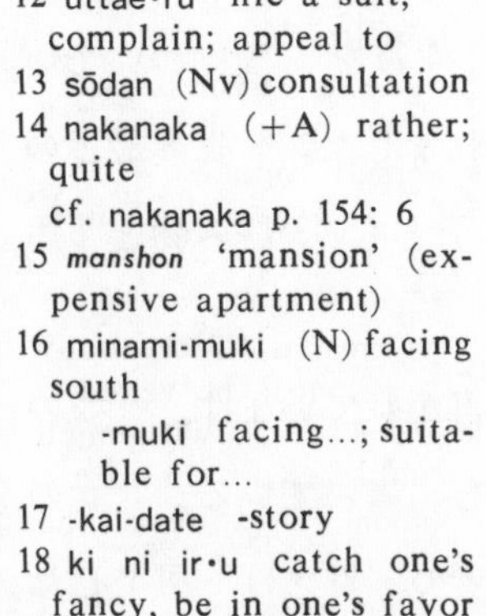

12 uttae·ru file a suit, complain; appeal to
13 sōdan (Nv) consultation
14 nakanaka (+A) rather; quite
cf. nakanaka p. 154: 6
15 *manshon* 'mansion' (expensive apartment)
16 minami-muki (N) facing south
-muki facing...; suitable for...
17 -kai-date -story
18 ki ni ir·u catch one's fancy, be in one's favor
19 asobi (N) play, pastime ←asob·u

日本の　文学—1

日本の　文学作品の[1]　中で、　いちばん　古い　作品は　「古事記」や　「日本書紀」の[2]　中の　歌です。　この　時代には、　特定の[3]　作者も[4]　なく、　人人の　口から　口へ　伝えられたと　言われています。

▼From *Kojiki*

八世紀の　中ごろ、「万葉集」が[5]　できましたが、この　ころ、すでに[6]　日本人によって　漢詩集も[7]　作られていました。

九世紀は、　日本の　政治・文化が　すべて　中国風に　なったので、　国風暗黒時代[8]と　言われています。しかし、　やがて　国粋文化が[9]　復活して[10]　905年に　「古今集」[11]ができました。

「古事記」や　「日本書紀」や　「風土記」[12]などの　中の　伝説が　人々に　語り伝えられ、[13]「竹取物語」[14]などの　物語が　生まれました。

また、歌の　説明から　長い　物語が　生まれました。その　代表が[15]　「伊勢物語」[16]です。

有名な　「源氏物語」は　この　二種類の　物語の　性質を[17]　受けついでいます。[18]　「源氏物語」は　十一世紀の　初めに　書かれました。　世界最古の[19]　すばらしい　文学作品の　一つですが、　当時は　女子どもの　読み物[20]と　思われていました。

「源氏物語」より　古い　「土佐日記」[21]も　かなで　書かれています。　この　「土佐日記」の　初めに、　「男が　日記という　ものを　書いている。　女の　わたしも　書いてみよう。」　と　言っています。　作者の　貫之は[22]　男でしたが、　女の　立場で　日記を　書く　つもりでした。　かな文学は[23]　このように[24]　当時は　女性の　文学でした。

Japanese Literature—1

The oldest Japanese literary works are said to be the anonymous poems handed down orally and finally recorded in the *Kojiki* and *Nihonshoki*.

Manyoshu was produced in mid-eighth century, by which time there were already Japanese anthologies of Chinese poetry.

While all aspects of Japanese culture was "Sino-ized" in the ninth century and native customs fell into eclipse, Japanese traditions were soon revived and *Kokinshu* was compiled in 905.

The legends in *Kojiki*, *Nihonshoki*, *Fudoki*, and others are folk tales, giving rise to stories such as *Taketori-Monogatari*. There were also long stories created to explain poems, of which *Ise-Monogatari* is typical.

Genji-Monogatari was influenced by both types. Although one of the world's oldest great works of literature, having been written early in the eleventh century, this was at first thought of as a story for women and children.

Tosa-Nikki, written even before *Genji-Monogatari*, also uses *kana* script. While it begins "Men are writing things called diaries, and I think I too will keep one even though a woman," the author, Tsurayuki, was actually a man trying to write from a female perspective using the "feminine" *kana*.

語句

1 bungaku-sakuhin literary works
   sakuhin a piece of work
2 Nihon-shoki ("history" book compil ed in 720)
3 tokutei no specific
4 sakusha author, artist
5 Man'yō-shū (the oldest anthology of Japanese poems, compiled in the 8th century) -shū collection
6 sude-ni=mō already (Formal)
7 Kanshi-shū anthology of Chinese poems
8 Kokufū-ankoku-jidai the Dark age of nationalism
9 kokusui-bunka nationalistic culture
10 fukkatsu (Nv) revival
11 Kokin-shū (anthology of Japanese poems compiled in the 10th century)
12 Fudo-ki (local documents of ancient times)
13 katari-tsutae•ru hand down orally from generation to generation
14 Taketori Monogatari (the title of a romance)
15 daihyō (Nv) represent; representative
16 Ise Monogatari (the title of a romance)
17 seishitsu nature, temper, character
18 uke-tsug•u inherit
19 sekai sai-ko the oldest in the world
   sai-ko the oldest
20 yomi-mono reading matter, things to read
21 Tosa Nikki (the title of a diary)
22 Tsurayuki (?-945)
23 kana-bungaku (literature written in *hiragana*)
24 kono yō-ni in this way, like this

第 19 課

彼の こと

TAPE
No. 5
Side 2

❶彼(かれ)は 来(く)る[1]でしょうか。

——わかりませんね。 来(こ)ないかもしれません[2]。 この間(あいだ)から青(あお)い 顔(かお)をして、 よく つかれたと 言(い)っていました。どこか[3] からだが 悪(わる)いのでしょうか。 病気(びょうき)かもしれませんね。

——そうかもしれません。しかし あの ようす[4]では ほか[5]に 何(なに)か なやみ[6]が あるにちがいありません[7]。

❷そうですね。 近(ちか)ごろの 彼(かれ)は ようすが 少(すこ)し おかしい[8]ですね。 よく お酒(さけ)を 飲(の)んだり、夜(よる) おそく 帰(かえ)ったりしています。きっと 何(なに)かが あったにちがいありません。

——仕事(しごと)の ことでしょうか。それとも 失恋(しつれん)[9]したのかもしれません。何(なに)か 言(い)っていましたか。

語句

1 deshō See §79
2 ...kamo shirenai it may be that, See §80
3 doko ka somewhere
4 yōsu (N) appearance, state of affairs
5 hoka (N) other
6 nayami trouble, worry
7 ...ni chigai na·i it is certain that...; it must be See §81
8 okashi·i strange; funny

❸いいえ。 彼は もともと 明るい[10] 元気な 青年[11]です。

その うち[12] きっと 元気な 顔を 見せる[13]でしょう。

——わたしも そうだろう[14]と 思います。 しかし 一度 ゆっくり 話し合った ほうが いいですね。 一度 彼の 所[15]へ いっしょに 行ってみましょう。

❹それは いいかもしれませんね。 きっと 喜ぶでしょう。

早い ほうが いいですね。 あすは どうですか。

——いいです。 それでは わたしが 彼に 連絡[16]します。

---

9 shitsuren (Nv) lost love, broken heart
10 akaru·i bright, light; cheerful
11 seinen young man
12 sono uchi before long
13 mise·ru (Vt) show, let...see
14 ...darō (Plain style of deshō) See §79
15 tokoro place
16 renraku (Nv) contact, get in touch

Dai 19-ka
Kare no Koto

1 Kare wa kuru deshō ka?

——Wakarimasen ne. Konai kamo shiremasen. Kono aida kara aoi kao o shite, yoku tsukareta to itte-imashita.

Doko ka karada ga warui no deshō ka? Byōki kamo shiremasen ne.

——Sō kamo shiremasen. Shikashi ano yōsu dewa hoka ni nani ka nayami ga aru ni chigai arimasen.

2 Sō desu ne. Chika-goro no kare wa yōsu ga sukoshi okashii desu ne. Yoku o-sake o nondari, yoru osoku kaettari shite-imasu. Kitto nani ka ga atta ni chigai arimasen.

——Shigoto no koto deshō ka? Soretomo shitsuren-shita no kamo shiremasen. Nani ka itte-imashita ka?

3 Iie. Kare wa motomoto akarui genki-na seinen desu. Sono uchi kitto genki-na kao o miseru deshō.

——Watashi mo sō darō to omoimasu. Shikashi ichi-do yukkuri hanashi-atta hō ga ii desu ne. Ichi-do kare no tokoro e issho-ni itte-mimashō.

4 Sore wa ii kamo shiremasen ne. Kitto yorokobu deshō. Hayai hō ga ii desu ne. Asu wa dō desu ka?

——Ii desu. Soredewa watashi ga kare ni renraku-shimasu.

▲A back street in Shinjuku

Lesson 19

A Friend

1 I wonder if he will come.

——Who knows? Maybe not. He has looked pale for a while and talks of being tired a lot.

Maybe there is something wrong with him. Maybe he is sick.

——Maybe. But the way he was, I am sure it is something else, that something is troubling him.

2 You are right. He has been a little strange lately. He has been drinking a lot and staying out late at night. There must be something wrong.

——I wonder if it could be his work. Or maybe he has fallen out of love. Has he said anything to you?

3 No. He has always been a bright and cheerful lad. In time, his face will regain its cheerfulness.

——I think so too. But still, maybe it would be best to sit down and have a long talk with him. Shall we go to his place sometime?

4 Maybe that would be a good idea. It would surely cheer him up. The sooner the better. How about tomorrow?

——Fine. I will tell him we are coming.

19

ANSWERS 〈pp. 232, 233〉

I. A. desu, desu B. desu, deshō C. kuru deshō D. ryokō-shinai deshō

II. 1. (She will go to the sea tomorrow.) 2. (She will likely go to the sea tomorrow.) 3. (It may be that she will go to the sea tomorrow.) 4. (She will surely go to the sea tomorrow.)

III. 1. ugokanai 2. omoi 3. benri 4. yunyū-hin

IV. 1. noboru 2. iku 3. ikanai 4. ōi 5. miru 6. subarashii 7. samui 8. motte-ikō

V. 1. Kare wa kan-ji o yomu koto ga dekimasen kara, kono hon ga wakaranai kamo shiremasen. 2. Kare wa Nippon-go de tegami o kaku koto ga dekimasu. Sukunakutomo ichi-nen (wa) benkyō-shita ni chigai arimasen.

●文法

§ 79 Expressions of Guessing (1)

The Present forms of Predicates may be used to express the speaker's opinion about what will happen in the future.

e.g. Ashita wa ame desu. 'It will rain tomorrow.'

Tarō wa kyō kimasu. 'Taro will come today.'

When the speaker is less sure, however, the Auxiliary form **-deshō** (**darō** in the Plain style) is added to the Present or Past forms of the Predicates. In the case of 'N/Na/A+desu,' deshō replaces desu.

N/Na A (present or past) V (present or past)	**deshō.**	'I guess....' 'Probably....'

e.g. Ashita wa ame deshō. 'I guess it will rain tomorrow.'

Ashita wa atsui deshō. 'It will probably be hot tomorrow.'

Tarō wa kyō kuru deshō. 'Taro will probably come today.'

Hanako wa konai deshō. 'I guess Hanako won't come.'

Tarō wa mō kaetta deshō. 'I guess Taro has gone home already.'

Adverbs such as **tabun** and **osoraku**, meaning 'maybe' and 'probably,' often occur with the 'deshō form.'

§ 80 Expressions of Guessing (2)

When the speaker is still less sure, or when he thinks that there is only a slight possibility, the form '**-kamo shiremasen/shirenai**' is used instead of deshō.

e.g. Ashita wa ame kamo shiremasen.

'It might rain tomorrow.' 'It might happen that it rains tomorrow.'

Tarō wa kita kamo shiremasen. 'It is possible that Taro came.'

When the sentence ends with -kamo shiremasen, adverbs such as **hyotto**

suru to or **moshi ka suru to** often precede the Predicate to indicate that the speaker is uncertain about what he is going to state.

e.g. Hyotto suru to ashita wa ame kamo shiremasen.

'It just might rain tomorrow.'

Tarō wa moshi ka suru to kyō konai kamo shiremasen.

'It just might be Taro does not come today.'

§ 81 Expressions of Guessing (3)

On the other hand, if the speaker wants to emphasize that he is quite sure about what he is saying, he may add **-ni chigai arimasen/nai**.

e.g. Ashita wa ame ni chigai arimasen.

'It will rain tomorrow for sure.'

Tarō wa kuru ni chigai arimasen.

'Taro will certainly come.'

The adverb **kitto** is very often used with such Predicates.

e.g. Ashita wa kitto ame ni chigai arimasen.

'I am sure it will rain tomorrow no doubt.'

Kare wa kitto sensei ni chigai arimasen.

'There is no doubt about it that he is a teacher.'

These adverbs, kitto, tabun, osoraku, hyotto suru to, and so on, are called 'Modal Adverbs,' because they are in agreement with the speaker's mental attitude. They help the listener to anticipate what the speaker is going to say, which is always expressed by the final form of the sentence.

●練習 ANSWERS→p. 229

I. Complete the sentences using 'desu' or 'deshō.'

A. Kinō wa Getsu-yōbi deshita.
Kyō wa Ka-yōbi _____.
Ashita wa Sui-yōbi _____.

B. Kinō wa ame deshita.
Kyō wa kumori[1] _____.
Ashita wa tabun hare _____.

C. Kare wa kinō daigaku e kimashita.
Ashita mo tabun daigaku e _____.

D. Kare wa kyo-nen no natsu ichi-do mo ryokō-shimasen deshita.
Kotoshi mo tabun _____.

II. Compare the following sentences.

1. Kanojo wa ashita umi e ikimasu.
2. Kanojo wa ashita umi e iku deshō.
3. Kanojo wa ashita umi e iku kamo shiremasen.
4. Kanojo wa ashita umi e iku ni chigai arimasen.

III. Substitute the key words for the underlined parts.

Ex. (operated by hand) A: Kono kikai wa te[2] de ugoku kamo shiremasen.
B: Kono kikai wa te de ugoku ni chigai arimasen.

語句

1 kumori cloudy weather ←kumor·u (get cloudy)
2 te hand, arm
3 ren-kyū consecutive holidays
4 ani elder brother cf. ane (elder sister), otōto (younger brother), imōto (younger sister)
5 kaze o hik·u catch cold

1. (doesn't work)

2. (heavy)

3. (convenient)

4. (imported article)

IV. Fill in the blanks.

Ashita to asatte wa ren-kyū[3] desu kara, watashi wa ani[4] to Fuji-san ni (1. climb) tsumori desu. Chichi mo watashi-tachi to issho-ni (2. go) kamo shiremasen. Haha mo yama ga suki desu ga, ima kaze o hiite[5]-imasu kara, tabun (3. not go) deshō. Ima wa daigaku mo natsu-yasumi-chū[6] desu kara, doko demo gakusei-tachi ga (4. many) to omoimasu. Watashi-tachi wa Fuji-san no chōjō[7] de asa-hi[8] o (5. see) tsumori desu. Sono nagame[9] wa kitto (6. wonderful) ni chigai-arimasen. Fuji-san no chōjō niwa mada yuki ga atte, (7. cold) kamo shiremasen kara, *sētā* o (8. will bring) to omoimasu.

V. Put the following into Japanese.

1. As he cannot read *kanji*, he might not understand this book.
2. He can write a letter in Japanese. He must have studied Japanese for at least[10] a year.

---

6 -chū (N/Adv) during...; in the midst of...

7 chōjō summit

8 asa-hi morning sun, rising sun

9 nagame view ←nagame・ru (look around)

10 sukunakutomo at least

19

●会話

DŌZO KOCHIRA E

Uketsuke wa kochira deshō ka?

—Hai, sō desu.

Kokusai[1]-bu no Maeda[2]-san ni aitai no desu ga.

—Maeda bu-chō[3] de gozaimasu[4] ne.

Shitsurei desu ga, o-kyaku-sama wa nan to osshaimasu[5] ka?

Igirisu no *Buraun* desu. Yamada-san no shōkai desu ga, bu-chō-san wa go-zonji[6] nai kamo shiremasen.

—Renraku-shite-mimasu. Shibaraku soko ni o-kake ni natte o-machi-kudasai.

(Denwa ni) Kochira uketsuke desu ga, Maeda bu-chō oraremasu[7] ka? *Buraun*-san to iu kata[8] ga miete[9]-imasu.

O-tōshi[10]-shimashō ka?...

Hai, shōchi[11]-shimashita.

O-matase-shimashita. Bu-chō wa ma-

Is this the reception desk?
—Yes, it is.
I'd like to see Mr. Maeda of the International Division.
—Do you mean Division Chief Maeda? Excuse me, but may I have your name, please?
I'm Mr. Brown from England. I have an introduction from Mr. Yamada, but I don't think Mr. Maeda knows me.
—I'll contact him.
Please be seated for a minute.
(on the phone)
This is the reception desk. Is Mr. Maeda there? A Mr. Brown is here to see you. Shall I send him up?...Yes, sir.
I'm sorry to have kept you waiting. Mr. Maeda

語句

1 kokusai- international
2 Maeda (a family name)
3 bu-chō department chief
4 ...de gozaimasu (very Polite form of desu)
5 osshar•u (Honorific form of i•u)
6 go-zonji (N) being informed of; acquainted with
7 orare•ru (Honorific form of i•ru)
8 kata =hito (Polite)
9 mie•ru (Honorific form of kuru, i•ru)
10 tōs•u let...pass, show in (visitor)
11 shōchi (Nv) understand, know, agree
12 ma-mo-naku soon, presently
13 -te-mairimas•u (Humble

will be down shortly. Will you wait in that room, please? Oh, no, I'm sorry. Some people may be using that room. Let me show you to another room. This way, please.

Thank you. Being a receptionist seems to be a busy job, isn't it?

—Well, I don't know. But it is an important job and we all do our best. This room, please. I'll bring you a cup of tea soon.

Thanks.

mo-naku[12] orite-mairimasu.[13]

Soko no ōsetsu-shitsu[14] de o-machi-kudasai. Iya, shitsurei-shimashita,[15] soko wa ima shiyō-chū[16] kamo shire-masen. Betsu[17] no o-heya ni go-annai-mōshiagemasu.[18] Dōzo kochira e.

Arigatō. Uketsuke no o-shigoto wa iso-gashii deshō ne?

—Ē, mā .... Demo, taisetsu-na shigoto desu kara, watashi-domo[19] isshō ken-mei[20] yatte-orimasu.[21]

Kono heya desu. Dōzo.

Sugu-ni[22] o-cha o o-mochi-shimasu.[23]

Dōmo.

19

form of -te-kuru)
14 ōsetsu-shitsu drawing/reception room
15 Shitsurei-shimashita (Cph: used in apologizing)
16 shiyō-chū (N) be occupied, be in use
    shiyō (Nv) use
17 betsu (N) something else, different
18 -mōshiagemasu (Humble form of suru)
19 watashi-domo we (Humble)
20 isshō kenmei with all one's might
21 or•u =i•ru See § 37
22 sugu(-ni) (Adv) soon, immediately
23 o-mochi-suru (Polite form of motte-iku/-kuru)

▼Office buildings in Tokyo

経済生活[1]

日本の　経済成長率[2]は　世界第一位と　言われている。1971年の　国民総生産[3]、GNPは　1955年に　比べて[4]、9.17倍になり、　アメリカ、ソ連に　ついで、　世界第三位である。しかし　国民　一人当たりの　所得[5]は　1971年現在[6]、　世界第13位である。　物価[7]は　毎年[8]　上昇[9]して、　インフレ[10]の　傾向にある。公共施設[11]の　不足[12]も　目立[13]っている。

日本の　失業率[14]は、低くて、　わずか[15]　1.2％であるが、　労働条件[16]は　あまり　よくない。労働時間[17]は　平均[18]　週42時間ぐらいであり、その　平均賃金は　税金を　ふくめて　月66,000円ぐらいだ。

いろいろな　社会保障制度は　一応[19]　あるが、　その　内容[20]や　額は　まだまだ[21]　不十分[22]である。今、社会保障の　一人当たりの　給付額[23]は　イタリアや　イギリスの　$\frac{1}{4}$から　$\frac{1}{5}$、西ドイツ[24]の　$\frac{1}{8}$である。今後[25]、社会保障はもっと　充実するだろうが、スウェーデンや　西ドイツに　追いつく[26]までには、何年も　かかるにちがいない。

日本は　この　経済成長の　うらに[27]　もう　一つ　大きな　問題を　もっている。それは　公害の　問題だ。これについては　別の　章[28]で　述べよう。

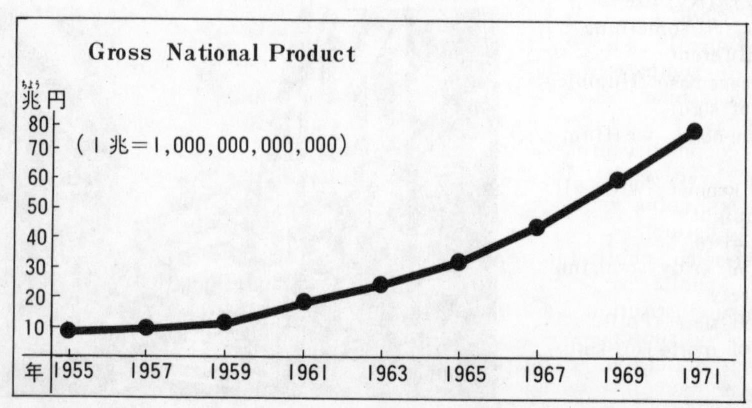

The Japanese Economy

Japan's economic growth rate is the highest in the world, GNP marking a 9.17-fold expansion between 1955 and 1971 to become third-largest in the world, surpassed only by the U.S. and the U.S.S.R. However, per-capita income was still 13th in 1971, prices have shown inflationary annual increases, and the social infrastructure is strikingly inadequate.

While Japanese unemployment is a low 1.2%, working conditions are not so favorable, people averaging a 42-hour week yet earning only ¥66,000 per month before taxes.

Although various social security systems have been provided, they are deficient both qualitatively and quantitatively. For example, social security payments are only 1/4 to 1/5 those of Italy, England, and other nations—and only 1/8 those in West Germany! Even though improvements may be expected, it will be some years before Japan catches up with Sweden or West Germany.

In addition, Japanese economic growth has also been accompanied by the very important problems of pollution generated, but this issue is taken up elsewhere.

19

語句

1 keizai-seikatsu economic life
2 keizai-seichō-ritsu economic growth rate
　seichō (Nv) growth
3 kokumin-sō-seisan gross national product (GNP)
　sō- general..., all...
4 kurabe·ru compare (with)
5 shotoku income
6 -genzai as of...
7 bukka commodity prices
8 mai-nen every year
9 jōshō (Nv) going up, rise
10 *infure* 'inflation'
11 kōkyō-shisetsu public facilities
　kōkyō public
　shisetsu institution, facilities
12 fusoku (Nv) shortage
13 medats·u stand out, be conspicuous
14 shitsugyō (Nv) unemployment
15 wazuka (Na) only, no more than
16 rōdō-jōken working conditions
　jōken condition
17 rōdō-jikan working hours
18 heikin (N/Adv) average
19 ichiō (N/Adv) to speak tentatively/roughly
20 naiyō content
21 mada-mada still; not yet (more emphatic than mada)
22 fu-jūbun (Na) not enough
23 kyūfu-gaku delivery, payment
　kyūfu (Nv) payment
24 Nishi-*Doitsu* West Germany
　nishi west
25 kongo from now on, in the future
26 oitsuk·u overtake, catch up with
27 ura back/reverse side
　cf. omote (surface, face)
28 shō chapter

第 20 課

わたしの　ふるさと

TAPE
No. 5
Side 2

❶ 昨夜(さくや)[1]、ゆめを　見(み)ました。ふるさとの　ゆめです。わたしの　ふるさとは　信州(しんしゅう)[2]の　小(ち)さな　村(むら)です。東京(とうきょう)へ出(で)て来(き)てから　仕事(しごと)が　忙(いそが)しくて、めったに　帰(かえ)れ[3]ません。今度(こんど)の　年末(ねんまつ)[4]には　五年(ごねん)ぶり[5]に　帰(かえ)る　つもりです。

❷ 信州(しんしゅう)は　日本(にほん)アルプス[6]の　山々(やまやま)や　湖(みずうみ)など　美(うつく)しい　景色(けしき)で有名(ゆうめい)です。また　そば[7]や　みそが　おいしくて　よく　知(し)られています。いまでは　全国(ぜんこく)　どこででも　買(か)えます。先日(せんじつ)も　ふるさとの　みそが　恋(こい)しくて[8]　デパートへ　買(か)いに　行(い)きました。評判(ひょうばん)[9]が　よくて　よく　売(う)れて[10]います　と　店員(てんいん)[11]も　言(い)っていました。

▲Kamikochi in Shinshu

❸ わたしの　家(いえ)から　日本(にほん)アルプスの　山々(やまやま)が　見(み)えます[12]。

語句

1 saku-ya　last night
　saku-　last... cf. saku-jitsu (yesterday), saku-nen (last year)
2 Shinshū　(a district name)
3 -e•ru　See §82
4 nen-matsu　(N/Adv) (toward) the end of the year
　-matsu　the end of...　cf. getsu-matsu
5 -buri　after an interval of..., for the first time in...
6 Nihon *Arupusu*　the Japan Alps
7 soba　(a kind of Japanese noodle)
8 koishi•i　that one longs for/misses
9 hyōban　reputation
10 ure•ru　sell (well)　See §83
11 ten-in　attendant, store clerk
12 mie•ru　be visible, can be seen　See §83
13 naki-goe　(sounds of animals in general) cry, whine, call, sing, chirp, twit-

夏(なつ)は　とても　すずしくて、　ときどき　うぐいすの　美(うつく)しい　鳴(な)き声(ごえ)[13]が　聞(き)[14]こえます。　また　すぐ　近(ちか)くの　きれいな　川(かわ)で　泳(およ)げます。　冬(ふゆ)は　たいへん　寒(さむ)いですが、　雪(ゆき)は　とても　美(うつく)しいです。　近(ちか)くで　スキー[15]も　スケート[16]も　できます。　冬(ふゆ)の　寒(さむ)い　夜(よる)、　いろり[17]を　かこんで　いろいろ　話(はな)し合(あ)う　ことも　とても　楽(たの)しいです。

❹　父母(ふぼ)[18]は　どうしているでしょうか。　父母(ふぼ)の　ことが　思(おも)い出(だ)されます。　何度(なんど)か[19]　東京見物(とうきょうけんぶつ)に　さそいましたが、　畑(はたけ)[20]の　仕事(しごと)などが　忙(いそが)しくて　なかなか　出(で)て来(こ)られ[21]ません。

❺　もう　向(む)こうは　かなり　寒(さむ)いだろうと　思(おも)います。　雪(ゆき)が　降(ふ)っているかもしれません。　この　冬(ふゆ)は　久(ひさ)しぶり[22]に　本場(ほんば)[23]の　そばが　食(た)べられます。　今(いま)から　楽(たの)しみ[24]です。

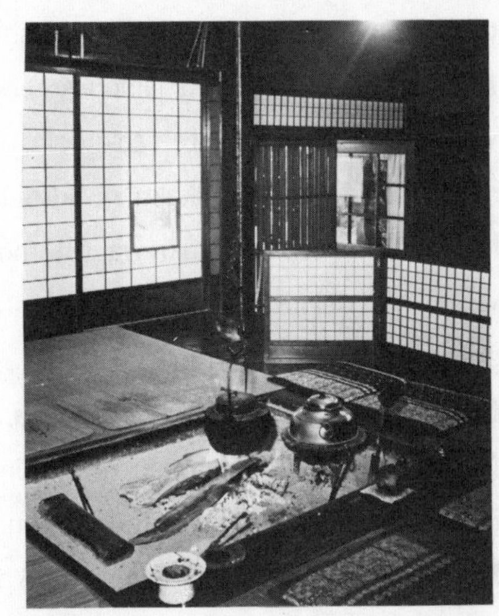

▲An *irori*

---

ter, etc.; crying (sobbing, weeping, etc.) of people
　nak·u　weep, cry, whine, call, sing, chirp, etc.
14 kikoe·ru　be audible, can be heard　See §83
15 *suki*　'skiing'
16 *sukēto*　'skating'
17 irori　(a Japanese-style fireplace)
18 fubo　father and mother
19 nan-do ka　several times
20 hatake　(farm) field
21 -rare·ru　See §82
22 hisashi-buri　(N) after a long interval
23 hon-ba　(N) the home of, the best place for
24 tanoshimi　pleasure, what one looks forward to ←tanoshim·u (enjoy)

Dai 20-ka
Watashi no Furusato

1 Saku-ya, yume o mimashita. Furusato no yume desu.

Watashi no furusato wa Shinshū no chiisa-na mura desu. Tōkyō e dete-kite kara shigoto ga isogashikute, mettani kaeremasen. Kondo no nen-matsu niwa go-nen-buri ni kaeru tsumori desu.

2 Shinshū wa Nihon-*Arupusu* no yama-yama ya mizuumi nado utsukushii keshiki de yūmei desu. Mata soba ya miso ga oishikute yoku shirarete-imasu. Ima dewa zen-koku doko de demo kaemasu. Sen-jitsu mo furusato no miso ga koishikute *depāto* e kai ni ikimashita. Hyōban ga yokute yoku urete-imasu to ten-in mo itte-imashita.

3 Watashi no ie kara Nihon-*Arupusu* no yama-yama ga miemasu. Natsu wa totemo suzushikute, toki-doki uguisu no utsukushii naki-goe ga kikoemasu. Mata sugu chikaku no kirei-na kawa de oyogemasu. Fuyu wa taihen samui desu ga, yuki wa totemo utsukushii desu. Chikaku de *sukī* mo *sukēto* mo dekimasu. Fuyu no samui yoru, irori o kakonde iroiro hanashiau koto mo totemo tanoshii desu.

4 Fubo wa dō shite-iru deshō ka. Fubo no koto ga omoi-dasaremasu. Nan-do ka Tōkyō-kenbutsu ni sasoimashita ga, hatake no shigoto nado ga isogashikute nakanaka dete-koraremasen.

5 Mō mukō wa kanari samui darō to omoimasu. Yuki ga futte-iru kamo shiremasen. Kono fuyu wa hisashi-buri ni hon-ba no soba ga taberaremasu. Ima kara tanoshimi desu.

▶A farmhouse

Lesson 20

My Home Town

1 I had a dream last night. It was a dream about my home town. It is a small village in the Shinshu region. I have been so busy with my work since I came to Tokyo that I have not been able to go back very often. I plan to go back this December for the first time in five years.

2 Shinshu is famous for the beautiful scenery of the mountains and lakes of the Japan Alps. It is also well-known for its delicious *soba* and *miso*. Now you can buy them anywhere in Japan. The other day I was longing for some *miso* from Shinshu and went to a department store to buy it. The clerk said it is very popular and sells well.

3 I can see the Japan Alps from my home. The summers are very cool and we can sometimes hear the nightingale's beautiful song. We can also swim in a clear river nearby. The winters are very cold, but the snow is just beautiful. We can ski and skate nearby. During the cold winter nights, it is great fun to gather around the hearth and talk.

4 I wonder how my parents are. I often think about them. I have invited them to come sight-seeing in Tokyo several times, but they are too busy with farming and everything to get away easily.

5 It is probably rather cold in Shinshu already. There may even be snow. This winter I will be able to enjoy real *soba* for the first time in many years. I am looking forward to it already.

ANSWERS 〈pp. 244, 245〉

I. 1. Anata wa *Supein*-go ga hanasemasu ka? 2. ...*uiskī* ga nomemasu ka? 3. ...mō is-shū-kan matemasu ka? 4. ...ie ga kaemasu ka? 5. ...sashimi ga taberaremasu ka? 6. ...asa hayaku okiraremasu ka? 7. ...Nippon-go de denwa ga kakeraremasu ka? 8. ...kuruma ga unten dekimasu ka? 9. ...kaigi ni shusseki-dekimasu ka? 10. ...mō ichi-do koko e koraremasu ka?

III. 1. noremasen deshita 2. tsukemasen deshita 3. kikoemasu 4. dekimasen 5. miemasu 6. mieru 7. miemasen

IV. 1. "Koko wa dōro no jidōsha no oto ga kikoemasen ka?" "Hai. Kono heya wa taihen shizuka desu kara, yoku benkyō-dekimasu." 2. Kinshi desu kara, kokuban no ji ga miemasen. 3. Kono hon wa taihen yoku urete-ite, kotoshi no *besuto-serā* no hito-tsu desu.

●文法

§ 82 Expressions of Ability

As has already been noted, the idea 'someone can do (is able to do) something,' can be expressed with the pattern: (§ 66)

X wa (**N** o) **V** (Dict. form) koto ga dekimasu.

This pattern can be simplified by using what is called the 'Potential form' of the Verb.

X wa {**V**-(Stem) (1st Group) **-e-** / **V**-(Stem) (2nd Group) **-rare-**} masu.

e.g. Watashi wa shinbun o yomu koto ga dekimasu. 'I can read the paper.'

→Watashi wa shinbun ga yom-**e**-masu.

Anata wa Ei-go o oshieru koto ga dekimasu ka? 'Can you teach English?'

→Anata wa Ei-go ga oshie-**rare**-masu ka?

The Irregular Verb suru becomes dekiru.

e.g. Anata wa unten-suru koto ga dekimasu ka? 'Can you drive?'

→Anata wa unten dekimasu ka?

The other Irregular Verb kuru changes to either **koreru** or **korareru**.

e.g. Anata wa ashita hito-ri de koko e koremasu/koraremasu ka?

'Can you come here tomorrow by yourself?'

NB: (1) The Potential form of Verbs is inflected just like 2nd Group Verbs.

(2) When a Verb takes the Potential form, it gains an Adjective-like quality, so that the (original) object of the Verb (e.g. shinbun in the first example above) becomes the Subject of the Predicate, taking the Particle ga, instead of o, as seen in above examples.

cf. 'I can read the paper.'→'The paper is *readable*.'

§ 83 Expressions of 'Spontaneity'

Expressions in English such as 'I can see Mt. Fuji from my window,' 'Can you hear me?' (over the telephone), or 'Do you understand this?' often appear in Japanese as 'Mt. Fuji is visible from my window.' 'Is my voice audible?' 'Is this understandable?' (or, 'Is this clear?'). The forms of the verbs used here are the same as the Potential forms, with a few exceptions as shown below. They are called the 'Spontaneous forms,' as distinct from the Potential forms, because they do not mean that something (Mt. Fuji or the voice in the above examples) has a certain ability to do something, but rather that such came about spontaneously, or that something has such and such innate property.

One of the striking differences between Japanese and English is that in expressions involving feeling (like, dislike, hate, etc.), perception (see, hear, smell, etc.), or conception (think, regard, etc.), Japanese prefers expressing as 'subject' what is usually expressed as 'object' in English. Some examples have already come up.

Compare the following English and Japanese expressions.

'I love you.' Anata ga suki desu.

'I want coffee.' *Kōhī* ga hoshii desu.

'I need a million yen now.' (Watashi wa) ima hyaku-man-en irimasu.

'Can you teach English?' (Anata wa) Ei-go ga oshieraremasu ka?

'We can see Mt. Fuji clearly today.' Kyō wa Fuji-san ga yoku miemasu.

'Can you hear me?' (Watashi no koe ga) kikoemasu ka?

Compare also such expressions as the following.

'This book sells well.' Kono hon wa yoku uremasu.

'This knife doesn't cut well.' Kono *naifu* wa yoku kiremasen.

'Do you understand this?' Kore ga wakarimasu ka?

20

●練習

ANSWERS→p. 241

I. Make questions and answers with the key phrases as shown in the example.

Ex. (write *kanji*) Q: Anata wa kan-ji ga kakemasu ka?

A: Hai, kakemasu. (or, Iie, kakemasen.)

1. (speak Spanish)
2. (drink whisky)
3. (wait another week)
4. (buy a house)
5. (eat *sashimi*)
6. (get up early in the morning)
7. (make a telephone call in Japanese)
8. (drive a car)
9. (attend[1] the meeting)
10. (come here once again)

II. Answer the following questions.

1. Anata wa *gitā*[2] ga hikemasu ka?
2. Anata wa *taipu* ga utemasu ka?
3. Anata wa saikin yoku nemuremasu ka?
4. Anata wa kan-ji ga iku-tsu gurai yomemasu ka?
5. Anata wa hyaku-*mētoru* o jū-byō[3] inai[4] de hashiremasu ka?
6. Anata wa *rajio* no shūri ga dekimasu ka?
7. Anata wa nan-*mētoru* gurai oyogemasu ka?

語句

1 shusseki (Nv) attendance, presence
2 *gitā* 'guitar'
3 -byō second(s)
4 ...inai within...
5 itsumo no usual, as always
6 uta-goe singing voice
7 oto sound
8 hiru-yasumi lunch break

III. Fill in the blanks.

Watashi no kaisha wa Tōkyō no kōgai ni arimasu. Watashi no ie kara kaisha made *basu* de san-jup-pun gurai desu. Shikashi, kesa wa ku-ji goro ni okimashita kara, itsumo no[5] *basu* ni (1. could not board). Sukoshi aruite, densha ni norimashita. Shikashi, itsumo no jikan niwa (2. could not arrive).

Kaisha no chikaku ni ongaku-gakkō ga atte, itsumo kirei-na uta-goe[6] ya *piano* no oto[7] ga (3. can be heard). Hiru-yasumi[8] niwa *biru* no okujō[9] e ikimasu. Soko dewa wakai hito-tachi ga *barē-bōru* o shite-imasu. Watashi wa *barē-bōru* ga (4. cannot play) kara, tomodachi to hanashitari, atari no keshiki o nagame-tari[10] shimasu. *Biru* no okujō kara wa Tōkyō-*tawā*[11] ga yoku (5. can be seen). Fuji-san ga (6. can be seen) koto ga arimasu. Shikashi, kumori no hi ya ame no hi niwa dochira mo (7. cannot be seen).

20

IV. Put the following into Japanese.

1. "Don't you hear (the noise of) the cars in the street here?"

   "No. It is very quiet in this room. I can study well."

2. Being near-sighted,[12] I cannot see (the writing[13] on) the blackboard.

3. This book is selling very well; and is one of this year's best sellers.[14]

---

9 okujō roof (topmost floor) of a building
10 nagame·ru look at, view
11 *tawā* 'tower'
12 kinshi =kin-gan (N) near-sighted
13 ji letter, character, handwriting
14 *besuto-serā* 'best seller'

●会話

SOROIMASHITA KA?

A: Mō minna soroimashita[1] ka? Shuppatsu-dekimasu ka?

B: Iie, Kobayashi[2]-san to Yamada-san ga mada desu.

A: Iya, Yamada-san wa kyūyō[3] de korarenai to denwa ga arimashita.

B: Suruto,[4] ato wa Kobayashi-san dake desu ne?

C: Kare wa jikan ni ***rūzu***[5] da kara, okureru kamo shiremasen ne.

B: Densha wa nan-ji ni demasu ka?

A: Hachi-ji ni-jū-go-fun ni demasu. Daijōbu desu, mada jikan wa arimasu yo.

C: Kyō wa yukkuri to Chūzenji-ko[6] ga miraremasu ka ne?

A: Chūzenji-ko to Kegon-no-taki[7] o mawatte, roku-ji niwa ryokan ni tsukemasu. Yuttari-shita[8] ***sukejūru*** desu.

A: Are we all here now? Can we get started?

B: No, Mr. Kobayashi and Mr. Yamada are not here yet.

A: Mr. Yamada phoned to say that something has come up suddenly making it impossible for him to come.

B: Then, that leaves only Mr. Kobayashi.

C: He's very careless about time, so he may be late.

B: What time does the train leave?

A: It leaves at 8:25. It's all right, we still have time.

C: Can we take our time seeing Lake Chuzenji today?

A: After looking round Lake Chuzenji and Kegon Falls, we can get to the inn by six o'clock. This is a leisurely schedule.

語句

1 soro•u complete preparations (in the sense of having everyone/everything needed ready)
2 Kobayashi (a family name)
3 kyūyō urgent business
4 suruto then
5 ***rūzu*** 'loose'
6 Chūzenji-ko Lake Chuzenji
7 Kegon-no-Taki Kegon Falls
8 yuttari-shita (+N)

B: Ah, there he is! Mr. Kobayashi has arrived. Kobayashi! Over here!
K: Sorry to be late. No excuse for it. I thought I might not get here in time, so I came by taxi.
B: In your haste, are you sure you didn't forget anything?
K: There's nothing to worry about. I got everything ready before I went to bed last night.
A: Now that everyone's here, we have to hurry. I'm afraid we might miss the train.

B: Ā, kita! Kobayashi-san ga kimashita yo.
Kobayashi-san, kotchi[9] desu yo!
K: Iyā..., okurete-shimaimashita.[10]
Dōmo mōshiwake arimasen.[11]
Ma ni awanai[12] ka to omotte,
takushī de kimashita.
B: Sonna-ni awatete,[13] wasure-mono[14] wa arimasen ka?
K: Sore wa shinpai irimasen.
Saku-ya junbi-shite kara nemashita kara.
A: Sā, kore de zen'in[15] soroimashita.
Sukoshi isoganakereba[16] narimasen.
Ressha ni norenai kamo shiremasen yo.

20

without squeezing
9 kotchi this way; here cf. atchi (that way), dotchi (which way, where)
10 -te-shima·u See § 88
11 mōshiwake na·i inexcusable, unpardonable
12 ma ni a·u be in time
13 awate·ru make haste, rush, hurry, be frantic
14 wasure-mono something left behind
15 zen'in all the members
16 isog·u hurry

日本の 芸能[1]

▲*No*

お正月です。 笛[2]や 太鼓[3]の 音が 聞こえてきます。 あれは 「しし舞[4]」です。

ししは 普通[5]は ライオンの ことで、このような おどりは アジア[6]の 各地[7]で 見られます。 日本では、 昔の 人が この おどりで 田畑[8]から しかや いのしし[9]を 追い出しました。

日本の 農村[10]では、 昔から 田の 神を まつって[11]、 おどりました。 その おどりは 「田楽[12]」と 言われました。 千年ほど 前、 朝鮮から アジア大陸[13]の 音楽が 伝えられました。 それを 「散楽[14]」と 言います。 それが 「猿楽[15]」と なり、 これと 田楽とから 「能[16]」が できました。

十四世紀ごろ 世阿弥[17]という 人が 「花伝書[18]」を 書き、 能の 理論を 完成[19]しました。 能では 「幽玄[20]」と いう ことばが よく 使われます。 たとえば、 世阿弥は 「岩[21]に 花が 咲く。 それが 幽玄だ。」と 言っています。 あなたの 心の 目[22]に 幽玄の 花が 見えませんか。

「狂言[23]」は 短い 劇で、 こっけいな[24] ものが 多く、 普通は 能の 間に 上演[25]されますが、 それだけでも 上演できます。

「文楽[26]」は 散楽の 中の 人形劇[27]です。 十六世紀の 中ごろから びわ[28]に かわって[29] 三味線[30]が 伴奏[31]に 使われました。 十八世紀ごろ 近松[32]という 人気作家[33]が 出て、 文楽が 民衆[34]に 愛[35]されました。

「歌舞伎」は、 十七世紀ごろ 出雲の お国[36]という 女が 京都で 人々に 見せ、 たいへん 評判に なりました。 江戸時代[37]、 能は 武士の 芸術、 歌舞伎は 町人[38]の 芸術と され、 武士は 表向き[39]には 歌舞伎を 見に 行けませんでした。

Japanese Arts

The sound of drums and flutes at New Year's signals the coming of the "lion dance." Common throughout Asia, "lion dances" were once performed in Japan to drive deer and wild boar from the fields. Farmers in ancient times also had the *Dengaku* festival dedicated to the god of the rice paddies. In addition, there was the *Sangaku* music introduced from the Asian mainland by way of Korea some 1,000 years ago. This later became *Sarugaku*, and it is the combination of these two, *Dengaku* and *Sarugaku*, which gave birth to *No*.

The ideals of *No* were set forth in a book called *Kadensho* written by Zeami around the 14th century, and one of the words commonly used to express this esthetic is *yugen*. For example, Zeami wrote "A flower blooms upon a rock. This is *yugen*." Can you picture this fanciful flower?

Kyogen are short, usually comical, plays. Although typically performed between *No* segments, they can also be played alone.

Bunraku is a puppet theater form within the *Sangaku* tradition. After *shamisen* replaced *biwa* accompaniment in the mid-16th century, *Bunraku* became popular with the masses in the 18th century with the emergence of the playwright Chikamatsu.

Kabuki was acclaimed in the 17th century when an actress named Okuni from Izumo performed in Kyoto. Still, *No* was theater for the *samurai* and *Kabuki* was for the common man, *samurai* not openly attending *Kabuki* performances.

語句

1 geinō performing arts, entertainment
2 fue flute
3 taiko drum
4 shishi-mai lion dance mai dance
5 *raion* 'lion'
6 *Ajia* 'Asia'
7 kaku-chi each place, every part of the country
kaku- each cf. sekai-kak-koku (each/every nation in the world)
8 ta-hata rice paddies and vegetable fields ta rice field
9 inoshishi wild boar
10 nō-son agricultural village cf. gyo-son (fishing village)
11 matsur·u enshrine, deify
12 Dengaku (a traditional dance)
13 *Ajia*-tairiku Asian Continent
14 Sangaku (a traditional dance)
15 Sarugaku (a traditional dance)
16 Nō(-gaku) *No* theater
17 Zeami (founder of *No*; 1363-1443)
18 Kaden-sho (title of a book)
19 kansei (Nv) complete
20 yūgen (N) subtle and profound
21 iwa rock
22 me eye
23 Kyōgen (an interlude comedy)
24 kokkei (Na) funny, humorous
25 jōen (Nv) put on (a show)
26 Bunraku (a puppet drama)
27 ningyō-geki puppet play
28 biwa (a traditional musical instrument)
29 ...ni kawatte taking the place of...
30 shamisen (a traditional musical instrument)
31 bansō (Nv) accompaniment
32 Chikamatsu (1653-1724)
33 ninki-sak-ka popular writer
34 minshū people, general public; common people
35 ai (Nv) love
36 Izumo no Okuni (?-1607)
37 Edo-jidai Edo Period (1603-1867)
Edo (the old name for Tokyo)
38 chōnin townsman (in Edo Period)
39 omote-muki (N) officially, on the surface (implying that the real state of affairs is hidden behind)

第 21 課

久しぶりの 訪問

TAPE
No. 6
Side 1

❶ 先日 久しぶりに 友人の 山口[1]さんを たずねました。彼は 小説を 書いていますが、まだ あまり 有名では ありません。彼の 家は 郊外の 団地[2]に あります。

❷ 彼は 音楽が たいへん 好きですから、レコードを 持って行きました。ドボルザーク[3]の「新世界より」[4]です。彼は ドボルザークが とても 好きです。

❸ 彼は 仕事ちゅう[5]は いつも ドアに かぎ[6]を かけておき[7]ます。そこで、前もって[8] 電話を しておきました。

雨上がり[9]でしたから、団地の どの[10] 家の ベランダ[11]にも かさや せんたく物[12]が ほして[13]ありました[14]。

❹ 彼は 久しぶりの 訪問を とても 喜んでいました。「好きな レコードを 持って来てくれて ありがとう。」と 言いました。机の 上には 本や ペンや 原稿用紙[15]が いっぱい 置いてありました。彼は きょうじゅうに 原稿を 書いてしまわなければならないと 言いながら さっそく ウイスキーを 出してきました。わたしは「だいじょうぶかい、仕事を してしまった ほうが いいんじゃないか[16]。きょうは もう すぐ

語句

1 Yamaguchi (a family name)
2 danchi large (apartment) complex
3 *Doboruzāku* 'Dvořák'
4 Shin-sekai yori 'From the New World'
5 shigoto-chū (N) at work, while working
6 kagi key, lock
kagi o kake·ru lock (V)
7 -te-ok·u See §85
8 mae-motte in advance, beforehand
9 ame-agari (N) after the rain
←ame ga agar·u (it stops raining)
10 dono...mo every...
11 *beranda* 'verandah'

帰るよ。」と 言いましたが、 彼は 「だいじょうぶだ。 もう ほとんど できている。」と 言って 引き止め[17]ました。

❺ 彼は もう 何日も 人と 会わないで 仕事を していたからでしょうか、 小説の こと、 音楽の ことなどを 夢中[18]に なって しゃべり[19]ました。 彼は 「おなかが すいてきたね。 ご飯に しようか。」と 言いましたが、 仕事の じゃまに なっては[20] いけないので、 断わって[21] 帰って来ました。 帰りに、 彼は 今度の 小説は 自信[22]が あるから、 ぜひ 読んで みてくれと 言いました。

▲An apartment complex in Tokyo

---

12 sentaku-mono washing, laundry
13 hos•u (Vt) dry (in the sun)
14 -te-aru See §84
15 genkō-yōshi manuscript paper
 genkō manuscript
16 ja =dewa (Colloquial)
17 hiki-tome•ru ask someone to stay
18 muchū (N) utter absorption
19 shaber•u chatter; talk
20 jama ni nar•u be in the way
21 kotowar•u refuse, decline; warn
22 jishin self-confidence

Dai 21-ka
Hisashi-buri no Hōmon

1 Sen-jitsu hisashi-buri ni yūjin no Yamaguchi-san o tazunemashita. Kare wa shōsetsu o kaite-imasu ga, mada amari yūmei dewa arimasen. Kare no ie wa kōgai no danchi ni arimasu.

2 Kare wa ongaku ga taihen suki desu kara, *rekōdo* o motte-ikimashita. *Doboruzāku* no "Shin-sekai yori" desu. Kare wa *Doboruzāku* ga totemo suki desu.

3 Kare wa shigoto-chū wa itsumo *doa* ni kagi o kakete-okimasu. Sokode, mae-motte denwa o shite-okimashita.

Ame-agari deshita kara, danchi no dono ie no *beranda* nimo kasa ya sentaku-mono ga hoshite-arimashita.

4 Kare wa hisashi-buri no hōmon o totemo yorokonde-imashita. "Suki-na *rekōdo* o motte-kite-kurete arigatō." to iimashita. Tsukue no ue niwa hon ya *pen* ya genkō-yōshi ga ippai oite-arimashita. Kare wa kyō-jū ni genkō o kaite-shimawanakereba naranai to iinagara sassoku *uisukī* o dashite-kimashita. Watashi wa "Daijōbu kai? Shigoto o shite-shimatta hō ga ii n ja nai ka? Kyō wa mō sugu kaeru yo." to iimashita ga, kare wa "Daijōbu da. Mō hotondo dekite-iru." to itte hiki-tomemashita.

5 Kare wa mō nan-nichi mo hito to awanaide shigoto o shite-ita kara deshō ka, shōsetsu no koto, ongaku no koto nado o muchū ni natte shaberimashita. Kare wa "Onaka ga suite-kita ne. Gohan ni shiyō ka?" to iimashita ga, shigoto no jama ni natte wa ikenai node, kotowatte kaette-kimashita. Kaeri ni, kare wa kondo no shōsetsu wa jishin ga aru kara, zehi yonde-mite-kure to iimashita.

Lesson 21

A Visit to a Friend

1 I visited my friend Yamaguchi the other day for the first time in a long time. He is a novelist, but he is not very well known yet. He lives in a housing development in the suburbs.

2 Since he is very fond of music, I took him a record. It was Dvořák's *New World*. He likes Dvořák a lot.

3 He always keeps the door locked when he is working. So I had called ahead to tell him I was coming.

Since it had just rained, all of the verandahs had umbrellas and wash hanging out to dry.

4 He was very pleased at having me visit. "Thank you for bringing me this good record," he said. His desk was covered with books, pens, manuscript paper, and the like. He said he had to finish writing something by tomorrow, but while saying that, he got out a bottle of whisky for us. I said, "Is it okay? Shouldn't you finish your work? I won't stay very long today." but he stayed me with "It's all right. It's almost finished."

5 Maybe it was because he had been working for days without talking with anyone. He talked nonstop about novels, music, and everything. Although he said he was hungry and suggested we eat, I turned down the offer and came home because I didn't want to keep him from his work too long. As I was leaving, he told me he had confidence in the story he was writing and told me to be sure to read it.

ANSWERS 〈pp. 256, 257〉

I. 1. tabete-shimaimashita 2. kaite-shimaimashita 3. benkyō o shite-shimaimashita 4. shirabete-shimaimashita 5. tsukatte-shimaimashita

IV. 1. B: motte-iki A: motte-ika 2. B: tabete-iki 3. A: tsurete-ike B: tsurete-itte

V. 1. katte-kite 2. tsurete-ki 3. yonde-ki

VI. 1. kimashita 2. kimashita 3. ikimasu 4. ikimasu 5. kimashita

●文法

§ 84 V-te + Auxiliary Verbs (1)

V-te-aru (V: active, transitive)

This form indicates that something is in a certain state, but it is different from other stative expressions in that this implies that the state has been brought about by an unidentified person.

e.g. *Doa* ni kagi ga kakete-arimasu. 'The door is locked.'

(Almost synonymous with '*Doa* ni kagi ga kakatte-imasu.')

In addition this pattern often involves the meaning of being ready.

e.g. Heya ga totte-arimasu. (toru 'take')

'There is a room reserved.'

§ 85 V-te + Auxiliary Verbs (2)

V-te-oku (V: active, transitive or intransitive)

This means 'to put or leave something in a certain state' with the implication that the action is intended as preparation for some future use or occasion.

e.g. Denki o tsukete-okimashō.

'Let's leave the light on (because we are coming back soon, etc.).'

Denwa o kakete-oita hō ga ii desu. 'You'd better call (ahead).'

§ 86 V-te + Auxiliary Verbs (3)

V-te-iku 'do...and go' or 'go...ing'

e.g. Gohan o tabete-ikimashō. 'Let's finish lunch and then go.'

Kodomo wa hashitte-ikimashita. 'The child went running.'

§ 87 V-te + Auxiliary Verbs (4)

V-te-kuru

(1) 'do...and come' or 'come ...-ing'

e.g. Gohan o tabete-kimashita. 'I ate before I came.'

Kamera o motte-kite-kudasai. 'Please bring your camera.'

(2) Event in progress—toward the speaker:

e.g. Samuku natte-kimashita ne. 'It's gotten colder, hasn't it?'

§ 88 V-te + Auxiliary Verbs (5)

V-te-shima(w)u 'bring an action (V) to an end' or 'finish...'

e.g. Ano hon o yonde-shimaimashita ka? 'Have you finished the book?'

NB: This form is used mainly to emphasize, in one way or another, the completion of an action or event, the effect varying depending upon the form (Past, Imperative, Volitional, etc.) and the context.

e.g. Baka-na koto o itte-shimatta. 'I have said a foolish thing.'

Hayaku tabete-shimai-nasai. 'Come on. Finish up (eating) quickly!'

Kyō-jū ni kono shigoto o shite-shimaō.

'Let's finish this work today.'

21

§ 89 V-te + Auxiliary Verbs (6)

V-te-miru 'do...and see (how it will turn out)' or 'try ...ing and see'

e.g. Ichi-do haite-mite-kudasai. 'Please try them on (and see if they fit).'

Yamada-san wa uchi ni iru deshō ka? 'I wonder if Yamada's at home.'

—Sā . . . Denwa o kakete-mimashō.

'Who knows? Why don't we call him up (and find out)?'

●練習

ANSWERS→p. 253

I. Make questions and answers with the key phrases using '-te-shimau' as shown in the example.

Ex. (kono hon o yomu)

Q: Anata wa mō kono hon o yonde-shimaimashita ka?

A: Hai, mō yonde-shimaimashita.
(or Iie, mada desu.)

1. (hiru-gohan o taberu)
2. (ronbun o kaku)
3. (shiken no benkyō o suru)
4. (mondai o shiraberu[1])
5. (o-kane o tsukau)

II. Describe the interior of the room using '-te-aru' as shown in the example.

Ex. Mado ga akete-arimasu.

III. Using the picture above, make dialogs with '-te-oku' as shown in the example.

Ex. Q: Mado o akete-okimashō ka?

A: Hai, akete-oite-kudasai. (or Iie, akete-okanaide-kudasai.)

語句

1 shirabe·ru examine, investigate, check

2 dōbutsu-en zoo

dōbutsu animal cf. shokubutsu (plants)

3 hito-hako one box/package

IV. Practice the following dialogs adding the appropriate '-te-iku' forms.

1. A: Ashita yama e ikimashō.

   B: *Kamera* o (   )mashō ka?

   A: Iie, *kamera* wa (   )nai hō ga ii deshō.

2. A: Ima kara Nara e ikimasu ga, mukō ni tsuite kara hiru-gohan o tabemashō ka?

   B: Iya, koko de (   )mashō.

3. A: Watashi no kodomo wa dōbutsu-en[2] e ikitagatte-imasu ga, watashi wa isogashikute (   )masen.

   B: Soredewa, watashi ga (   )-agemashō.

V. Complete the sentences using the appropriate forms of '-te-kuru.'

1. *Tabako*-ya e itte, *tabako* o hito-hako[3] (   )-kudasai.
2. Kanojo wa *pātī* ni kodomo o (   )mashita.
3. Haha ga byōki desu kara, watashi wa isha o (   )masu.

VI. Fill in the blanks with the appropriate forms of 'kuru' or 'iku.'

1. Higashi no sora ga akaruku-natte-(   ).
2. Ame ga futte-(   ).
3. Niji[4] ga dandan kiete[5]-(   ).
4. Kokoro to kokoro ga hanarete-(   ).
5. Kare no kangae[6] ga wakatte-(   ).

21

---

4 niji rainbow
5 kie·ru disappear
6 kangae thought, idea ←kangae·ru

●会話

NOKOSHITE-OKITAI

—Kore ga Kyōto no Minami-za[1] desu.

Takusan no kanban[2] ga kakete[3]-arimasu ne.

—Ē, yakusha[4] no namae ga kaite-arimasu. 'Maneki'[5] to iimasu.

Sā, hairimashō.

Kippu o katte-kimashō ka?

—Iya, kippu wa mō katte-arimasu.

Kono mae Kyōto e kita toki ni katte-okimashita.

Sono hi niwa nakanaka kaemasen.

Sore wa arigatai. . . .

....

—Dō desu, omoshirokatta desu ka?

Ē, taihen omoshirokatta desu ga, kotoba ga wakarimasen deshita.

—Kotoba wa Nippon-jin nimo nakanaka wakari-nikui[6] desu yo.

Wakai hito wa amari mi ni ikimasen.

—This is the Kyoto Minami-za Theater.

There sure are a lot of signboards hanging outside.

—Yes, the names of the actors are written on them.

They're called "maneki."

Let's go in.

Shall I get the tickets?

—No, I already have our tickets. I bought them the last time I came to Kyoto.

It's quite difficult to buy same-day tickets.

That's very nice of you.

....

—How did you like it? Interesting?

Yes, it was very interesting, although I didn't understand the words.

—The language is difficult for Japanese too. Young people don't go to see it very often.

語句

1 Minami-za (the name of the *Kabuki* theater in Kyoto)
  -za ...theater
2 kanban signboard, advertising billboards
3 kake•ru hang
4 yakusha actor
5 Maneki billboards ← manek•u (invite)
6 -nikui difficult to...

Sō desu ne. O-toshiyori[7] ga ōkatta desu ne.

—Kabuki mo kono-mama dewa horonde[8]-shimau kamo shiremasen. Nokoshite[9]-okitai desu.

Nō ya Kyōgen mo onaji desu ka?

—Onaji yō-ni sutarete[10]-imasu.

Nippon no koten[11]-geijutsu ga nakunatte-iku no wa zannen desu ne.

You're right. There were a lot of old people there.

—If this continues, *Kabuki* may die out. I'd like to see this preserved.

Are *No* and *Kyogen* in the same state?

—They're dying out, too. It's regrettable that the traditional arts of Japan are perishing, isn't it?

▲The *maneki* at Minami-za

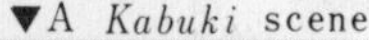

▼A *Kabuki* scene

21

---

7 toshiyori (N) old (person)

8 horob·u =horobi·ru (Vi) cease to exist, decline, decay

9 nokos·u (Vt) leave behind, preserve
cf. nokor·u (Vi)

10 sutare·ru go out of use, die out, decline

11 koten classics

企　業

日本は、大企業[1]がふえてきたが、まだまだ中小企業[2]が多い。事業所[3]総数[4]の約99％が、従業員[5]300人未満[6]の中小企業である。逆[7]に、従業員1,000人以上の大企業は、全体の0.2％ぐらいしかない。従業員数では、中小企業が全体の67％以上を占めている。一般に、中小企業は、大企業に比べて[8]、労働条件が悪く、生産性[9]も低い。大企業は、部品[10]などを賃金の安い中小企業に下請け[11]させている。

一方、鉄鋼産業[12]や自動車産業、電機産業などの中には、世界有数[13]の大企業もある。三井[14]、三菱[15]、住友[16]、安田[17]などの戦前[18]の財閥[19]も依然として[20]、主要[21]な位置[22]を占め、多くの産業部門[23]に、それぞれの系列会社[24]を持っている。

明治[25]以来[26]、資本主義[27]の発展が非常に急速だった。国家[28]の保護が、急速な発展の要因[29]だったと言える。このような政策が、日本経済の中に、二重構造[30]をもたらし[31]、大企業と中小企業の格差[32]を拡大[33]してきた。

現在、日本の企業は、国営[34]、公営[35]、私営[36]に分け[37]られる。日本国有鉄道[38]（国鉄）、たばこなどの専売事業[39]、国有林業[40]などは、国営である。地下鉄、市電[41]、市バス[42]などは公営で、あとは私営である。また、会社事業の中では、株式会社[43]組織[44]のものがいちばん多い。

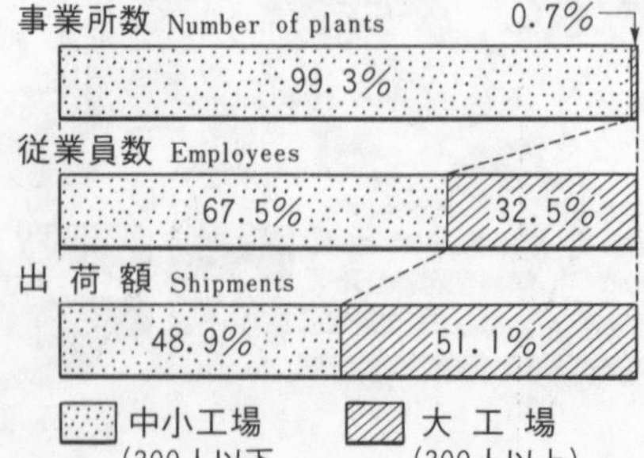

▼An ironworks

Industry

Although large-scale industries have expanded, most of Japanese industry is still small, approximately 99% of all places of work employing fewer than 300 people. By contrast, industries employing 1,000 or more account for only 0.2% of the total. Thus small business employs more than 67% of the working population. Generally, labor conditions are worse and productivity is lower in small businesses. Yet the major companies subcontract the manufacture of parts etc. to these smaller companies where wages are lower.

At the same time, Japanese steel, automobile, electrical equipment, and other companies are among the world's leaders. The prewar Mitsui, Mitsubishi, Sumitomo, Yasuda, and other *zaibatsu* groups are still important and still have their affiliates throughout the industrial structure.

Spurred on by state protections, Japanese capitalism has grown rapidly since the Meiji Restoration, yet these policies have induced a dual structure with increasing disparities between large and small companies.

Japanese industry includes such state-run enterprises as the Japanese National Railways, the Japan Monopoly Corporation, and the national forest services; public-operated utilities such as subways, streetcars, buses, and others; and all the rest private enterprises, most of them joint-stock companies.

語句

1 dai-kigyō big business
  kigyō business, enterprise
2 chūshō-kigyō small- and medium-size business
3 jigyō-sho place of business
  jigyō enterprise
4 sō-sū the total number
  sū the number of...
5 jūgyō-in employee, worker
6 ...miman less than...
7 gyaku (N) reverse
  gyaku ni conversely
8 ...ni kurabete as compared with
9 seisan-sei productivity
10 buhin parts of a machine
11 shita-uke subcontract
12 tekkō iron and steel
13 sekai-yūsū among the greatest in the world
14, 15, 16, 17 Mitsui, Mitsubishi, Sumitomo, Yasuda (names of *zaibatsu* groups)
18 sen-zen (N/Adv) prewar time cf. sen-go (postwar time)
19 zaibatsu gigantic business concerns, capital cliques
20 izen to shite still, as it used to be
21 shuyō=omo (Na) main
22 ichi position
23 bumon field, section
24 keiretsu-gaisha member company of a big business group
25 Meiji (name of an Emperor [1852-1912] and era [1868-1912])
26 ...irai since...
27 shihon-shugi capitalism
  shihon capital
28 kokka nation, state
29 yōin main factor/cause
30 ni-jū-kōzō dual structure
  -jū -fold
31 motaras·u bring about
32 kakusa difference
33 kakudai (Nv) expansion, enlarging
34 koku-ei (N) government-operated
35 kō-ei (N) public-operated
36 shi-ei (N) privately operated
37 wake·ru classify; divide, distribute
38 Nippon-kokuyū-tetsudō=Koku-tetsu Japanese National Railways
  kokuyū state-owned
39 senbai-jigyō monopoly business
  senbai (Nv) exclusive selling, monopoly
40 ringyō forestry
41 shi-den city streetcar
42 shi-*basu* city bus
43 kabushiki-gaisha joint-stock company
  kabu shares, stocks
  -shiki form cf. yō-shiki
44 soshiki organization, system

21

第 22 課

冬の 手紙

TAPE
No. 6
Side 1

❶ だんだん 寒(さむ)く なってきましたが、 その後(ご)[1] お変(か)わり[2] ありませんか。 わたしは かぜを ひいてしまいました。 毎朝(まいあさ)の 出勤(しゅっきん)[3]が とても つらい[4]です。 あなたも 奥(おく)さんも 気(き)を つけてください。

❷ 先日(せんじつ)は 突然(とつぜん)[5] おじゃまして ご迷惑(めいわく)[6]を かけました。 久(ひさ)しぶりでしたので、 つい[7] ゆっくりしてしまいました。 奥(おく)さんにも 親切(しんせつ)に してもらって たいへん うれしかったです。

❸ もう 三(さん)か月(げつ)で あなたも 一児(いちじ)[8]の 父親(ちちおや)[9]に なりますね。 何(なに)かと[10] たいへんでしょうが、 家庭(かてい)が いっそう[11] 楽(たの)しく にぎやかに なるでしょうね。

❹ あの 夜(よる) 帰(かえ)り道(みち)[12] 少(すこ)し お酒(さけ)に よっていた[13]ので、 川(かわ)べり[14]を ぶらぶら[15] 歩(ある)きました。 風(かぜ)が ヒューヒュー[16]と 吹(ふ)いていましたが、 あまり 寒(さむ)く 感(かん)じませんでした。 それは お酒(さけ)の せいばかり[17]ではなくて、 あなたがたの ことが ほのぼの[18]と むね[19]の 中(なか)に あったからでしょう。

語句

1 sono go after that, from that time on, since then
2 o-kawari arimasen ka? (Cph) Hope you are still well. (←lit. Have there been any changes in your situation?)
3 shukkin (Nv) go to work
4 tsura·i hard, painful, hard to bear
5 totsuzen (Adv) suddenly
6 meiwaku (Nv/Na) annoyance, nuisance, bother
meiwaku o kake·ru cause trouble, make a bother of oneself
7 tsui in spite of oneself, without intending
8 ichi-ji one child
9 chichi-oya =chichi father cf. haha-oya (mother)
10 nani ka to in various ways, with this or that, somehow
11 issō (Adv) all the more

　その　夜(よる)は　都会(とかい)には　めずらしく　星(ほし)が　きらきらと[20]　かがやいて[21]いました。

❺　もう　すぐ　お正月(しょうがつ)ですね。　これから　しばらく　忙(いそが)しくなって、　なかなか　会(あ)えないでしょうが、　おたがいに　しっかり[22]　がんばって[23]　よい　年(とし)を　むかえましょう。

❻　さくらの　ころには　赤(あか)ちゃん[24]に　会(あ)えますね。

　それでは、　お元気(げんき)で。　奥(おく)さんと　おなかの　赤(あか)ちゃんによろしく。

12月(がつ)3日(か)

22

▲Dotonbori in Osaka

---

12 kaeri-michi　the way back
13 yo·u　get drunk
14 kawa-beri　river bank
15 bura-bura (to)　(onomat) idly, aimlessly
16 hyū-hyū (to)　(onomat) (sound of whistling wind)
17 ...no sei　owing to..., caused by..., the fault of...
18 hono-bono (to)　(onomat) warmly; dimly, faintly
19 mune　chest, heart
20 kira-kira(to)　(onomat) twinkle, glitter
21 kagayak·u　glitter, glisten, twinkle
22 shikkari (to)　(onomat) firmly, tightly, decidedly, positively
23 ganbar·u　exert oneself, put up a good fight, persist, stand firm, hang in
24 aka-chan　baby

Dai 22-ka
Fuyu no Tegami

1 Dandan samuku natte-kimashita ga, sono go o-kawari arimasen ka? Watashi wa kaze o hiite-shimaimashita. Mai-asa no shukkin ga totemo tsurai desu. Anata mo oku-san mo ki o tsukete-kudasai.

2 Sen-jitsu wa totsuzen o-jama-shite go-meiwaku o kakemashita. Hisashi-buri deshita node, tsui yukkuri-shite-shimaimashita. Oku-san nimo shin-setsu-ni shite-moratte taihen ureshikatta desu.

3 Mō san-ka-getsu de anata mo ichi-ji no chichi-oya ni narimasu ne. Nani ka to taihen deshō ga, katei ga issō tanoshiku nigiyaka-ni naru deshō ne.

4 Ano yoru kaeri-michi sukoshi o-sake ni yotte-ita node, kawa-beri o bura-bura arukimashita. Kaze ga hyū-hyū to fuite-imashita ga, amari samuku kanjimasen deshita. Sore wa o-sake no sei bakari dewa nakute, anata-gata no koto ga hono-bono to mune no naka ni atta kara deshō.

Sono yoru wa tokai niwa mezurashiku hoshi ga kira-kira to kagayaite-imashita.

5 Mō sugu o-shōgatsu desu ne. Kore kara shibaraku isogashiku natte, nakanaka aenai deshō ga, o-tagai-ni shikkari ganbatte yoi toshi o mukae-mashō.

6 Sakura no koro niwa aka-chan ni aemasu ne.

Soredewa, o-genki de. Oku-san to onaka no aka-chan ni yoroshiku.

12(jū-ni) gatsu 3(mik-)ka

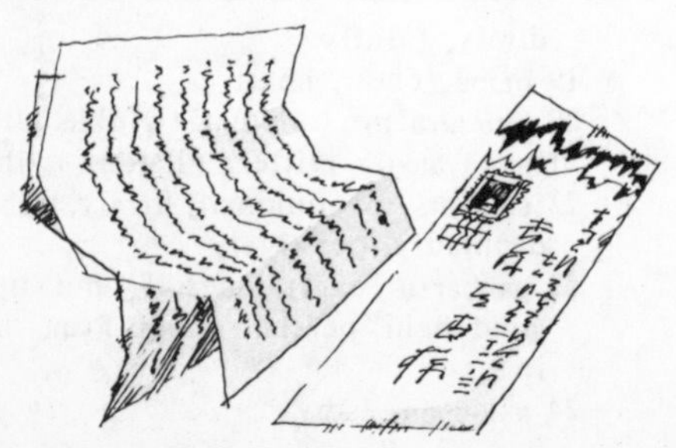

Lesson 22
A Winter Letter

December 3

1 It is getting colder, but how have you been? I have caught a cold. It is very hard to get up and go to work every morning. You and your wife please take care not to catch colds.

2 I am sure my sudden appearance was an imposition on you both the other day. And since I had not seen you for so long I absently overstayed myself. I was very happy that your wife was also so kind to me.

3 In just another three months you will be a father. I am sure it will be very demanding, but it will also brighten up and enliven your household.

4 After leaving your home, I was still a little high from the wine and walked amblingly along the river bank. Although the wind was whistling by, I did not feel very cold. I think this is attributable not only to the wine but also to the warm glow which seeing you both had left in me.

Unusual for the big city, the stars were also out brightly that night.

5 Soon it will be New Year's. We will probably be too busy for a while to get together again, but let us both continue doing our best and have a good year next year.

6 I will be around to see the baby in cherry blossom time.

Farewell and good health to you. Please also give my best to your wife and unborn baby.

ANSWERS 〈pp. 268, 269〉

I. 1. ...ippai-ni narimashita. 2. ...kirei-ni narimashita. 3. ...takaku narimashita. 4. ...hima-ni narimashita. 5. ...isogashiku narimashita. 6. ...benri-ni narimashita. 7. ...kuraku narimashita. 8. ...yūmei-ni narimashita.

II. 1. kirei-ni 2. yasuku 3. hayaku 4. shizuka-ni 5. karuku 6. osoku 7. ōku 8. akaruku

III. 1. wan-wan 2. nyā-nyā 3. zā-zā 4. pyū-pyū 5. gata-gata 6. ton-ton 7. rin-rin 8. pachi-pachi 9. gū-gū 10. suya-suya

IV. Watashi no machi wa onsen de taihen yūmei-ni narimashita. Mukashi wa ryokō-sha mo hotondo nakute, shizuka-na mura deshita. Shikashi kono-goro wa machi-jū ga nigiyaka-ni narimashita. Atarashiku tetsudō ga dekite, kōtsū mo benri-ni narimashita. Mata soko no hito-bito wa ryokō-sha ni totemo shinsetsu desu.

●文法

§ 90 Adverbs (3)

A-ku **Na-ni** } (+V)	cf.	**A-i** **Na-na** } (+N)	

e.g. Samuku narimashita. 'It has gotten cold.'

cf. Kyō wa samui desu. 'It is cold today.'

samui hi 'a cold day'

Kanojo wa kirei-ni narimashita ne.

'She has gotten pretty, hasn't she?'

cf. Kanojo wa kirei desu. 'She is pretty.'

kirei-na hito 'a pretty person (girl)'

§ 91 'A-ku' form used as N

Some of the -ku (adverbial) forms of adjectives are used as Nouns.

e.g. Gakkō no <u>chikaku</u> ni sunde-imasu.

'I live near (in the neighborhood of) the school.'

Kane no oto ga <u>tōku</u> kara kikoete-kimasu.

'The sound of a bell can be heard from afar.'

Kono sensō de <u>ōku</u> no hito ga shinimashita.

'Many people died in this war.'

NB: ×ōi hito ga . . .

§ 92 Adverbs (4): 'Onomatopoeia'

Like some other languages, Japanese abounds in what is called 'onomatopoeia' or 'onomatopoetic words.'

Some of them are used just to imitate sounds.

e.g. *Pisutoru* o pan-pan to utta. '(He) shot the pistol bang-bang!'

Inu ga wan-wan to hoeru. 'The dog barks bow-wow.'

More difficult for the non-native speaker, however, are those that are used to describe various manners in which an action or event takes place. Following are some of the most frequently used onomatopoetic expressions.

hakkiri (**to**) 'clearly,' 'articulately.'

e.g. Motto hakkiri kaite-kudasai. 'Please write more clearly.'

Hakkiri wakarimasen. 'I don't know exactly.'

yukkuri (**to**) 'leisurely,' 'without rush,' 'slowly'

e.g. Motto yukkuri hanashite-kudasai. 'Please speak more slowly.'

Dōzo yukkuri mite-kudasai. 'Please take your time looking at it.'

don-don 'rapidly,' 'without restraint'

e.g. Bukka ga don-don agarimasu. 'Prices are skyrocketing.'

Don-don shitsumon-shite-kudasai.

'Please don't hesitate to ask questions.'

Yushutsu ga don-don fuete, ichi-oku-en o koemashita.

'Exports increased rapidly, and exceeded 100 million yen.'

shikkari 'hard,' 'tightly,' 'with precision,' 'without fail'

e.g. *Rōpu* o shikkari musunde-kudasai. 'Tie the rope tightly.'

Shikkari benkyō-shi-nasai yo. 'Study hard.'

22

§ 93 Some Idiomatic Expressions Involving Onomatopoeia

at-to iu ma ni 'While I was saying, 'Attt!' ='Before I could say Jack Robinson.' ='In the wink of an eye'

e.g. Nippon e kite, atto iu ma ni is-shū-kan tachimashita.

'A week has passed in just a twinkling since I came to Japan.'

At-to iu ma ni hi wa hirogarimashita.

'The fire spread in a flash.'

soro-soro

e.g. Mō soro-soro jikan desu. 'It's about time (to start/end something).'

●練習

ANSWERS→p. 265

I. Transform the sentences as shown in the example.

Ex. (Atama ga itai desu.) Atama ga itaku narimashita.

1. (Onaka ga ippai desu.)
2. (Kanojo wa chika-goro kirei desu.)
3. (Bukka ga takai desu.)
4. (Shigoto ga hima desu.)
5. (Kaisha ga isogashii desu.)
6. (Kōtsū ga benri desu.)
7. (Soto ga kurai desu.)
8. (Kono kaisha wa *toranjisutā-rajio*[1] de yūmei desu.)

II. Transform the sentences as shown in the example.

Ex. (Kono *zubon*[2] wa nagai desu.) Kono *zubon* wa nagai desu kara, mō sukoshi mijikaku shite-kudasai.

1. (Kono heya wa kitanai[3] desu.)
2. (Heya-dai[4] ga takai desu.)
3. (Jidōsha no *supīdo*[5] ga osoi desu.)
4. (Sawagashii desu.)
5. (Nimotsu[6] ga omoi desu.)
6. (Kaigi no jikan ga hayai[7] desu.)
7. (Kyūryō ga sukunai desu.)
8. (Kono heya wa kurai desu.)

語句

1 *toranjisutā-rajio* 'transistor radio'
2 *zubon* trousers
3 kitana·i dirty
4 heya-dai room rent
5 *supīdo* 'speed'
6 nimotsu luggage, load
7 haya·i early; rapid, fast
8 nyā-nyā (to) (onomat) mew, meow
9 rin-rin (to) (onomat) (sound of a small bell)
10 pyū-pyū (to) (onomat) (sound of wind)
11 zā-zā (to) (onomat) (sound of pouring rain)
12 ton-ton (to) (onomat) (sound of someone knocking)
13 suya-suya (to) (onomat) (a manner of

III. Choose a suitable word from group (A) and fill in the blanks in the sentences of group (B).

(A) nyā-nyā,[8] rin-rin,[9] pyū-pyū,[10] zā-zā,[11] ton-ton,[12] suya-suya,[13] wan-wan[14], pachi-pachi[15], gū-gū[16], gata-gata[17]

(B) 1. Inu ga (   ) naite[18]-imasu.

2. Neko ga (   ) naite-imasu.

3. Ame ga (   ) futte-imasu.

4. Tsuyoi kaze ga (   ) fuite-imasu.

5. To ga (   ) natte[19]-imasu.

6. Dare ka ga to o (   ) tataite[20]-imasu.

7. *Beru*[21] ga (   ) natte-imasu.

8. Minna ga te o (   ) tatakimashita.

9. Chichi ga (   ) nete-imasu.

10. Aka-chan ga (   ) nete-imasu.

IV. Put the following into Japanese.

My town became well-known for its hot springs.[22] It had been a quiet village with few visitors[23] before, but nowadays the whole town has become lively. A new railway was built and it is easier now to get to the town. People there are also very kind to visitors.

▲The Unzen spa in Nagasaki

sleeping soundly)
14 wan-wan (to) (onomat) bowwow
15 pachi-pachi (to) (onomat) (cracking or clapping)
16 gū-gū (to) (onomat) (sound of someone sleeping, mostly snoring)
17 gata-gata (to) (onomat) (rattling sound)
18 nak•u weep, cry, whine, call, note, chirp, etc.
19 nar•u (something) make a sound or noise
20 tatak•u strike, hit, knock, tap
21 *beru* 'bell'
22 onsen hot spring
23 ryokō-sha traveler, visitor

●会話

AME GA YAMIMASHITA

A: Daibu[1] atatakaku natte-kimashita ne.

B: Ē, soro-soro[2] ume[3] no kisetsu desu ne.

A: Ima demo yappari[4] anata wa o-cha no o-keiko[5] ni kayotte[6]-irasshaimasu ka?

B: Ē, mada tsuzukete-imasu no yo.

A: Yoku tsuzukimasu wa ne.
Misete-itadakō ka shira?

B: Dewa, chotto shitaku[7] o shite-kimasu kara, sukoshi o-machi-kudasai ne.

....

B: Ikaga desu ka?

A: Taihen kekkō deshita.
Kibun[8] ga sukkiri[9]-shimashita.
O-cha wa hontō-ni ii desu ne.

B: O-cha o tatete-iru toki wa, kibun ga yuttari-shimasu wa.

A: Urayamashii wa. Watashi nante,[10]

A: It has gotten warmer, hasn't it?

B: Yes, it'll soon be time for the plum blossoms.

A: Are you still taking tea ceremony lessons?

B: Yes, I still keep it up.

A: That's good that you do.
Will you show me?

B: Well, since I'll have to get things ready, can you wait a little?

....

B: How do you like it?

A: I like it very much.
It's very refreshing.
The tea is really good.

B: I always feel so at ease while I'm making tea.

A: I envy you. As for me,

語句

1 daibu=daibun considerably
2 soro-soro (to) (onomat) slowly; little by little; pretty soon
3 ume plum
4 yappari=yahari (Adv) as was expected
5 keiko (Nv) practice, training, lessons
6 kayo・u commute
7 shitaku (Nv) preparations, arrangements
8 kibun feeling, mood
9 sukkiri (to) (onomat) refreshed; clear-cut
10 ...nante such a wretched thing as
11 nen-jū all the year round

I'm too busy all year to do things like this.

B: Look, the rain's stopped, and it's clearing up. Let's open the *shoji*.

A: Oh, how splendid your garden is. Isn't the color of the moss so much prettier after a rain? And in a little while the flowers will gradually blossom and the garden will be gay.

B: I make my flower arrangements with flowers from the garden.

A: Did you also arrange the flowers in the *toko-no-ma*?

B: Yes. But flower arrangement is very difficult, and it's hard to get good at it.

nen-jū[11] bata-bata[12] isogashikute. . . .

B: Ara, ame ga yande, soto ga akaruku narimashita ne.
Shōji[13] o akemashō.

A: Mā, rippa-na o-niwa desu ne.
Ame ni nurete,[14] koke no iro ga utsukushiku narimashita ne.
Kore kara don-don[15] hana ga saki-hajimete, o-niwa ga nigiyaka-ni naru deshō ne.

B: Niwa kara o-hana o kitte[16]-kite iketari[17] shimasu no yo.

A: Ano toko-no-ma[18] no o-hana mo anata ga o-ike ni natta[19] no?

B: Ē, dakedo,[20] o-hana[21] wa muzukashii wa. Nakanaka jōzu-ni naranai no.

12 bata-bata (to) (onomat) bustling about
13 shōji sliding door of paper on a framework (Japanese)
14 nure•ru get wet
15 don-don (to) (onomat) (expressing force or rapidity)
16 kir•u (Vt) cut
17 ike•ru arrange (flowers)
18 toko-no-ma alcove (Japanese)
19 o-...ni nar•u (Honorific of suru) See § 118
20 dakedo however (←da keredomo)
21 o-hana=ike-bana flower arrangement

都市問題

人口は大都市[1]に集中しているが、1965年ごろからは、大都市の人口増加のテンポ[2]がにぶく[3]なって、大都市周辺[4]地域[5]で人口がどんどん増加している。大都市の中心部の過密[6]がひどくなった[7]ので、その周辺部の通勤[8]の可能[9]な地域に向かって[10]人口が移動[11]し、ドーナツ型[12]と言われる現象[13]が起こって[14]きた。1970年には、首都圏[15]、中京圏[16]、京阪神圏[17]の三大都市圏[18]の人口が、全人口の43％を占めた。

この結果、東北[19]、北陸[20]、山陰[21]、四国、九州などの地域、特に、いなか[22]では人口が非常に減少[23]して、過疎[24]の現象が現われた[25]。

過密の地域と過疎の地域で、いろいろな問題が表面化[26]してきた。大都市やその周辺地域では、朝夕[27]の交通停滞[28]、満員電車[29]の混雑[30]ぶり[31]がすさまじい[32]。地価[33]は高くなり、住宅不足[34]は深刻[35]になっている。せまい家に、テレビ、冷蔵庫[36]、せんたく機[37]などの電気製品[38]や、たんす[39]などの家具[40]がぎっしり[41]置かれて[42]いる。そのうえ[43]、大気[44]や水のよごれ[45]はひどく、生活環境[46]は、ますます[47]悪くなってきた。一方、農村では人口流出[48]がはげしく[49]なり、医師[50]がいなくなったり、鉄道が廃止[51]されたりして、だんだん暮らしにくくなってくる。これがいっそう、過疎化を進め[52]、集団[53]離村[54]が、あちこち[55]で問題になっている。

Urban Problems

Although people continue to crowd into the big cities, the pace has slowed since 1965 and population increases have shifted to outlying areas. Extreme overcrowding in downtown districts has deflected people to suburban towns within commuting range, thus giving rise to the doughnut phenomenon. By 1970, 43% of the total Japanese population lived in the Capital Tokyo Sphere, Chukyo Sphere, and Keihanshin Sphere.

As a result, Tohoku, Hokuriku, San'in, Shikoku, Kyushu, and other rural areas have been drained of their people.

People in and around the big cities face commuter traffic jams, commuter trains filled to overflowing, soaring land prices, and a housing shortage. Their small apartments are packed with television sets, refrigerators, washing machines, dressers and other electrical appliances and furniture. In addition, they face the threat of air and water pollution making the life environment even worse.

On the other hand, desolute rural villages are often without doctors, their train service is cut off, and life there has become more difficult. There have even been cases of entire villages being abandoned in the face of this isolation.

語句

1 dai-toshi big city, metropolis
2 *tenpo* 'tempo'
3 nibu•i dull
4 shūhen (N) outskirts, circumference
5 chiiki area
6 kamitsu (Na) overcrowding cf. kaso
7 hido•i awful, cruel, terrible
8 tsūkin (Nv) commute, go to work/the office
9 kanō (Na) possible
10 muka•u turn toward, be headed for
11 idō (Nv) movement
12 *dōnatsu* 'doughnut'
13 genshō phenomenon
14 okor•u happen, occur
15 shuto-ken Capital Sphere
  -ken area, zone, circle
16 Chūkyō (Nagoya and vicinity)
17 Keihanshin Kyoto, Osaka, and Kobe
18 san-dai- the three biggest...
19, 20, 21 Tōhoku, Hokuriku, San'in (areas within Japan)
22 inaka countryside; one's home town
23 genshō (Nv) decrease cf. her•u
24 kaso desolution, depopulation
25 araware•ru appear
26 hyōmen-ka (Nv) coming to the surface hyōmen surface
27 asa-yū (N/Adv) morning and evening
28 kōtsū-teitai traffic congestion
  teitai (Nv) stagnation
29 man'in-densha jam-packed train
30 konzatsu (Nv) crowding, confusion
31 -buri manner, way, style
32 susamaji•i terrifying
33 chi-ka price of land
34 jūtaku-busoku housing shortage
35 shinkoku (Na) serious, grave
36 reizōko refrigerator
37 sentaku-ki washing machine
38 denki-seihin electrical appliance
39 tansu cabinet (for clothes), dresser
40 kagu furniture
41 gisshiri (to) (onomat) (the way many things are squeezed into a small space)
42 ok•u put, set
43 sono ue (Adv) moreover, on top of that
44 taiki air, atmosphere
45 yogore spot, smudge, contamination ←yogore•ru (get dirty/polluted)
46 kankyō environment
47 masu-masu increasingly
48 ryūshutsu (Nv) outflow
49 hageshi•i violent
50 ishi=isha (medical) doctor
51 haishi (Nv) abolishment
52 susume•ru (Vt) push forth, promote, hasten cf. susum•u (Vi)
53 shūdan group
54 rison (Nv) leaving a hamlet
55 achi-kochi (N) here and there

第 23 課

文章

TAPE
No. 6
Side 2

❶あなたは　文章を　書く　ことが　とても　じょうずだと　山田さんが　言っていました。

——いや、　そうでも　ありません。　文章を　書く　ことは　たいへん　好きですが………。　文章と　言えば[1]　小説の「書き出し」[2]などは　たいへん　参考[3]に　なりますね。「国境[4]の　長い　トンネル[5]を　抜ける[6]と[7]　雪国[8]であった。夜の　底[9]が　白く　なった。　信号所[10]に　汽車が　止まった。」　これは　川端康成の　「雪国」[11]の　「書き出し」です。

❷わたしも　知っています。　たいへん　有名な　文章ですね。小説が　好きな　人なら[12]　たいてい　知っていますね。

——とても　印象的[13]な　文章ですからね。　小説家は　特に小説の「書き出し」に　気を使いますね。　わたしだったら[14]　とても[15]　こんな　文章は　書けません。　夏目漱石[16]の「草枕」[17]も　有名ですね。

語句

1 ...to ieba　speaking of...
2 kaki-dashi　opening paragraph
　-dashi ←-das•u　(begin to...)
3 sankō　reference
4 kuni-zakai　(national/country) border
5 *tonneru*　'tunnel'
6 nuke•ru　go through
7 -to　See § 96
8 yuki-guni　snow country
9 soko　bottom
10 shingō-jo　signal station
11 Yuki-guni　(the title of a novel)
12 ...nara　See § 95
13 inshō-teki　(Na) impressive
　inshō　impression
14 -tara　See § 94
15 totemo　very much; (not...) by any means
16 Natsume Sōseki　(novelist; 1867-1916)
17 Kusa-makura　(the title of a novel)
　kusa　grass　makura pillow
18 chi=chie　wisdom

❸どんな 文章(ぶんしょう)ですか。

——「山路(やまみち)を 登(のぼ)りながら こう 考(かんが)えた。 智(ち)[18]に 働(はたら)けば[19] 角(かど)が 立(た)つ[20]。 情(じょう)[21]に さお[22] させば 流(なが)される。 意地(いじ)[23]を 通(とお)せば[24] きゅうくつ[25]だ。 とかくに[26] 人(ひと)の 世(よ)[27]は 住(す)みにくい。」

❹とても おもしろい 文章(ぶんしょう)ですね。 一度(いちど) その 小説(しょうせつ)を 読(よ)んでみたいです。 漱石(そうせき)は あまり 読(よ)んでいません。 どんな 作品(さくひん)を まず 読(よ)んだら いいでしょうか。

——わたしなら 「心(こころ)」を すすめます[28]。 外国人(がいこくじん)は これを 読(よ)むと 日本人(にっぽんじん)の ものの 考(かんが)え方(かた)が よく わかると 言(い)いますね。 続(つづ)いて、「それから」[29]や 「門(もん)」[30]も 読(よ)んでみたら いいでしょう。 図書館(としょかん)へ 行(い)けば 全集(ぜんしゅう)[31]が あります。 よかったら[32] わたしのを 貸(か)しましょうか。

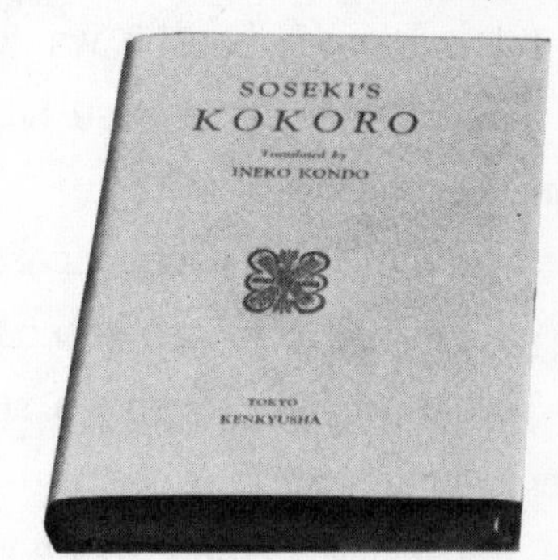

SOSEKI'S
KOKORO
Translated by
INEKO KONDO
TOKYO
KENKYUSHA

❺だれかが 借(か)り出(だ)して[33]いて、もし 図書館(としょかん)に なかったら、貸(か)してもらえますか。

---

19 -ba See §95
20 kado ga tats·u the corners stick out (and hurt people)
21 jō sentiment, emotion cf. kanjō
22 sao (bamboo) pole, rod, oar
23 iji pride, will, stubbornness
24 tōs·u (Vt) let...through
25 kyūkutsu (Na) stuffy, squeezing, not free, restricting, cramped
26 tokaku (ni) (Adv) be apt to
27 hito no yo this world of men, this earthly life
28 susume·ru recommend
29 Sore kara (the title of a story)
30 Mon (the title of a story)
mon gate
31 zenshū complete works (usually literature)
32 yokattara if it's all right, if you don't mind See §94
33 kari-das·u check out (a book from a library)

Dai 23-ka

Bunshō

1 Anata wa bunshō o kaku koto ga totemo jōzu da to Yamada-san ga itte-imashita.

——Iya, sō demo arimasen. Bunshō o kaku koto wa taihen suki desu ga.... Bunshō to ieba shōsetsu no 'Kaki-dashi' nado wa taihen sankō ni narimasu ne. "Kuni-zakai no nagai *tonneru* o nukeruto yuki-guni de atta. Yoru no soko ga shiroku natta. Shingō-jo ni kisha ga tomatta." Kore wa Kawabata Yasunari no 'Yuki-guni' no 'kaki-dashi' desu.

2 Watashi mo shitte-imasu. Taihen yūmei-na bunshō desu ne. Shōsetsu ga suki-na hito nara taitei shitte-imasu ne.

——Totemo inshō-teki-na bunshō desu kara ne. Shōsetsu-ka wa tokuni shōsetsu no 'kaki-dashi' ni ki o tsukaimasu ne. Watashi dattara totemo konna bunshō wa kakemasen. Natsume Sōseki no 'Kusamakura' mo yūmei desu ne.

3 Donna bunshō desu ka?

——"Yama-michi o noborinagara kō kangaeta. Chi ni hatarakeba kado ga tatsu. Jō ni sao saseba nagasareru. Iji o tōseba kyūkutsu da. Tokaku ni hito no yo wa sumi-nikui."

4 Totemo omoshiroi bunshō desu ne. Ichi-do sono shōsetsu o yonde-mitai desu. Sōseki wa amari yonde-imasen. Donna sakuhin o mazu yondara ii deshō ka?

——Watashi nara 'Kokoro' o susumemasu. Gaikoku-jin wa kore o yomuto Nippon-jin no mono no kangae-kata ga yoku wakaru to iimasu ne. Tsuzuite, 'Sore kara' ya 'Mon' mo yonde-mitara ii deshō. Tosho-kan e ikeba zen-shū ga arimasu. Yokattara watashi no o kashimashō ka?

5 Dare ka ga kari-dashite-ite, moshi tosho-kan ni nakattara, kashite-moraemasu ka?

Lesson 23

On Writing

1 Mr. Yamada tells me you write very well.

——Not really. I like very much to write, but.... Speaking of writing, I find it helps me a lot to read the lead-ins to novels. "The train came out of the long tunnel into the snow country. The earth lay white under the night sky. The train pulled up at a signal stop." This is the beginning of Kawabata Yasunari's *Yuki-guni* ('Snow Country'). (trans. Edward G. Seidensticker)

2 Yes, I know it. It is quite a famous passage. Anyone who likes to read is probably familiar with it.

——It is really a striking bit of writing. Novelists are especially careful of how they start their novels. I could never write sentences like these. Natsume Soseki's *Kusa-makura* ('The Three-Cornered World') is also very well known.

3 How does it go?

——"Going up a mountain track, I fell to thinking. Approach everything rationally, and you become harsh. Pole along in the stream of emotions, and you will be swept away by the current. Give free rein to your desires, and you become uncomfortably confined. It is not a very agreeable place to live, this world of ours." (trans. Alan Turney)

4 It is very interesting. I would like to read that novel sometime. I have not read much of Soseki. What would you suggest I start with?

——I would recommend *Kokoro.* It is supposed to be good for foreigners who want to understand the Japanese way of thinking. And then it would probably be good to read *Sore kara* and *Mon.* If you go to the library, they would have his complete works. Shall I lend you mine?

5 Would you let me borrow yours if someone has checked out the library's and I can not get it there?

ANSWERS ⟨pp. 280, 281⟩

I. 1. kaitara/kakeba Neg.→kakanakattara; kakanakereba 2. benkyō-shitara/benkyō-sureba Neg.→benkyō-shinakattara; benkyō-shinakereba 3. futtara/fureba Neg.→furanakattara; furanakereba 4. tsutaetara/tsutaereba Neg.→tsutaenakattara; tsutaenakereba 5. takakattara/takakereba Neg.→takaku nakattara; takaku nakereba 6. yokattara/yokereba Neg.→yoku nakattara; yoku nakereba 7. shizuka dattara/shizuka-nara Neg.→shizuka de nakattara; shizuka de nakereba 8. byōki dattara/byōki nara Neg.→byōki de nakattara; byōki de nakereba 9. shinshi dattara/shinshi nara Neg. →shinshi de nakattara; shinshi de nakereba

II. 1. ...jōzu dattara, ... 2. ...kanemochi dattara, ... 3. ...ōkikattara, ... 4. ...oyogetara, ... 5. ...otoko dattara, ...

III. 1. kōsa-ten 2. ginkō 3. yūbin-kyoku 4. hon-ya 5. gakkō

IV. Kare ga kitara, oshiete-kudasai. Kare ga konakattara, anata ga kawari ni kenkyū-sho e itte-kuremasen ka? Kyō watashi ga hima dattara, issho-ni ikitai desu ga.... Mukō de jikken no kekka o setsumei-shite-kureru deshō. Wakaranai koto ga attara, enryo-naku kiite-kudasai.

●文法

§ 94 Conditional Expressions (1)

V-**tara, ...**	'If..., ...'
A-**kattara, ...**	'When...has done..., ...'
N/Na **dattara, ...**	'Provided..., ...'
	(Form: the Past form (§ 41)+ra)

e.g. Ame ga furimasu (furu). 'It rains.'

Ame ga futtara, watashi wa ikimasen. 'If it rains, I won't go.'

Hiru-gohan o tabetara, watashi no heya e kite-kudasai.

'When you have eaten lunch, please come to my room.'

Yasukattara (←yasui), kaimasu. 'If it is cheap, I will buy it.'

Gakusei dattara (←gakusei da/desu), han-gaku desu.

'It is half-price (=There is a 50% discount) if you are a student.'

NB: (1) The adjective ii (=yoi) becomes yokattara (not ikattara).

(2) The negative forms:

furimasen→furanai→furanakattara 'if it doesn't rain'

samui→samuku nai→samuku nakattara 'if it is not cold'

gakusei da→gakusei de(wa) nai→gakusei de nakattara

'if you are not a student'

§ 95 Conditional Expressions (2)

V { (1st Group) (Stem+) **-eba, ...**
(2nd Group) (Stem+) **-reba, ...**
sureba (←suru)/**kureba** (←kuru), ... 'If..., ...'

A-**kereba, ...**

N/Na **nara, ...**

e.g. Ame ga fureba, shigoto wa yasumi desu. 'If it rains, there's no work.'

Nichi-yōbi nara, uchi ni imasu. 'If it's Sunday, I will be home.'

NB: The adjective ii becomes yokereba (not ikereba).

§ 96 Conditional Expressions (3)

V A N/Na **da**	(Plain Present form) + **-to, ...**	'(If you) do..., then...' 'If..., then...'

e.g. Ano kado o magaruto, yūbin-kyoku ga miemasu.

'If you turn that corner, you'll see a post office.'

('Turning the corner, you will...')

Ni ni ni o tasuto, yon ni narimasu.

'If you add 2 to 2, it will become 4.' '2 and 2 makes 4.'

§ 97 Comparison of the Three Conditional Expressions

The ranges of meaning covered by the three Conditionals **-tara**, **-(r)eba**, and **-to** overlap to a large extent, almost so much that they appear to be synonymous and freely interchangeable. There are, however, some slight differences in nuance and use. Following are some of the main points that should be noted here. For convenience, we will let 'P' stand for the first sentence (clause) ending with one of the Conditional forms, and 'Q' for the following 'consequent' sentence (clause).

23

(1) 'P-reba Q' and 'P-to Q' imply that Q is a necessary or natural consequence of P, and therefore these two are more commonly used in mathematics, logic, physics, etc. than 'P-tara,' which has an implication that the speaker is reserving judgment on Q. Thus 'P-tara Q' is preferred when the whole sentence involves invitation or suggestion ('-mashō'), request or order ('-te-kudasai' or '-nasai'), permission ('-temo ii desu'), prohibition ('-tewa ikemasen'), etc.

(2) 'P-tara' is mostly used in the spoken language; 'P-reba' is rather limited to the written, and 'P-to' is both spoken and written.

●練習

ANSWERS→p. 277

I. Fill in the blanks with the Conditional forms and then make the sentences negative.

Ex. Anata ga kono *kamera* o (kattara/kaeba), watashi mo kaimasu. (buy)

Neg.→Anata ga kono *kamera* o kawanakattara (kawanakereba), watashi mo kaimasen.

1. Anata ga tegami o (　　　　), kare mo tegami o kaite-kureru deshō. (write)
2. Yoku (　　　　), anata wa shiken ni tōru[1] deshō. (study)
3. Ashita ame ga (　　　　), watashi wa yama e ikimasen. (rain)
4. Kare ni sono koto o (　　　　), kare wa kaette-kuru deshō. (inform)
5. Moshi[2] heya-dai ga (　　　　), watashi wa sono heya o karimasen. (expensive)
6. Kono hon ga (　　　　), imōto ni yomasemasu. (good)
7. Sono heya ga (　　　　), soko de shigoto o shimasu. (quiet)
8. Kanojo ga (　　　　), watashi-tachi wa ryokō ni ikimasen. (sick)
9. Kare ga (　　　　), watashi wa kare to kekkon-shimasu. (gentleman[3])

II. Make sentences using the Conditionals as shown in the example.

Ex. Watashi wa tori dewa arimasen.→Moshi watashi ga tori dattara, anata no tokoro e tonde-iku deshō.

1. Watashi wa Nippon-go ga jōzu dewa arimasen.
2. Watashi wa kanemochi[4] dewa arimasen.
3. Watashi no uchi wa ōkiku nai desu.

語句

1 tōr・u　pass
2 moshi　(Adv) if, provided
3 shinshi　gentleman
4 kanemochi　(N) rich; a rich man/class
5 massugu　(Adv) straight
6 magar・u　(Vi) turn; bend
cf. mager・u　(Vt)
7 hidari-gawa　(N) the left side

4. Watashi wa oyogemasen.

5. Watashi wa otoko dewa arimasen.

III. Use the map to fill in the blanks.

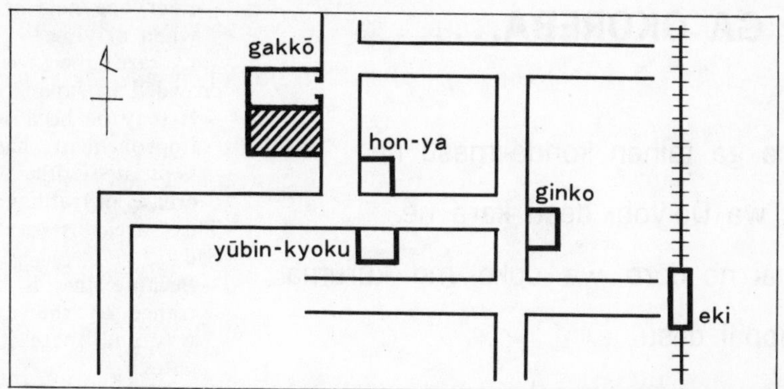

Eki kara massugu[5] ikuto, (1.   ) ga arimasu. Migi e magaruto,[6] sugu (2.   ) ga arimasu. Soko o hidari e magatte sukoshi ikuto, hidari-gawa[7] ni (3.   ) ga arimasu. Sono mae ni (4.   ) ga arimasu. Sono yoko no michi o kita e sukoshi ikuto, (5.   ) ga arimasu.

IV. Put the following into Japanese.

When he comes, please let me know. If he doesn't come, will you go to the research institute[8] in his stead? If I were free today, I would like to go with you. There they will explain the results of their experiment.[9] If there is anything you don't understand, please feel free[10] to ask.

---

8 kenkyū-sho research institute
9 jikken (Nv) experiment
10 enryo-naku without hesitation/reserve
enryo (Nv) reserve, hesitation, modesty

23

●会話

JIKO GA OKOREBA....

Kuruma ga taihen konde-imasu ne.

—Kyō wa Do-yōbi desu kara ne.
Shinai no dōro wa doko mo kuruma de ippai desu.

Konna noro-noro-unten[1] nara, aruita hō ga hayai kamo shiremasen yo.

—Kuruma o unten shite-iruto minna ira-ira[2]-shimasu.

Nippon no dōro wa naze konna-ni[3] komu no desu ka?

—Kōtsū-ryō[4] ga konna-ni fuetemo, dōro-seibi[5] ga oitsuite-ikanai kara deshō ne.

Koko wa tokuni hidoi desu ne.

—Koko wa kōsoku-dōro[6] no iri-guchi de, ryōkin-sho[7] ga aru kara desu.

Ryōkin-sho'tte[8]?

—Yū-ryō-dōro[9] desu kara, ryōkin o torareмasu.[10]

There're so many cars.

—Because today's Saturday. All the city roads are full of cars.

At this snail's pace, it may be faster to walk.

—Everyone gets irritated when driving.

Why are the roads so crowded in Japan?

—It may be because road improvement has not kept up with the increase in traffic volume.

This area is especially bad.

—Because this is the entrance to the expressway and there are toll gates.

Toll gates?

—This is a toll road and so we have to pay to use it.

語句

1 noro-noro-unten (Nv) driving slowly (in a traffic jam)
   noro-noro (to) (onomat) slowly, lazily
2 ira-ira (to) (onomat) irritated, impatient
3 konna-ni (Adv) like this
4 kōtsū-ryō traffic volume
   ryō quantity, amount
5 dōro-seibi road construction
   seibi (Nv) build, provide, maintain, arrange, improve
6 kōsoku-dōro express-way, highway
   kōsoku (N) high speed
7 ryōkin-sho toll gate
8 ...-tte? Did you say...? What is...? See § 106
9 yū-ryō-dōro toll road
   yū-ryō (N) charged cf.

What? You have to pay to use the road?

....

—Once we get past this part, the rest is easy. From there on the speed limit is 100 km per hour.

But, it would be terrible if there were an accident.

—Yes. If you're careless on the expressway, there'd be a big accident before you knew it.

You're all right though, aren't you?

—Yes, leave it to me.

Hē[11]? Tsūkō[12] ni o-kane ga iru no desu ka?

....

—Koko o sugiruto,[13] ato wa raku[14] desu. Sokudo-seigen[15] wa hyak-*kiro* desu kara.

Shikashi, moshi jiko ga okoreba[16] taihen desu ne.

—Ē, kōsoku-dōro dewa, ukkari[17]-shite-iruto, at-to iu ma ni[18] dai-jiko ni nari masu.

Anata wa daijōbu deshō ne?

—Ē, makasete[19]-oite-kudasai.

mu-ryō, tada (free)

10 tor•u take

11 Hē? What a surprise!

12 tsūkō (Nv) passing, transit

13 sugi•ru go past; exceed

14 raku (Na) easy, comfortable

15 sokudo-seigen speed limit sokudo speed seigen (Nv) limit

16 okor•u happen, occur

17 ukkari (to) (onomat) carelessness, absent-minded

18 at-to iu ma ni before you can say Jack Robinson, in the twinkling of an eye

19 makase•ru leave (something) to (someone), trust (somebody) with (something)

23

日本の芸術

日本の芸術は自然[1]をたいせつにする。たとえば、お茶やお花でも、四季おりおり[2]の道具[3]を使う。俳句にも、必ず、季語[4]があって、伝統的[5]な約束[6]を守らなければならない。歳時記[7]を見ると、季語がくわしく[8]説明してある。

菊[9]の香[10]や[11]　奈良には古き[12]仏[13]たち　　芭蕉

この句[14]の季語は「菊」で、これは秋の句である。菊は春でも、夏でも、冬でも咲いているが、春の菊だったら、「菊苗[15]」とか、「菊若葉[16]」と言わなければならない。夏の菊だったら、「夏菊[17]」と言わなければならない。冬なら、「寒菊[18]」と言わなければならない。

自然のままをたいせつにすることも、日本の芸術の特徴[19]である。庭園[20]を例[21]にとってみよう。西欧の庭なら、円形[22]や三角形[23]の幾何学的[24] 図形[25]の花壇を造ったり、噴水[26]をこしらえたり[27]する。しかし、日本人は、庭に木を植えたり[28]、石[29]を置いたり、池や水の流れ[30]を作ったりするときにも、できるだけ[31]、自然の美しさ[32]をとどめよう[33]とする。ときには[34]、へい[35]の外のけしきも庭のながめの一部と考えて、庭を造る。これを借景[36]という。

このように、日本の芸術はつねに[37]自然との永遠[38]の一致[39]を求める[40]。

▶The garden at Daisenin

Japanese Arts

Nature plays an important part in Japanese arts, as in the tea ceremony or flower arrangement with their seasonal accessories. *Haiku* too has a traditional commitment to seasonal terms, and these are explained in *Saijiki.*

Kiku no ka ya	The scent of chrysanthemums and
Nara ni wa furuki	Long resident in Nara
Hotoketachi	Buddhist spirits

In this *haiku* by Basho, *kiku* (chrysanthemum) is used as the seasonal clue to autumn. While these do also bloom in other seasons, spring chrysanthemums would have to be indicated by *kikunae* or *kikuwakaba*, summer ones by *natsugiku*, and winter ones by *kangiku.*

It is characteristic of Japanese art to present nature as it truly is. Whereas the typical Western garden would have a geometrically designed flower bed and a fountain, the Japanese strive to retain the beauty of nature by planting trees, placing rocks, and providing a flow for water in the pond. Gardens are sometimes even created so as to incorporate the outside view as part of the setting. This is called borrowing the scenery.

In all these ways, Japanese arts constantly seek eternal oneness with nature.

語句

1 shizen (N/Na) nature; natural
2 shiki oriori (N) for each season
  oriori (N) occasion cf. ori
3 dōgu tool
4 ki-go special seasonal terms in *haiku* poems to show the seasons
5 dentō-teki (Na) traditional
6 yakusoku (Nv) promise, appointment
7 Saiji-ki (a glossary of *ki-go*)
8 kuwashi·i detailed
9 kiku chrysanthemum
10 ka =kaori scent, smell
11 ...ya (special ending for *haiku* poems)
12 furuki (archaic)=furu·i
13 hotoke Buddha
14 ku a *haiku* phrase
15 kiku-nae young chrysanthemum plant nae young plant
16 kiku-waka-ba young chrysanthemum leaves waka-ba young leaves
17 natsu-giku summer chrysanthemum
18 kan-giku winter chrysanthemum
  kan coldness, winter
19 tokuchō characteristic, distinctive feature
20 teien=niwa garden
21 rei example
22 en(-kei) (N) circle
  -kei shape
23 san-kaku(-kei) (N) triangle (←three cornered shape)
24 kikagaku-teki (Na) geometrical
  kika-gaku geometry
25 zukei (geometrical) figure
26 funsui fountain
27 koshirae·ru make
28 ue·ru (Vt) plant
29 ishi stone, rock
30 nagare (N) flow ←nagare·ru (Vi)
31 dekiru dake as...as possible
32 utsukushi-sa beauty←utsukushi·i
33 todome·ru detain; stop; leave...as it is
34 toki niwa sometimes
35 hei fence
36 shakkei making use of the scenery (e.g. mountains) behind the garden (lit. 'borrowing scenery')
37 tsune ni always
38 eien (N) eternity
39 itchi (Nv) oneness, coincidence, agreement
40 motome·ru seek; ask for, demand; buy

23

第 24 課

広告・宣伝・コマーシャル

TAPE
No. 6
Side 2

❶あそこに 止まっている 電車に 乗りますか。

――いいえ、 あれは 京都へ 行く 電車です。 わたしたちが 乗る 電車は もう すぐ 来るでしょう。

❷ところで、 近ごろ 駅には きれいな ポスター[1]が たくさん はって[2]ありますね。 あれには「Discover Japan」と 書いてありますよ。 このごろ 英語を 使った 広告が 多いですね。

――まちがった[3] 英語の 使い方[4]も よく 見かけます[5]。 あまり たくさん 英語が 使ってある 広告も 困りますね。 この間、「クール[6]な タッチ[7]で ハード[8]な アクション[9]を ダイレクト[10]に サービスする『ナポレオン・ソロ[11]』」という 映画の 宣伝[12]が ありました。 一度 聞いただけで どういう[13] 意味か わかりますか。

❸うーん[14]…。 英語だけでなく フランス語や 中国語などを 使った 広告も 多いですね。

――そうですね。 必要以上[15]に 外国語を 使う ことは よく

語句

1 *posutā* 'poster'
2 har・u stick, paste, affix
3 machigatta (+N) ←machigatte-i・ru mistaken, wrong
  machiga・u =machigae・ru make a mistake/an error, be wrong
4 tsukai-kata usage, how to use
5 mikake・ru see/find/notice by chance
6 *kūru* (Na) 'cool'
7 *tatchi* 'touch'
8 *hādo* (Na) 'hard'
9 *akushon* 'action'
10 *dairekuto* (Na) 'direct'
11 *Naporeon Soro* 'Napoleon Solo' (the title of a TV film series)
12 senden (Nv) advertisement, publicity, propaganda
13 dō iu… what kind of…

ないですね。

❹近ごろ わたしの 子どもが テレビコマーシャル[16]で 言った ことばを よく 使うので 困っています。「がんばらなくっちゃ[17]」と いう ことばが よく 流行[18]していますね。

——薬の テレビコマーシャルでしょう。 薬を のんでまで[19] がんばる 必要が あるか どうか[20] 疑問[21]ですね。

❺おしつけがましい[22] 広告や 日本語を 混乱[23]させる 宣伝は ほんとうに 困りますね。

---

14 Ūn Hmmm
15 hitsuyō ijō ni more than is needed
16 ***terebi-komāsharu*** 'TV commercial'
 komāsharu 'commercial'
17 ...nakutcha (Colloquial)=...nakutewa/nakereba narimasen have to...
18 ryūkō (Nv) fashion, popularity
19 -te made even taking the trouble of ...ing
20 ...ka dō ka whether...or...
21 gimon question, doubt
22 oshitsuke-gamashi·i wishing to have one's own way
 oshitsuke·ru press against/down, force
 -gamashi·i look/sound like
23 konran (Nv) confusion

Dai 24-ka

Kōkoku, Senden, *Komāsharu*

1 Asoko ni tomatte-iru densha ni norimasu ka?

——Iie, are wa Kyōto e iku densha desu. Watashi-tachi ga noru densha wa mō sugu kuru deshō.

2 Tokorode, chika-goro eki niwa kirei-na *posutā* ga takusan hatte-arimasu ne. Are niwa "Discover Japan" to kaite-arimasu yo. Kono-goro Ei-go o tsukatta kōkoku ga ōi desu ne.

——Machigatta Ei-go no tsukai-kata mo yoku mikakemasu. Amari takusan Ei-go ga tsukatte-aru kōkoku mo komarimasu ne. Kono aida, "*Kūru*-na *tatchi* de *hādo*-na *akushon* o *dairekuto*-ni *sābisu*-suru '*Naporeon Soro*'" to iu eiga no senden ga arimashita. Ichi-do kiita dake de dō iu imi ka wakarimasu ka?

3 Ūn.... Ei-go dake de naku *Furansu*-go ya Chūgoku-go nado o tsukatta kōkoku mo ōi desu ne.

——Sō desu ne. Hitsuyō ijō ni gaikoku-go o tsukau koto wa yoku nai desu ne.

4 Chika-goro watashi no kodomo ga *terebi-komāsharu* de itta kotoba o yoku tsukau node komatte-imasu. "Ganbaranakutcha" to iu kotoba ga yoku ryūkō-shite-imasu ne.

——Kusuri no *terebi-komāsharu* deshō. Kusuri o nonde made ganbaru hitsuyō ga aru ka dō ka gimon desu ne.

5 Oshitsuke-gamashii kōkoku ya Nippon-go o konran-saseru senden wa hontō-ni komarimasu ne.

Lesson 24

Advertising

1 Do we get on that train stopped over there?
——No, that is the train to Kyoto. Our train will be along soon.

2 Say, there has been an abundance of beautiful posters in the stations lately. That one says, "Discover Japan." A lot of the advertising uses English now.
——There is also considerable English used incorrectly. Advertisements that use too much English really turn me off. The other day I saw a movie advertisement for "Napoleon Solo—straight-served hard action with a cool touch." How are we supposed to understand that the first time through?

3 Hmmm... And it is not only English but also French, Chinese, and all the others which are used a lot.
——You are right. Foreign words are used far more than necessary.

4 My kid has gotten into the bad habit of using the catch-phrases from television commercials. "Gotta try harder" was a big one a while ago.
——That was from a health-drink commercial. But I wonder if it is really necessary to try harder to the extent of taking that stuff.

5 Something ought to be done about hard-sell commercials and advertising which debases the Japanese language.

24

ANSWERS 〈pp. 292, 293〉

I. 1. Watashi ga/no kaita shōsetsu wa nagai desu. 2. Kare ga/no totta shashin wa kirei desu. 3. Watashi ga sensei kara karita hon wa omoshirokatta desu. 4. Watashi wa chichi ga (watashi ni) tsukutte-kureta tsue o mai-nichi tsukatte-imasu. 5. Watashi ga tomodachi kara/ni moratta *raitā* wa gaikoku-sei desu.

II. 1. Anata wa kono *rajio* ga ikura ka shitte-imasu ka? 2. Anata wa kare ga megane o kakete-ita ka dō ka oboete-imasu ka? 3. Yamada-san wa mata kuru ka dō ka wakarimasen. 4. Yamada-san no tsutomete-iru kaisha wa doko ka oshiete-kudasai. 5. Watashi wa jibun no kangae-kata ga tadashii ka dō ka wakaranakatta.

III. 1. doko e iku 2. doko de katta 3. Watashi ga hanashite-ita 4. susumeru/ichiban ii to omou 5. tsukurarete-iru/tsukurareru/tsukutte-iru 6. shite-iru 7. Kono kōjō de hataraite-iru 8. Koko de tsukurareru/tsukurarete-iru

IV. Kinō watashi wa, *Ōsutoraria* de Nippon-go o benkyō-shite-iru tomodachi kara, tegami o moraimashita. Kanojo wa Nippon no uta no *rekōdo* o okutte-kudasai to kaite-kimashita. Watashi wa *popyurā*-ongaku no suki-na otōto ni sōdan-shimashita. Otōto wa kare no tomodachi ga hataraite-iru *rekōdo*-ya-san e watashi o tsurete-itte-kuremashita. Kare-ra ga erande-kureta ongaku wa taitei watashi no zenzen shiranai uta deshita. San-mai katte, *Ōsutoraria* e kōkū-bin de okurimashita.

●文法

§ 98 Using a Sentence as a Noun Modifier

In Japanese, a modifier always precedes what is modified. This section is concerned with the Noun-modifying constructions. Observe the following:

hon 'a book'

sono hon 'that book'

Nippon-go no hon 'a book in Japanese'

watashi no Nippon-go no hon 'my book in Japanese'

sono akai hyōshi no Nippon-go no hon 'that book in Japanese with the red cover'

This general order is maintained even when a Noun is modified by what could be a complete sentence, no matter how long or complex it may be.

e.g. Watashi ga kinō Kyōto de katta hon wa omoshiroi desu.

'The book (which) I bought in Kyoto yesterday is interesting.'

Sore wa anata ga kyonen Tai e itta (←iku) toki (anata ga) katta (←kau) hon desu ka? (Literally translated and left in the same word order, this would be: 'that, you, last year, Thailand, to, went, time, (you) bought, book, is?')

'Is that the book you bought when you went to Thailand last year?'

NB: In using a sentence-equivalent as a Noun Modifier, a few adjustments are required ((1)-(3) below) or preferred (4).

(1) The Particle wa, since it shows the Topic of the (whole) sentence, cannot be used within the Noun-modifying construction. Ga must be used when N is the subject (as is usually the case), and o or ni when N shows the object or location of V.

e.g. Watashi wa hon o katta. 'I bought a book.'

→watashi ga katta hon 'the book which I bought'

Kono hon wa watashi no tomodachi ga kakimashita.

'A friend of mine wrote this book.'

→kono hon o kaita watashi no tomodachi

'a friend of mine who wrote this book'

(2) The Predicate of the Noun-modifying clause normally takes the Plain form, since the politeness is expressed by the main clause.

e.g. Watashi wa kinō hon o kaimashita. 'I bought a book yesterday.'

→Watashi ga kinō katta hon wa omoshiroi desu. 'The book which I bought yesterday is interesting.'

Sono hi wa samukatta desu. 'It was cold that day.'

→samukatta sono hi 'that day when it was cold' (='that cold day')

(3) When the Predicate of the Noun-modifying clause is a Na-adjective, it takes the '-na form.'

e.g. Ano hito wa *kōhī* ga suki desu. 'That person likes coffee.'

→*kōhī* ga suki-na hito 'a person who likes coffee'

(4) When the Predicate of the Noun-modifying clause ends with 'Noun+desu,' it changes to 'N no.'

e.g. Ano hito wa byōki desu. 'That person is sick.'

→byōki no hito 'a person who is sick' (='a sick person')

(5) In the modifying clause, 'N ga' and 'N no' are interchangeable.

24

§ 99 Using an Interrogative Sentence as part of another Sentence

An Interrogative sentence can be used as part of another sentence with the same modifications as noted in (1) and (2) above. When it contains no Interrogative word such as nani, doko, dare, etc., however, 'dō ka' must be added to '...ka.'

e.g. Kare wa doko e ikimashita ka? 'Where did he go?'

→Kare ga doko e itta ka anata wa shitte-imasu ka?

'Do you know where he went?'

Kare wa ikimashita ka? 'Did he go?'

→Kare ga itta ka dō ka watashi wa shirimasen.

'I don't know whether he went or not.'

●練習

ANSWERS→p. 289

I. Combine the sentences with the second sentence as the main clause.

Ex. Watashi wa *Furansu* de budō-shu o kaimashita. Sore wa oishii desu.

→Watashi ga *Furansu* de katta budō-shu wa oishii desu.

1. Watashi wa shōsetsu o kakimashita. Sore wa nagai desu.
2. Kare wa shashin o torimashita. Sore wa kirei desu.
3. Watashi wa sensei kara hon o karimashita. Sore wa omoshirokatta desu.
4. Chichi wa watashi ni tsue[1] o tsukutte-kuremashita. Watashi wa sore o mai-nichi tsukatte-imasu.
5. Watashi wa tomodachi ni *raitā*[2] o moraimashita. Sore wa gaikoku-sei desu.

II. Combine (a) and (b) with (a) as the main clause.

1. (a) Anata wa shitte-imasu ka?

   (b) Kono *rajio* wa ikura desu ka?
2. (a) Anata wa oboete-imasu[3] ka?

   (b) Kare wa megane o kakete-imashita ka?
3. (a) Wakarimasen.

   (b) Yamada-san wa mata kimasu ka?
4. (a) Oshiete-kudasai.

   (b) Yamada-san no tsutomete-iru kaisha wa doko desu ka?
5. (a) Watashi wa wakaranakatta.

   (b) Jibun no kangae-kata wa tadashii ka?

語句

1 tsue walking stick, cane
2 *raitā* 'lighter'
3 oboete-i•ru remember, keep in mind
oboe•ru memorize, remember, learn

III. Fill in the blanks to complete the translations.

1. Where does this train go?

→Kore wa (   ) densha desu ka?

2. Where did you buy this watch?

→Kore wa (   ) tokei desu ka?

3. The man I was talking with is Yamada.

→(   ) hito wa Yamada-san desu.

4. Which dictionary do you recommend?

→Anata ga (   ) jisho wa dore desu ka.

5. This factory makes mostly transistor radios.

→Kono kōjō de (   ) omo-na seihin wa *toranjisutā-rajio* desu.

6. What kind of work does he do?

→Ano hito ga (   ) shigoto wa nan desu ka.

7. About how much do the people who work in this factory get paid?

→(   ) hito-tachi no chingin wa ikura gurai desu ka?

8. Where do they export the radios produced here?

→(   ) *rajio* wa doko e yushutsu-saremasu ka?

IV. Put the following into Japanese.

Yesterday I received a letter from my friend who is studying Japanese in Australia. She wrote asking me to send her some records of Japanese songs. I talked it over with my brother, who loves popular music,[4] and he took me to a record shop where a friend of his is working.

Most of the music (records) that they chose for me were songs which I didn't know at all. I bought three, which I sent to Australia by air mail.[5]

---

4 *popyurā*-ongaku 'popular,' pop music

5 kōkū-bin air mail   kōkū aviation

●会話

MOKUTEKI WA?

Watashi no hanasu kotoba ga wakarimasu ka?

—Ē, yoku wakarimasu.

Watashi wa Nippon e kite mada ichi-nen tarazu[1] desu. Sorede, amari jōzu-ni hanasemasen.

—Sonna koto wa arimasen, rippa-na mon[2] desu yo. Tokorode, Nippon e kite, ichiban komatta mondai wa nan desu ka?

Yahari,[3] kotoba desu ne. Nippon-go wa taihen muzukashii desu.

—Nippon e kita mokuteki[4] wa nan desu ka?

Nippon no chūsei[5]-bungaku no kenkyū desu.

—Sorejā, chūsei-bungaku de tsukawarete-iru kotoba wa gendai no Nippon-go to kanari chigaimasu kara, taihen deshō ne.

Do you understand what I say?

—Yes, very well.

It's a little less than a year since I came to Japan, so I'm not so fluent.

—Oh, that's not true. You're quite good. By the way, what was your biggest problem after you got here?

As might be expected, the language. Japanese is very difficult.

—What was your purpose in coming to Japan?

To study Japanese medieval literature.

—Then, since the language used in medieval literature is quite different from modern Japanese, you must be having a hard time.

語句

1 ...tarazu less than...
2 mon (Colloquial)=mono
3 yahari=yappari as expected
4 mokuteki purpose, objective
5 chūsei the medieval age
6 bungo literary language
7 kyōju professor; (Nv)

You have to study literary Japanese, don't you?
That's right. The classes at the university are not enough, so I'm learning from a friend my professor introduced me to.
—Is he Japanese?
No, another English student. But he's been studying in Japan for 3 years, and his Japanese is very good. Moreover, since he's doing research on the *waka*, he understands the old Japanese very well.
—That's very good.
The classical writings are difficult even for Japanese. Study hard.
Thank you.

Bungo[6] no benkyō o shinakereba narimasen ne.

Sō desu. Daigaku no jugyō dake dewa ma ni awanai node, kyōju[7] ga shōkai-shite-kureta tomodachi ni oshiete-moratte-imasu.

—Sono hito wa Nippon-jin desu ka?

Iya, onaji *Igirisu* no gakusei desu.

Demo, kare wa san-nen mo Nippon de benkyō-shite-imasu kara, Nippon-go wa pera-pera[8] desu. Soreni, kare ga kenkyū-shite-iru kadai[9] ga 'waka'[10] desu kara, furui kotoba mo yoku shitte-imasu.

—Sore wa yokatta desu ne.

Bungo-bun[11] wa Nippon-jin ni tottemo muzukashii kotoba desu.

Shikkari benkyō-shite-kudasai.

Dōmo arigatō.

instruction
8 pera-pera (onomat) (speak) fluently
9 kadai theme/problem to be solved, task
10 waka (Japanese poem of 5-7-5-7-7 syllables)
11 bungo-bun Japanese in written style

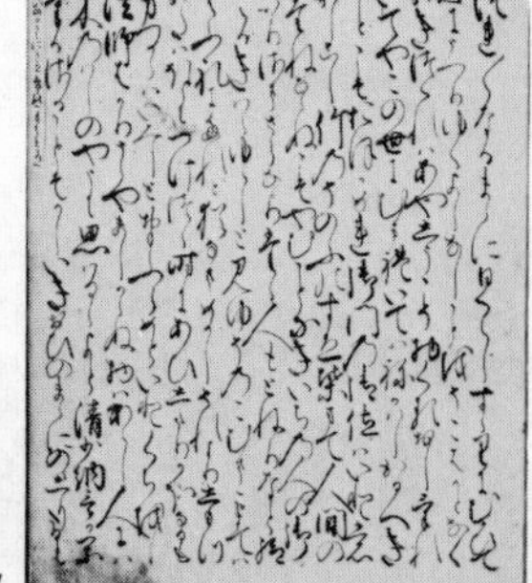

▶From *Tsurezure-gusa*

24

公　害

日本の公害問題は、世界のどの国よりも深刻だ。「公害先進国[1]」とまで言う人もいる。日本経済は、戦後、高度[2]に成長して、「経済大国[3]」になった。しかし、そのかげで国土[4]は急速に荒廃[5]して、公害が表面化してきた。

水俣[6]と新潟[7]の水銀中毒[8]、四日市[9]の大気汚染[10]、東京、大阪近郊[11]の光化学スモッグ[12]、新幹線沿線[13]の騒音と震動[14]など、日本全土[15]で公害は数えきれない[16]。そのうえ、PCB[17]など、一つの地域に限られない[18]公害も出てきた。

工場廃液[19]によって、河川[20]や海が汚染され、さかなに水銀、カドミウム[21]、PCBなどが蓄積[22]された。さかなをよく食べる日本人にとって、これは大きな問題だ。公害病[23]にかかった[24]住民[25]は、治療法[26]もなく、苦しんで[27]いる。

問題が深刻化[28]するにつれて[29]、被害者[30]の住民が公害反対運動[31]に立ち上がった[32]。公害企業に損害賠償[33]を求める裁判[34]が起こされ[35]、四日市の大気汚染訴訟[36]などで、いずれも[37]住民側が勝った[38]。

これらの結果から、企業側も真剣[39]に公害対策[40]に取り組む[41]姿勢[42]をやっと[43]見せはじめた。経済成長を考える前に、まず、公害対策を考えなければならないという意見[44]が強くなっている。政府なども多くの法律を作って、対策に乗り出し[45]ている。しかし、問題はまだ残されていて、公害はこれからの政治の大きな課題だ。

▼Keihin industrial area

Pollution

Japan is said to have the worst pollution in the world and has been called an "advanced pollution nation." Although the economy has grown to a position of prominence since the War, this has also ravaged the land and generated intolerable pollution.

Be it the mercury poisoning in Minamata and Niigata, air pollution in Yokkaichi, photochemical smog in Tokyo and Osaka, the noise and vibration caused by super-express railways, or what have you, Japan has countless cases of environmental disruption.

When the industrial effluents pollute waterways, fish build up concentrations of mercury, cadmium, PCB, and other pollutants, and fish-eating Japanese are stricken with pollution-diseases. This has become a major social problem recently, especially as the people afflicted must suffer with no cure in sight.

As the situation has gotten worse, citizens have banded together to fight pollution. Court suits have even been instituted seeking, and winning, indemnification from polluting industries.

Many people have come to feel that pollution prevention should come before economic growth. The Government too has formulated legislation and shown concern, yet the problem remains a major unresolved political issue.

語句

1 senshin-koku advanced country
2 kōdo (Na) height, high degree, rapid, sophisticated
3 tai-koku Great Power
4 kokudo the land of a country
5 kōhai (Nv) devastation
6 Minamata (a place name)
7 Niigata (a place name)
8 suigin chūdoku mercury poisoning
suigin mercury
chūdoku (Nv) poisoning
9 Yokkaichi (a place name)
10 taiki-osen air pollution
osen (Nv) pollution, contamination
11 kinkō suburbs, area near the city
12 kōkagaku-*sumoggu* 'photochemical smog' *sumoggu* 'smog'
13 ensen (N) along the (railroad) line
14 shindō (Nv) vibration, trembling
15 zendo the whole land
16 kazoe-kirenai countless, innumerable
kazoe•ru count
17 *PCB* polychlorinated biphenyl
18 kagir•u limit
19 haieki waste fluid
20 kasen =kawa (more common) rivers
21 *kadomiumu* 'Cadmium'
22 chikuseki (Nv) accumulation
23 kōgai-byō pollution-caused diseases
byō←byōki disease
24 (byōki ni) kakar•u fall ill, suffer from a disease
25 jūmin inhabitants, residents
26 chiryō-hō remedy, cure
chiryō (Nv) cure, medical treatment
hō method, measure
27 kurushim•u suffer, be afflicted
28 shinkoku-ka becoming more serious
29 ...ni tsurete in proportion to, as...
30 higai-sha victim, sufferer
higai damage
31 hantai-undō movement/campaign protesting against...
hantai (Nv) opposition, objection; reverse, contrary undō (Nv) movement, campaign; physical exercise
32 tachi-agar•u stand up, set oneself to
33 songai-baishō compensation
34 saiban (Nv) trial (in court)
35 okos•u (Vt) start (a movement); organize; generate (electricity)
36 soshō (Nv) lawsuit, legal action
37 izure mo each/all of them
38 kats•u win
39 shinken (Na) earnest, sincere, serious
40 taisaku countermeasure, policy to cope with...
41 torikum•u wrestle/come to grips with
42 shisei posture, attitude
43 yatto (Adv) at last; with difficulty; barely
44 iken opinion
45 taisaku ni noridas•u embark upon countermeasures

24

第 25 課

映画を 見る

TAPE
No. 7
Side 1

❶　きのうは　久しぶりに　ひまが　できた[1]ので、　友人と　いっしょに　映画を　見に　行く　ことに　しました。

友人は　今　上映[2]している　中で　いちばん　見たいの[3]は　チャップリン[4]の　「モダン・タイムス[5]」だと　言いました。　わたしは　その　映画は　ずっと　昔、　子どもの　ときに　一度　見た　ことが　ありました。　それで、　今　評判の　日本映画を　見たかったのですが、　友人が　どうしても[6]　「モダン・タイムス」を　見たいと　言うので、　それを　見る　ことに　しました。

＊　＊　＊

❷　たいへん　おもしろかったです。　子どもの　ときは、　見て　ただ[7]　ゲラゲラ[8]　笑っていただけですが、　今度は　いろんな[9]　ことを　考えさせられました。　まず、　第一に[10]　その　新鮮さ[11]に　おどろかされました。　何十年も　前に　作られているのに　その　新しさ[12]は　まったく[13]　おとろえて[14]いません。

❸　映画を　見おわってから、　友人と　喫茶店で　コーヒーを　飲みながら　この　映画の　よさ[15]や　おもしろさ[16]を　論じ合い[17]ま

語句

1 deki•ru　be ready; come into being, form; be possible; be able to
2 jōei　(Nv) show (a movie)　cf. jōen
3 …no　See §101 (2)
4 *Chappurin*　'Chaplin'
5 *Modan Taimusu*　'Modern Times'
6 dō shitemo　at any cost, by any means
7 tada　only
8 gera-gera (to)　(onomat) a manner of laughing loudly and continuously
9 ironna ＝iroiro-na　various
10 dai-ichi ni　firstly
11 shinsen-sa　fresh ←shinsen (Na)
12 atarashi-sa　newness
13 mattaku　totally; (not) in the least
14 otoroe•ru　become weak, wither, decline

した。

❹　チャップリンの　言いたい　ことが　よく　わかったと　思います。　近ごろ、　わたしも　友人も　忙しくて、　なかなか映画を　見る　ことが　できませんが、　これからは　できるだけよい　映画は　見ようと　いう　ことに　[18]なりました。

❺　よい　映画を　見る　ことは　たいへん　いい　ことです。[19]ところが、　今の　日本映画には　なかなか　よい　作品が　ありません。　[20]エロ・グロ・ナンセンスの　映画が　多いです。これは　作る　人にも　見る　人にも　問題が　あると　思われます。

　ほんとうに　すぐれた　映画と　[21]いうのは　[22]いつまでも　[23]生きつづける　映画の　[24]ことなのでしょう。

---

15 yo-sa　good point ←yo•i (good)
16 omoshiro-sa　fun; the point of a story
17 ronji-a•u　discuss
18 ...to iu koto ni nar•u　That means...
19 tokoroga　however
20 *ero-guro-nansensu*　pornographic, grotesque, and nonsense
　ero　'erotic'
　guro　'grotesque'
　nansensu　'nonsense'
21 ...to iu no wa　...means
22 itsu made mo　forever
23 iki-tsuzuke•ru　continue to live
　-tsuzuke•ru　continue ...ing
24 (N/Na) na no desu　See § 101 (4)

25

Dai 25-ka
Eiga o Miru

1 Kinō wa hisashi-buri ni hima ga dekita node, yūjin to issho-ni eiga o mi ni iku koto ni shimashita.

Yūjin wa ima jōei-shite-iru naka de ichiban mitai no wa *Chappurin* no *'Modan Taimusu'* da to iimashita. Watashi wa sono eiga wa zutto mukashi, kodomo no toki ni ichi-do mita koto ga arimashita. Sorede, ima hyōban no Nippon-eiga o mitakatta no desu ga, yūjin ga dō shitemo *'Modan Taimusu'* o mitai to iu node, sore o miru koto ni shimashita.

* * *

2 Taihen omoshirokatta desu. Kodomo no toki wa, mite tada gera-gera waratte-ita dake desu ga, kondo wa ironna koto o kangaesaseraremashita. Mazu, dai-ichi ni sono shinsen-sa ni odorokasaremashita. Nan-jū-nen mo mae ni tsukurarete-iru noni sono atarashi-sa wa mattaku otoroete-imasen.

3 Eiga o mi-owatte kara, yūjin to kissa-ten de *kōhī* o nominagara kono eiga no yo-sa ya omoshiro-sa o ronji-aimashita.

4 *Chappurin* no iitai koto ga yoku wakatta to omoimasu. Chika-goro, watashi mo yūjin mo isogashikute, nakanaka eiga o miru koto ga dekimasen ga, kore kara wa dekiru dake yoi eiga wa miyō to iu koto ni narimashita.

5 Yoi eiga o miru koto wa taihen ii koto desu. Tokoroga, ima no Nippon-eiga niwa nakanaka yoi sakuhin ga arimasen. *Ero-guro-nansensu* no eiga ga ōi desu. Kore wa tsukuru hito nimo miru hito nimo mondai ga aru to omowaremasu.

Hontō-ni sugureta eiga to iu no wa itsu made mo iki-tsuzukeru eiga no koto na no deshō.

Lesson 25

Going to a Movie

1 Since I had some free time yesterday, I decided to go to a movie with a friend. My friend said he wanted to see Chaplin's *Modern Times* more than anything else showing. I had already seen it a long time ago when I was little. So I wanted to see one of the popular Japanese movies playing, but my friend insisted that he just had to see *Modern Times*, so we went to see it.

* * *

2 It was very interesting. When I saw it as a child, it only made me laugh, but this time it also made me think. I was especially surprised at how timeless it is. Even though it was made decades ago, it still has an astonishing freshness about it.

3 After the movie, we went to a coffee shop for some coffee and talked about how good and how interesting the movie was.

4 I think I understand what Chaplin wanted to say. We have both been too busy to go to movies of late, but we decided we want to see as many good movies as possible from now on.

5 It is a very good thing to see a good movie. But there are not very many good movies among the Japanese products. There is just a lot of sex, sadism, and stupidity. I think this is the fault of both the people who make movies and the people who go to see them.

A really good movie, I believe, is one that never loses its appeal.

ANSWERS 〈pp. 304, 305〉

I. 1. Watashi wa kinō no ban jishin ga atta koto/no o shinbun de shirimashita. 2. Anata wa ima Kyōto de ōki-na kokusai-kaigi ga hirakarete-iru koto/no o shitte-imasu ka? 3. Raigetsu kara *basu*-dai ga agaru koto/no wa tashika desu ka? 4. Watashi wa mō sugu sōsenkyo ga aru koto/no o *rajio* no *nyūsu* de shirimashita. 5. Watashi wa kono hon ga zeppan ni natte-iru koto/no o tomodachi kara kikimashita. 6. Ano kaisha ga tōsan-shita no/koto wa hontō desu ka?

II. 1. ... benkyō-suru koto ni shimasu (shimashita). 2. ... yameru koto ni shimasu (shimashita). 3. ... nomanai koto ni shimasu (shimashita). 4. ... suwanai koto ni shimasu (shimashita). 5. ... awanai koto ni shimasu (shimashita).

III. 1. koto 2. koto/no 3. koto 4. koto 5. koto 6. koto 7. no 8. no 9. koto

IV. "Watashi ga kare kara *gitā* o katta koto/no o shitte-imasu ka? Kore ga kare kara katta *gitā* desu." "Kare wa *gitā* o hiku koto ga dekimasu ka? Watashi wa kare ga hiku no o kiita koto ga arimasen." "Iie, kare wa hikemasen. Sorede kare wa watashi ni *gitā* o uru koto ni shita no desu."

●文法

§ 100 The Use of koto

(1) Koto meaning 'matter, thing' is used just like any other Noun.

e.g. Kore wa daiji-na koto desu. 'This is an important matter.'

Watashi ga/no itta koto o oboete-imasu ka?

'Do you remember what (=the thing which) I said?'

(2) Koto is also used as a Pseudo Noun, whose function is to give a Noun-like quality to a V (as we have already seen in § 67) as well as to other types of Predicates. It can thus function to nominalize a sentence, i.e. to change a sentence into a Noun Clause.

Sentence + **koto**	'that (Sentence)'

e.g. { Kinō asoko de kaji ga arimashita. 'There was a fire there yesterday.'
Anata wa sore o shitte-imasu ka? 'Do you know that?'

→Anata wa kinō asoko de kaji ga atta koto o shitte-imasu ka?

'Do you know that there was a fire there yesterday?'

NB: The modifications necessary (or preferred) in using a Sentence as a Noun Modifier (See NB: (1)-(5) in § 98) generally apply here, except (4), i.e., 'N desu' changes to 'N de aru (koto)' or 'N da to iu (koto),' rather than 'N no (koto).'

(3) The Pseudo Noun koto is also used in the following fixed pattern:

V (Dict. form) **koto ni** { **shimasu**	'I have decided to...'
narimasu	'It is decided to...'

e.g. Watashi wa mō ichi-nen Nippon ni iru koto ni shimashita.

'I have decided to stay in Japan for another year.'

Mō ichi-nen Nippon ni iru koto ni narimashita.

'It has been decided that I am to stay in Japan for another year.'

§ 101 The Use of no

(1) The Particle no sometimes plays the same roles as koto.

e.g. Anata wa kinō asoko de kaji ga atta koto/no o shitte-imasu ka?

'Do you know that there was a fire there yesterday?'

Koko de *tabako* o suu koto/no wa kiken desu.

'It is dangerous to smoke here.'

No cannot replace koto, however, when koto is used in some fixed (or idiomatic) patterns, e.g., '...koto ga dekimasu,' '...koto ga arimasu,' '...koto ni shimasu/narimasu,' etc.

(2) The Emphatic Construction using **no**:

...no wa...desu 'It is...that...'

e.g. Kare wa kyo-nen *Indo* e ikimashita. 'He went to India last year.'

→Kyo-nen *Indo* e itta no wa kare desu.

'It is he who went to India last year.'

→Kare ga *Indo* e itta no wa kyo-nen desu.

'It was last year that he went to India.'

(3) The Object of Perception:

N ga/no V **no o mimasu/kikimasu**, etc. 'see/hear/etc. N doing...'

e.g. Watashi wa hen-na otoko ga heya kara dete-kuru no o mimashita.

'I saw a strange man come (or coming) out of the room.'

(4) The Explanatory Sentence: Sentence + **no/n desu**

When the speaker intends to explain a reason, cause, or circumstance, the Predicate is followed by 'no desu.'

e.g. Anata wa kinō kimasendeshita ne. 'You didn't come yesterday.'

—Hai, kuni kara haha ga kita no desu.

'(That was because) Mother came to visit me yesterday.'

Seeing someone looking pale, one will ask:

Dō shita no/n desu ka? 'What is the matter?'

—Kesa kara atama ga itai no/n desu.

'I've had a headache since this morning.'

25

●練習 ANSWERS→p. 301

I. Combine the sentences as shown in the example.

Ex. Rai-shū shiken ga arimasu. Watashi wa sore o shirimasen deshita.

→Watashi wa rai-shū shiken ga aru koto/no o shirimasen deshita.

1. Kinō no ban jishin[1] ga arimashita. Watashi wa sore o shinbun de shirimashita.
2. Ima Kyōto de ōki-na kokusai-kaigi[2] ga hirakarete[3]-imasu. Anata wa sore o shitte-imasu ka?
3. Rai-getsu kara *basu*-dai[4] ga agarimasu.[5] Sore wa tashika desu ka?
4. Mō sugu sō-senkyo[6] ga arimasu. Watashi wa sore o *rajio* no *nyūsu* de shirimashita.
5. Kono hon wa zeppan[7] ni natte-imasu. Watashi wa sore o tomodachi kara kikimashita.
6. Ano kaisha wa tōsan[8]-shimashita. Sore wa hontō desu ka?

II. Transform the sentences as shown in the example.

Ex. Rai-getsu kuni e kaerimasu.

→Rai-getsu kuni e kaeru koto ni shimasu (shimashita).

1. Mai-asa Nippon-go o benkyō-shimasu.
2. Shigoto o yamemasu.
3. O-sake o nomimasen.
4. *Tabako* o suimasen.
5. Kanojo to aimasen.

語句

1 jishin earthquake

2 kokusai-kaigi international conference

3 hirakare・ru be held

4 *basu*-dai bus fare

5 agar・u (Vi) rise cf. age・ru (Vt)

III. Fill in the blanks using 'koto' or 'no.'

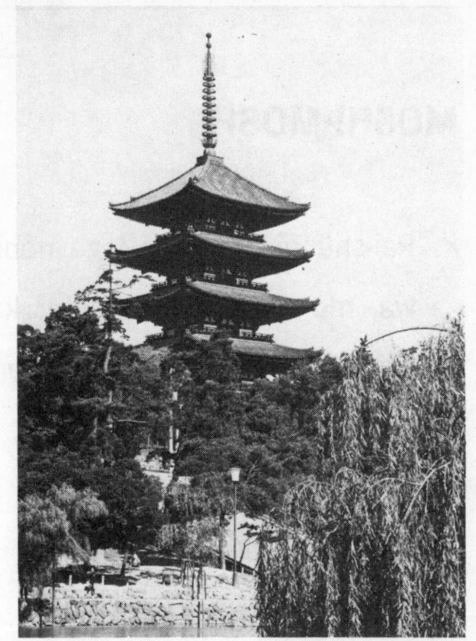

Nippon wa taihen subarashii to iu (1.) o tomodachi kara kiite, watashi wa kyo-nen Nippon e kimashita. Nippon e kite, odoroita (2.) wa, doko e ittemo hito ga taihen ōi (3.) desu. Asa no *basu* ni noru (4.) ga dekinakute, *takushī* de gakkō e iku (5.) mo arimasu. *Takushī* ga nakanaka konakute, taihen komatta (6.) mo arimasu.

Sen-shū wa gakkō ga yasumi datta node, Nara e ikimashita. Furui o-tera ya butsuzō[9] ga sono mama nokosarete-iru (7.) o mite, hontō-ni subarashii to omoimashita. Tomodachi ga ii to omotta (8.) mo, tabun ano o-tera ya butsuzō o mita kara deshō. Kondo no natsu-yasumi niwa Kyōto e mo itte-miru (9.) ni shite-imasu.

IV. Put the following into Japanese.

"Did you know that I bought a guitar from him? This is the guitar I bought from him."

"Can he play the guitar? I have never heard him play it."

"No, he can't. That's why he decided to sell me his guitar."

---

6 sō-senkyo general election
 senkyo (Nv) election
7 zeppan (N) out of print
8 tōsan (Nv) bankrupt
9 butsuzō statue of Buddha

●会話

MOSHI-MOSHI

K: Rai-shū ni bōnen-kai[1] ga nobita[2] koto wa, mō mina ni shiraseta[3] kai?

T: Iya, mada renraku ga tsukanai[4] hito ga futa-ri iru n da.

K: Sore wa komatta na.[5]

Dare-dare[6] dai[7]?

T: Yamada to Satō[8] da yo.

K: Yamada no tokoro niwa denwa ga aru darō? Soko no kōshū-denwa[9] kara denwa o kakeyō yo.[10]

T: Un, boku ga kakete-miru yo.

....

T: Moshi-moshi, Yamada-san no o-taku desu ka?

Y: Hai, Yamada desu ga.

T: Masao[11]-kun wa imasu ka?

Y: Hai, Masao wa orimasu ga, dochira-sama deshō ka?

T: Dō-kyū[12] no Takada[13] desu.

Y: Ā, Takada-san desu ka.

K: Have you notified everyone that the year-end party has been postponed to next week?

T: No, I have two more people to contact.

K: We can't leave them uninformed. Who are they?

T: Yamada and Sato.

K: Yamada has a phone, doesn't he? Let's call him from that phone-booth.

T: Yeah, I'll try it.

....

T: Hello, is this the Yamada's?

Y: Yes, it is.

T: Is Masao there?

Y: Yes, he is. May I ask who's calling?

T: His classmate Takada.

Y: Oh, Mr. Takada.

語句

1 bōnen-kai year-end party (lit. party to forget the year gone by)
2 nobi•ru (Vi) extend, expand; be postponed
3 shirase•ru inform
4 renraku ga tsuk•u (Vi) get in touch with...
cf. renraku o tsuke•ru (Vt)
5 ...na (vaguely exclamatory ending)
6 dare-dare who and who
7 ...dai? (Colloquial) (WH-question) desu ka?
8 Satō (a family name)
9 kōshū-denwa public phone
kōshū (N) public

Thank you for everything you've done for Masao. Please wait a minute while I call him.

....

M: Hello.
T: Hello, Yamada? Takada here. How are you?
M: Oh, Takada. It's been a long time.
T: To get right to the point, it's about that year-end party. It had to be moved back to next week. Sorry I'm so late getting in touch with you.
M: And, when is it for now?
T: Next Saturday. It'll be still at the same place, but I haven't been able to contact Sato.
M: Since I'll be seeing him this Sunday, I'll tell him.
T: Great! I'll leave it all to you.
M: OK, I'll do it.

Itsumo Masao ga o-sewa ni natte-imasu. Yonde-kimasu kara, sukoshi o-machi-kudasai.

....

M: Moshi-moshi.

T: Yā, Yamada-kun kai?
Takada da yo. Genki kai?

M: Ō,[14] Takada ka, hisashi-buri da ne.

T: Sassoku da ga ne, rei no bōnen-kai no koto da ga, tsugō[15] de, rai-shū ni nobasu[16] koto ni natta n da. Renraku ga okurete mōsiwake-nai ga.

M: De,[17] itsu ni natta?

T: Rai-shū no Do-yōbi na n da. Kaijō wa kono mae kimeta tokoro da ga, Satō-kun nimo renraku ga tsukanakute ne.

M: Kare to wa kondo no Nichi-yōbi ni au koto ni natte-iru kara, boku ga itte-oku yo.

T: Soitsu[18] wa ii. O-negai-suru yo. Yoroshiku na.

M: Ii yo, hiki-uketa.

---

10 ...yo. ..., I say. ..., I assure you.
11 Masao (a given name(m))
12 dō-kyū (N) the same class/grade
 dō- the same...
 -kyū class, grade
13 Takada (a family name)
14 Ō oh
15 tsugō convenience
16 nobas·u (Vt) postpone; extend, expand
 cf. nobi·ru (Vi)
17 De And, then
18 soitsu (Colloquial, derogatory) that one (thing or person)

25

日本の歴史—3

日本でも封建社会[1]に商品[2]経済が発達し、徳川幕府の支配力[3]は弱くなっていった。そのころ、ヨーロッパの資本主義諸国[4]が、相ついで[5]幕府に、鎖国をやめて貿易することを求めてきた。幕府は、この圧力[6]に負け[7]て、1858年以後、アメリカ、その他[8]の国々[9]と条約[10]を結び[11]、貿易することにした。このことが、一つのきっかけ[12]になって、270年間続いた「徳川幕府」は倒れた[13]。

1868年、幕府にかわって、天皇を中心とした新しい政府が生まれた。この革命[14]を「明治維新[15]」と呼んでいる。新しい明治政府は、ヨーロッパ諸国に追いつこうとして、「富国強兵策[16]」を打ち出した[17]。以後、日本の産業は、飛躍的[18]に発展したが、その発展は、国家からの多額[19]の援助[20]と、農民[21]や労働者の長時間労働[22]と低賃金によってもたらされたものであった。産業が発達した結果、日本は国内市場だけではまにあわなくなり、大陸に市場を求めた。

一方、1890年に第一回の衆議院議員[23]の選挙が行なわれた[24]が、投票[25]できたのは、全人口のわずか1％にすぎなかった[26]し、言論[27]や出版も自由ではなかった。そうした中[28]でも、選挙権[29]の拡大を求める運動や、労働組合[30]の運動が続けられた。特に、第一次世界大戦[31]が終わった1918年ごろから、労働運動は、一段と[32]はげしくなった。しかし、こうした動き[33]に対する[34]政府の弾圧[35]はきびしく[36]、年々、運動も弱められ[37]、すべての民主的[38]な権利[39]や思想[40]が否定されていった。こうして、長くて[41]、暗い戦争の時代が続くことになった。

▲Perry's visit to Japan (1853)

Japanese History—3

During Japan's feudal age, a mercantile economy was developed and the power of the Tokugawa Shogunate weakened. At the same time, Western capitalism was calling upon the Shogunate to open the country to overseas trade. Yielding to such pressures, the Government concluded trade agreements with America and other nations, leading to the fall of the Shogunate 270 years after its establishment.

In 1868, a new Government was formed around the Emperor, this revolution being referred to as the Meiji Restoration. The new Government adopted a policy of "Rich Nation, Strong Army" to catch up with the West and Japan began its spectacular growth, growth supported by massive governmental assistance as well as by farmers and laborers working long hours for slight wages. As industrialization progressed, Japan sought to expand to the continental Asian market.

Although the first election was held in 1890, only a mere 1% of the population was able to vote, and there was very little freedom of speech or the press. Even so, campaigns to extend suffrage and labor union movements grew, the labor movement becoming especially active after World War I. Nevertheless, the Government moved to surpress and slowly crushed these movements, denying all democratic thoughts and rights. Thus it was that Japan entered the long, dark years of World War II.

語句

1 hōken-shakai feudal society
cf. hōken-seido (feudal system)
2 shōhin merchandise, commodity
3 shihai-ryoku ruling power
shihai (Nv) rule, govern, control
-ryoku power, force
4 shokoku (many) countries
5 aitsuide in succession, one after another
6 atsuryoku pressure
7 make•ru be defeated; lose
8 ta no=hoka no other...
9 kuni-guni countries
10 jōyaku treaty
11 musub•u tie; conclude
12 kikkake chance, turning point
13 taore•ru (Vi) fall over; collapse
cf. taos•u (Vt)
14 kakumei revolution
15 Meiji-ishin Meiji Restoration
16 fukoku-kyōhei-saku (lit. 'rich-country-strong-military policy')
-saku policy
17 uchidas•u set forth; launch
18 hiyaku-teki (Na) leaping
hiyaku (Nv) jump, leap
19 ta-gaku (N) great amount (of money)
20 enjo (Nv) aid
21 nōmin farmer cf. gyomin
22 chō-jikan (N/Adv)(for) many hours
23 Shūgiin-giin member of the House of Representatives
Shūgiin the House of Representatives giin assembly man
24 okona•u (formal expression of suru)
25 tōhyō (Nv) vote
26 ...ni suginai no more than...
27 genron speech (as in 'freedom of speech')
28 sō shita naka de in such a situation, under such circumstances
29 senkyo-ken suffrage
-ken ←kenri (right)
30 rōdō-kumiai labor/trade union
kumiai union
31 Dai-ichi-ji-sekai-taisen World War I
32 ichi-dan to (Adv) a grade higher/more, all the more
33 ugoki motion; trend; movement ←ugok•u
34 ...ni taisuru against, toward
cf. ...ni taishi(te) (Adv)
35 dan'atsu (Nv) oppression
36 kibishi•i harsh, rigid
37 yowame•ru (Vt) make...weak/feeble
38 minshu-teki (Na) democratic
cf. minshu-shugi (democracy)
39 kenri right
40 shisō (political/philosophical) thought
41 kō-shite thus, in this way

25

第 26 課

ステレオを 買う

TAPE
No. 7
Side 1

❶山田さん、 いい ところで 会いました。 これから、 ステレオを 買いに 行く[1] ところですが、どこか 安くて いい 店を 知りませんか。

——ステレオ! それは いいですね。 わたしも 買いたいと 思っていた ところです。 いっしょに 見に 行きましょうか。 日本橋[2]の 店が いいと いう 話です。

* * *

❷ステレオが ほしいのですが。

——どれぐらいのが いいですか。

そうですね。 わたしが 楽しむ[3] ため[4]に 買うと いうより[5] 子どもたちの ために 買うのです。すぐ こわし[6]たり しますから、 安ければ[7] 安い ほど いいですが……。

——これは どうですか。 手ごろ[8]だと 思いますが……。

❸一度 音を 聞かせてもらえますか。……少し 音が かたい[9]ですね。 山田さん、 どうですか。

——わたしも そう 思います。 向こうに あるのは どうでしょう。 あれは 広告で いい 音が 出ると 言っ

語句

1 tokoro See §102
2 Nippon-bashi (a place name)
3 tanoshim•u (Vt) enjoy
4 tame See §103
5 …to iu yori rather than…
6 kowas•u (Vt) break, destroy
cf. koware•ru (Vi)
7 …-ba…hodo See §104
8 te-goro (Na) handy, easy to handle
9 kata•i hard, solid cf. yawaraka•i (soft)
10 tōri See §105

ていましたよ。

❹少し　高いですが、あなたの　言う　とおり　いい　音[10]ですね。

——これは　いいですよ。　これぐらいのが　よく　売れて　います。　これは　聞く　人の　思う　とおりの　音が　出[11]せます。　この　五つの　つまみ[12]は　低音[13]や　高音[14]を　調節[15]する　ための　ものです。

❺これは　なかなか　いいですね。　山田さん　どうですか。

——たいへん　いいですね。　わたしも　これぐらいの　ものが　ほしいです。　この　クラス[16]では　これほど[17]の　ものは　ちょっと　ないでしょう。

❻わたしは　今まで　忙しかった　ために　ゆっくり　音楽を　楽しむ　ことも　できませんでしたが、　これからは　ひまを　見つけ[18]て　よい　音楽を　聞こうと　思います。　音楽を　聞く　ための　ひまぐらいは　ぜひ　作りたいですね。

---

11 das·u (Vt) put/take out; send; mail (a letter) cf. de·ru (Vi)
12 tsumami knob
13 tei-on low-pitched sound
14 kō-on high-pitched sound
15 chōsetsu (Nv) adjust
16 *kurasu* 'class'
17 kore hodo as (N) to this degree
18 mitsuke·ru (Vt) find out, discover cf. mitsukar·u (Vi)

Dai 26-ka
Sutereo o Kau

1 Yamada-san, ii tokoro de aimashita. Kore kara, *sutereo* o kai ni iku tokoro desu ga, doko ka yasukute ii mise o shirimasen ka?

——*Sutereo*! Sore wa ii desu ne. Watashi mo kaitai to omotte-ita tokoro desu. Issho-ni mi ni ikimashō ka? Nippon-bashi no mise ga ii to iu hanashi desu.

* * *

2 *Sutereo* ga hoshii no desu ga.

——Dore gurai no ga ii desu ka?

Sō desu ne. Watashi ga tanoshimu tame ni kau to iu yori kodomo-tachi no tame ni kau no desu. Sugu kowashitari shimasu kara, yasukereba yasui hodo ii desu ga....

——Kore wa dō desu ka? Te-goro da to omoimasu ga....

3 Ichi-do oto o kikasete-moraemasu ka? ...Sukoshi oto ga katai desu ne. Yamada-san, dō desu ka?

——Watashi mo sō omoimasu. Mukō ni aru no wa dō deshō. Are wa kōkoku de ii oto ga deru to itte-imashita yo.

4 Sukoshi takai desu ga, anata no iu tōri ii oto desu ne.

——Kore wa ii desu yo. Kore gurai no ga yoku urete-imasu. Kore wa kiku hito no omou tōri no oto ga dasemasu. Kono itsu-tsu no tsumami wa tei-on ya kō-on o chōsetsu-suru tame no mono desu.

5 Kore wa nakanaka ii desu ne. Yamada-san dō desu ka?

——Taihen ii desu ne. Watashi mo kore gurai no mono ga hoshii desu. Kono *kurasu* dewa kore hodo no mono wa chotto nai deshō.

6 Watashi wa ima made isogashikatta tame ni yukkuri ongaku o tanoshimu koto mo dekimasendeshita ga, kore kara wa hima o mitsukete yoi ongaku o kikō to omoimasu. Ongaku o kiku tame no hima gurai wa zehi tsukuritai desu ne.

Lesson 26

Buying a Record Player

1 Mr. Yamada, just the man I wanted to see. I'm on my way to buy a stereo set, and I wondered if you might know of someplace that is good but inexpensive.
——A stereo set! That's very nice. I've been wanting to get one myself. Why don't we go looking together? There's supposed to be a good place near Nippon-bashi.

* * *

2 We'd like to see some stereo sets.
——What sort of a set did you have in mind?
Let's see. I'm not buying it so much for my own enjoyment as for my children to have fun with. Since it will probably get broken fairly soon, the cheaper the better.
——How about this one? It's not too expensive.

3 Could I hear how it sounds? ... Sounds a little harsh to me. What do you think, Yamada?
——I think so too. What about that one over there? The advertisements say it has good reproduction.

4 It's a little expensive, but the sound is good.
——This is a good set. And sets in this range are selling very well. You can adjust the sound the way you like it. These five controls here are to adjust the tone.

5 This is a nice set, isn't it? What do you think, Yamada?
——It's very nice. I'd like something like this myself. It's rare to find a set this good in this price range.

6 I've been too busy until now to sit down and enjoy good music, but from now on I want to find the time to listen to good music. Surely I can find the time for music.

ANSWERS 〈pp. 316, 317〉

I. 1. (A) kaku (B) kaite-iru (C) kaita 2. (A) yomu (B) yonde-iru (C) yonda 3. (A) toru (B) totte-iru (C) totta 4. (A) hairu (B) haitte-iru (C) haitta 5. (A) kakeru (B) kakete-iru (C) kaketa 6. (A) shiraberu (B) shirabete-iru (C) shirabeta 7. (A) benkyō-suru (B) benkyō-shite-iru (C) benkyō-shita 8. (A) suru (B) shite-iru (C) shita

II. (A) 1. ...iku tame ni 2. ...shiraberu tame ni 3. ...iwau tame ni
(B) 1. ...neta tame ni 2. ...ki ga chiisai tame ni 3. ...amari dekinai/dekinakatta tame ni

III. 1. Yoyaku wa hayakereba hayai hodo ii desu. 2. Aeba au hodo kanojo ga suki ni narimasu. 3. Kōjō ga fuereba fueru hodo kōgai ga ōku narimasu.

IV. 1. tame ni 2. tōri ni 3. hodo/gurai 4. tōri; hodo 5. tōri ni 6. hodo 7. tame ni; tame ni

V. "Ima nani o shite-iru tokoro desu ka?" "Jikken ga owatte, ie ni kaeru tokoro desu." "Nan no jikken desu ka?" "*Masutā*-ronbun no tame no jikken desu. Jikan ga amari nakatta node, isoganakereba narimasen deshita. Isogeba isogu hodo takusan machigai o shimashita." "Kyōju ga itta tōri ni shimashita ka?" "Hai, mochiron. Shikashi kyōju ga watashi ni itte-ita hodo yasashiku wa arimasen deshita."

●文法

§ 102 The Use of tokoro

(1) Tokoro, as an ordinary Noun, means 'place.'

e.g. O-tokoro wa doko desu ka? 'Where is your place (=Where do you live)?'

Koko wa Natsume Sōseki ga umareta tokoro desu.

'This is the place where Natsume Soseki was born.'

(2) Tokoro, on the other hand, is used as a kind of Pseudo Noun in some fixed patterns like the following; here tokoro means something like 'a certain point (in time or in a process).'

V(Dict. form)+tokoro desu 'be about to... (at this moment)'

e.g. Ima ginkō e iku tokoro desu. 'I am on my way to the bank.'

V(Past form)+tokoro desu 'have just finished...ing now'

e.g. Ima anata ni denwa o kaketa tokoro desu.

'I have just phoned you.'

V-te-iru tokoro desu 'I am in the process of ...ing'

e.g. Ima rokuon-shite-iru tokoro desu. 'I am recording now.'

§ 103 The Use of tame (ni)

(1) Reason or Cause:

e.g. Kinō kaminari ga ochita tame ni teiden ni narimashita.

'There was a power failure because of the lightning yesterday.'

Teiden no tame ni nani mo dekimasen deshita.

'Because of the power failure, I couldn't do anything.'

(2) Purpose:

e.g. Kekkon-suru tame ni o-kane o tamete-imasu.

'I am saving money (in order) to get married.'

cf. Gohan o tabe ni ikimasu/kimasu/kaerimasu. (See § 34)

§ 104 The Use of **hodo** as a Pseudo Noun

e.g. Kare wa anata ga iu hodo warui ningen dewa arimasen.

'He is not so bad a person as you say he is.'

Kyōto wa Ōsaka hodo ōkiku nai desu. 'Kyoto is not so large as Osaka.'

Anata wa Nippon-go ga jōzu desu ne. 'You speak very good Japanese.'

—Iie, sore hodo dewa arimasen.

'No, not all that much (=not to the extent that you praise me.)'

Hodo, preceded by the Conditional '-(r)eba form' (See § 95), forms the following fixed pattern:

Predicate (-(r) eba form)+Predicate (Dict. form) **hodo...**

'The more..., the more...'

e.g. Hayakereba hayai hodo ii desu. 'The earlier the better.'

Kangaereba kangaeru hodo wakaranaku narimasu.

'The more I think about it, the more difficult it is to understand.'

§ 105 The Use of **tōri**

e.g. Watashi ga iu tōri ni kaite-kudasai.

'Please write it as I say it (=the way I say it).'

Kore wa mina ga iu hodo kantan-na mondai dewa arimasen.

'This is not so simple a problem as everyone says it is.'

—Sono tōri desu. 'That's right.'

26

§ 106 **-tte**: A Contraction in Informal Conversation

e.g. O-mikoshi-tte nan desu ka? (←O-mikoshi to iu (mo)no wa nan desu ka?)

'What is *omikoshi*, anyway?'

Yamada-san kyō kuru-tte. (←Yamada-san wa kyō kuru to itte-imasu.)

'Yamada says he will come today.'

●練習

ANSWERS→p. 313

I. Practice the pattern '...tokoro desu' as shown in the example.

Ex. (gohan o taberu)

(A) Gohan o taberu tokoro desu.

(B) Gohan o tabete-iru tokoro desu.

(C) Gohan o tabeta tokoro desu.

1. (tegami o kaku)
2. (shinbun o yomu)
3. (shashin o toru)
4. (furo ni hairu)
5. (denwa o kakeru)
6. (jiko no gen'in[1] o shiraberu)
7. (benkyō-suru)
8. (ryokō no junbi o suru)

II. Connect (a) and (b) using 'tame (ni).'

(A) Ex. (a) Kare wa kekkon-shimasu. (b) O-kane o tamete[2]-imasu.

→Kare wa kekkon-suru tame ni o-kane o tamete-imasu.

1. (a) Kanojo wa gaikoku e ikimasu. (b) Kaisha o yamemashita.[3]
2. (a) Kono mondai o shirabemasu. (b) Iin-kai[4] o tsukurimashō.
3. (a) Sotsugyō o iwaimasu. (b) *Pāti* o hirakimashō.

(B) Ex. (a) Tomodachi to hanashite-imashita. (b) Osoku narimashita.

→Tomodachi to hanashite-ita tame ni osoku narimashita.

1. (a) Yūbe osoku nemashita. (b) Kesa wa asa-nebō[5] o shimashita.
2. (a) Kanojo wa ki ga chiisai[6] desu. (b) Jibun no iken o iu koto ga dekimasen.
3. (a) Kare wa Nippon-go ga amari dekimasen. (b) Kurō[7]-shimashita.

語句

1 gen'in cause
2 tame・ru (Vt) save (money), accumulate
3 yame・ru (Vt) quit; stop
4 iin-kai committee
iin member of a committee
5 asa-nebō (Nv) sleeping till late in the morning
nebō (Nv) late rising/riser
6 ki ga chiisa・i timid, cautious

III. Make sentences using the key phrases as shown in the example.

Ex. (shiken) (yasashii) (ii)→Shiken wa yasashikereba yasashii hodo ii desu.

1. (yoyaku[8]) (hayai) (ii)
2. (au) (kanojo ga suki ni naru)
3. (kōjō ga fueru) (kōgai ga ōku naru)

IV. Fill in the blanks with 'tōri (ni),' 'hodo,' 'gurai,' or 'tame (ni).'

1. *Sutoraiki*[9] no (   ) kyō wa densha ga tomarimasu.
2. Kono mihon[10] no (   ) tsukutte-kudasai.
3. Kare wa zenzen ugokenai (   ) tsukarete-imasu.
4. Kan-ji wa omotte-ita (   ) taihen muzukashii desu ga, kaiwa wa omotte-ita (   ) muzukashiku nai desu.
5. Anata ga watashi ni hanashita (   ) shimashita ga shippai[11]-shimashita.
6. Nippon no natsu wa taihen atsui desu ga, fuyu wa sore (   ) samuku nai desu.
7. Anata wa taberu (   ) hataraite-imasu ka, hataraku (   ) tabete-imasu ka?

V. Put the following into Japanese.

"What are you doing now?" "I have just finished an experiment, and now I'm going home." "What is the experiment for?"

"It's for my Master's thesis.[12] I didn't have enough time, so I had to rush. But the more I hurried, the more mistakes I made."

"Did you do it just as your professor had told you?"

"Yes, of course. But it was not as easy as it sounded (as he had said)."

---

cf. ki ga ōki・i (bold, generous, broad-minded)
7 kurō (Nv) hardship, suffering
8 yoyaku (Nv) reservation
9 *sutoraiki* 'strike,' walk-out
10 mihon sample
11 shippai (Nv) failure
12 *masutā*-ronbun Master's thesis
masutā 'master'

26

●会話

WASSHOI, WASSHOI!

—Mō soro-soro, o-matsuri no gyōretsu[1] ga kuru koro desu yo. O-shaberi[2] wa yamete, mi ni ikimasen ka?

Mochiron, ikimasu yo. O-matsuri o miru tame ni kita n desu kara.

—O-mise-suru hodo rippa-na mono dewa arimasen ga ne.

Iya, zehi, Nippon no matsuri wa mite-ikitai to omoimasu.

....

—Hora,[3] fue ya kane no oto ga kikoete-kita deshō? Yatte-kimashita[4] yo. Takusan no hito ga katsuide[5]-iru mono ga aru deshō? Are o o-mikoshi[6] to iimasu.

Hohō, o-mikoshi desu ka?

—Sō desu. Chiisai hō ga kodomo no mikoshi de, ato kara otona no mikoshi mo kimashita yo.

Nani o sakende[7]-iru no desu ka?

—It's almost time for the festival procession to pass by here. Shall we stop talking and go see it?

Of course, let's go. I came here mainly for the festival.

—Though, honestly, it isn't really all that great.

Oh, but please. I really want to see a Japanese festival before I leave.

....

—Listen, can you hear the sounds of the flutes and bells? Here it comes. Do you see that thing all those people are carrying? That's called an "omikoshi."

So that's an "omikoshi"!

—That's it. The small one is for children, and the adults' "omikoshi" is coming later.

What are they shouting?

語句

1 gyōretsu (Nv) procession; queue
2 o-shaberi (Nv) chattering ←shaber・u (speak, chatter)
3 Hora Look, There!
4 yatte-kuru come
5 katsug・u carry on the shoulder; play a trick on; be superstitious
6 mikoshi (a portable shrine used in Shinto festivals)
7 sakeb・u cry out, shout
8 Wasshoi, wasshoi! Heave-ho, heave-ho!
9 kake-goe encouraging shout

—They're shouting their chant of "Wasshoi, wasshoi!"
Isn't that a "shishimai" coming from behind?
—Hey, you know all about this. It certainly is.
I've seen photographs of them before. By the way, how many people are there in this parade?
—Let's see.... Probably about a hundred or so, wouldn't you say?
So many! Where do they go?
—I'm sure they're going to the shrine a little way beyond here.
Shall we follow?
—No, let's not. Even if you go to the shrine, there's nothing special there.

—Are wa "Wasshoi, wasshoi![8]" to
kake-goe[9] o kakete-iru tokoro desu.
Ushiro no hō kara kuru no wa
'shishi-mai' dewa nai desu ka?
—Hē, yoku shitte-imasu ne.
Sono tōri desu yo.
Izen, shashin de mita koto ga arimasu.
Tokorode, kono *parēdo*[10] niwa nan-nin
hodo no hito ga imasu ka?
—Sō desu ne... hyaku-nin gurai
ja nai desu ka.
Takusan no hito desu ne.
Doko made iku no deshō ka?
—Tashika, kono saki ni aru jinja made
da to omoimasu yo.
Tsuite-ikimashō[11] ka?
—Iya, yoshimashō.[12]
Jinja made ittatte, betsu-ni[13]
dōt-te koto wa nai[14] desu yo.

---

kake-goe o kake•ru shout time/encouragement
10 *parēdo* 'parade'
11 tsuite-iku accompany cf. tsuite-kuru See § 86
12 yos•u =yame•ru stop/refrain from
13 betsu-ni (...nai) (not) in particular, special
14 dōt-te koto wa nai=dō to iu koto wa nai It is nothing to get excited about.; It's nothing to surprise (or worry) you.

▶ *Omikoshi*

26

日本の政治

1945年、日本が負けて、第二次世界大戦[1]は終わった。この悲惨[2]な戦争に対する反省[3]から、日本国民は、再び[4]戦争のための武器[5]はとらないことを強く誓い合った[6]。日本国憲法[7]の第9条[8]では、戦争を永久[9]に放棄[10]すると述べている。

ところが、今の日本には「自衛隊[11]」がある。この「自衛隊」が憲法に違反[12]しているかどうかについて、活発[13]な議論[14]がたたかわされてきた[15]。この問題をはじめとして、経済、外交[16]、民生問題[17]など、国政[18]の重要な問題を討議[19]し、決定[20]するところが国会[21]である。この国会は、衆議院と参議院[22]とに分かれているが、それぞれの議員は、選挙によって直接、国民から選ばれる。選挙は、20歳以上のすべての国民が、自分の考えるところを政治に反映させるたいせつな機会である。しかし、その投票率はそれほど高くはなくて、いつも65％ぐらいである。

現在、日本にある政党[23]は五つである。自民党[24]、社会党[25]、共産党[26]、公明党[27]、民社党[28]である。自民党は、戦後ほとんどの期間、政権[29]を担当[30]してきたが、その支持率[31]は徐々に減ってきている。今の日本には、国際平和[32]の問題や、物価、農業、住宅、教育、老人などの問題がたくさんあって、すべて政治的[33]解決[34]が必要になってきている。しかし、投票率の低さにも見られるとおり、政治に対する無関心[35]層[36]はたいへん多い。これらの問題を政府に解決させるためには、どうしても国民ひとりひとり[37]が、政治について、もっと真剣に考えなければならない。

▼The Diet building

▼The Diet (House of Representatives)

Japanese Politics

With Japan's defeat and the end of the War in 1945, the Japanese people reacted to the tragedy of war by vowing to never again take up arms for war. Article 9 of the Japanese Constitution notes this renunciation forever of war.

However, Japan currently maintains "Self-Defense Forces" and there is considerable arguement over whether or not this is in violation of the Constitution. This issue, as well as other economic, diplomatic, welfare, and other important policy questions, is to be debated and resolved in the Diet. The Diet is divided into the House of Representatives and House of Councillors, members of both houses being selected by direct popular election. While elections are thus an important chance for all adults to influence government, the voter turnout is lower than one would expect, holding steady at about 65%.

The five Japanese political parties at present are the Liberal Democratic Party (LDP), Japan Socialist Party (JSP), Japan Communist Party (JCP), *Komeito*, and Democratic Socialist Party (DSP). Although the LDP has been in power for almost all of the postwar period, its voter support has gradually fallen off.

Japan is today faced with a vast number of problems requiring political solutions, such as those of international peace, prices, agriculture, housing, education, and the aged, yet there is considerable apathy toward politics, as reflected in the low voter turnouts. However, every citizen must show more interest in politics if the Government is to solve these problems.

語句

1 Dai-ni-ji-sekai-taisen World War II
2 hisan (Na) miserable
3 hansei (Nv) looking back on what one has done and trying to find what went wrong
4 futa-tabi again
5 buki weapon
  buki o tor•u take up arms
6 chikai-a•u promise each other, mutual vows cf. chika•u (promise, vow)
7 Nippon-koku-kenpō the Japanese Constitution
8 dai-...-jō the...-th article
9 eikyū (N) eternity
10 hōki (Nv) give up, abandon
11 Jieitai the (Japanese) Self-Defense Forces jiei- (Nv) self-defense
  -tai force, army
12 ihan (Nv) violating (a rule)
13 kappatsu (Na) active
14 giron (Nv) discussion, debate
15 tatakawas•u =tatakawase•ru set...to fight cf. tataka•u (fight)
16 gaikō diplomacy cf. gaikō-kan (diplomat)
17 minsei civil administration
18 kokusei national administration
19 tōgi (Nv) discuss
20 kettei (Nv) decision
21 kokkai the National Diet/Parliament
22 Sangiin the House of Councillors
23 seitō political party
24 Jimin-tō the Liberal Democratic Party tō (political) party
25 Shakai-tō the Socialist Party
26 Kyōsan-tō the Communist Party
27 Kōmei-tō the *Komei* Party
28 Minsha-tō the Democratic Socialist Party
29 seiken administrative power
30 tantō (Nv) being in charge of, being responsible for
31 shiji (Nv) support, backing
32 kokusai-heiwa =sekai-heiwa world peace heiwa peace
33 seiji-teki (Na) political
34 kaiketsu (Nv) solution
35 mu-kanshin (N/Na) indifference
36 sō layer; class
37 hitori-hitori each of us/them

第 27 課

魚つり

TAPE
No. 7
Side 2

❶急(きゅう)に[1]　寒(さむ)く　なりましたね。

——寒(さむ)い　はず[2]ですよ。　きょうは　「大寒(だいかん)[3]」ですから。

そうですか。　あなたは　年(とし)の　わりに[4]　そういう　ことを　よく　知(し)っていますね。

——ええ、　わたしは　ずっと　祖母(そぼ)[5]に　育(そだ)てられましたから。　そんな　わけ[6]で、　日本(にっぽん)の　古(ふる)い　こよみ[7]や　行事(ぎょうじ)の　ことは　わりあい[8]　よく　知(し)っているのです。　たしか[9]　二月(にがつ)四日(よっか)が　「立春(りっしゅん)[10]」で、　三月二十一日(さんがつにじゅういちにち)が　「春分(しゅんぶん)[11]」の　はずです。

❷「春分(しゅんぶん)」は　「お彼岸(ひがん)[12]」とも　言(い)いますね。　昔(むかし)から　「暑(あつ)さ　寒(さむ)さも　彼岸(ひがん)まで」と　言(い)いますから、　「春分(しゅんぶん)」までは　まだまだ　寒(さむ)い　わけですね。

——ところで、　山田(やまだ)さんは　おそいですね。　もう　来(く)る　はずですが……。

❸そうですね。　きょうの　魚(うお)つり[13]は　彼(かれ)が　いちばん　期待(きたい)[14]し

語句

1 kyū-ni　suddenly
2 hazu　(N) supposed to　See § 107
3 Dai-kan　the coldest day of the year
4 …no wari ni　considering…;　for… (as in 'He looks young *for* his age.')
5 sobo　grandmother cf. sofu (grandfather)
6 wake　See § 108　7 koyomi　calendar
8 wariai　(N/Adv)　ratio, proportion; comparatively, rather
9 tashika　if I remember right, surely
10 Risshun　(the period when signs of spring show up here and there, around February 4 in the solar calendar)
11 Shunbun　vernal equinox (around the 21st of March in the solar calendar)
12 Higan　the week around March 21 and the week around Sept. 23 in the solar calendar

ていたのですから、 遅れる はずは ないでしょう。 あなたは 初づり[15]に 行ったのでしょう。 どうでしたか。

——あまり つれませんでしたが、 楽しかったですよ。 朝早く まっかな[16] 太陽[17]が 海から 上る[18]のを 見ながら、大好きな つりを するのですから。

❹わたしは 行けなくて 残念でした。 ですから、 きょうが初づりと いう わけです。山田さんは 行ったのでしょうか。

——あれほど[19] つりの 好きな 人が 行かなかった はずはないでしょう。

❺近ごろは 公害で 海も 川も きたなく なりましたね。わたしたち 「つり好き[20]」にとっては 悲しい[21] ことですね。

——つった さかなも 安心[22]して 食べられませんし、 ほんとうに 困りますね。 家の 近くにも 昔は よい つり場[23]が あったのに、こんなに 遠くまで 出かけなければなりません。

なんとかすれば[24] 海も 川も もっと きれいに できる はずなんですがね[25]……。

---

13 uo-tsuri =sakana-tsuri fishing
uo =sakana fish
14 kitai (Nv) expectation, hope
15 hatsu-zuri the first fishing trip
hatsu- the first...of the new year
16 makka (Na) crimson, bright red
17 taiyō sun
18 nobor·u rise, go up
19 are hodo that much
20 tsuri-zuki fishing fan
-zuki (N/Na) lover/fan of ←suki
21 kanashi·i sad, sorrowful
22 anshin (Nv) peace of mind, freedom from care, feeling easy
23 tsuri-ba fishing spot
24 nan toka suru muddle through, manage to do
25 ...ga ne ..., I dare say

Dai 27-ka
Uo-tsuri

1 Kyū-ni samuku narimashita ne.

——Samui hazu desu yo. Kyō wa 'Dai-kan' desu kara.

Sō desu ka. Anata wa toshi no wari ni sō iu koto o yoku shitte-imasu ne.

——Ē, watashi wa zutto sobo ni sodateraremashita kara. Sonna wake de, Nippon no furui koyomi ya gyōji no koto wa wariai yoku shitte-iru no desu. Tashika Ni-gatsu yok-ka ga 'Risshun' de, San-gatsu ni-jū-ichi-nichi ga 'Shunbun' no hazu desu.

2 'Shunbun' wa 'O-higan' to mo iimasu ne. Mukashi kara "Atsu-sa samu-sa mo Higan made" to iimasu kara, 'Shunbun' made wa mada-mada samui wake desu ne.

——Tokorode, Yamada-san wa osoi desu ne. Mō kuru hazu desu ga....

3 Sō desu ne. Kyō no uo-tsuri wa kare ga ichiban kitai-shite-ita no desu kara, okureru hazu wa nai deshō. Anata wa hatsu-zuri ni itta no deshō? Dō deshita ka?

——Amari tsuremasen deshita ga, tanoshikatta desu yo. Asa hayaku makka-na taiyō ga umi kara noboru no o minagara, dai-suki-na tsuri o suru no desu kara.

4 Watashi wa ikenakute zannen deshita. Desukara, kyō ga hatsu-zuri to iu wake desu. Yamada-san wa itta no deshō ka?

——Are hodo tsuri no suki-na hito ga ikanakatta hazu wa nai deshō.

5 Chika-goro wa kōgai de umi mo kawa mo kitanaku narimashita ne. Watashi-tachi 'tsuri-zuki' ni totte wa kanashii koto desu ne.

——Tsutta sakana mo anshin-shite taberaremasen shi, hontō-ni koma-rimasu ne. Ie no chikaku nimo mukashi wa yoi tsuri-ba ga atta noni konna-ni tōku made dekakenakereba narimasen.

Nan toka sureba umi mo kawa mo motto kirei-ni dekiru hazu na n desu ga ne....

Lesson 27

Fishing

1 It sure has gotten cold all of a sudden, hasn't it?
——What do you expect? Today's *Daikan*, the coldest day of the year.
Is that so? You know the old traditions very well for your age.
——I was brought up by my grandmother. So I have a fair acquaintance with the old Japanese customs and festivals. If I remember right, February 4 is *Risshun*, the first day of spring, and March 21 is *Shunbun*, the vernal equinox.

2 The equinoxes are also called *O-higan*, aren't they? There used to be an old saying that both hot and cold last until *Higan*, so I guess we've got some more cold weather ahead of us until the equinox.
——Yamada's late, isn't he? He should be along any time now.

3 You're right. He was looking forward to today's fishing the most, so I don't expect he'll be late. You went on that New Year's fishing trip, didn't you? How was it?
——Didn't catch much, but it was fun. Got up early in the morning and watched the bright red sun come up over the sea while we fished.

4 I'm sorry I couldn't go. Today will be my first time this year. Did Yamada go too?
——You'd hardly expect him not to have gone, the way he loves fishing.

5 But the pollution sure has dirtied the rivers and oceans. It's enough to make a fisherman want to cry.
——We can't even feel safe eating our catches, it's such a messed up situation. There used to be some good fishing spots in our neighborhood, but no more.
It ought to be possible somehow to clean up the rivers and seas, but….

ANSWERS 〈pp. 328, 329〉

I. (A)2+(B)8 Kyūryō-bi mae desu kara, kare wa o-kane ga nai hazu desu. (A)3+(B)2 Kanojo wa jū-nen mae ni kekkon-shimashita kara, mō kodomo ga ni-san-nin iru hazu desu. (A)4+(B)4 Sono ie wa yama no naka ni arimasu kara, shizuka-na hazu desu. (A)5+(B)1 O-tō-san mo o-kā-san mo kirei-na hito desu kara, musume-san mo kirei-na hazu desu. (A)6+(B)7 Kare wa han-jikan mae ni ie o demashita kara, mō sugu koko e kuru hazu desu. (A)7+(B)5 *Dizuni* no eiga desu kara, tanoshii hazu desu. (A)8+(B)6 Tsukue no ue ni *memo* o oite-okimashita kara, kare wa mita hazu desu. (A)9+(B)9 Kare wa san-nen mae ni sotsugyō-shimashita kara, ano sensei ni naratta hazu desu.

II. 1. Anata ga sonna koto ni kyōmi o mochi-hajimeta wake o hanashite-kudasai.
2. Kan-ji ni nan-tōri mo yomi-kata ga aru wake ga, kono hon ni kaite-arimasu.
3. Bukka ga konna-ni takai wake o keizai-gakusha ni kikimashita.
4. Kōbe no niku ga konna-ni oishii wake wa, ushi ni *biru* o nomaseru kara desu.
5. Kare ga kekkon-shinai wake wa, kare ni o-kane ga nai kara desu.
6. Kanojo ga kono-goro tokuni kirei-na wake wa, kanojo ga ren'ai-shite-iru kara desu.

III. 1. Kono keikaku ni tsuite nan-do mo kare ni setsumei-shite-arimasu kara, yoku shitte-iru hazu desu. Kare ga ima kono keikaku ni hantai-suru wake ga wakarimasen.
2. Anata ga Nippon no Bukkyō ni kyōmi o motta wake wa nan desu ka? —Ni-nen mae ni Ryōan-ji no niwa o mite, taihen kandō-shimashita. Sono toki, Bukkyō o shiranakereba, Nippon no niwa no hontō no imi ga wakaru hazu ga nai to oshieraremashita. Sorede, Bukkyō o benkyō-shi-hajimeta wake desu.

27

●文法

§ 107 The Use of the Pseudo Noun hazu

Sentence + **hazu desu.** 'It is supposed to be that....'
'It should be that....'

NB: Negative:... ga/wa arimasen/nai.

This pattern indicates that the speaker supposes that something is a certain way and has a reason for supposing it to be so.

e.g. *Marisa* wa kyō konai hazu desu.

'I don't suppose Marisa will come today.'

This sentence means that the speaker thinks Marisa is not coming because, for instance, she told him that she was not coming, he knows that she left town the previous day, she is sick, etc.

Some more examples:

Ima denwa shitara, kare wa uchi ni iru hazu desu.

'If you call him now, he should be at home.'

Yamada-san kara denwa ga atta hazu desu ga, anata wa shirimasen ka?

'Yamada is supposed to have called me. Do you know anything about it?'

Marisa wa Nippon-go ga jōzu-na hazu desu yo. Go-nen mo Nippon ni iru no desu kara.

'It's quite natural (or, it's no wonder, it's nothing to be surprised at, etc.) that Marisa is good at Japanese, since she has been in Japan for five years.'

Shuppatsu wa ashita desu ka? 'Is (your) departure tomorrow?'

—Hai, sono hazu desu. 'Yes, it is supposed to be.'

Marisa ga sore o shiranai hazu wa arimasen.

'It can't be (or, it is impossible) that Marisa doesn't know this.'

§ 108 The Use of the Pseudo Noun wake

(1) Reason:

e.g. Kare wa naze anna-ni okotte-iru no desu ka? 'Why is he so angry?'

Anata wa sono wake o shitte-imasu ka? 'Do you know why?'

These two sentences can be combined into one as in the following.

→Kare ga anna-ni okotte-iru wake o anata wa shitte-imasu ka?

'Do you know why he is so angry?'

(2) Explaining the situation:

Sentence + wake desu.

e.g. Kanojo wa go-nen mo Nippon ni ita no dakara, Nippon-go ga jōzu-na wake da. 'She has been in Japan for five years. No wonder (=that's the reason) she is fluent in Japanese.'

NB: In this context wake is interchangeable with hazu.

Rai-getsu shuppatsu no hazu deshita ga, is-shūkan hayaku narimashita. Sorede awatete-iru wake desu.

'My departure was supposed to be next month, but it has been moved up a week. That is why I am in such a rush.'

Kaisha ga gappei-shite kara, shigoto ga amari omoshiroku arimasen. Kuni no haha wa byōki desu shi, kanai mo kuni ni kaeri-tai to itte-imasu. Sonna wake de, kuni e kaeru koto ni shimashita.

'Since my company merged, I haven't been very happy with my work. My mother is ill at home, and my wife says she wants to go home. Thus (the circumstances being such), I have decided to go home.'

§ 109 The Use of noni 'In spite of the fact that....'

e.g. Watashi ga kawanai hō ga ii to itta noni, kare wa sono *kamera* o katte-shimatte, komatte-imasu. 'Although (Even though) I had told him he should not buy it, he went ahead and bought the camera anyway.'

NB: N/Na desu+noni →N/Na na noni

●練習

ANSWERS→p. 325

I. One of the sentences in (A) is the basis, in one way or another, supporting a statement in (B). Combine them and conclude the whole sentence with 'hazu desu.'

Ex. (A)1＋(B)3 Ima jū-ji go-fun mae desu kara, *depāto* wa mō sugu aku hazu desu.

(A)	(B)
1. Ima jū-ji go-fun mae desu.	1. Musume-san wa kirei desu.
2. Kyūryō-bi[1] mae desu.	2. Mō kodomo ga ni-san-nin imasu.
3. Kanojo wa jū-nen mae ni kekkon-shimashita.	3. *Depāto* wa mō sugu akimasu.
4. Sono ie wa yama no naka ni ari-masu.	4. Shizuka desu.
5. O-tō-san mo o-kā-san mo kirei-na hito desu.	5. Tanoshii desu.
6. Kare wa han-jikan[2] mae ni ie o demashita.	6. Kare wa mimashita.
7. *Dizuni*[3] no eiga desu.	7. Mō sugu koko e kimasu.
8. Tsukue no ue ni *memo*[4] o oite-okimashita.[5]	8. Kare wa o-kane ga arimasen.
9. Kare wa san-nen mae ni sotsugyō-shimashita.	9. Ano sensei ni naraimashita.

II. Combine (a) and (b) with 'wake,' as shown in the example.

Ex. (a) Watashi niwa wakaranai.

(b) Kare wa naze okotte[6]-imasu ka?

→Watashi niwa kare ga okotte-iru wake ga wakaranai.

語句

1 kyūryō-bi pay day
2 han-jikan half an hour
3 *Dizuni* 'Walt Disney' (1901-66)
4 *memo* 'memo'
5 oite-ok·u leave...behind and come
6 okor·u get/be angry
7 dō shite How, Why
8 -tōri (N) different ways/methods

1. (a) Hanashite-kudasai.

   (b) Anata wa dō shite[7] sonna koto ni kyōmi o mochi-hajimemashita ka?

2. (a) Kono hon ni kaite-arimasu.

   (b) Kan-ji ni naze nan-tōri[8] mo yomi-kata ga arimasu ka?

3. (a) Keizai-gaku-sha[9] ni kikimashita.

   (b) Naze konna-ni bukka ga takai desu ka?

4. (a) Ushi ni *bīru* o nomaseru[10] kara desu.

   (b) Kōbe no niku[11] wa naze konna-ni oishii desu ka?

5. (a) Kare niwa o-kane ga nai kara desu.

   (b) Dō shite kare wa kekkon-shimasen ka?

6. (a) Kanojo wa ren'ai[12]-shite-iru kara desu.

   (b) Naze kanojo wa kono-goro tokuni kirei desu ka?

III. Put the following into Japanese using 'wake' or 'hazu.'

1. I have explained this plan[13] to him many times, so he should understand it well.

   I can't see why he is opposed to this plan now.

2. Tell me how you came to be interested in Buddhism.

   —Two years ago, I visited the garden at Ryoan-ji Temple[14] and was greatly impressed. I was then told that I could not understand the real meaning of Japanese gardens without knowing about Buddhism. That is why I began to study Buddhism.

27

▶The garden at Ryoan-ji Temple

9 keizai-gaku-sha economist
10 nomas·u=nomase·ru make/let... drink
11 niku meat
12 ren'ai (Nv) love between man and woman
13 keikaku (Nv) plan
14 Ryōan-ji (a temple in Kyoto)

●会話

IRASSHAIMASE

Gomen kudasai.

—Irasshaimase.

Ōsaka-dō[1] no 'Kokugo-gaku[2] Jiten' o kudasai.

—Mōshiwake arimasen ga,
tada-ima[3] shina-gire[4] desu.

Okashii desu ne. Sen-shū denwa de chūmon-shita toki, kyō atari[5] hairu hazu da to iu koto deshita yo.

Sorede kyō yotta wake desu.

—Ima sugu o-shirabe-shimasu ga,
nan-yōbi ni go-chūmon-itadakimashita ka?

Ē . . . to, are wa, tomodachi no ie ni itta hi da kara, tashika, sen-shū no Doyōbi no hazu desu.

—(Chūmon-*kādo* o shirabenagara)
Ā, tashika-ni chūmon wa o-uke-shite-imasu ne. Mōshiwake arimasen ga, kyō no gogo atari hairu hazu desu

Excuse me.

—Welcome.

I'd like the Osaka-do *Dictionary of Japanese Linguistics*, please.

—I'm sorry, but we don't have it in stock.

That's strange. When I phoned in my order last week, I was told it would be here today or so. That's why I came by for it today.

—I'll check for you.
On what day exactly did we have your order?

Well, let me see. That was the day I visited my friend's place, so it must have been last Saturday.

—(Checking the orders)
Yes, we certainly received your order. I'm sorry, but your book will be in this

語句

1 -dō (Suf. to a name of a shop)
2 kokugo-gaku study of the national language, Japanese (traditional) linguistics
koku-go national language
3 tada-ima (N/Adv) this moment, in a minute; (Cph: used when one has come home)

ga . . . .

Jā, ni-san-nichi shite kara[6]

mata kimasu.

—Hontō-ni ai-sumimasen.[7]

Tokorode, Okada-shoten[8] kara dete-iru 'Nippon-go no Rekishi' wa sorotte-imasuka?

—Ē, zenbu aru hazu desu. Ano oku no tana[9] no ue no hō desu.

Zenbu de ikura desu ka?

—Roku-sen-yon-hyaku-en desu.

O-isogi[10] de nakereba

o-todoke[11]-shimasu ga . . . .

Jā, todokete-moraimashō.

O-negai-shimasu.

afternoon.

Then, I'll come back in a couple of days.

—I'm really sorry about this.

By the way, do you have a complete set of *The History of the Japanese Language* published by Okada-shoten?

—Yes, we should have them all. On one of the top shelves at the far end of the room.

How much for the set?

—6,400 yen. If you're not in a hurry, we can deliver them.

In that case, I'd like them delivered.

Would you please?

4 shina-gire (N) out of stock
5 atari (N/Adv) around...
6 (time) shite (kara) after...has passed
7 ai-sumimasen (Cph) very sorry
8 shoten book shop; publishing company
9 tana shelf
10 isogi (N) haste←isog·u
11 todoke·ru deliver; report (to an office)

▼Bookshops in Kanda

日本の文学—2

武家政治によって、貴族階級[1]はおとろえた。したがって[2]、貴族社会[3]をえがいた「源氏物語」などの王朝文学[4]にかわって、戦争をえがいた物語がさかんになった。その代表的[5]なものが「平家物語」[6]である。ここでわすれてならない[7]のは、漢語[8]をうまく使って[9]、きびきびした[10]文体を作り出した[11]ことだ。

和歌の世界でも、新しい手法[12]が生まれた。多くの戦争を経験した[13]人々は、現実[14]の世界が信じ[15]られなくて、遠い過去[16]の世界やゆめなどをえがくことが多かった。「方丈記」[17]や「徒然草」[18]もくりかえし[19]無常[20]を説いた[21]。

やがて、庶民文学[22]として、俳句や近世小説[23]が生まれ、芭蕉や西鶴[24]が活躍[25]した。劇の世界では近松が活躍する。この三人のそろった元禄時代[26]は、わが文学史[27]のルネッサンス[28]と言われることもある。西鶴も近松も、人間の恋愛[29]を大胆に[30]表現した。彼らの文学は、この方向[31]で発展すれば、当然[32]、人間解放[33]の文学となるはずであったのだが、封建社会の壁[34]にはばまれて[35]、義理[36]人情[37]の世界に迷いこんで[38]しまった。近松のほとんどの劇は、心中[39]で終わっている。自己否定[40]の文学と言われるわけである。

▼Chikamatsu　▼Saikaku　▼Basho

Japanese Literature—2

As the nobility was weakened by the various warrior clans, monarchic literature such as *Genji-Monogatari* depicting the nobles' life was replaced by tales of war. *Heike-Monogatari* is typical of this genre, and these are memorable for their skillful use of Chinese words and their sharp writing.

Even in the *waka*, new techniques were born when, the many wars experienced having made it impossible for them to believe any longer in reality, people turned to the distant past and dreams for their motifs. *Hojoki*, *Tsurezure-gusa*, and others repeatedly invoke the insignificance of life.

In the mean time, *haiku* and modern novels came into being as popular literature, with Basho and Saikaku active. In the theater, Chikamatsu was active. The Genroku Era which these three led is sometimes called a renaissance in Japanese literary history. Both Saikaku and Chikamatsu wrote boldly of love, and had their work developed in this direction it most likely would have become a literature of liberation. However, they ran up against the barriers of feudal society and floundered on the problem of duty versus compassion. Most of Chikamatsu's plays end in suicide, such that they have been called a literature of self-denial.

語句

1 kizoku nobleman/-woman, aristocrat
2 shitagatte therefore, consequently
3 egak・u describe, depict
4 ōchō dynasty
5 daihyō-teki (Na) representative, typical
6 Heike Monogatari *The Tale of the Heike Family*
7 -te naranai = -te(wa) ikenai must not
8 kan-go old Chinese words/language
9 umaku skillfully, well ←uma・i (skillful, good at)
10 kibi-kibi (to) (onomat) brisk, lively; efficient
11 tsukuri-das・u produce, create
12 shuhō technique, method
13 keiken (Nv) experience
14 genjitsu (N) reality
15 shinji・ru believe
16 kako (N) the past
17 Hōjō-ki (an essay written by Kamo-no-Chomei around 1212)
18 Tsurezure-gusa (an essay written by Yoshida Kenko in 1324-31)
19 kurikaeshi repeatedly ←kurikaes・u (repeat)
20 mujō transiency of life
21 tok・u explain, preach, persuade
22 shomin the common people, the masses
23 kinsei the pre-modern period (Edo Period)
24 Saikaku (a novelist-poet in the early Edo Period; 1642-93)
25 katsuyaku (Nv) being active, playing an important role
26 Genroku-jidai the Genroku Era (early Edo Period)
27 bungaku-shi history of literature
  -shi history ←rekishi
28 *Runessansu* 'Renaissance'
29 ningen human-being
30 daitan (Na) bold, daring, fearless
31 hōkō direction
32 tōzen (N/Adv) as a matter of course
33 kaihō (Nv) liberation
34 kabe obstacle; wall
35 habam・u hinder, obstruct
36 giri the way that a man is supposed to act in relations with other people; obligation
37 ninjō love (or hatred) or other emotions that a man naturally has as a man
38 mayoi-kom・u wander into a maze and get lost
39 shinjū (Nv) double suicide
40 jiko oneself, self, ego

27

第 28 課

日本研究

TAPE
No. 7
Side 2

❶ウィル[1]さん、 あなたは 日本の 文学を 研究しているそう[2]ですね。

——はい。 近代文学を 研究しています。 アンさんも 日本の 文学を 研究していますが、 彼女のように[3] 日本語がうまく[4]ないので 困っています。

❷あなたも たいへん じょうずですよ。 彼女は 日本の 古典も 読めるらしい[5]ですね。 ところで、 新聞によれば[6] 近く[7]京都の 国際会議場[8]で 「日本文化研究[9]国際会議」が 開かれるそうですね。 外国の ジャパノロジスト[10]が おおぜい 来るらしいですよ。

——そうらしいですね。 キーン[11]教授や グルスキナ[12]女史[13]のような 有名な 研究者[14]が おおぜい 出席するそうです。

❸わたしは 専門外[15]ですが、 それは たいへん おもしろそうですね。 その 成果[16]は あなたには 大いに[17] 参考に なりそうですね。

語句

1 *Uiru* 'Will' (a given name)
2 sō be said to; look like See § 111
3 yō the same way as..., like...
4 uma·i skillful, good (at); tasty
5 rashi·i seem to See § 112
6 ...ni yoreba according to...
7 chikaku in the near future
8 Kokusai-kaigi-jō International Conference Hall
9 Nippon-bunka-kenkyū study of Japanese culture
10 *Japanorojisuto* 'Japanologist'
11 *Kin* 'Keene'
12 *Gurusukina* 'Gruskina' (a famous Soviet Japanologist)
13 joshi Mrs., Miss, Ms. (for famous women)
14 kenkyū-sha researcher
15 senmon-gai (N) out of one's field/specialty -gai out of

——山田さん、　そろそろ　帰りましょうか。

雨が　降りそうですから、　少し　急いだ　ほうが　よさそうですね。

*　*　*

❹ウィルさん、例の　国際会議は　どうでしたか。新聞に　よると　いろいろ　問題が　あったそうですが……。ペンクラブ[18]の　主催[19]でしたが、　会議の　持ち方[20]について　一部の　作家から　いろいろと　批判[21]が　出ていたらしいですね。

——ええ……、　分科会[22]も　少なすぎた[23]ようでしたし、討論[24]も　日本語と　英語だけで　行なわれて、　不都合[25]も　あったようです。　しかし、　世界の　ジャパノロジストが　初めて[26]　集まり[27]を　持った　ことは　たいへん　意義深い[28]　ことだと　思います。

❺そうですね。その　ことには　問題は　なさそうですね。

——それに、　日本研究が　戦後　いちじるしく[29]　発達し、くわしい　研究が　行なわれるように　なった　ことが　よく　わかりました。

---

16 seika　great success, achievement
17 ōi-ni　greatly, to a great extent
18 *pen-kurabu*　'P.E.N. Club'
19 shusai　(Nv) sponsorship, promoting
20 mochi-kata　how to hold
21 hihan　(Nv) criticizing
22 bunka-kai　sub-committee meeting
23 -sugi·ru　too..., excessively...
24 tōron　(Nv) debate, discussion
25 fu-tsugō　(Na) inconvenience
26 hajimete　for the first time
cf. hajime wa　at first　　hajime ni　first of all
27 atsumari　meeting
←atsumar·u　(assemble, gather)
28 igi-buka·i　significant, fruitful
igi　significance; sense, meaning
-bukai ＝fuka·i　deep
29 ichijirushi·i　remarkable, distinguishing, considerable

Dai 28-ka
Nippon-kenkyū

1 *Uiru*-san, anata wa Nippon no bungaku o kenkyū-shite-iru sō desu ne.

——Hai, kindai-bungaku o kenkyū-shite-imasu. *An*-san mo Nippon no bungaku o kenkyū-shite-imasu ga, kanojo no yō-ni Nippon-go ga umaku nai node komatte-imasu.

2 Anata mo taihen jōzu desu yo. Kanojo wa Nippon no koten mo yomeru rashii desu ne. Tokorode, shinbun ni yoreba chikaku Kyōto no Kokusai-kaigi-jō de "Nippon-bunka-kenkyū Kokusai-kaigi" ga hirakareru sō desu ne. Gaikoku no *Japanorojisuto* ga ōzei kuru rashii desu yo.

——Sō rashii desu ne. *Kīn*-kyōju ya *Gurusukina*-joshi no yō-na yūmei-na kenkyū-sha ga ōzei shusseki-suru sō desu.

3 Watashi wa senmon-gai desu ga, sore wa taihen omoshirosō desu ne. Sono seika wa anata niwa ōi-ni sankō ni narisō desu ne.

——Yamada-san, soro-soro kaerimashō ka?

Ame ga furisō desu kara, sukoshi isoida hō ga yo-sasō desu ne.

* * *

4 *Uiru*-san, rei no kokusai-kaigi wa dō deshita ka? Shinbun ni yoruto, iroiro mondai ga atta sō desu ga.... *Pen-Kurabu* no shusai deshita ga, kaigi no mochi-kata ni tsuite ichi-bu no sak-ka kara iroiro to hihan ga dete-ita rashii desu ne.

——Ē..., bunka-kai mo sukuna-sugita yō deshita shi, tōron mo Nippon-go to Ei-go dake de okonawarete, fu-tsugō mo atta yō desu. Shikashi, sekai no *Japanorojisuto* ga hajimete atsumari o motta koto wa taihen igi-bukai koto da to omoimasu.

5 Sō desu ne. Sono koto niwa mondai wa na-sasō desu ne.

——Soreni, Nippon-kenkyū ga sen-go ichijirushiku hattatsu-shi, kuwashii kenkyū ga okonawareru yō-ni natta koto ga yoku wakarimashita.

Lesson 28

Japanology

1 I hear you're studying Japanese literature, Will.

——Yes, I'm doing research on modern literature. Ann is also studying Japanese literature, but I'm having trouble because my Japanese is not as good as hers.

2 But you're quite proficient. I hear she can even read the classics. Say, I see by the paper that there's going to be an international conference on Japanese culture at the International Conference Hall in Kyoto. A lot of foreign Japanologists are supposed to come.

——That's what I hear. There are supposed to be a lot of famous scholars coming, like Keene and Gruskina.

3 It's not my field, but it sounds very interesting. I expect you'll find the results of the conference very helpful.

——I guess we'd better be getting home, Yamada.

It looks like rain, so we'd better hurry.

* * *

4 How was the conference, Will? The newspapers said there were some problems, but what was it? It was sponsored by the P.E.N. Club, but it seems there was considerable criticism from some writers about the way it was done.

——Well, there weren't enough group sessions, and the discussion was only in Japanese and English, so some people were not very happy, I hear. But I think it was still very significant as the first gathering of the world's Japanologists.

5 I guess you're right. There doesn't seem to be any disagreement on that point.

——Also it showed me that Japanology has made great strides since the War and that detailed research is being done.

ANSWERS ⟨pp. 340, 341⟩

28

I. 1. a. ame ga furi b. ame ga furu 2. a. oishii b. oishi 3. a. yoi b. yo-sa 4. a. benri b. benri da 5. a. na-sa/nai b. nai

II. 1. ...byōki rashii desu. 2. ...kita rashii desu. 3. ...oishii rashii desu. 4. ...nai rashii desu. 5. (none) 6. ...datta rashii desu.

III. 1. Kare wa kane-mochi rashii. 2. Kare wa kane-mochi rashikatta. 3. Kare wa sensō mae wa kanemochi datta rashii. 4. Watashi wa sono hito ni ni-nen mae Kyōto de atta. Kare wa sono toki o-kane ni komatte-ite, tochi o urō to shite-ita. Kare wa mukashi wa taihen kanemochi datta rashikatta.

IV. 1. (yō-ni) Please write the way I write. 2. (yō-na) I once heard a story as follows. 3. (yō-ni) She gradually became able to walk. 4. (yō-ni) I did as my teacher had told me to, but it did not work. 5. (yō-na) Her cheeks are like apples. 6. (yō-ni) She prayed to God that her child would recover soon. 7. (yō-ni) She stood up suddenly as if remembering something.

●文法

§ 110 Presumption or Estimation based upon an Observation

V(Conj. form)
A (stem)
Na
} + **-sō desu.**

N no yō desu.

'It { looks like....' / looks....' / appears....'

e.g. Ame ga furisō desu. 'It looks like rain.'

Himo ga kiresō desu. 'The string looks like it's going to break.'

Kono ringo wa oishisō desu ne. 'This apple looks delicious, doesn't it?'

Kono eiga wa amari omoshirosō dewa arimasen ne.

'This movie doesn't look very interesting, does it?'

Are wa sha-chō no yō desu ne. 'That man looks like the boss.'

NB: (. . .)nai becomes (. . .)na-sasō

ii becomes yo-sasō

§ 111 Hearsay

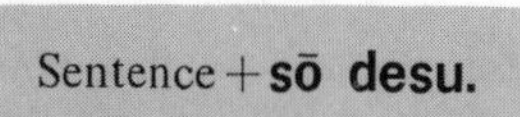
Sentence + **sō desu.**

'I hear that....'
'They say that....'

e.g. Ame ga furu sō desu. 'They (radio, newspaper, etc.) say it will rain.'

Kinō Hokkaidō de ō-yuki ga futta sō desu.

'They say there was a heavy snow in Hokkaido yesterday.'

Shinbun ni yoruto, ano eiga wa taihen ii sō desu.

'According to the newspaper, that movie is very good.'

Ano hito wa yūmei-na joyū da sō desu.

'They say she is a famous actress.'

Ano hito wa yūmei-na joyū datta sō desu.

'They say she used to be a famous actress.'

§ 112 Appearance

V (present/past)
A (present/past)
Na
N
} +**rashii desu.**

'It seems that....'

'It appears that....'

'...rashii desu' is ambiguous in the sense that it is not clear whether the speaker makes that statement (of presumption or estimation) based upon his own observation or based upon information he got from some other source.

e.g. Ame ga furu rashii desu ne. 'It seems that it's going to rain.'

Ame ga futta rashii desu ne. '(Since the road is wet,) it looks like it rained.'

Kono eiga wa omoshiroi rashii ne. 'This movie is said to be interesting.' or 'This movie looks interesting.'

NB: 'N rashii desu' is slightly different from 'N no yō desu.' Both mean 'N looks like...' or 'N seems/appears to be...,' but 'N no yō desu' can mean that N seems to be...but is not really, as in:

'She is just like a flying fish.' →Kanojo wa (maru de) tobi-uo no yō desu. (or, tobi-uo mitai desu which is slightly colloquial).

'N rashii' cannot be used in this descriptive way.

§ 113 Other Use of yō

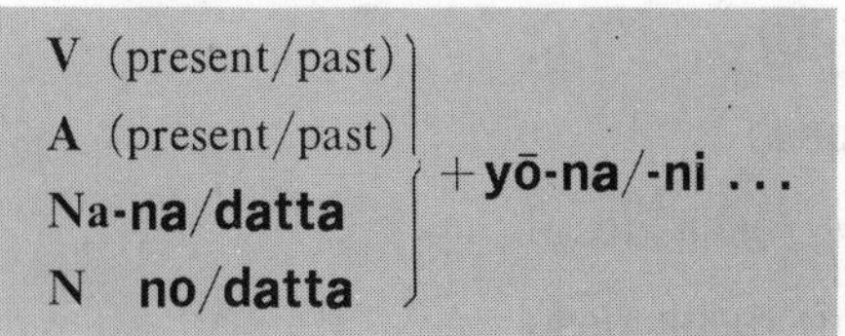

'In the manner of....'

'Like....'

'Just like....'

28

e.g. Kanojo wa tobi-uo no yō-ni hayaku oyogu.

'She swims as fast as a flying fish.'

Kanojo wa Nippon-jin no yō-na kao o shite-iru.

'She has a Japanese-looking face.'

Anata ga itta yō-ni (=itta tōri), are wa muzukashii shigoto deshita.

'As you said, that was tough work.'

●練習

ANSWERS→p. 337

I. Fill in the blanks using the key words.

1. (rain) a. Sora ga kumotte[1]-ite, (　　　) sō desu.

   b. *Rajio* ni yoruto, gogo kara (　　　) sō desu.

2. (delicious) a. Ane no hanashi dewa, akai ringo no hō ga (　　　) sō desu.

   b. Kono ringo wa akakute, (　　　) sō desu.

3. (good) a. Gakusei-tachi ni kiite-miruto, kono *taipu-raitā* wa hontō-ni (　　　) sō desu.

   b. Chotto miruto, kono *taipu-raitā* wa (　　　) sō desu ga, hontō wa[2] amari yoku nai desu.

4. (convenient) a. Kono daidokoro[3] wa sekkei[4] ga yokute, (　　　) sō desu.

   b. Kanojo ni yoruto, kanojo no atarashii ie no daidokoro wa (　　　) sō desu.

5. (there is no...) a. Kore yori hōhō[5] wa (　　　) sō desu.

   b. Sekkei-sha[6] no setsumei ni yoruto, kore yori hōhō wa (　　　) sō desu.

II. Correct the errors, if any.

1. Kanojo wa byōki da rashii desu.
2. *Takushī* ga kimashita rashii desu.
3. Ano mise no *kōhī* wa oishi rashii desu.
4. Kanojo wa o-kane ga amari nakute rashii desu.
5. Konban gakusei-tachi no *pātī* ga aru rashii desu.
6. Kare wa mukashi sensei da rashii desu.

語句

1 kumor･u get cloudy/dim
2 hontō wa the truth is, in reality
3 daidokoro kitchen
4 sekkei (Nv) planning, design (for a building or a city)
5 hōhō means, method

III. Put the following into Japanese (in the Plain style).

1. He seems to be rich.
2. He seemed to be rich.
3. He seems to have been rich before the War.
4. I met the man two years ago in Kyoto. He was in financial trouble at that time and was going to sell his land. He seemed to have been very rich a long time ago.

IV. Fill in the blanks with the appropriate forms of 'yō (da),' and then translate the sentences.

1. Watashi no kaku (   ) kaite-kudasai.
2. Tsugi no (   ) hanashi o kiita koto ga aru.
3. Kanojo wa dandan arukeru (   ) natta.
4. Sensei kara oshierareta (   ) shita ga, dame datta.
5. Kanojo wa ringo no (   ) hoho[7] o shite-iru.[8]
6. Kanojo wa kodomo no byōki ga hayaku yoku naru (   ) kami-sama[9] ni o-inori[10] o shita.
7. Kanojo wa nani ka omoidashita (   ), totsuzen tachi-agatta.

28

---

6 sekkei-sha designer
7 hoho cheek(s)
8 ...o shite-i•ru have (some feature)
See § 115
9 kami(-sama) God, Goddess
10 inori prayer ←inor•u (pray)

●会話

GO-SHINPAI NE....

A: Anata no o-kā-san, nyūin[1]-nasatta[2] sō ne?

B: Un, i-kaiyō[3] rashii n da.

A: Sore wa go-shinpai ne.
Ichi-do mimai ni ikō ka shira?

B: Sonna hitsuyō wa nai yo.
Sugu taiin[4]-dekiru rashii kara.

A: Demo....

B: Sore yori,[5] eiga ni demo ikanai?
'Aka-hige'[6] ga omoshiroi rashii yo.

A: O-kā-san ga byōki-na noni?

B: Sore mo sō[7] da ne. Jā, yappari, byōin e ikō ka? Koko kara sonna-ni tōku mo nai shi.

A: Ē, sō shimashō yo.
Watashi, nani ka katte-iku wa.

B: Sonna-ni ki o tsukawanakutemo ii yo.

A: Demo.... Nani ga ii ka shira?
Kudamono nanka[8] dō?

A: I hear your mother has been in the hospital.
B: Yes, it seems she's got an ulcer.
A: You must be worried. Shall I go and look in on her some time?
B: There's no need. I've been told that she'll be able to leave the hospital soon.
A: But....
B: Why don't we go to a movie instead? I hear "Red Beard" is interesting.
A: When your mother is ill?
B: Well, you're right.... OK, shall we go to the hospital, then? It's not so far from here.
A: Yes, let's. I'll buy something to take her.
B: You don't need to bother.
A: But.... What shall it be? How about fruit?

語句

1 nyūin (Nv) entering/going into the hospital, being hospitalized
2 nasar·u (Honorific form of suru)
3 i-kaiyō stomach ulcer
  i stomach kaiyō ulcer
4 taiin (Nv) leaving/being discharged from the hospital
5 sore yori rather than that, more than that
6 Aka-hige "Red Beard" (the title of a film)
  hige mustache, beard, whiskers
7 Sore mo sō da That's true too; I guess you're

B: No. I was told she's not allowed to eat anything but hospital food. Seems everything else is out.
A: OK, then how about magazines or flowers?
B: Umm..., that'd be all right.

* * *

A: Excuse me, I'd like some of these white carnations.
C: Yes, thank you, thank you. Always a pleasure. Are they for a gift?
A: Yes, for someone in the hospital. Could you wrap them appropriately?
C: Here you are. Sorry to have taken so long.
A: Thank you.
OK, let's go.

B: Iya, byōin no shokuji igai wa kinji-[9] rarete-iru sō da.
Issai[10] dame rashii yo.

A: Jā, zasshi ka o-hana ni shimashō ka?

B: Un, ii darō.

* * *

A: Oji-san, kono shiroi *kānēshon*[11] o kudasai na.

C: Hai, mai-do[12] arigatō gozaimasu.
Okuri-mono ni nasaru n desu ka?

A: Byōki mimai[13] desu.
Sono yō-ni tsutsunde[14]-chōdai.[15]

C: Hai, o-machidō-sama.

A: Arigatō.
Sā, ikimashō.

---

right.
8 ...nanka (Colloquial)= nado ...or the like
9 kinji·ru forbid
10 issai (N/Adv) all, whole, entire
11 *kānēshon* 'carnation'
12 mai-do every time, always
13 byōki mimai inquiry after a sick person
14 tsutsum·u wrap, pack, envelop; conceal
15 -te-chōdai (Colloquial and Intimate) =-te-kudasai

28

日本の宗教

日本には、仏教、神道[1]、キリスト教など、多くの宗教[2]がある。ある調査によると、宗教別[3]の人口の合計[4]は、全人口の2.7倍ぐらいになったそうだ。日本では、一人の人が二つ以上の宗教をもっていることが多いのだ。この辺に日本の宗教の特徴がありそうだ。

日本人の大部分[5]は、形式的[6]には仏教徒[7]である。しかし、たいていの家庭には、仏壇[8]と並んで[9]、神だな[10]も祭ってある。神社とお寺の行事に同じように参加[11]するのが、多数[12]の日本人の習慣である。これは、キリスト教などの立場から見れば、きわめて奇妙[13]なことだが、日本では、仏教伝来[14]の初めから、比較的[15]自然に行なわれてきたようだ。

古代の日本人は、自然界[16]の山や川や森[17]には、目に見えない精霊[18]が無数[19]にいて、これらの精霊や祖先[20]の霊[21]が、人間を幸福[22]にも、不幸[23]にもすると考えた。これらの精霊はカミと呼ばれた。人々は、カミのめぐみ[24]を求めるために、あるいは、カミのたたり[25]をさけるために、宗教儀礼[26]を行なった。これが神道の起こり[27]らしい。

六世紀に仏教が朝鮮を経[28]て日本に伝えられた。一般に外国から新しい宗教がはいったときは、衝突[29]らしいものは、あまり[30]見られなかった。それは、外国の神を合わせ[31]て祭ったほうがききめ[32]がありそうだと考えたかららしい。こういう意味で、日本の仏教では、あらゆる[33]時代を通じて[34]呪術[35]が重要な役割[36]を演じ[37]ている。

今日、神道は、新年[38]を祝い、豊作をいのる[39]とか、新しく建てられる建物の安全[40]をいのるとか、災害[41]の予防[42]に用いられる[43]ことが多いようだ。結婚も神前[44]でする人が多い。一方、仏教は葬式[45]やおぼんなど[46]の死んだ人の霊をなぐさめる[47]行事として、人々の生活につながって[48]いるわけである。

Japanese Relegion

There are many religions in Japan, including Buddhism, Shinto, and Christianity. Yet according to one survey, the sum of all religious affiliations comes to 2.7 times the total population. This is because each person has more than one religion, a feature characteristic of Japan.

While most Japanese are formally Buddhist, there is also a small Shinto altar next to the Buddhist altar in most homes. It is customary for people to go to both temples and shrines in the same way. While this may seem very strange in Christian eyes, it has persisted naturally since Buddhism's earliest days in Japan.

The ancient Japanese believed that there were innumerable holy spirits in nature, and that these divine spirits and ancestoral spirits could act to make men blessed or damned. These divine spirits were called *kami*, and men performed religious ceremonies in order to call down their blessings and to ward off their curses. This is the origin of Shinto.

In the 6th century, Buddhism was brought to Japan by way of Korea. Because it was felt that it might be more efficacious to pray to these foreign gods as well, there has generally been little outward conflict when new religions were introduced from abroad. In this sense, superstition has played a major role in Japanese Buddhism throughout the ages.

Today, Shinto rites are used to celebrate the New Year or plentiful harvests, to pray for the safety of new building projects, and to protect against accidents, as well as for many weddings. Buddhism is used for funerals, *bon*, and otherwise to placate the dead. Thus the two are intermixed within Japanese life.

語句

1 Shintō Shintoism
2 shūkyō religion
3 -betsu (N) according to the classification/distinction of...; by...
4 gōkei total
5 dai-bubun (N/Adv) most
6 keishiki-teki (Na) formally
7 Bukkyō-to Buddhist cf. *Kirisuto*kyō-to (Christian), Kaikyō-to (Moslem)
8 butsudan a Buddhist altar
9 ...to narande ranking/together with
10 kami-dana a family *Shinto* altar
11 sanka (Nv) participate, join in
12 tasū (N/Adv) a large number
13 kimyō (Na) strange, queer
14 denrai (Nv) coming from
15 hikaku-teki comparatively
16 shizen-kai the world of nature
  -kai area, field ←sekai
17 mori forest
18 seirei holy spirit
19 musū (N) numberless, countless
20 sosen=senzo ancestor
21 rei spirit, soul (of a dead person)
22 kōfuku (N/Na) happiness, happy
23 fukō (N/Na) unhappiness, misfortune
24 megumi blessing, mercy, charity ←megum•u (bless, give in charity)
25 tatari divine punishment, curse
26 girei ritual, courtesy
27 okori origin ←okor•u (originate, begin)
28 he•ru go through, via...
29 shōtotsu (Nv) collision; discord
30 ...rashi•i mono something like...
31 awasete put together, in addition ←awase•ru (Vt) put together, fit
32 kikime effect
33 arayuru (+N) all sorts of
34 ...o tsūjite all through...
35 jujutsu witchcraft
36 yakuwari part, role (in a drama, plot)
37 enji•ru play (a part)
38 Shinnen New Year
39 inor•u pray
40 anzen (N/Na) safety
41 saigai disaster
42 yobō (Nv) prevention
43 mochii•ru utilize, employ, use
44 shinzen (N) in the gods' presence
45 sōshiki funeral
46 shinda (+N) ←shinde-iru (be dead)
47 nagusame•ru console, soothe, cheer
48 tsunagar•u (Vi) be connected/tied cf. tsunag•u (Vt)

第 29 課

後悔

TAPE
No. 8
Side 1

❶ 外は 雨が 降っているようです。 ときおり[1] 風が 吹いて 雨が パラパラと[2] まどを 打ちます。 わたしは さきほどから ぼんやり[3]しています。 たばこの けむりが すうっと[4] 一すじ[5] 立ち上って[6]います。 わたしは さきほどから じいっと[7] それを ながめています。 ときおり まどを 打つ 風の 音に はっと[8] われに[9] 帰ります。

❷ あなたは どうして いるだろう……。 この 間は どうして あのような 別れ方を してしまったのだろう……。 今になって[10] あなたの 気持ち[11]が いたい ほど[12] よく わかります。

❸ あなたは ほんとうに 悲しそうな 目を していました。 あなたは 今にも[13] なき出し[14]そうな 顔を していました。 そして くるりと[15] 背[16]を 向けて[17]、 さようならも 言わずに[18] 走り去って[19]しまいました。

語句

1 toki-ori occasionally
2 para-para (to) (onomat) pattering
3 bon'yari (onomat) absent-mindedness, not clear
4 sūtto (onomat) straight, quietly
5 hito-suji one straight line
  suji straight line
6 tachi-nobor·u ascend, go up
7 jitto (onomat) fixedly, patiently, quietly, intently, motionlessly
8 hatto (onomat) with a start, in surprise
9 ware myself
  ware ni kaer·u come to/return to oneself
10 ima ni natte now things have to come to this pass, after so long a time, at this juncture
11 kimochi feeling
12 itai hodo to the extent that one feels pain
13 ima nimo at any moment
14 naki-das·u burst into tears
15 kururi to (onomat) (turn) around, wheel (about)
16 se the back (side)
17 se o muke·ru turn one's back
  muke·ru (Vt) turn...toward
18 iwazu ni without saying...
19 hashiri-sar·u run away (out of sight)

❹ わたしは 今(いま) その ときの あなたの うしろ姿(すがた)[20]を 思(おも)い浮(う)かべ[21]ています。 それは とても さびしそうな 感(かん)じ[22]が しました。 その とき わたしは たいせつな ものを 失(うしな)[23]って しまったと いう 気(き)[24]が しました。

❺ わたしは ほんとうに どうかしていた[25]のです。 仕事(しごと)が うまく いかず[26]、毎日(まいにち) いらいらしていたのです。自信(じしん)も まったく なくなっていました。あなたの 真剣(しんけん)な はげまし[27]や なぐさめ[28]も わずらわしく[29] 感(かん)じるだけでした。 やけに なって[30] 飲(の)んだ お酒(さけ)も ただ 苦(にが)い[31] 後悔(こうかい)[32]の 味(あじ)[33]が するだけでした。

❻ けさ 起(お)きて 鏡(かがみ)[34]を 見(み)たら 自分(じぶん)でも おどろく ほど[35] すさんだ[36] 顔(かお)に なっていました。

これでは わたしは だめです。 今(いま) 心(こころ)から 立(た)ち直(なお)[37]りたいと 思(おも)います。 たぶん、 あすは 旅先(たびさき)[38]です。 旅(たび)は きっと わたしを なぐさめてくれるでしょう。 心身(しんしん)とも[39] 元気(げんき)に なって あなたを たずねます。

それでは、 また 会(あ)う 日(ひ)まで。

---

sar·u go away, leave
20 ushiro-sugata view of someone from behind sugata figure, look (whole body)
21 omoi-ukabe·ru imagine; recollect
22 kanji feeling, touch, impression See § 114 ...kanji ga suru feel...
23 ushina·u lose
24 ...ki ga suru feel (like)
25 dō ka shite-i·ru something must be wrong
26 umaku ik·u work well, be successful
27 hagemashi encouragement ←hagemas·u (encourage, cheer up)
28 nagusame consolation, comfort ←nagusame·ru (console)
29 wazurawashiku troublesome, annoying
30 yake ni nar·u turn desperate/bitter
31 niga·i bitter
32 kōkai (Nv) regret
33 aji taste
34 kagami mirror
35 odoroku hodo astonishingly, to a surprising extent
36 susanda (+N) desolate, barren
37 tachi-naor·u regain one's footing, recover
38 tabi-saki place visited, be on a trip tabi=ryokō (Nv) trip, travel
39 shin-shin tomo in both mind and body, physically and mentally

Dai 29-ka
Kōkai

1 Soto wa ame ga futte-iru yō desu. Toki-ori kaze ga fuite ame ga para-para to mado o uchimasu. Watashi wa saki-hodo kara bon'yari-shite-imasu. *Tabako* no kemuri ga sūtto hito-suji tachi-nobotte-imasu. Watashi wa saki-hodo kara jitto sore o nagamete-imasu. Toki-ori mado o utsu kaze no oto ni hatto ware ni kaerimasu.

2 Anata wa dō shite-iru darō.... Kono aida wa dō shite ano yō-na wakare-kata o shite-shimatta no darō.... Ima ni natte anata no kimochi ga itai hodo yoku wakarimasu.

3 Anata wa hontō-ni kanashisō-na me o shite-imashita. Anata wa ima nimo naki-dashisō-na kao o shite-imashita. Soshite kururi to se o mukete, sayōnara mo iwazu ni hashiri-satte-shimaimashita.

4 Watashi wa ima sono toki no anata no ushiro-sugata o omoi-ukabete-imasu. Sore wa totemo sabishisō-na kanji ga shimashita. Sono toki watashi wa taisetsu-na mono o ushinatte-shimatta to iu ki ga shimashita.

5 Watashi wa hontō-ni dō ka shite-ita no desu. Shigoto ga umaku ikazu, maini-chi ira-ira-shite-ita no desu. Jishin mo mattaku naku natte-imashita. Anata no shinken-na hagemashi ya nagusame mo wazurawa-shiku kanjiru dake deshita. Yake ni natte nonda o-sake mo tada nigai kōkai no aji ga suru dake deshita.

6 Kesa okite kagami o mitara jibun demo odoroku hodo susanda kao ni natte-imashita.

Koredewa watashi wa dame desu. Ima kokoro kara tachi-naoritai to omoimasu. Tabun, asu wa tabi-saki desu. Tabi wa kitto watashi o nagu-samete-kureru deshō. Shin-shin tomo genki ni natte anata o tazunemasu.

Soredewa, mata au hi made.

Lesson 29
Regret

1 It is raining outside. Sometimes the wind blows and the rain pitter-pats against my window. I have been just sitting here lazily for some time. With the smoke from my cigarette wafting dreamily upward, I just sit here watching it. Occasionally, the sound of the rain against my window abruptly recalls me to myself.

2 I wonder what you are doing. Why did we have to part that way? I know now how you must have felt then, know so much it hurts.

3 You looked so forlorn. You looked about to cry at any moment. Then suddenly you turned and were gone without so much as a fare-thee-well.

4 Even now I still recall the sight of your fleeting figure. It is a very saddening feeling. I feel as though I have lost something very important.

5 I must have been out of my mind. My work had not been going well and I was wracked with irritation every day. I had lost all confidence in myself. Your well-meant encouragement and sympathy seemed to me but mockery. The *sake* drunk to drown my self-pity left only a bitter after-taste.

6 This morning when I got up and looked at myself in the mirror, even I was surprised at how washed-out I looked.

I can not go on this way. I feel I must refresh my spirit. Tomorrow I will probably be far from here. A trip will surely do me good. When I am well again in mind and body, I will visit you again.

Until we meet again....

▼An old inn in Takayama

ANSWERS ⟨pp. 352, 353⟩

I. 1. nioi 2. oto 3. nioi 4. ki 5. kanji 6. ki/kanji 7. nioi/aji 8. ki 9. nioi 10. kanji

II. 1. katachi/kakkō 2. kao 3. yōsu 4. kakkō/kao 5. yōsu 6. kao 7. katachi

●文法

§ 114 Idiomatic Expressions (1): '... ga suru'

(yō-na)	aji nioi kanji ki	ga shimasu	'have a {taste / smell / feeling (impression) / mind (feeling)} (like)...'

e.g. Sono *sūpu* wa donna aji ga shimasu ka (=aji desu ka)?

'What does the soup taste like?'

—Henna/ii/kusuri no yō-na aji ga shimasu.

'It tastes strange/good/like medicine.'

Kono kudamono wa kawatta/kusatte-iru yō-na/*banana* no (yō-na) nioi ga shimasu. 'This fruit smells strange/rotten/like a banana.'

Ano hito to hanashite-iruto, (marude) *robotto* to hanashite-iru yō-na kanji ga shimasu. 'When I talk with him, I feel as if I am talking with a robot.'

Kyō wa kaisha e iku ki ga shinai. 'I don't feel like going to work today.'

§ 115 Idiomatic Expressions (2): '... shite-iru'

(yō-na)	katachi iro kao kakkō	o shite-imasu	'have a {shape / color / face (look) / appearance} of/that...'

e.g. Ano tatemono wa omoshiroi katachi o shite-imasu.

'That building has an interesting shape.'

Anata wa aoi kao o shite-imasu ne.

'You look pale.'

Sono otoko wa kojiki no yō-na kakkō o shite-imashita.

'That man was dressed like a beggar.'

§ 116 A Remark on Omission

As you have probably already noticed, Japanese allows far greater freedom for the omission of sentence elements than do most other languages. The speaker often leaves out what he believes is known or understood by the hearer in a dialog between two persons, where the principals to the conversation share common situations or interests.

e.g. (Watashi wa) An desu. Dōzo yoroshiku. '(I am) Ann. Glad to meet you.'

(Anata wa) gohan o tabe ni ikimasu ka? '(Are you) going to eat?'

This general tendency often results in constructions which may look 'illogical' or strange if translated literally into English.

e.g. Shutchō wa tsukaremasu. 'Business trips are (things that make me) tired.'

Sore wa komarimasu. 'It is (something that will cause me to be) troubled.'

The pattern in the next section may thus be regarded as typical condensation.

§ 117 'N **wa** N **desu**' as Condensed Predicates

The very basic sentence pattern with which we began Lesson 1 in this book is capable of containing virtually all kinds of predicates, with their meanings depending entirely upon the previous statement or situation.

e.g. Watashi wa tenpura o tabemasu. Anata wa?

—Watashi wa sushi desu. (←Watashi wa sushi o tabemasu.)

Watashi wa Haneda kara shuppatsu-shimasu. 'I am departing from Haneda.'

—Sō desu ka. Watashi wa Itami desu. 'I am (departing from) Itami.'

Uchi no musuko wa rai-nen Tōkyō Daigaku o ukemasu.

'Our son is going to take the University of Tokyo entrance exam next year.'

—Sō desu ka. Uchi wa Keiō desu.

'Is that so? Ours is (going to take the exam for) Keio (Univ.).'

●練習

ANSWERS p.→349

I. Fill in the blanks with 'nioi,'[1] 'aji,' 'kanji,' 'ki,' or 'oto.'

1. Doko ka de sakana o yaku[2] (   ) ga suru.
2. Ni-kai o dare ka ga aruite-iru (   ) ga suru.
3. Kono hana wa ii (   ) ga suru.
4. Kare wa kyō konai yō-na (   ) ga suru.
5. Kinu[3] no kimono wa doko ka yawarakai[4] (   ) ga suru.
6. *Erebētā-gāru*[5] ga kyū-ni warai-dashita[6] node hen[7]-na (   ) ga shita.
7. Kono *sarada* wa tamanegi[8] no (   ) ga suru.
8. Kare wa kanojo to kekkon-suru yō-na (   ) ga suru.
9. Kono kōsui[9] wa bara no (   ) ga suru.
10. Kanojo wa tsumetai (   ) ga suru hito da.

II. Fill in the blanks with 'katachi,'[10] 'yōsu,' 'kakkō,'[11] or 'kao.'

1. Ano tatemono wa kyōkai[12] no yō-na (   ) o shite-iru.
2. Kare wa o-sake o nonda yō-na akai (   ) o shite-ita.
3. Kare wa sha-chō no mae de nanda ka[13] ochitsukanai (   ) deshita.
4. Kanojo wa *piero*[14] no yō-na (   ) o shite-ita.
5. Ni-kai no (   ) ga hen da. Nani ka okotta rashii.
6. Kanojo wa aoi (   ) o shite-iru. Kibun ga warui yō da.
7. Kono jidōsha wa mita koto mo nai yō-na (   ) o shite-iru.

語句

1 nioi smell, odor, fragrance
←nio·u (smell)
...nioi ga suru smell (of)...
2 yak·u bake, burn, scorch, fry
3 kinu silk
4 yawaraka·i soft, tender, pliant
5 *erebētā-gāru* 'elevator girl,' elevator operator
6 warai-das·u begin to laugh
7 hen (Na) strange, unusual

III. Practice patterns with the key phrases.

(A) Ex. (kiku no hana) Ano ie no chikaku o tōruto kiku no hana no nioi ga suru.

1. (*karē-raisu*)

2. (*pan* o yaku)

3. (ii)

4. (o-cha o hiite[15]-iru yō da)

(B) Ex. (sankaku) Sono isu wa sankaku no katachi o shite-iru.

1. (marui[16])

2. (dōbutsu)

3. (hako no yō da)

(C) Ex. (kaze) Soto de kaze no oto ga shite-iru.

1. (jidōsha)

2. (sawagashii)

3. (ame ga futte-iru yō da)

IV. Continue the dialogs as shown in the example.

Ex. a) O-cha to *kōhī* to dochira ga ii desu ka?

b) Watashi wa o-cha desu. Anata wa?

a) Watashi wa *kōhī* desu.

1. a) Nippon no eiga to gaikoku no eiga to dochira o yoku mimasu ka?

2. a) Hokkaidō to Kyūshū to dochira e ikitai desu ka?

3. a) Kare to kanojo to dochira ga suki desu ka?

4. a) Anata wa shingaku-shimasu ka, shūshoku-shimasu ka?

5. a) Anata wa densha de kayotte-imasu ka, *basu* de kayotte-imasu ka?

---

8 tamanegi onion
9 kōsui perfume
10 katachi shape
11 kakkō shape, appearance
12 kyōkai church
13 nanda ka somewhat, kind of
14 *piero* 'pierrot,' clown
15 hik·u grind
16 maru·i round, circular

●会話

YORU NI NARUTO...

—Tōkyō dewa ima takai tatemono ga don-don taterarete-imasu.

Nippon wa jishin no ōi kuni da to kiite-imasu ga, daijōbu na n deshō ne?

—Mā, gijutsu mo shinpo[1]-shite-imasu kara, kitto anzen-na n deshō. Shikashi, san-juk-kai ya yon-juk-kai de shigoto o suru no wa, amari ii kanji no mono dewa nai deshō ne.

Kono atari mo, mukashi to wa taihen-na kawari-yō[2] na n deshō ne.

—Kono mae inaka kara jū-nen-buri ni dete-kita chichi ga, yume no yō-na ki ga suru to itte, me o mawashite-[3]imashita.

Sō deshō ne. Shikashi, kono yō-ni machi ga kindai-teki[4]-ni nareba naru hodo, Nihon-rashisa[5] ga ushinawarete-iku n ja arimasen ka?

—There are a lot of tall buildings being built in Tokyo nowadays.

I hear Japan has many earthquakes, but are these buildings all right?

—Well, engineering techniques are very advanced, so I'm sure they are safe. But I'll bet it's no fun to work on the 30th or 40th floor.

This area must be very different from what it was like in the old days.

—The other day when my father came from the country for the first time in 10 years, he was very surprised and said he must be dreaming.

I'll bet. But the more a city is modernized like this, the more Japanese characteristics will be lost, don't you think?

語句

1 shinpo (Nv) progress, advance

2 kawari-yō change, how ...has changed
-yō manner, way

3 me o mawas·u be stunned, swoon; be astonished
mawas·u (Vt) revolve; send/hand round
cf. mawar·u (Vi)

4 kindai-teki (Na) modern

5 -rashisa (N) -ness, characteristic quality
cf. ningen-rashisa, otoko-rashisa, kodomo-rashisa
←rashi·i See § 112

6 ...bakari ka not only... (but also)

7 *ofuisu*-gai 'office' street,
-gai town, street
cf. chika-gai (underground shopping area)

8 hakaba graveyard, cemetery

—That's not all. The population of central Tokyo is decreasing. For example, I hear the business centers are as quiet as graveyards at night.

Really? How could all these cars and people disappear so completely? Just thinking of it gives me an eerie feeling.

—Well, look at it in the daytime too. What with being surrounded by exhaust fumes and stinking canals, this is no place for people to live in. It's probably just that urban modernization and human happiness don't necessarily go together.

—Sore bakari ka,[6] Tōkyō no chūshin-bu no jinkō wa sukunaku natte, *ofuisu*-gai[7] nado wa, yoru ni naruto, hakaba[8] no yō-ni hissori[9]-shite-shimau sō desu yo.

Hē..., konna-ni takusan no kuruma ya hito ga kiete-shimau no desu ka.... Nanda ka, kaidan[10]-meita[11] kanji ga shimasu ne.

—Hiru-ma wa hiru-ma de, kuruma no haiki-*gasu*[12] ni torimakare,[13] dobu-gawa[14] wa iya-na nioi ga suru, to iu wake de, tōtei[15] ningen no sumeru tokoro dewa arimasen. Toshi no kindai-ka[16] to ningen no shiawase[17] to wa, kanarazu-shimo[18] pittari[19] to ikanai, to iu koto deshō ne.

haka grave, tomb
9 hissori (onomat) silent, deserted
10 kaidan ghost story
11 -meita (+N) seeming to be..., something of a...
12 haiki-*gasu* engine exhaust
haiki (Nv) exhaust; ventilation *gasu* 'gas'
13 torimak·u surround
14 dobu-gawa muddy river
dobu gutter, drainage ditch
15 tōtei...nai by no means
16 kindai-ka (Nv) modernization
17 shiawase =kōfuku (Na) happiness
18 kanarazu-shimo...nai not necessarily/always...
19 pittari (to) (onomat) the state of matching just right or fitting perfectly

29

日本の文学—3

近代文学(きんだいぶんがく)のあけぼの[1]は、明治十五年(めいじじゅうごねん)の「新体詩抄(しんたいししょう)[2]」である。西欧詩(せいおうし)の直訳(ちょくやく)[3]のにおいがするが、何(なん)といっても[4]、清新(せいしん)[5]の気(き)にあふれている[6]。散文(さんぶん)[7]の世界(せかい)でも、明治二十年(めいじにじゅうねん)に「浮雲(うきぐも)[8]」が二葉亭四迷(ふたばていしめい)[9]によって書(か)かれた。この小説(しょうせつ)は、それまでの小説(しょうせつ)とちがって[10]、登場人物(とうじょうじんぶつ)[11]も平凡(へいぼん)[12]な一市民(いちしみん)[13]であり、文体(ぶんたい)も言文一致(げんぶんいっち)[14]で、まさに[15]新時代(しんじだい)[16]を代表(だいひょう)する感(かん)[17]があった。

▲Futabatei Shimei

しかし、間(ま)もなく政治的(せいじてき)にも反動期(はんどうき)[18]になり、文学(ぶんがく)においても[19]、古典(こてん)が復活(ふっかつ)し、小説(しょうせつ)も古(ふる)い文体(ぶんたい)で書(か)かれるようになる[20]。

▲Mori Ogai

ドイツやイギリスへの留学(りゅうがく)から帰(かえ)ってきた森鷗外(もりおうがい)[21]や夏目漱石(なつめそうせき)は、最初(さいしょ)、日本(にっぽん)の現実(げんじつ)を高(たか)いところからながめているような顔(かお)をしていたが、やがて自然主義者(しぜんしゅぎしゃ)[22]と同(おな)じように、日露戦争(にちろせんそう)[23]後(ご)の社会(しゃかい)の矛盾(むじゅん)[24]に立(た)ち向(む)かって行(い)く[25]ようになる。しかし、彼(かれ)らも晩年(ばんねん)[26]には「レジニアション[27]」や「則天去私(そくてんきょし)[28]」の心境(しんきょう)[29]にはいっていった。

▲Natsume Soseki

他(た)の自然主義作家(しぜんしゅぎさっか)たちも現実分析(げんじつぶんせき)[30]をあきらめて[31]、単(たん)なる[32]私生活(しせいかつ)[33]の記録(きろく)[34]を無批判(むひはん)[35]に書(か)きとどめた[36]。これを私小説(ししょうせつ)[37]といい、日本(にっぽん)の近代小説(きんだいしょうせつ)の大(おお)きな特徴(とくちょう)となった。

社会的(しゃかいてき)[38]にもめざめ[39]、自我(じが)[40]を追求(ついきゅう)[41]しようとする、ほんとうの意味(いみ)での近代文学(きんだいぶんがく)が一般的(いっぱんてき)[42]になったのは、1945年(ねん)の敗戦後(はいせんご)[43]からといえる。

Japanese Literature—3

The dawn of modern literature was with *Shintaishi-sho* in 1882. Although at times reading like literal translations from the West, these poems were still undeniably fresh. Prose too changed with *Ukigumo* written by Futabatei Shimei in 1887. This differed from previous novels in that the chraracters are all ordinary townsfolk and it is written in a colloquial style, making it truly representative of the new age.

However, political reaction soon set in and literature too reverted to its classical forms. Back from their studies in Europe, Mori Ogai, Natsume Soseki, and others initially wrote as people observing the Japanese scene from on high, but they soon joined with the naturalists in speaking out on society's contradictions after the Russo-Japanese War. In later years, however, they adopted attitudes of resignation.

The other naturalists too gave up on social analysis and contented themselves with uncritical records of private life. These "I-novels" are a unique feature of the modern Japanese novel. Nevertheless, modern literature in the true sense of the term did not begin until after Japan's defeat in 1945.

語句

1 akebono dawn, daybreak
2 Shintaishi-shō (the name of an anthology of poems)
  shi poetry, poem
  -shō selection, extract, abstract
3 choku-yaku (Nv) literal/word-for-word translation cf. i-yaku
4 nan to itte mo when all is said and done, after all
5 seishin (Na) fresh
6 afure•ru overflow
7 sanbun prose cf. inbun, shi
8 Uki-gumo (the title of a novel)
9 Futabatei Shimei (novelist; 1864-1909)
10 ...to chigatte differently from...
11 tōjō-jinbutsu dramatis personae, cast
  tōjō (Nv) come on stage
  jinbutsu person; personality
12 heibon (Na) commonplace, ordinary
13 ichi-shimin a citizen, a member of the society
14 gen-bun-itchi accord of the spoken and the written languages; writing as one speaks
  itchi (Nv) accord, agreement
15 masa-ni exactly, precisely
16 shin- new
17 ...kan feeling, impression
18 handō-ki reaction period
  handō reaction; anti-revolutionary
  cf. handō-teki (reactionary)
  -ki=kikan period
19 ...ni oite mo in... too
20 ...yō-ni nar•u turn out to be...
21 Mori Ōgai (novelist; 1862-1922)
22 Shizen-shugi-sha Naturalist (literature)
  Shizen-shugi Naturalism (literature)
23 Nichi-Ro-sensō Russo-Japanese War (1904-5)
24 mujun (Nv) contradiction
25 tachi-muka•u confront, fight against
26 ban-nen (N/Adv) one's closing years, late in life (lit. 'evening years')
27 rejiniashiyon (Ogai's term) ←*resignation* (Fr.)
28 sokuten-kyoshi to indentify oneself with nature and get rid of one's ego
29 shinkyō state of mind
30 bunseki (Nv) analysis
31 akirame•ru give up, resign
32 tannaru (PreN) mere
33 shi-seikatsu private life
34 kiroku (Nv) record, document
35 mu-hihan (Na) without criticism
36 kaki-todome•ru write down for the record
37 shi-shōsetsu (a particular type of novel in which the writer confines himself to describing daily happenings around him)
38 shakai-teki (Na) social
39 mezame•ru wake to
40 jiga self, ego
41 tsuikyū (Nv) pursuit; chase
42 ippan-teki (Na) general
43 haisen-go (N/Adv) after the lost war, after World War II
  haisen (N) lost war, defeat

第 30 課

先生への 電話

TAPE
No. 8
Side 1

❶——もしもし、 吉田先生[1]の お宅でしょうか。 奥さま[2]で いらっしゃいますか。 わたし 学生時代に 吉田先生に お世話に なりました 山田と 申します[3]。 先生は おいでに なり[4]ますか。 今 お出かけですか。 七時ごろには お帰りに なりますね。 それでは、 七時過ぎ[5]に もう 一度 お電話させていただき[6]ます。

* * *

❷——吉田先生で いらっしゃいますか。 わたし 山田です。 ごぶさた[7]いたし[8]ております。 先生も お変わりなく、 お元気ですか。 ところで、 近々[9]、 先生を お囲みして 同窓会[10]を 開きたいと 思っております。 先生に ぜひ ご出席願い[11]たいと 思いまして……。

❸——はい、 ありがとうございます。 元気で やっております。 いつも 先生が おっしゃっていましたように、

語句

1 Yoshida (a family name)
2 oku-sama =oku-san wife (Polite)
3 ...to mōs・u (Humble form of...to i・u)
4 o-ide ni nar・u (Honorific form of i・ru, ik・u, kuru)
5 ...sugi (N) past, after...
6 -sasete-itadak・u (Humble form of suru)
7 gobusata-suru fail to keep in touch (e.g. not calling or writing as frequently as one should)
8 -itas・u (Humble form of suru)
9 chika-jika one of these days, before long, in the near future
10 dōsō-kai alumni meeting
dōsō (N) graduates of same school
11 go /o-...nega・u ask you to please...

「千里[12]の　道も　一歩[13]から」[14]で　がんばっております。

❹——はい、　木下[15]君も　山本[16]さんも　元気だそうです。

はい、　ぜひ　また　その　うちに　おうかがい[17]したいと思っております。　ところで、　先生は　毎日　大学へ出ておられ[18]ますか。　一度　研究室[19]の　方へも　おじゃましたいと　思っております。　先生が　なさった　翻訳[20]のお仕事　たいへん　ごりっぱな　ものだと　評判です。

❺——それでは、　みなで　お待ちいたしております。　木下君が　四時ごろ　お宅へ　車で　おむかえ[21]に　まいります。

それでは、　きょうは　これで　失礼いたします。

---

12 sen-ri (N) thousand *ri* (1 ri=2.44 miles)
13 ip-po one step
14 Sen-ri no michi mo ip-po kara (proverb) A journey of a thousand miles must begin with the first step. (=High buildings have low foundations.)
15 Kinoshita (a family name)
16 Yamamoto (a family name)
17 ukaga·u (Humble) ask; visit
18 orare·ru (Honorific form of i·ru)
19 kenkyū-shitsu study room, laboratory
20 hon'yaku (Nv) translation
21 mukae coming for; going to see ←mukae·ru

Dai 30-ka
Sensei e no Denwa

1——Moshi-moshi, Yoshida-sensei no o-taku deshō ka?
Oku-sama de irasshaimasu ka? Watashi gakusei-jidai ni Yoshida-sensei ni o-sewa ni narimashita Yamada to mōshimasu.
Sensei wa o-ide ni narimasu ka?
Ima o-dekake desu ka? Shichi-ji goro niwa o-kaeri ni narimasu ne.
Soredewa, shichi-ji sugi ni mō ichi-do o-denwa-sasete-itadakimasu.

* * *

2——Yoshida-sensei de irasshaimasu ka? Watashi Yamada desu.
Go-busata-itashite-orimasu. Sensei mo o-kawari naku, o-genki desu ka? Tokorode, chika-jika, sensei o o-kakomi-shite dōsō-kai o hiraki-tai to omotte-orimasu. Sensei ni zehi go-shusseki negaitai to omoi-mashite....

3——Hai, arigatō gozaimasu. Genki de yatte-orimasu. Itsumo sensei ga osshatte-imashita yō-ni, "Sen-ri no michi mo ip-po kara" de ganbatte-orimasu.

4——Hai, Kinoshita-kun mo Yamamoto-san mo genki da sō desu.
Hai, zehi mata sono uchi ni o-ukagai-shitai to omotte-orimasu.
Tokorode, sensei wa mai-nichi daigaku e dete-oraremasu ka? Ichi-do kenkyū-shitsu no hō e mo o-jama-shitai to omotte-orimasu. Sen-sei ga nasatta hon'yaku no o-shigoto taihen go-rippa-na mono da to hyōban desu.

5——Soredewa, mina de o-machi-itashite-orimasu. Kinoshita-kun ga yo-ji goro o-taku e kuruma de o-mukae ni mairimasu.
Soredewa, kyō wa korede shitsurei-itashimasu.

Lesson 30

Telephoning a Teacher

1 —Hello, is this Professor Yoshida's house? ... Mrs. Yoshida? ... This is Mr. Yamada, a former student of Professor Yoshida's. Is the Professor in? ... Oh, he's out now, is he? But he'll be back around seven o'clock, will he? If I may then, I'll call back around seven.

* * *

2 —Professor Yoshida? This is Yamada. I'm sorry to have been out of touch for so long. ... How have you been? ... The reason I called is that we would like to have a reunion and would like to invite you. We thought if you could please come....

3 —Yes, thank you. I'm fine. I'm plugging away one step at a time just like you told us to. ...

4 —Yes, Mr. Kinoshita and Miss Yamamoto are fine. ...
Yes, we would all like to come and see you some time. Do you go to the university every day? ... Someday I would like to visit you at your office there too. Everybody's talking about what an excellent job you did with that translation. ...

5 —Then we will all be looking forward to seeing you then. Mr. Kinoshita will be around about four to pick you up. ...
Thank you, and good-bye until the reunion.

ANSWERS 〈pp. 364, 365〉

I. 1. kakareru; o-kaki ni naru 2. matareru; o-machi ni naru 3. kawareru; o-kai ni naru 4. akerareru; o-ake ni naru 5. omowareru; o-omoi ni naru

II. 1. mōshimasu 2. irasshaimasu/oraremasu 3. -oraremasu/-irasshaimasu 4. kaerareru/o-kaeri ni naru 5. o-machi-shitemo 6. o-kake (ni natte-) 7. Donata 8. o-kyaku-san 9. ossharu/iwareru 10. o-machi ni natte-irasshaimasu 11. o-matase-shita 12. go-yō 13. mōshimasu 14. mairimashita 15. o-kaki ni natta/kakareta 16. o-hanashi 17. o-kiki-shitai 18. ukagaimashita 19. itadaita 20. gozaimasu

III. O-wakare no hi ga tōtō kimashita. Watashi ga Kyōto o tatta hi wa ame deshita. Tomodachi no Tarō-san ga mi-okuri ni eki e kite-kuremashita. Kare no o-kā-san mo kite-kudasaimashita. O-kā-san wa "Shujin mo mairu tsumori deshita ga, kyūyō no tame ni mairu koto ga dekimasen deshita. Anata ni yoroshiku to mōshite-imashita." to osshaimashita. O-kā-san wa utsukushii *tēburu-kurosu* o kudasaimashita. Watashi no tame ni somete-kudasatta no desu. Tarō-san ga "Goran. Koko ni anata no namae ga kan-ji de somete-aru yo." to iimashita.

Hassha no *beru* ga nari-hajimemashita. O-kā-san wa, "Mata irasshai ne. O-machi-shite-imasu." to osshaimashita.

●文法

§ 118 The System of 'Honorifics'

Japanese is a language having an intricate system of what are generally called 'honorific' forms, by means of which the speaker expresses his particular respect for the person mentioned in a sentence.

The prefix o- or go- attached to a Noun referring to a person or a thing belonging to the person is one such form, as you have already seen, especially in the Conversation sections. These prefixes can be attached to adjectives too when they show the state of the person the speaker respects. Generally speaking, o- is attached to native Japanese Nouns or Adjectives, and go- to Chinese-origin Nouns or Adjectives.

e.g. Anata no o-tō-san no go-iken wa dō desu ka?

'What is your father's opinion?'

cf. Watashi no chichi no iken wa…desu. 'My father's opinion is….'

Imōto-san wa o-kirei desu ne. '(Your) sister is pretty, isn't she?'

cf. Kare no imōto wa kirei desu. 'His sister is pretty.'

Verbs also take the Honorific forms when the speaker wants to express respect for the person who performs the action expressed by the Verb. There are two general ways by which you can make the Honorific forms: one is to use the Passive form (§ 71), and the other is to use the pattern 'o-/go- V(Conj. form) ni narimasu (Plain style: naru).

e.g. Yamada-san ga kore o kakimashita. 'Mr. Yamada wrote this.' (Neutral)

→Yamada-san ga kore o kakaremashita. (Honorific by Passive)

→Yamada-san ga kore o o-kaki ni narimashita. (Honorific)

Ano hito wa nani o kenkyū-shite-imasu ka? (Neutral)

'What is he doing research on?'

→Ano hito wa nani o kenkyū-sarete-imasu ka? (Honorific by Passive)

→Ano hito wa nani o go-kenkyū ni natte-imasu ka? (Honorific)

There are some Honorific forms, however, where it is difficult to find any formal similarities with their 'neutral' counterparts, and these are the ones that are most frequently used in daily conversation.

Neutral	Honorific
ikimasu ('go'), kimasu ('come'), imasu ('be, stay')	irasshaimasu or oide ni narimasu
iimasu ('say')	osshaimasu
mimasu ('see')	go-ran ni narimasu

e.g. Anata wa ashita doko e irasshaimasu ka? 'Where are you going tomorrow? —Kyōto e ikimasu. 'I am going to Kyoto.'

Sha-chō-san wa irasshaimasu ka? 'Is your President in?'

—Hai, imasu. —'Yes, he is in.'

§ 119 The Humble Forms

The speaker can express his respect not only by using the Honorific forms as seen above, but also by using 'Humble' Verb forms to refer to himself and other members of his group. What he does is to 'elevate' others relatively by 'lowering' himself. Most frequently used Humble forms include: **mōshimasu** in place of iimasu (e.g. Watashi wa *Jon* to mōshimasu. 'I call myself John.' or 'My name is John.'); **mairimasu** in place of ikimasu or kimasu (e.g. Mō ichi-do mairimasu. 'I will come again.'); and **itashimasu** in place of shimasu.

§ 120 Additional Remark

The Honorific and Humble forms should be distinguished from the Polite and Plain styles of § 41, although all are related to the speaker's intention to be polite.

In the Polite style, the politeness is always directed to the person spoken to, whereas in the honorific (or humble) expressions it is directed to the particular person mentioned in the sentence, who may or may not be the hearer.

Ano hito wa sō itta. →Ano hito wa sō osshatta.

'He said so.'

Ano hito wa sō iimashia. →Ano hito wa sō osshaimashita.

30

●練習

ANSWERS→p. 361

I. Make the Honorific forms as shown in the example.

Ex. yomu→yomareru; o-yomi ni naru.

1. kaku
2. matsu
3. kau
4. akeru
5. omou

II. Replace the underlined parts with their Honorific or Humble forms.

Buraun: Gomen-kudasai. Watashi wa *Buraun* to iimasu (1). Yamada-sensei wa imasu (2) ka?

Joshu[1]: Yamada-sensei wa ima kaigi ni dete-imasu (3).
Mō sugu kaeru (4) to omoimasu ga....

B: Ā, sō desu ka. Sukoshi koko de mattemo (5) ii desu ka?

J: Kono isu ni kakete (6)-kudasai.

Yamada: Dare (7) ka kyaku (8) desu ka?

J: Hai, *Buraun*-san to iu (9) kata ga saki-hodo kara matte-imasu (10).

Y: Ā, sō desu ka. Mataseta (11) yō desu ne. Watashi ga Yamada desu ga donna yō[2] (12) desu ka?

B: Watashi wa *Buraun* to iimasu (13). *Igirisu* kara kimashita (14). Sensei no kaita (15) hon o yonde, zehi ichi-do hanashi (16) o kikitai (17) to omotte tazunemashita (18). Koko ni watashi no kyōju ni moratta (19) shōkai-jō[3] ga arimasu (20).

語句

1 joshu assistant
2 yō =yōji errand, business
3 shōkai-jō letter of introduction/ recommendation
4 tōtō at last, finally
5 tats·u start, leave
6 mi-okur·u see off
7 shujin master; husband

III. Put the following into Japanese, using Honorific and Humble forms where appropriate.

The day of parting finally[4] came. It was raining the day I left[5] Kyoto. My friend Taro came to the station to see me off.[6] His mother came too. She said, "My husband[7] was going to come too, but could not come because of unexpected business. He sends you his best regards." She gave me a beautiful tablecloth.[8] She had dyed[9] it for me. "Look,[10]" Taro said, "here is your name in *kanji*." The bell signaling the train's departure[11] began to ring. His mother said, "Come again. We'll be waiting for you."

▼Kyoto

30

8 **tēburu-kurosu** 'tablecloth'
9 some·ru dye
10 goran (Honorific) (Imperative) Look
11 hassha (Nv) starting of train, bus, etc.

●会話

MOCHIRON YOROKONDE ....

—Yā, o-matase-shimashita. Kikaku[1]-bu no Tanaka to mōshimasu. Daitai[2] no o-hanashi wa Kawai[3]-bu-chō kara kiite-orimasu ga, kyō wa saishū-teki[4]-na *puran*[5] o o-mochi-itadaita wake desu ne.

Hai, watashi-domo no hō demo, sono go iroiro to kentō[6] o kasanemashita kekka, kono mae ni o-shimeshi[7]-kudasatta dai-san-*puran* de ikō, to iu koto ni iken ga itchi-shimashita.

Kore ga keikaku-sho[8] desu.

—Naruhodo..., kore de ikimasuto, hiyō[9] no ten[10] demo, daibu raku ni narimasu ne....

Chōdo yokatta. Jitsu wa[11] gogo san-ji kara, watashi-domo no kikaku-kaigi ga gozaimasu node, yoroshikattara,[12] *obuzābā*[13] to shite go-shusseki-kudasaimasen ka?

—Sorry to have kept you waiting. I'm Mr. Tanaka of the Planning Division. I've gotten most of the story from Mr. Kawai. I understand you've brought the final plans today?

Yes. After looking everything over, we've agreed on Plan 3 that you showed us last time. And I have the plan right here.

—Now let's see.... If we do it this way, financially too, it is fairly easy. You've come at just the right time. Actually we're having a planning meeting at 3 p. m. today. If you'd like why don't you attend as an observer?

語句

1 kikaku (Nv) planning
2 daitai (N) outline
3 Kawai (a family name)
4 saishū-teki (Na) final
5 *puran* 'plan'
6 kentō (Nv) investigation, scrutiny, examination
7 shimes·u show, suggest
8 keikaku-sho plan, blueprint
9 hiyō expense, cost
10 ten point
11 jitsu wa the fact is, to tell the truth
12 yoroshikattara if you don't mind, if you like
13 *obuzābā* 'observer'
14 yorokonde with pleasure
15 kensetsu (Nv) construction, founding
16 hakobi arrangement, stage, process

Mochiron yorokonde[14] shusseki-sasete-itadaki-mashō.

—Rai-nen no hajime niwa, shin-kōjō no kensetsu[15] to iu hakobi[16] ni naru hazu desu ga, sono mae ni genchi[17] ni watashi-domo no sha-in o go-mei[18] bakari okuri, yōchi[19] no kakuho[20] no shigoto o sasetai to omotte-imasu.

Watashi-domo mo, kōji[21]-kankei dake de naku, sono hōmen[22] demo kyōryoku[23] o oshimanai[24] tsumori desu kara, nan-nari[25] to o-mōshitsuke[26]-kudasai.

—Ikaga deshō, kaigi made ni mada ni-jikan bakari aru yō desu shi, go-issho-ni shokuji demo?

Ē, kekkō desu.

—Jā . . . . Ā, Nishida[27]-kun, kuruma o yonde-kuren ka ne? Sore kara, o-kyaku-sama o o-tsure-shite sukoshi gaishutsu-shite-iru to Kawai-bu-chō ni tsutaete-oite-kure-tamae.[28] Jā, dekakemashō. Keikaku-sho wa hisho[29] ni azukete-[30] okimashō. Dōzo, kochira desu.

Of course, I'd be glad to.

—I expect the construction of the new factory will probably begin the beginning of next year. Before that we'll send five or so of our staff to secure the site.

We're not limited to construction work, so if there's anything else we can do to help, please don't hesitate to say so.

—Say, we seem to have a couple of hours before the meeting. Why don't we go for lunch together?

Yes, thank you.

—Fine...Hey, Nishida, get us a taxi, will you? And tell Mr. Kawai that I'll be out for a while with our guest. Well, let's go. We can leave the plan here with the secretary. Please come this way.

---

17 genchi (N) on the spot
18 -mei (Count. for persons)
19 yōchi site for...
20 kakuho (Nv) ensure, secure
21 kōji (Nv) construction, building work
22 hōmen direction; area
23 kyōryoku (Nv) cooperation
24 oshim•u grudge, hold dear; regret
25 nan-nari to anything, whatever it is
26 mōshitsuke•ru give orders, bid
27 Nishida (a family name)
28 -tamae (Polite request usually to juniors)
29 hisho secretary
30 azuke•ru give...in trust, deposit

はぎの露　—「源氏物語」から—

明石中宮[1]さまは、近く御所[2]にお帰りにならなければなりませんので、紫の上[3]が、おやすみになっているおへやに、お別れのごあいさつを申しあげる[4]ために、いらっしゃいました。おりしも[5]秋風[6]が吹いて、はぎが[7]、ほの白く[8]夕やみ[9]の中にゆらいで[10]おりました。

そこへ源氏の君[11]がいらっしゃいました。源氏は、ふとんから[12]身[13]を起こされて、庭をながめていらっしゃる紫の上をごらんになり、たいそうおどろかれて[14]、「起きていらっしゃっても、およろしい[15]のでございますか。姫君[16]とごいっしょで、少しはお気もお晴れに[17]なりましたか。」とおっしゃいました。紫の上は、源氏の君のおやさしいお心づかい[18]にむねをおいため[19]になりながら、歌[20]をお作りになって、はぎの露[21]のように、すぐ消えさる[22]であろう[23]ご自身[24]の生命[25]のはかなさを述べ[26]られました。

庭のはぎがはげしくゆれ動いて[27]、まさに露がこぼれ落ち[28]そうなのをごらんになりながら、源氏の君ははらはらと[29]なみだをお流しになって、お歌をお返し[30]になり、露と争って[31]消えてゆくこの世[32]に、だれが先[33]に死に、だれが生き残る[34]などということがないようにしたい[35]ものですとなげかれ[36]ました。

このようにして、紫の上は、明け方[37]近く、中宮にお手を取られ[38]ながら、露のように、はかなくおなくなりに[39]なりました。

▼A scene from *Genji-Monogatari*

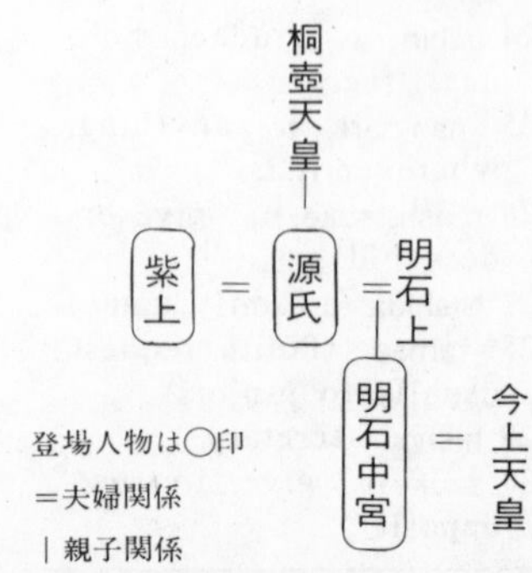

Dew on the Clover—from *The Tale of Genji*

As the Empress Akashi was soon to have to return to the Imperial Court, she went to the room where the ill Lady Murasaki was resting to bid her farewell. As they were talking, the autumn wind blew and the clover fluttered blazing white in the twilight.

Prince Genji came upon this scene and, surprised at seeing Lady Murasaki up and gazing out on the garden, asked if it was all right for her to be up and if she felt better and happier by spending some time with the Empress. Lady Murasaki, moved so deeply by Prince Genji's tender considerations, composed a poem comparing her fleeting life to the soon-disappearing dew on the clover.

Watching the clover in the garden as it shook and seemed indeed to drop its dew, Prince Genji shed profuse tears and composed a poem in reply lamenting that it is not possible in this world where men's lives vie with the dew for transitoriness to break the pattern of some's passing away first and others' staying behind.

In this way, her hand clasped by the Empress, Lady Murasaki ended her dewly brief life and passed away near dawn.

語句

1 Akashi Chūgū Empress Akashi
Chūgū (the title given to the Crown Princess)
2 Gosho residence of a member of the Imperial family
3 Murasaki-no-ue (the name of the wife of Hikaru Genji; the current empress; mother-in-law of Akashi no Chugu)
4 mōshi-age•ru (Humble form of i•u)
5 orishimo (Archaic) just then, on that occasion
6 aki-kaze cold autumnal wind
7 hagi (the name of a flower)
8 hono-jiroku (Adv) pale white, dimly
9 yū-yami evening twilight, dusk
10 yurag•u sway; shake; flicker
11 Genji-no-Kimi His excellency/highness Genji
Genji =Hikaru Genji (the main character of *The Tale of Genji*)
Kimi honorable person; prince
12 futon quilt
13 mi body
14 taisō=totemo, hijō-ni
15 yoroshi•i all right
16 hime-gimi princess
17 hare•ru turn nice, clear up
18 kokoro-zukai care, consideration
19 itame•ru hurt, give pain, injure
20 uta poem, song
21 tsuyu dewdrop, dew
22 kie-sar•u vanish, disappear
23 ...de arō be likely to...
24 jishin oneself
25 seimei =inochi life
26 hakana-sa transiency ←hakana•i (short-lived, momentary)
27 yure-ugok•u sway, quake, heave
yure•ru (Vi) shake, rock
28 kobore-ochi•ru overflow and drop off
kobore•ru (Vi) fall, spill
29 hara-hara (to) (onomat) (the way in which things very light and feeble drop one after another)
30 kaes•u (Vt) answer; return
31 araso•u compete; dispute; struggle
32 kiete-yuk•u die away, vanish
-te-yuk•u =-te-ik•u
33 saki ni ahead, previously
34 iki-nokor•u survive, live longer than
35 -tai mono desu would like to...if possible
36 nagek•u lament, grieve
37 ake-gata (N/Adv) at daybreak
38 te o tor•u grasp/take another's hand
39 nakunar•u die (=shin•u); disappear

APPENDIX I

Conjugation of Verbs, Auxiliaries, Adjectives, and Copula

		Dictionary form	Conjunctive form	te form	ta form (Past)	tara form (Conditional)	tari form
VERBS	1st Group	kak·u	kaki	kaite	kaita	kaitara	kaitari
		oyog·u	oyogi	oyoide	oyoida	oyoidara	oyoidari
		os·u	oshi	oshite	oshita	oshitara	oshitari
		yom·u	yomi	yonde	yonda	yondara	yondari
		shin·u	shini	shinde	shinda	shindara	shindari
		yob·u	yobi	yonde	yonda	yondara	yondari
		mats·u	machi	matte	matta	mattara	mattari
		nor·u	nori	notte	notta	nottara	nottari
		ka(w)·u	kai	katte	katta	kattara	kattari
	2nd Group	tabe·ru	tabe	tabete	tabeta	tabetara	tabetari
		mi·ru	mi	mite	mita	mitara	mitari
	Irreg.	suru	shi	shite	shita	shitara	shitari
		kuru	ki	kite	kita	kitara	kitari
AUX.	Polite	−masu		−mashite	−mashita	−mashitara	−mashitari
	Passive	−(r) are·ru	−(r)are	−(r) arete	−(r) areta	−(r) aretara	−(r) aretari
	Causative	−(s) ase·ru	−(s) ase	−(s) asete	−(s) aseta	−(s) asetara	−(s)asetari
Adj.		samu·i	samuku	samukute	samukatta	samukattara	samukattari
Copula		da		de	datta	dattara	dattari
		desu		deshite	deshita	deshitara	deshitari

NB (1) All 1st Group Verbs whose stems end with the same consonant are conjugated in the same way. For instance, ur-u('sell'), tor-u('take'), and kaer-u ('go home') are conjugated in the same way as nor-u above. The only exception to this general rule is ik-u('go'), which, although its stem ends with 'k', is conjugated iki, itte, itta, ittara, ittari, ikō, ike, ikeba, ikanai, ikareru, ikeru, ikaseru.

(2) The grouping of a Verb into 1st Group or 2nd Group is indicated in the footnote where it first appears. In this book, 1st Group Verbs are shown as '...·u,' and 2nd Group Verbs as '...·ru.'

(3) 'Na Adjectives' consisting of the Stem (the form preceding na) plus a Copula, conjugation is done with the Copula.

Presumptive/ Volitional form	Imperative form	reba form (Conditional)	Negative form	Passive form	Potential form	Causative form
kakō	kake	kakeba	kakanai	kakareru	kakeru	kakaseru
oyogō	oyoge	oyogeba	oyoganai	oyogareru	oyogeru	oyogaseru
osō	ose	oseba	osanai	osareru	oseru	osaseru
yomō	yome	yomeba	yomanai	yomareru	yomeru	yomaseru
shinō	shine	shineba	shinanai	shinareru	shineru	shinaseru
yobō	yobe	yobeba	yobanai	yobareru	yoberu	yobaseru
matō	mate	mateba	matanai	matareru	materu	mataseru
norō	nore	noreba	noranai	norareru	noreru	noraseru
kaō	kae	kaeba	kawanai	kawareru	kaeru	kawaseru
tabeyō	tabero	tabereba	tabenai	taberareru	taberareru	tabesaseru
miyō	miro	mireba	minai	mirareru	mirareru	misaseru
shiyō	{ shiro (seyo)	sureba	shinai	sareru	(dekiru)	saseru
koyō	koi	kureba	konai	korareru	{ korareru koreru	kosaseru
−mashō	(−mase)	(−masureba)	masen			
−(r) areyō	−(r) arero	−(r) arereba	−(r) arenai			
−(s) aseyō	−(s) asero	−(s) asereba	−(s) asenai	-(s) aserareru -(s) asareru	-(s) aserareru	
samukarō		samukereba	samuku nai			
darō		nara	de(wa) nai			
deshō			de(wa) arimasen			

(4) The Presumptive/Volitional forms of Verbs expressing voluntary actions indicate 'volition' as in will, intention, or invitation (See §49 & §76), and those of Verbs expressing non-voluntary actions, events, or states; Adjectives; and the Copula indicate the speaker's presumption or assumption.

(5) The negative forms of Verbs are conjugated in almost the same way as 'i Adjectives,' becoming kakanai, kakanakatta, kakanakereba, etc. For '-nakute', however, '-naide' or '-zu-ni' is sometimes used, as in Kakanaide-kudasai. ('Please do not write.') and Kakazu-ni kaerimashita. ('I went home without writing.').

APPENDIX II

Numerals and the Counting System

	Chinese-origin Numerals	Abstract Number + Counter (See § 14)					Native Japanese	
	Abstract Numbers	+ mai	+ satsu	+ hon	+ dai	+ tsū	Things	People
1	ichi	ichi–mai	is–satsu	ip–pon	ichi–dai	it–tsū	hito–tsu	hito–ri
2	ni	ni–mai	ni–satsu	ni–hon	ni–dai	ni–tsū	futa–tsu	fata–ri
3	san	san–mai	san–satsu	san–bon	san–dai	san–tsū	mit–tsu	san–nin
4	shi	yo(n)–mai	yon–satsu	yon / shi } –hon	yon–dai	yon–tsū	yot–tsu	yo–nin
5	go	go–mai	go–satsu	go–hon	go–dai	go–tsū	itsu–tsu	go–nin
6	roku	roku–mai	roku–satsu	rop–pon	roku–dai	roku–tsū	mut–tsu	roku–nin
7	shichi	shichi / nana } –mai	nana–satsu	nana–hon	nana–dai	nana–tsū	nana–tsu	shichi / nana } –nin
8	hachi	hachi–mai	has–satsu	{ hachi–hon / hap–pon	hachi–dai	hat–tsū	yat–tsu	hachi–nin
9	{ kyū / ku	kyū–mai	kyū–satsu	kyū–hon	kyū–dai	kyū–tsū	kokono–tsu	kyū–nin
10	jū	jū–mai	jus–satsu	jup–pon	jū–dai	jut–tsū	tō	jū–nin

11 jū-ichi
12 jū-ni
13 jū-san
14 jū-shi, jū-yon
15 jū-go
16 jū-roku
17 jū-shichi, jū-nana
18 jū-hachi
19 jū-kyū, jū-ku
20 ni-jū
21 ni-jū-ichi
24 ni-jū-shi, ni-jū-yon
30 san-jū
40 yon-jū
50 go-jū
60 roku-jū
70 nana-jū,
80 hachi-jū
90 kyū-jū
99 kyū-jū-kyū

100 hyaku
156 hyaku-go-jū-roku
200 ni-hyaku
300 san-byaku
400 yon-hyaku
500 go-hyaku
600 rop-pyaku
700 nana-hyaku
800 hap-pyaku
900 kyū-hyaku
1,000 sen
1,973 sen-kyū-hyaku-nana-jū-san
2,000 ni-sen
3,000 san-zen
4,000 yon-sen
5,000 go-sen
6,000 roku-sen
7,000 nana-sen
8,000 has-sen
9,000 kyū-sen

10,000 ichi-man
100,000 jū-man
1,000,000 hyaku-man
4,000,000 yon-hyaku-man
10,000,000 sen-man
30,000,000 san-zen-man
100,000,000 ichi-oku
1,000,000,000 jū-oku
10,000,000,000 hyaku-oku
100,000,000,000 sen-oku
1,000,000,000,000 it-chō

0 rei (or zero)
0.5 rei-ten-go
0.176 rei-ten-ichi-nana-roku
1/2 ni-bun-no-ichi
3/4 yon-bun-no-san

APPENDIX III

Education System

1. Primary (or Elementary) School
2. Junior High (or Middle) School
3. High School
4. Technical College
5. University (or College)
6. School of Medicine
7. Junior College
8. Graduate School
   a. Master's Course
   b. Doctorate Course

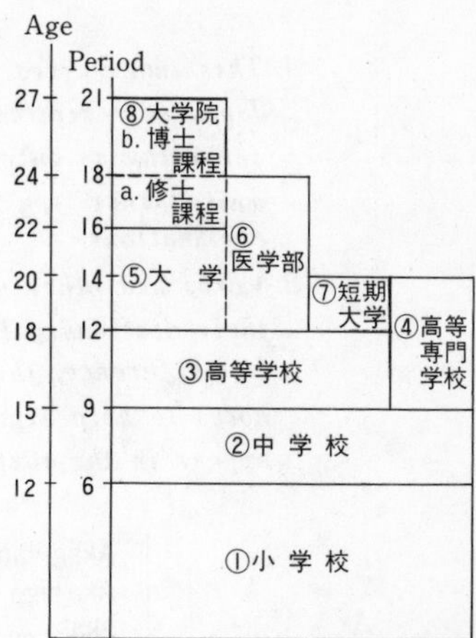

Main Fields of Study

Bungaku	literature	Igaku	medical science
Koku-bungaku or Nihon-bungaku	Japanese literature	nai-ka	general medicine
		ge-ka	surgery
Ei-bungaku	English literature	Shi-gaku	dentistry
Gengo-gaku	linguistics, philology	Yaku-gaku	pharmacology
		Kenchiku(-gaku)	architecture
Tetsugaku	philosophy	Doboku-kōgaku	civil engineering
Shakai-gaku	sociology	Toshi-keikaku	urban planning
Shinri-gaku	psychology	Kikai-kōgaku	mechanical engineering
Rekishi(-gaku)	history	Senpaku-kōgaku or Zōsen-kōgaku	shipbuilding
Chiri(-gaku)	geography		
Hōritsu(-gaku)	law, jurisprudence	Denki-kōgaku	electrical engineering
Seiji-gaku	political science	Denshi-kōgaku	electronic engineering
Keizai(-gaku)	economics	Yakin-gaku	metallurgy
Keiei-gaku	business administration	Jōhō-kōgaku	information science
Tōkei-gaku	statistics	Nō-gaku	agriculture
Kyōiku-gaku	education	Ringyō	forestry
Sūgaku	mathematics	Nōgyō-keizai-gaku	agricultural economics
Butsuri(-gaku)	physics	Suisan-gaku	fishery
Kagaku	chemistry	Bijutsu	fine arts
Dōbutsu-gaku	zoology	Ongaku	music
Shokubutsu-gaku	botany	Engeki(-gaku)	theater
Seibutsu-gaku	biology		

INDEX

1. *This index gives each entry first in romanized and then in Japanese script as it is commonly written. The first number following an entry is the page on which it first appears, while larger-type page numbers are for relevant grammatical explanations.*
2. *Verbs and other words which change with use are given in their dictionary forms.*
3. *For reference, this index also includes words given in footnotes to help explain other words, even when these do not appear in the text proper.*

D

E

F

G

I

J

K

O

P

Y

Z